IFISM
The Complete Works of Òrúnmìlà

Volumes
Ten • Eleven • Twelve • Thirteen

The Odus of Ogunda

The Odus of Osa

The Odus of Etura

The Odus of Irete

Dr. C. Osamaro Ibie, J.D.
B. SC. ECONS. (HONS.) LONDON B.A. ECONS. (HONS.)
STRATHCLYDE FIAMN (HONS.)

ATHELIA HENRIETTA PRESS
PUBLISHING IN THE NAME OF ÒRÚNMÌLÀ

Editorial and Production:	Roger Francis
	Rudolph Francis
Interior Design:	Rudolph Francis
Type Design and Typography	Joshua Knights

Library of Congress Cataloging-in-Publishing Data   2001 135751

ISBN 1-890157-30-9
Printed in USA

Distributed by Athelia Henrietta Press
Publishing In The Name Of Òrúnmìlà

· **ATHELIA HENRIETTA PRESS**
Publishing In The Name Of Òrúnmìlà
1194 Nostrand Avenue
Brooklyn, New York 11225
Tel. (718) 493-4500   Fax (718) 467-0099
Email: Atheliahenriettapress@yahoo.com

IFISM
The Complete Works of Òrúnmìlà

Volume Ten
The Odus of Ogunda

Volume Eleven
The Odus of Osa

Volume Twelve
The Odus of Etura

Volume Thirteen
The Odus of Irete

Other Titles by C. Osamaro Ibie

Ibie, C. Osamaro
IFISM: THE COMPLETE WORKS OF ÒRÚNMÌLÀ
251pp. 2 b/w, 11line, Illust. Cloth - *ISBN 1-890157-04-X*

Ibie, C. Osamaro
IFISM: THE COMPLETE WORKS OF ÒRÚNMÌLÀ
Vol. 2 - The Odus of Eji-Ogbe
How Man Created His Own God
242pp. 5 b/w, 41line, Illust. - *ISBN 1-890157-05-8*

Ibie, C. Osamaro
IFISM: THE COMPLETE WORKS OF ÒRÚNMÌLÀ
Vol. 3 - The Odus of Oyeku-Meji
101pp. 1 b/w - *ISBN 1-890157-06-6*

Ibie, C. Osamaro
IFISM: THE COMPLETE WORKS OF ÒRÚNMÌLÀ
Vol. 4 - The Odus of Iwori
172pp. 1 b/w - *ISBN 1-890157-07-4*

Ibie, C. Osamaro
IFISM: THE COMPLETE WORKS OF ÒRÚNMÌLÀ
Vol. 5 - The Odus of Idi
144pp. 1 b/w - *ISBN 1-890157-08-2*

Ibie, C. Osamaro
IFISM: THE COMPLETE WORKS OF ÒRÚNMÌLÀ
Vol. 6 & 7 - The Odus of Obara and Okonron
153pp. - *ISBN 0-9638787-6-X*

Ibie, C. Osamaro
IFISM: THE COMPLETE WORKS OF ÒRÚNMÌLÀ
Vol. 8 & 9 - The Odus of Irosun and Owanrin
178pp. - *ISBN 1-890157-09-0*

Table of Contents

IFISM
The Complete Works of Òrúnmìlà
Volume Ten
The Odus of Ogunda

About the Author
A Quintessential Mother
Prologue-How To Appease Esu

Chapter 4
Ogunda-Idi
Ogunda-Di-Ugbin

Chapter 5
Ogunda-Obara

Chapter 6
Ogunda-Okonron

Chapter 7
Ogunda-Irosun

Chapter 8
Ogunda-Owanrin
Ogunda-Mi-Lerin
Ogunda-Derin

Chapter 9
Ogunda-Osa
Ogunda-Maa-Saa

Chapter 10
Ogunda-Etura
Ogunda-Te-Tura-La

IFISM
The Complete Works of Òrúnmìlà
Volume Eleven
The Odus of Osa

Chapter 4
Osa-Idi

Chapter 5
Osa-Obara

Chapter 6
Osa-Okonron
Osa-Kunrin

Chapter 7
Osa-Irosun

Chapter 8
Osa-Owanrin
Osa-Olubi

Chapter 9
Osa-Ogunda
Osa-Ogunleja
Osagun-Ero

Chapter 10
Osa-Etura
Osa-Alawure
Osa-Ilefiri

Chapter 11
Osa-Irete
Osa-Oloyan

IFISM
The Complete Works of Òrúnmìlà
Volume Twelve
The Odus of Etura

Chapter 1
Etura-Ogbe
Etura-Eleji
Etura-Orilana
Etura-Arodemi
Etura-Jobi
Etura-Rina

Chapter 9
Etura-Ogunda
Etura-Arira
Etura-Takuta Sole
Etura-Ta-Gitan

Chapter 10
Etura-Osa

Chapter 11
Etura-Irete
Etura-Ago
Itonlo-Etura-Itonlo
Etura Olugba-Ete

Chapter 12
Etura-Eka

Chapter 13
Etura-Eturukpon
Etura-Tiku
Etura-Olomu

Chapter 14
Etura-Ose
Etura-Alashe
Etura-Ori-Wese

Chapter 15
Etura-Ofun

IFISM
The Complete Works of Òrúnmìlà
VOLUME THIRTEEN
THE ODUS OF IRETE

Chapter 1
Irete-Ogbe
Irete-Te-Nu-Olu

Chapter 15
Irete-Ofun
Irete-Afun

About the Author

Mr. C. Osamaro Ibie was born in the defunct Benin Empire's capital City of Benin mid- Western Nigeria on the 29th of September, 1934 to Chief and Mrs. Thompson Ibie Odin. He hailed from a Christian family. When his naming ceremony was, however being performed eight days after his birth, experts in the esoteric analysis of newly born infants, with special reference to the late Chief Obalola Adedayo, who confirmed to journalists when Ifism: *The Complete Works of Òrúnmìlà Vol. One* was being launched in 1987, predicted that God created the infant as a servant to Òrúnmìlà, God's own servant and divinity of wisdom, and that the world was going to know about Òrúnmìlà and the distorted, falsified and fabricated truth about the true nature of the one and only good God through the infant whose future problems and prospects were being analyzed. In fact, Chief Obalola confessed that he himself wondered why Òrúnmìlà left the whole of Yorubaland, which was his base, to come to Benin, which he first visited but could not reside in, to pick his *viva voce*.

According to the author's father the augury was totally ignored as farfetched because the man was talking to a Christian family who could not imagine any connection with Òrúnmìlà.

The author went through his primary and secondary education in Benin City, during which he generally operated as a man-server in the Catholic Church. In 1947, he joined some of his friends to enlist in the priesthood of the Catholic Church, but his father intervened with the Bishop to insist that his son was not cut out for the Christian priesthood, and the Bishop deferred to the wish of his father by releasing him.

Upon the completion of his primary and secondary education, the author was employed in the Nigerian Federal Public Service where he rose from the post of a Clerical Officer to the lofty position of an Executive Officer in 1959. At the same time, he won a Federal Government Scholarship to read Economics in London. He went to London in 1960 and obtained a Second Class Honor Degree in both Strathclyde, Glasgow and the University of London.

He returned to the Nigerian Federal Public Service where he was appointed as an Assistant Secretary, becoming Deputy Permanent Secretary in 1973 and Permanent Secretary in 1975.

He was appointed as a member of the Nigerian Economic and Finance Committee on the same year, which was charged with the management of the Nigerian economy. At the same time, he was appointed as a member of the Nigerian Government delegation to the intergovernmental consultative conference between the American and Nigerian governments, on which he served between 1976 and 1980.

Between 1980 when he retired voluntarily from the Nigerian Federal Public Service, and 1989, he operated exgratiation as an economic analyst; writing many newspaper articles on the categorical and hypothetical imperatives of economic policy and management. He also addressed several public and private sector institutions on the directions of economic policy, including the Nigerian Institute of Bankers, the Manufacturers Association of Nigeria, Nigerian Institute of Strategic Studies, several tertiary educational institutions, etc.

From 1985 and to the present, he has been serving as a member of the governing Council of the Federal Government owned University of Benin, in Edo State. Since his retirement from the Civil Service in 1980, he has actively engaged in business in the private sector. He was in 1992 awarded an Honorary Fellowship of the Institute of Administrative Management of Nigeria (FIAMN - Hon.) and recognized as a certified and Distinguished Administrator (CDA). In 2000, Mr.C.Osamaro Ibie received his Doctorate of Jurisprudence, University of Marlborough, Honolulu, Hawaii, U.S.A.

According to Orunmila, there are three main factors conducive to a blissful sojourn on earth. One of some questions which I have been asked on a number of occasions, it will be necessary at the outset to define what a blissful or successful life is, because all too often, there is a tendency for people to define true happiness and satisfaction hedonistically, that is, in terms of material satisfaction and synthetic pleasure.

True happiness on earth can only come from deriving satisfaction from simple needs and desires, a life spent in accordance with the natural endowments of the true God, the manifestation of genuine and veritable dreams come true, and longevity. What shortens our lives on earth are not the pursuits of our needs, for which God and nature amply provide, but the never-ending hunt for greed. The birds of the air, the animals of the bush and the fishes of the rivers and seas, live happily from nature's simple endowment in their respective habitats. What truncates human life on earth is not our needs but the pursuit of greed for which God and nature forgot to provide.

The happiness herein referred to is not the synthetic greed for monetary satisfaction. How many people ever stop to sympathise with government functionaries and extortionate businessmen, who after mortgaging ethical objectivity and their conscience to loot billions of dollars, as if they were going to live forever, were subsequently denied by the higher powers, the undeserved right to live to enjoy their ill-gotten acquisitions? It is the maximization of the success and happiness deriving from living long enough to enjoy satisfaction from small wants and simple desires.

Against the foregoing background, I will now proceed to illustrate Orunmila's three prescriptions for lasting happiness in our planet. These three factors are: To come through one's destined parents to the world; to have the fortune of meeting one's destined marital partner on earth; and to be born into the right ambience.

Let me illustrate what I mean by referring to the experience of a late pupil and admirer, the intrepid journalist Dele-Giwa of blessed memory.

Three weeks before he became the victim of bureaucratic homicide, I invited him for a dinner to provide the opportunity of telling him some home truths. The first question I aksed him was whether his mother was alive and equal to the task that his audacity necessitated. When he did not seem to comprehend the point I was making, I told him that unless he had a mother who was teleguiding his survival, it would be catastrophic for him to continue to singe the tiger's beards. I reminded him of the Bini aphorism that before challenging the messenger of death a young man must have a reliable protective shield. I was therefore, not surprised when, less than three weeks later, he was reported to have died suddenly from a bomb allegedly mailed to him by the bureaucracy.

Between 1944 and 1989, I took so many moronic risks that were it not for the brand of parents that it pleased God to give me, I would have long gone to join my ancestors. Between 1942 and 1969, when I was still the victim of synthetic foreign religion, it was my mother that provided the means of dodging the bricks and mortars of life. At the time, I was convinced that she was, and I had occasions to call her, the agent of the devil. That was because she was always talking about enemies seeking to destroy me. She borrowed money from any and every body to perform idolatrous sacrifices purportedly to keep me alive. She had five children all of who lived to bury her. But her expenditure on me alone was more than all her other four children put together.

She was prepared to eat human waste in the interest of her children. She endured all kinds of indignities, especially from uncles in order to stay around to look after her children in my father's house.

Whenever, in my characteristic devil-may-care brazen effronteries, it was my mother, who often manipulated the brakes to apply forcibly, when I ignored the red traffic lights of life to race along at high speed. I should like to illustrate this oxymoron with two spectacular events in my formative years.

In September, 1955, I was working as a Shipping Assistant in the Department of Marketing and Exports at Warri in what is now the Delta State. I got a message from my mother that she had been told at augury to warn me to travel to Benin for the next three months to obviate the risk of becoming a victim of the evil machinations of esoterics and warlocks. As an ardent Roman Catholic fanatic, I had developed indomitable aversion against such idolatrous advice. I had no intention of heeding my mother's advice. Early in October, 1955, I had a fever and I went to the Warri General Hospital for treatment, I was given Quinacrine or Mepacrine and advised to take two tablets three times a day. I was taking the tablets as prescribed. When my guardian heard that I was ill, he came to visit me. Mr. Wilfred Osaoyomwanobo Osunde, the man who gave me my first job and harboured me for some months, was then an X-Ray Technician at the Warri General Hospital.

On hearing that I was ill, he came to my house to verify my condition. When he saw how high my temperature was, he advised me immediately to take a booster dose of mepacrine which had been given to me at the Warri General Hospital. After he left my house on that Friday, I immediately felt well enough to travel to Benin, in the company of my friend and next door neighbor, Mr. Joseph Okuofu. In book one, I have already told the story of how I lost my memory on my way to Benin and did not regain it partially until when I found myself at about 10pm after having strayed over five miles into the bush far away from Benin. A benevolent sympathiser subsequently backed me on his bicycle to my father's house. From then on, but for the indomitable disposition of my ever-caring mother, I would probably have ended up in an asylum or mental hospital.

It was the augury which my mother conducted that provided the esoteric solution to my problems. That was when a positive correlation was drawn between my previous incarnation and my indisposition. After the prescribed atonement sacrifices were made at the ancestral shrines in my maternal village, very close to the point in the bush into which I had mysteriously strayed on my way from Warri, I became perfectly well. That was also the setting in which my final initiation into Ifism was completed in October 1955. When Orunmila was reported to have complained that keeping him at the periphery of my life between 1944 and 1955 amounted to over-stretching my luck. That is why, at the instance of my parents, my Ifa was prepared without any further delay between the 7th and the 12th of October, 1955.

Except for some hiccups resulting from my first marriage between 1959 and 1969, my life had a reasonably smooth navigation.

After my first daughter was born in 1960, I went to study overseas on Nigerian Federal Government bursary. It is however, necessary to recall that during the final stages of my Ifa initiation in October, 1955, a ceremony which I can barely remember because I was at the time still suffering from severe hallucinations. I only began to know what was going on about the Ifa initiation on the fifth day when my life horoscope was disclosed, after being told that Orunmila, was the divinity God created me to serve? I fully regained my memory. I remember vividly that my parents were warned that if they did not wish to actuate any avoidable disruptions in my life they should not choose any wife for me unless it was one that I could choose myself and agree to marry.

In spite of that injunction, while I was preparing for the GCE Advance Level in 1957, with a view to furthering my education, my father proposed that I should marry a girl living on our street. Apart from the fact that the girl never went to school at all, I appealed strongly to my father that the time was not opportune for me to marry. He however, stood his ground and insisted that I had to obey his instructions. In the ensuing confrontation between father and son, I refused to visit Benin from Warri during the ensuing ten months. Before then, no fortnight expired without me coming to Benin to see my parents because I loved them.

Meanwhile, my mother besought my father to remember the injunction given to the two of them during the final stages of my Ifa initiation, "not to force me to marry any girl unless one chosen by myself." Since custom and tradition were on the side of my father at a time when Benin parents still had the last word on who, their children married, my father was in no mood to compromise his decision. For daring to challenge his authority, my father drove my mother from his house on the ground that she was supporting her son (my poor self) who had never theretofore disobeyed his instructions.

My mother, immediately travelled to Warri to beseech my guardian, Mr. W.O. Osunde to persuade me to save her from the wrath of my father. Mr. Osunde reminded me that as mortals, we have no armour against fate since we are only pawns on the chessboard of destiny. He used his own example to demonstrate that he never had any intention of marrying more than one wife and that when his mother told him several years before that he was destined to marry three wives, he dismissed the suggestion as a plastic joke, but that over time he came to have three wives, all living with him at the time he was talking to me.

He emphasized that it is only when we stray from the path of our destiny that we run into difficulties during our sojourn on this planet. He then asked me whether what my mother revealed to him, was what they told ok during my Ifa initiation? That anyone having Ifa, Ogunda-di-'gbin was bound to marry or have children from at least seven women was true. I confirmed the information but insisted that I never believed it. He ended by advising me to stop upsetting my father because his prayers and blessings would do me more good than his anguish and curse.

On that note, I agreed to accompany my mother to Benin that week-end to submit to the will of my father and asked for his forgiveness. I will skip the details and out-turn of that cave-in to another book I am writing at the instance of Orunmila about the "Dark Side of my Life." Suffice it to conclude at this stage that it almost cost me my life on the 23rd of September, 1969, but for the precautionary moves of my mother.

After agreeing to marry my first wife in deference to the will of my father, I was determined to brush her total illiteracy and fine-tune her to suit my station in life. On the surface, the woman proved to be so inoffensive that when I was going Overseas on Nigerian Federal Government scholarship in 1960, I promised to arrange for her to join me the following year.

I got to London for my university education. in September, 1960, when my first child was seven months old, having been born on the 6th of February, of that year. I immediately began to save money to get my wife to join me the following year. I immediately contacted my father to arrange to get my wife a passport to enable her to join me in August, 1961. My father was quite excited about my decision, but not my mother, who, in her characteristic aversion to "not looking thoroughly before leaping," decided to go places to "not looking thoroughly before leaping," decided to my decision.

At this point, it is necessary to recall an incident which transpired three weeks before I travelled to Britain in September, 1960.

My breakfast was esoterically poisoned by one of my father's wives, who I had trusted to the point of treating her more as a sister than a father's wife. The poison defied the competence of all the traditional doctors in Benin City. As I was about to give up the ghost, a paternal relative Mrs. Ozomwogie Isibor came in to to tell my father that she knew an Urhobo woman at Oghara junction near Sapele, who might help. I was immediately transported in a charted lorry, unconscious to the woman's place at about 8p.m. that night.

When we, (my mother, Madam Ozomwogie and I) got to Oghara, the woman told us that she could only determine the cause and cure of my problem after sleeping. She, however, alerted my mother that I should do whatever she told me to do when she woke up. Since I was in severe pain, I could not fall asleep. I was, therefore, wide awake after midnight when with a small clay pot in hand, she asked me to follow her on a journey towards the Benin road. After walking for about half a mile, singing an incantational song, she told me to follow her on a round the tree seven times. After that ritual, she gave me the pot to throw on the road towards Benin.

It was going on back to her house that she gave some liquid to drink after telling me that but for the special grace of God, the woman of taking it. Later that night, I began to vomit and out from my throat came a dead scorpion. Thereafter, I had no more pains and I slept throughout the rest of the night.

I did not know what happened between the Urhobo lady, Madam Keeke Efekeyan and my mother after I left for overseas for further studies. My mother was writing to update me but I was neither opening nor reading her letters because their weirdness were frightening to me.

I now move to August 1961 when my wife left for London. There were eight of us Nigerian students expecting our wives to arrive in the BOAC plane from Lagos to London. The normal arrival time of the plane was 6 a.m. At about 5.15 a.m. we heard a bizarre announcement through the public loud speaker system at the lounge that the BOAC plane from Lagos to London had crash landed in Barcelona due to engine problem, but that all the passengers were safe and that a relief plane had been depatched to fly them to London.

I subsequently wrote to thank my father and besought him to thank God for the safe arrival of my wife because the plane carrying them to London crash landed in Barcelona. I was to know the significance of the plane crash three years later, one year after arriving home.

Meanwhile, I got my wife enrolled with a private teaching institution to teach her from scratch. After a six month crash programme she was able to read, write and speak english and subsequently get through dress-making and cookery programmes. I bought an electric sewing machine and other gadgets for her to use. As stated earlier, in two years of living together in London and Glasgow, we did not have a single brawl in consequence of which I came to love her more than ever before . The only probem we had was that although she was treated by two of Britain's most proficient gynacologists, she did not once miss her period. I became worried when the wives of my other colleagues including a flat mate, were expecting second babies. The medical explanation for her condition was that her fallopian tube was blocked and the doctors did all they could to unblock it.

When her condition defied all clinical remedies, I decided to return home to seek traditional solutions. I was convinced that a womb which brought forth a first child should be able to accommodate other children. I was barely 29 years old then and still a very naive catholic. I had bluntly refused to cultivate any relationship with any other woman and vowed never to have an affair with any other woman until my wife had a second child.

We eventually returned home in September 1963, and narrated my abortive efforts to make my wife have another baby to my parents. I was even tested in London as to whether the medical fault was mine. My father's advice on getting home was that since I was mine. My father's advice on getting home was destined to have children by so many women, I should have as many girlfriends as I could afford. His advice fell on deaf ears, because I was in no mood to complicate my love life. My mother had suggested on several occasions that I should accompany her for augury to find out for myself why my wife could not have another child but I bluntly refused to *acquiesce*.

After persevering for two years, I decided to follow my father's suggestion of trying out other women. My first attempt was a disaster because as soon as the girl, a confidential secretary in the Ministry of External Affairs, became pregnant she confronted me with an untenable ultimatum to choose between having the child for me and doing away with my wife, because she could not share a husband with another woman. Coming as it did from a Bini woman, whose father was a polygamist, I told her that if I did away with my wife to marry her because of a child, I would equally most probably do away with her some day for another woman. Two days after turning down her proposal, she did a D and C to terminate the pregnancy. For the rest of her effective life, she neither had any other child nor spend one week of marriage with any other man.

Meanwhile, my mother persuaded me that I should accompany her to go and thank the Urhobo woman who dislodged the poison that nearly terminated my life before I travelled overseas. I readily agreed to accompany her and I went with clothes and drinks in addition to money with which to express my profound gratitude to Madam Keeke Efekeyan.

When we got to the woman's home at Oghara Junction she asked me whether my wife had another child? When I replied that she had not, her next remark startled me, when she said categorically that it was impossible for my wife to have another child for the rest of her life. She jolted me even more poignantly when she emphasized that no medicine or sacrifice could solve my wife's problem. When I *asked* whether that was her destiny or a situation brought about by medical or esoteric calamity, the old woman laughed and told me to calm down in order to understand the inexorable realities of life.

She started off with a local aphorism that no one can do much to alter what an individual has chosen to do for or with himself was destined to have seven children, that she subsequently preferred to surrender the remaining six when she was confronted with the harder option of losing her life. I was surprised to see that my mother was listening to the old woman's revelations with placid equanimity when I was rattled. The old woman then proceeded to narrate the most astonishing tale I had ever heard.

She explained that when I was coming to the world, I came with a mark on my forehead inserted by the cult of demons and warlocks. She added, that was why I had been having one problem after another since my childhood through the machinations of sorcerers. The woman then turned to face my mother. She asked her a curious question "Did one of your husband's lovers and two of your junior mates not do their utmost to end your son's (myself) life since he was born?" Is that not why his early years in life had to be spent with your mother? (my maternal grandmother). In confirming the woman's weird revelations, my mother gurgled into a wail of tears and since I was aware of most of what the woman was saying, I too instinctively burst into tears.

As if to restore some lucidity, the old woman congratulated my father and my mother for having the good sense to prepare Ifa for me very early in my life, adding that although they virtually forced me into it, I would have been reborn (reincarnated) four time since then if Orunmila had not been invited (via initiation) to my rescue.

Then came the grotesque disclosure which put me of completely. The old woman stunned me by revealing that when no one seemed able to end my lfe, my wife - who was, as far as I was concerned, the best spouse any man could pray to have - then got up in the cult of warlocks and volunteered to come and marry me to finish me off. The woman added that proffering to accomplish the long running task of terminating my life, she was given an enhanced promotion in the cult. The woman added that was why she did everything to advise my mother not to allow my wife to join me in London 1961 because that was going to give her the appropriate environment in which to achieve her nefarious objective against me. It was when I insisted on her coming to join me that the woman played her last card culminating in the crashed-landing of the air-craft bringing my wife to crash land in Barcelona in August 1961, to enable her to seize from my wife the esoteric weapons she was coming to use against me.

The price my wife had to pay for her inability to kill me, was the forfeiture of the six remaining children she was destined to have on earth and repeated emphatically that although I was totally adverse to marrying any other woman until my wife had a second child, she was absolutely incapable of having any other child. The situation became so bizzare for me that I had to leave the woman's house in anger for daring to prefer witchcraft charges against a young woman who could not even hurt a fly. Her last advice was that even if I tried to have another child through any other woman, I should do so in utmost secrecy because the pregnancy would abort as soon as my wife knew about it.

As I got into my car and halted on my mother to let us return home, the woman made a final prognostication. She told my mother and here, I will quote the woman verbatim "Edugie (my mother name) what I have just told your son that entered his head through one ear and he dismissed it through the other ear, he will only believe in five years' time. Your unrelenting task will be to ensure that he is alive then to appreciate the truth of what I have told him." There and then, I vowed never to see the woman ever again.

In an attempt to repudiate the woman's predictions, first, I left no stone unturned during the next eighteen months to use other traditional methods to get my wife to have another child. The more I tried, the nearer I inched into the immutable realities of my predicament.

My mother went on her knees several times to beg me to have an affair with other women. It was when my father, who gave me my wife, gave his support to my mother's supplications that I had the courage to befriend other girls. The first one, a Confidential Secretary, aborted her pregnancy when it was four months old. The second one, an Education Officer, and a Catholic like me, told me after two miscarriages that her eldest sister told her after traditional augury that no other woman would be able to have a child for me as long as my wife was with me. That was why I left the girl. Unhappily, a Yoruba church-seer called Michael later told me that my wife had damaged the woman's womb irreparably and so she could not have a child. She subsequently married another man for 25 years and could not have a child until she got to menopause. Each time I remember that poor Mary became barren for taking the risk of befriending me in her prime, I shed tears. I leave the judgment to God.

The next woman I befriended at the instance of the late Chief Slaede Azoba who took pity on my plight when we were next door neighbors at Bishop Street, Idi-Oro in Lagos, was the first relationship I managed to conceal for eight months. When the pregnancy was eight months old, I became afraid that I might have problems in proving the child's paternity if I did not introduce the woman to my parents. On my way to introduce her to my parents from her village, after I told my wife about it, I had an accident with my car at Uselu on the outskirts of Benin as a result of which the girl became unconscious. It was a friend, Mr. Eghujovbo who was passing by that provided cold water from his flask to revive her. She would have lost the pregnancy but for the fact that my father took charge of the situation when we got home. That was how my first son managed to come into my life, but unknown to me only because my mother was made to perform a special ritual by an Ifa Sage.

It was the man who advised my mother after augury to perform the ritual that later revealed to me the year I attempted to take my life, that he told her to make a special twenty-one days appeal to God, her guardian angel and ancestors, that although she was destined to have ten children on earth, they should transfer the remaining five to me. That explains why I had five children by five different women in 1970, following the termination of my first marriage in 1969, my year of realisation.

It was by the special grace of God and the efforts, activities and prayers of my parents, that I survived the quinquenium between August 1964 and September 1969 for which I remain eternally grateful to God, my guardian angel and my parents. That is why I often ponder to worry about fellow human beings, who are not endowed with the rare luck of being brought to the world throught the right ambience and parents. It makes all the difference to our lives.

This section of this book is merely a preview of the last book which I am writing at the instance Orunmila, God's own Servant of wisdom - when he enjoined me four years ago, 1995 on a flight from Lagos to London-that I should "Tell All About The Dark Side of My Life." Otherwise, it is not funny to recall these lugubrious phases of my life. Who will believe that I was in tears as

I was writing it! If my mother had to eat human waste to keep me alive, she would have done it and more. I could not stop crying and had to retire to go and sleep. If there are mistakes in this section of the book, it is because I did not read it a second time.

I have decided to jump the events of those five years because they have been amply covered in "The Dark Side of My Life." While still struggling with destiny to have more children from my wife, I had succeeded in having my first son and my second daughter from two other women. I do not know whether those developments marked a gloom and doom scenario in my life. In fairness to my parents and children, they turned out to become positive turning points in my life. Meanwhile, a climatic interval began in my life from the 8th of June, 1969 when I discovered that I could no longer copulate with any woman including my wife, and I was only 35 years old. I did everything medical, esoterical and psychological to overcome the problem until the 23rd of September, 1969. That was the night I tried to take my life. It was Orunmila, as I discovered later, who stopped me from performing the *harikari*. Again I prefer to skip the details because, I had previously referred to it in Book one of Ifism.

It was during Orunmila's first appearance to me at the Atlantic Hotel in Hamburg on the 23rd of June, 1979, ten years later, that I realised from his voice and words that he was the one God used to stop me from taking my life by hanging on the branch of an umbrella tree in front of the boys' quarters of my official residence at No. 2 Elmes Road in Yaba, Lagos at 3am on the 23rd of September. Mysteriously, Chief Igbinovia turned up at my house the following day in equally mysterious circumstances, to give me Orunmila's message that I was having problems because I abandoned him. The chief told me, that I should go back to the patron who happened to be my father who prepared the Ifa for me to appease Orunmila with a goat to enable him to remove from my house the woman who almost succeeded in terminating my life.

I followed the man's advice and went to Benin on the 25th of September 1969 to serve my Ifa. When Orunmila was being sounded for directions a few days later, my father invited *inter alios*, Chief Adedayo Obaola, who asked for my wife. When I told him that she was in Lagos, he asked a second question, who gave her to you? I replied that it was my father. He then told my father that the woman had already loaded my luggage in a boat ready to sail for heaven and that it was by the special grace of God, and the intervention of Orunmila that I was still alive to stand before him, lest I would have been dead. He then asked me two questions in the presence of my parents and I prefer to quote him "My son, is your body complete as you are standing before me?" When I answered negatively, he asked the second question - "Is that not why you tried to take your life, but for the timely intervention of Orunmila? I again answered affirmatively.

It was there and then that the decision was taken for me to return to Lagos to bring my wife home. I travelled to Lagos the next day and returned with her to Benin on the 27th of September, 1969. When I got home, instead of convenining a meeting of the two familes to discuss the termination of the marriage, my father's aunt Madam Imalele Uwangue had queried that it was not fair to decide the fate of my wife on the pronouncements of Chief Obalola alone, without seeking a second opinion. She convinced my father that it was advisable to refer the matter to an Olokun priestess - AKPOWA of Iyowa - who would provide a satisfactory solution to the problem because she divines by possession.

On my way to Benin 10.30 p.m. and 2am on the 27th of September, 1969, but for the timely intervention of my wife, who pulled the steering whell of my car to herself, we would probably have ended our lives in a ravine between Ajebandele and Onikparaga on Lagos - Benin Road.

It was when I got home on the 28th that I was told that we had to go and meet an Olokun priestess on the 29th of September, 1969, (which happened to be my 35th birthday) at Iyowa, on the old Benin - Lagos road.

My father's aunt, Madam Imalele Uwangue led my wife and myself to Akpowa's shrine at Iyowa the following morning. The first surprise packet I had was to be welcomed with a song by the priestess that "the man we have been expecting has finally arrived" - (Enakhere, Enakhere gho rere O). Next I saw the mother of my first son, who I had alienated since early 1969, when her six and a half months old pregnancy virtually disappeared for disobeying instructions never to enter my house in Lagos. She had come to find out from the same Olokun shrine why her pregancy receded and virtually disappeared. It appeared that when she went before the priestess for augury, she told her that her husband was on his way to her because Orunmila was directing him to her to unravel the *raison d'etre* of this indomitable problem. The priestess told me that she asked the woman to wait, because she would only understand the cause of her own problem, when she (the priestess) started talking to me.

When I finally appeared before the priestess, the embarrassing overture to her revelations (because she speaks in songs with musical accompaniment) was to ask everybody present to pronounce shame on me for allowing Christianity to becloud my vision, for so long. She next asked me pointedly and I prefer to quote her, "This woman (my wife) standing with you, did your mother of the night Madam Keke Efekeyan of Oghara not tell you five years ago that she will not have anymore children for you and will do her best to stop any other woman from having a child for you?" I answered affirmatively, and she responded by asking me how many children my wife had within that five years, and I replied, none.

She then faced my wife, "what has this man done to you that you made it your mission to destablise and if possible terminate his life? God who knows that he has done for you what few men can do for any woman has frustrated all your demonic designs against him, and it is in your own interest to know that it is a mission our Almighty Father will not allow you to accomplish." Next, the priestess made the second revelation that enhanced the credibility of whatever she was saying.

Still talking to my wife, the Priestness added "At the time your huband came to fetch you from Lagos, you knew that you were not going to return to him in Lagos because God, his divinities and your husbands' ancestors had swept your feet from his house.
"To prevent your secret from leaking, you decided to make his car tumble into a ravine, but when you realised that you too would die if the car fell into the ditch, you pulled the steering of his car. Am I lying, against you." She confirmed that was what happened.

Once more the priestess faced me saying "As long as you were quite happy with her only child, who she also tried unsuccessfully to kill to save her own life, following her failure to accomplish the task she set for herself. Thanks to your mother and your mother of the night, your wife did not become desperate. It was when you started trying to have children by other women that she decided to render you sexually impotent. Have you been a complete man in the past four months?"

When I answered negativelly, she then asked my wife to leave the consulting chamber and she was led outside. She then advised me that: (i) I should burn all the beddings with which I had been sleeping with my wife because she had installed a U-BOLT in my house so that if I passed through that point and later go to copulate with any other woman expecting a baby for me, the pregnancy would instantly disappear, or if any such woman passed through that place, her pregnancy would evaporate and (ii) My wife rendered me impotent to cage me and prevent me from trying any other woman for a child. The situation will reverse itself if you can muster the courage to get her out of your house and your life. But I warn you, if she is still with you in three days time, after unmasking her today, she will get hold of one of your pants and use it to make sure that you will not be able to have sex for the rest of your life.

I left the shrine on a somber note, and as soon as we returned home, I went before my father on my knees and reported the developments. I ended on the note that he should return my wife to wherever he got her from, because I was through with her as man-and-wife. I gave her an alimony and finished with her at 9.30p.m. on the 29th of September, 1969.

My mother's first reaction was to suggest that we should go and visit Madam Keke Efekeyan at Oghara to confirm that her prophesies had manifested beyond all expectations and to persuade her to follow us to my Lagos residence for sanctification. I was only too ready, and anxious to see her again to apologize to her personally for daring to *brook* misgivings on the veracity of her predictions. We travelled to her place on the 30th of September, 1969, and with drinks, money and clothes, I was on my knees to apologise to her. She only told me to thank my mother who held the fort while I was slumbering between 1960 and 1969, which I did not hesitate to do on the spot. I wonder how many people are endowed with the fortune of *having* such a prototypical mother! She was indeed one of the best things God did for me.

Madam Keke felt so elated that she got packed to travel with us immediately. We spent the night at Benin and left for Lagos the following morning. As soon as we got to my house in Lagos, she asked for water to drink and I called a nine year old junior male relative who was then staying with me and schooling at the time. As soon as the boy moved through the rear door to the direction of the refrigerator to fetch water, Madam Keke, in a paroxysm of bewilderment, asked me, "Who is that boy?" and I answered that he is the son on a relation sent to live with me. She then asked a more impugning question - "Why is it that you are always living with the wrong people? Of course I asked her what means I had of knowing who was good and who was evil? She then made a jest of me by remarking that "of course, I have forgotten that you do not have a second sight." She then invited the boy for a chat while I got up to fetch water for her to drink.

When the woman asked *him* for his name, he gave his familiar name. The woman then told him that she was asking for his cryptic name. At that point, the boy inclined his head on one of his shoulders. That was when the old *woman* got annoyed in a way I had never seen before. She challenged the boy whether he was testing her competence and authority. She proclaimed that she was the second in command among all the witches and wizards of Urhobo land, adding that as soon as a sorcerer inclined his/her head on the shoulder, nothing would make him/her to answer any more questions. The woman then disclosed that the name the boy had in the club of warlocks was a Yoruba name and that although she did not understand a word of the Yoruba language, (being Urhobo) she would translate the meaning of the name, as soon as he mentioned it. At that point all the inmates who spoke and understood the Yoruba language in my house had assembled for what was to say the least, an outlandish spectacle.

That was when, apparently, under the spell of the old woman, the boy gave his covert name as "OLOWOMIFO". There was total silence in my room. Nonetheless, of all the eight other individuals present, no one was adequately able to translate the meaning of the name. It was again Madam Keke who once more provided the clue to what was obviously a fiendish name. She explained that the name the boy took in the night meant "All the prosperous and successful people in his family would *be* permaturely dying. After asking him whether that was not why he manoeuvered himself into coming to live with me, the woman forced him to make a proclamation, changing the name instantly and he did. This is probably why the successful members of my family and myself are still alive.

The woman however had two more puzzles for him to unravel. She reminded him of the convenant *he* signed with my wife who had just left, to the effect, that (although no one gave any indication that she was leaving for good) she was not likely to return to Lagos, and therefore, she would send him something harmful to plant on my body. The woman then asked him whether she had sent it and he confirmed that she had not sent it. On that note, the woman warned him that if he accepted it and tried to plant it on my body, it would not only fail to work, but that he would not live to see the next morning.

Secondly, the woman made him to confirm that the umbrella tree in front of my boy's quarters was the staging post from which they (the club of warlocks) used to scan all the goings-on in my house and from where he used to send messages home to his mother for an update of whatever was going on in my house. Again, she warned him that if he ever tried to play the role of the inscrutable rapporteur on the happenings in my house and life anymore, he would not live to see the next new moon. On that note the woman dismissed him from the sitting room. She then suggested that later that night, the umbrella tree in front of my boy's quarters on which incidentally, I attempted to take my life the previous week, had to be cut down and uprooted. She added that after cutting down the tree, the boy would not be able to remain in my house for another five days. She also advised that whenever the boy elected to return to Benin, I should not only prepare new dresses for him but also promise to continue to pay his school fees from Lagos.

After dismissing the boy, the old lady turned to my mother to tell her in tete-a-tete to ask me whether I was still potent and whether I did not as a result of that, try to take my life. When my mother answered her questions affirmatively, she disclosed that my wife had planted an esteric U-BOLT in my house which not only made it impossible for any other woman to have a child for me, but also to render me impotent. The woman insisted that her visit to my house would be a failure if she could not locate the U-BOLT.

In fairness to the small boy, I was told two years later that while I was away to work one week day and he was on holiday, he cried all over the house that he was not happy at what the enemies were doing to me. He disclosed that they planted a U-Bolt in my house for any other woman not to have a child for me. He was reported to have threatened to spill the beans. My wife was still in the house and apparently told everybody not to let me know about the outburst of the boy.

Meanwhile, the woman and my mother had supper. Thereafter, from about 8pm until 1.45am they were searching for the U-Bolt. At the same time the umbrella tree was being mowed down. After trying and failing to locate the U-Bolt, the woman poured certain cryptical substances all over the rooms in my house, while assuring me that after her depature, I would discover it and I should get a wild melon ready in which I should stick it in and jettison it into the septic tank in the boys' quarters, since my wife probably never used the toilet there.

My driver returned the woman and my mother to Benin and Oghara the next morning. The following day my little boy went to the school and did not return home. I became so unsettled that I reported his disappearance to the Police Station and the NBC. It was as a result of the incessant radio announcements that someone spotted him by the side of the river and took him to the Yaba Police Station, from where he was escorted to my house. After the Police escorts had gone, I asked him why he behaved the way *he* had done and his reply was that he wanted to return to Benin. Two days later he was taken to Benin, with the assurance that I would pay his school fees up to whatever level of education he aspired to, which I did.

Three days after the boy left for Benin, I returned to St. Dominic's Catholic Church (High Mass) on a Sunday morning and went to *bed* after taking my breakfast. I was having a siesta when I had an apparition in which the Akpowa Priestess appeared to ask me why I had not removed the beddings on which I slept with my wife as she instructed. In fact, I deliberately refused to burn the beddings because I had just bought them during a trip to Europe. After that phantasm, I invited the inmates in my boys' quarters to help me remove the beddings. I had two mattresses on my bed, one cotton and one spring. After removing all the beddings, by the time we removed the two mattresses, there on the top of the tarpaulin was this mysterious U-Bolt, the type of which I had never seen before. I immediately went for the wild melon, stuck it into it and proceeded to dump it into the boys' quarters septic tank. Who would have believed this brand of fairy tale. But it happened to me. It was from that day that my sexual potency returned in earnest and I had five children by five different women between January and April, 1970. That was the first time I saw relief on my mother's face during the past ten years.

A Quintessential Mother

Prologue

How to Appease Esu

Before giving the details on how to make sacrifice to Esu, it is necessary to understand some fundamental features of the divinity of Evil. Orunmila has already established indubitably that the existence of Esu is as old as the existence of Olodumare. The one did not create the other because darkness could not have produced light or vice versa. The translucent enclave from which God commanded light to illuminate the void, existed at the same time *pari passu* as the darkness of the primeval.

There is however one point which Orunmila has not clarified to the author, which is underscored by the invocation of Esu. When supplicating Esu to accept any offering, reference is traditionally made to the parents of Esu, his wife and his friend. Normally, it is enough to mention Esu's name three times and he will accept any offering being made to him at any time and anywhere by saying:

E-Esu gba
E-esu gba
E-esu gba

So far, Orunmila has not confirmed to the author the genesis of the so-called relations and associates of Esu, often referred to by traditional Ifa priests, when invoking the divinity of evil. These are:-

1)   Agunmana Tidi Erukpe Olodi - as the father of Esu;
2)   Akuru mana nkpa - as his mother;
3)   Egba - as his wife;
4)   Ighoroko - His bosom friend who identifies all those who did or failed to perform the sacrifies prescribed for them at divination to Esu, for the purpose of helping or punishing them; and

5)   Agbirari, who delivers all sacrifices to Esu.

Orunmila ordered me to reveal everything for the benefit of posterity and misled mankind. Hence the corrections.

Invocation of Esu

I was informed by the traditional priest that Orunmila initially thought it fit to refer me to the traditional way of making offering to Esu is as follows:

To alert Esu to wake up if he is asleep, you begin at the Esu Shrine by using the Ifa Staff, Uranke to hit the protruding stone three times.

This is quickly followed by pouring cold water from a cup on the shrine three time with the words:-

Omi Esu
Omi Egba
Omi Ighoroko, Olukesu

If the offering is being made at day time, between sunrise and sunset, the offeror should again whilstle to say:

Esu Oologbe
Egba Oologbe
Ighoroko Oologbe.

Thereafter, the following incantation is pronounced if it is at day time (between 7am and 7pm)

Agbo Olonono -   (3 times)
Itaakun Tere fori laluja -   (3 times)
Oruko ton kpe' ejo.
Akuru mana nkpa   (3 times)
Oruko ton kpe iya Esu.
Agun mana tidi erukpe olodi   (3 times).
Oruko ti ankpe baba Esu.

Thereafter, touch the stone on Esu Shrine 3 times saying on each occasion - O o l o g b e !

Incidentally, that is the only nickname for Esu which Orunmila taught the author to utter to invite Esu to accept the sacrifice about to be offered - without all the other embellishments and affectations but including finally, Esu Tagrigba while muttering the word "O w i w i a" without anyone hearing, which was the primeval name of Esu.

If the offering is being made after dusk or in the night, the process that follows the water-pouring ritual changes, with the use of the following words:

Esu Oologbe
Egba Oologbe
Ighoroko Oologbe

Is no longer done by whistling but by words of mouth. That explains why it is forbidden to whistle in a house containing Ifa, at night, because Esu does not like the idea of inviting him by whistling, into frivolity and futility.

The ritual contines by adding:

Oruko ye kpe' Esu
Alamu lamu, Alamu lamu bataa - (3 times clapping both hands on each occasion)
Ofe bata Uja kun bam bam -   3 times
Oologbe - 3 times (Orunmila's version)
Esu tagrigba and muttering Owiwia.

Thereafter, break the four piece kolanut haralding the sacrifice and throw the four pieces on the ground to ask Esu whether the sacrifice is acceptable.

Since no one, including the divinities, shares kolanuts with Esu, all the kolanut pieces are left on the shrine. After the kolanut breaking and throwing ceremony, the food is then offered to Esu.

Finally, the pointed end of the Ifa Staff (Uranke) is pinned to the ground while beseeching God and His divinities, the offeror's guardian angel and ancestors, to add their ASEs to enable the sacrifice to manifest because it was God himself who taught his divinities and mortal creatures how to bribe Esu with food not to obstruct their activities in life.

At the end of the ceremony, the officiating Ifa Priest leads the way to Orunmila's shrine with the following song:-

Esu, mubo lowo otao, Ebibo bora olode, Ebibo
Mububo lowo Odi, Ebibo bora olode ebibo
Mubolowo Iku o, Ebibo bora olode, Ebibo
Mubo lowo Aisan, Ebibo bora olode, ebibo
Mubo lowo Aje o, Ebibo bora bora olode, ebibo,
Mubo lowo Aje o, Ebibo bora bora olode, ebibo
Mubo lowo Olosho, Ebibo bora olode, ebibo.

On getting to the Ifa shrine, the officiating Ifa priest orders everybody to kneel down including himself to report that the sacrifice has been made and beseech Orunmila to let it manifest. Thereafter, he says:

Oode Awo - Eeshi.

Although Esu is the creator, architect and generator of all evils, he is not altogether bereft of benign disposition. Unlike God who does not need to be fed by his creatures, Esu demands food from all organic beings created by God. That is why after creating them, God taught his divinities how to appease the evil divinity. In fact, after establishing a rapport with him, Esu once took Orunmila into confidence by telling him that if the divinity of wisdom could give him a part of whatever he eats, he (Esu) would always be by his (Orunmila's) corner to assist him in whatever he did. Esu can remove all obstacles from the path of those who feed him regularly. He can fight all battles for, and facilitate the passage through life of those who recognise and feed him. Let us now examine how this ambivalent amplitude of Esu, to be both amiable and hostile, has manifested itself through the passage of time.

The Contest for Seniority Between God's Divinities and Esu

It will be recalled that God created the earth as a new experiment on an evil-free universe after Esu had demonstrated in the divinosphere and heaven that the divine creatures could not enjoy any immunity from his disruptive machinations. As already revealed, incidentally, as the divinties were arriving on earth, they met Esu waiting for them on top of a stone inside the ocean.

As soon as God realised that Esu had pre-empted his designs for the world, he despatched Orisa-Nla to join the 200 divinities already on earth, as his personal surrogate. The arrival of Orisa-Nla to the world marked the beginning of another conflict among the divinities on who was to be recognised as the most senior of them all. Although Orisa-Nla was endowed by God to occupy the chair at the earthly meetings of the divinities, that did not automatically confirm him as being superior to his colleagues, since he was the last of the divinities to be created.

At the first meeting chaired by Orisa-Nla, they resolved the seniority dispute by declaring that beginning with the chair divinity, each of them should throw a feast for all the others at every meeting and that the first to succeed in hosting a feast would be recognised as the *primus inter pares*.

As soon as the decision was acclaimed, Esu appeared in their midst to raise a point of objection. He challenged them for daring to argue about seniority without deferring first to him. When they hushed him down by reminding him that he was not one of them and therefore did not have any *locus standi* at the divine council, he replied that he merely wanted to give them the opportunity of appreciating the aphorism that *first in time is first in law*. Esu then proceeded to explain that not even God their creator could claim to be senior to him. They retorted by insisting that they were discussing seniority among God's created-divinities and that unless he wanted to regard himself as God's own creature, he should leave them alone to continue with their deliberations.

Before taking leave of them, Esu told the divinities that the seniority they were contesting resolved itself into a competition for supremacy and therefore he was claiming the right to begin the feasting since he preceded them in arriving on earth. When he was eventually ordered to get lost, he warned them that none of them was going to succeed in pulling a feast through without allowing him to be the first to throw one.

Five days later, Orisa-Nla prepared an elaborate feast replete with plenty of food and drinks. As the chairman of the Council, Orisa-Nla had to say the opening prayers with the breaking of kola-nuts. No sooner did he start saying the prayers than screeches and squeals bellowed from the direction of Orisa-Nla's harem. Esu has esoterically winked his eyes to two of Orisa-Nla's little children, which instantaneously made them to develop convulsion. Before anyone could reach them, they both died. The sad event abruptly made the feast a non-event.

The same fatalities were repeated at the attempted feasts subsequently prepared by all other divinities until it came the the turn of Orunmila. To obviate the risk of losing his children to the feast, Orunmila consulted Ifa for directions. He was advised to serve Esu with a he-goat and the clay images of a rabbit and a lizard, and a piece of brass. He made the sacrifice after which he proceeded to arrange for his feast with down-beat despondency, not knowing what to expect.

On the day of his feast, as soon as Orisa-Nla was breaking the kolanuts with prayers, a comic yell was heard from the direction of Orunmila's backyard. Members of his household were astonished to find a live rabbit and live lizard both having brass pigmentation, fighting at the rubbish dump at the back of his house. The cries of amusement and bewilderment attracted the divinities to watch the strange spectacle. After watching the brass rabbit and lizard fighting for what lasted about an hour, the divinities returned to the feast table only to discover that fowls, ducks and other domestic pets had helped themselves to the food. Once again, the feast turned out to a non-event, but Orunmila did not lose a human soul on account of the sacrifice he had made.

That was the point at which the divinities realised the inexorability of Esu's proclamation, as a result of which they invited him albeit belatedly, and after tremendous cost in human lives, to start the feast. It is that feast made by Esu that all divinities and their human servants, pay for to this day in the form of sacrifices to Esu, which confirmed his pre-eminence over all the divinities created by God.

The event also explains why Esu is the only one-way receipient of sacrifice without recipro-cating or requitting. He receives sacrifice from all and sundry without the obligation to make sacrifice to anyone, which makes him *nulli secundus*.

Far from being a totally malevolent divinity therefore, Esu can be beneficent to, and sup-portive of, those who have the good sense to appreciate his importance by offering sacrifice to him. I will now illustrate this truism with the experience of the elephant and the tortoise on the one hand and the buffalo and toad on the other.

The Land Dispute Between the Elephant and the Tortoise

There was a piece of farm land in heaven the ownership of which was being contested between the mighty elephant and the meek tortoise. Both of them were arguing that the land belonged to them by inheritance from their parents. When the dispute assumed crisis propor-tions, God invited the divine council to intervene.

The council subsequently invited the elephant and the tortoise to indicate the physical land-mark or feature exemplifying their avowed title to the disputed land. They were given fourteen days within which to come with their attestations. The elephant, who was convinced that the innocuous tortoise stood no chance with him, went to the land and established his foot-prints all over it as proof that the land belonged to him. On his part, the tortoise went to Orunmila for divination, at which he was told to serve Esu with a he-goat and plently of raw beans. The tortoise made the sacrfice immediately.

After enjoying the sacrifice made to him, Esu went with a team of workers to cover up all the foot-marks of the elephant, and planted beans all over the land. Within a span of three days, the beans had germinated and sprouted into a thick farm of beans.

On the appointed day, both contestants appeared at the meeting of the divine council. Once again, they were both asked to establish their title to the land. The elephant re-iterated that the land was laden with the foot-marks of his late father and himself. However, the tortoise's guard-ian angel, acting as his advocate, observed the elephant's foot-marks were imminent in other stretches of the bush.

On his part, the tortoise averred that his parents and himself used to plant bean on the farm-land every year, and added that verifiers would see that there was a full-blown bean vegetation on it at that point in time. On that note, the divine council despatched a team of heavenly police-men to verify the averments of the two litigants.

When the verifiers got to the land, they saw no traces of the elephant's foot-marks. In contrast, they saw that it was completely covered up with bean plants that were already bearing fruits. Following the report of their findings to the divine council, the latter declared that the land truly belonged to the tortoise. Esu had favorably intervened on the side of the one who made sacrifice to him.

The Race Between the Toad and the Buffalo

Following God's decision that the Lion was to be the king of all quadruped animals, there was a subsequent conference to lay the ground rules for ensuring harmony and love among them. The meeting had gathered before they realised that they needed a red parrot's feather for the chairman to wear on his head as an ensignia of authority. To establish his supremacy, the lion called on the buffalo who instantly objected to the lion's derisive instruction, wondering why he did not send the smaller quadrupeds like the toad. The toad lost no time in taking umbrage to the irreverent remarks of the Buffalo. He added that much as he realised that he would move faster than the over-weighted buffalo, the latter had no right to challenge the authority of their God chosen leader. The lion however persuaded the toad to go quickly to fetch a red parrot's feather.

Since the Toad was familiar with the bush fountain where a flock of parrots went daily to have their baths and to drink water, he quickly dashed off to the spot where he found plenty of red parrot feathers. In a matter of minutes, he was able to turn up with three feathers, while keeping the rest for his own use whenever the need arose. The alacrity and agility with which the Toad produced the parrot's feathers earned him the appreciation of all the animals except the buffalo, who instinctively challenged the toad to a race. After some heated argument, it was resolved that the two of them were to be prepared for a race in nine days time.

The Toad, who did not disclose the secret of how he procurred the parrot's feathers, was a little more circumspect on what chance he stood in winning a race with the fast-moving buffalo. On getting home from the meeting, he quickly raced to Orunmila for divination, at which he was advised to serve Esu with a rat, a fish and a red parrot's feather. He made the sacrifice without delay.

Three days after the sacrifice, Esu transfigured into an amphibious knight of the heavenly grail and visited the toad in his abode to advise him on how to prepare for the up-coming contest with the buffalo. He asked the toad how many children he had and he disclosed that he had ten. The knight gave twelve red parrot's feathers to the toad and advised him that on the night of the eve of the contest, he was to line up his ten children throughout the route of the race, with each of them holding a red parrot's feather on its mouth. Since there is no remarkable difference between one toad and the other, the toad and his wife were also to wear a parrot's feather in their mouths. His wife was to begin the race with the buffalo while he was to conceal himself at a spot just before the finishing line of the race.

As soon as the race started between the toad's wife and the buffalo, she was to return home and at regular intervals, the children who were already lined up ahead of the buffalo were to call on the giant animal to hurry up as soon as he approached where they was waiting. The Toad thanked the Knight for his advice and the visitor went away.

Before the day of the contest, the Toad and his family had positioned themselves through-out the entire stretch of the route of the race, with each of them holding a red parrot's feather in its mouth.

As soon as the race began, the Buffalo soon got astounded at seeing that the Toad was always ahead of him. That made the former to run as fast as his legs and strenght could afford, until he became thoroughly enervated. At the last stretch before the finishing line, the Buffalo, who was now thoroughly exhausted, fell to the ground, dead. That was the point at which his challenger announced his arrival at the finishing line.

There is no other discernible way of serving Esu except by offering food to him from time to time. His favorite sacrifice is the he-goat or the cock and occasionally, ram. If one is undertaking a major project, travelling or going for a contest, even without going for divination, it is sufficient to offer akara, (bean buns) eko (maize porridge) meat of ram and fish, to Esu to solicit his support. In places where these materials are not available, it is enough to offer bread, cake, biscuits, fried corn, peanuts and local fruits. The offering can be made anywhere outside the house by calling on Esu in the name of Agbirari three times before depositing it, with the words; Esu gba, Esu gba.

Traditionally, all those who have been fully initiated into Ifism are ideally required to give out of whatever food they eat, to Esu. That is in accordance with the concordat reached at the beginning of time between Esu and Orunmila, when the latter promised to be sending a portion of whatever he eats, to the former. When any sacrifice is therefore being offered to Orunmila, a portion of it is first sent to Esu before anyone eats out of it. Such offerings are different from formal sacrifices to Esu, because although all and sundry are required to make sacrifice to him, he is neither obligated to serve, nor to make sacrifice to anyone, let alone share out of the sacrifices made to him with anyone else. That is why Esu is *nulli secundus* in terms of importance as recipient of sacrificial offerings.

Chapter 1

OGUNDA-OGBE

OGUNDA-SO-ORIRE
OGUNDA-OBORI-OGBE
OGUNDA-BE-EDE-OLE

He Made Divination for the Palm Tree

Lisa Liso, babalawo Okpe, odifa fun okpe, abufun Ifatoun ni
jo ti awon mejeji fi omi oju shubere omo tuutu tu.

Lisa Liso was the Ifa priest who made divination for the palm tree and a woman called Ifatoun, when each of them was desperately anxious to have a child. The Ifa that appeared for them was Ogunda-so-ori-re. Both of them were advised to make sacrifice to Ogun with a dog, gourd and bell to have children, but also to serve Esu with he-goat, cutlass, palm tree climber and tap-knife (ite in Yoruba and oya in Bini) that is, the instrument now used for tapping palm wine, so that enemies may not harm them and their children.

The palm tree made the first sacrifice to have children, but refused to make the second one on the ground that her captivating beauty and towering height were sufficient to deter any prospective enemy from daring her. Besides, she relied on her protective gadgets (thorns) to protect her from any aggressor.

On her part, Ifatoun made the two sacrifices after which she was told that her first child would be a boy but a trouble-shooter (Onijogbon in yoruba and Agberan-gbiri in Bini). Soon afterwards, she became pregnant and in the fullness of time, gave birth to a male child.

On the other hand, the palm had no problem in having children, but on account of the second sacrifice she refused to make, Esu went around to alert animals, birds and human beings that the children produced by the palm tree could be used for a variety of purposes. He told mankind that apart from cooking her children directly for food, they could also be crushed to produce palm oil, while the chaff remaining after squeezing out the oil, could be used as fuel for igniting fire. Besides that, Esu told human beings that the seeds or kernels could be eaten as food or used to produce kernel oil for use as pomade for creaming dry skins. The most rewarding revelation made to man by Esu, was that after cutting away her enchanting busts, the juice flowing out from them was one of the most exhilarating liquors ever known.

To experiment on the advice of Esu, man used the climber with which she failed to make sacrifice, to reach the height at which she held her children (palm fruits). When she saw a man climbing up to her, she rejoiced momentarily, saying that in spite of the predictions of Orunmila, a suitor was at last coming to chase her. Contrary to her expectation, however, on getting to her chest, the man used the cutlass (with which she failed to make sacrifice) to cut off all her protective gadgets (thorny palm branches). After clearing the way to her chest, the man used the cutlass to cut off the sheaf holding her children together and the bunch of them fell to the ground. As if berefting her of all her children was not enough, the man cut off one of her breasts and used the tap-knife to bore a hole into her chest and a pipe to funnel the liquid flowing from it into a gourd (with which she also failed to make sacrifice). As her blood was dropping into the gourd, she remembered the words of her diviner and began to cry "Lisa Liso, Lisa Liso" which is the sound that comes out of palm wine dropping into a container, gourd or bottle, and which was the name of the Awo who advised her to make the second sacrifice.

On her part, Ifatoun gave birth to a male child who grew up to be very rascally. The name given to him was Igara and he took to farming. He was the farmer that Esu instigated to attack the beautiful palm tree. He was the first man to use palm fruits to produce oil and to tap palm wine from her.

When this Ifa appears at Ugbodu, the person will be advised to make sacrifice to the new Ifa with a hen and five yams tied together, and to serve Esu with a he-goat, palm tree climber, gourd and tap-knife, to obviate the danger of losing his children to enemies and to avert the risk of a machete attack and the sickness of anaemia. At divination, the person should be advised to machete serve; Ogun with a cock, Ifa with a hen and five tubers of yam, and Esu with a he-goat, to prevent the danger of losing children and an attack by marauders. The person would give birth to a rascally male child, who should be given his own Ifa to enable him to weather the storms of life on earth.

Divination for Two Brothers - Ogunda and Ogbe

Oto-to-to-to ni mo kpe Ifa mi.
Oro-ro-ro-ro ni mo kpe Ifa mi,
Oto-to ni nje ekpa.
Oto-to ni a nje emu mi
I'n to re-to-re-o-to-re-to-o-re
Ni a nfun Oba mokin ni ode Iranje
Ki o le fi nkan ti o to-to-o-re,
to-o-re-ta eni ni ore.

These were the five Awos who made divination for Ese-kan-Ogunda when he was going to conceal his brother Ogbe with a pot in the bush to prevent him from being killed. He was advised to make sacrifice with a wild tuber called Abirishoko in yoruba and olikhoro in Bini, a giant pot and a he-goat. Without knowing that Ogbe was answering the call of nature in the bush, Ese-kan-Ogunda was told to take the sacrifice to the bush, by putting the pot on his head and inclining backwards to allow it to fall to the ground behind him.

When he got to the bush, Ogunda inclined his neck backwards and allowed the pot to drop face down to the ground. Unknown to him, the pot actually covered Ogbe, who tried unsuccess-fully to get out from the pot. At the same time, Esu held down the pot so firmly that there was nothing Ogbe could do to get out from it. Esu covered him up firmly on the ground because Death had been looking for Ogbe to kill him and take him to heaven. After looking for him in vain, Death gave up his search and went to capture someone else.

Subsequently, the two brothers came to realise how the sacrifice protected Ogbe from being killed by Death and they both sang in praise of the Awos who made divination and sacrifice for them.

When it appears at divination the person will be advised to make the same sacrifice to thwart the morbid contrivances of his enemies.

The Divination for Members of the Household of Odio

Kete ti eni di aiye ni eni ni aje.
Okete gun ori Ebe fono nomu,
Adifa won la akoko yegele ni ile Odio.

The moment a person is born to the world marks the beginning of his fortune. That was the Awo that made divination for the members of the household of Odio. They were advised to make sacrifice with one rat, and to serve their heads with pounded yam and soup prepared with dried fish. They made the sacrifice and began to enjoy life thereafter, and sang in praise of the Awo who divined for them.

His Experience with the People of Ife

Legbe Legbe eye, Legbe Legbe eye - were the two Awos who made divination for Ogunda-so-Orire when coming from heaven. He was advised to make sacrifice with a goat to his guardian angel, he-goat to Esu, and to make a feast with rats, fish, cooked yam, roasted corn, and ground-nuts to the animals of the forest, because of the hard time he was going to have before prosperity came to him on earth. He made the sacrifice and came out at Ife, where he became a proficient and popular Ifa priest. He became so prosperous that he had many wives and children. His success however generated enmity for him, so much that his children began to die soon after birth, as a result of the machination of witches.

He was hounded by problems from pillar to post which made him to become totally disillu-sioned. Eventually, he was physically driven out of his house at night and he took refuge in a cave which was known to be home to wild beasts like lions, tigers, pythons, hyenas and leopards. Paradoxically, the animals were quite happy to receive him as their guest. Every morning, he used to go around the village to make divination and sacrifice for people, as a result of which he often returned home with plenty of meat which he shared with the animals.

After living in the cave for the better part of one year, Ife was stricken with farmine, draught, destitution, deprivation and all manner of calamitous afflictions. There was no rain for the whole year, harvest failed woefully, several men became impotent, pregnant women had miscarriages, the people of Ife stopped paying any homage to the Olofin and death was plundering the population indiscrimately.

When the people began to say that the adversity which engulfed them was a function and indeed a reflection, of the hard-luck of the reigning Oba, there were rumors of imminent popular uprising to demand his banishment. The uncertainties culminated in the Olofin inviting his council of chiefs to summon divine priests, Ifa priests and seers to find out the cause of the catastrophe and to propose solutions. All the diviners invited for divination were unanimous in professing that the problems arose as a result of the Ifa priest they hounded into the forest, and that the divine council was so irritated about it that they invited Esu to visit his wrath on Ife. The diviners declared that the difficulties would only end if they sought the whereabouts of the man and persuaded him to return to his family in Ife.

The diviners recommended that the able-bodied young men of the town should be dispatched into the forests to hunt for animals with which to make sacrifice for the whole town. The young men were told to hunt for rabbits, hares, squirrels, rats, grass-cutters and hedge-hogs for sacrifice. After they had roamed the forest in vain for the small animals, they came across a huge cave and decided to rest at what looked like its entrance. After eating some food the young man began to hit the cave so forcefully that the vibration shook Orunmila below. Orunmila reacted with an incantation in the Ifa dialect as follows:-

He yelled "ORAA" - which the young men did not understand.
If they knew what it meant, they
would have replied with "ARAJE"
as the appropriate key.

When there was no reply, he continued "IGE WOMI" which the young men again did not understand, lest they should have replied with the key of "KUE-'RUBO-ORA." When he did not receive any reply, he subsequently reverted to literary Ife dialect by asking who it was that knocked the rock and they replied that they were the young men of Otu-Ife.

Thereafter, he asked what their mission was, and they replied that they were sent by the elders to fetch small animals from the forest for sacrifice. He retorted by professing that if they killed any small animals in the forest, all the remaining young men of Otu-Ife would die before they reached home. Not knowing the implication of that prophesy, the young men went about their business and subsequently succeeded in killing a number of small animals. They were so happy to have succeeded in their encounter, but became despondent when they got home to see all the male adolescents in the town had died and there was weeping and wailing in every house of Ife. Following that calamitous development, the elders decided that it was pointless making the sacrifice. They decided to make a second divination.

After divination, it was recommended that the able-bodied adults of Ife should be enjoined to fetch medium-sized animals from the forest for a town-wide sacrifice. The men got together and left with guns, spears, bows and poisoned arrows for the forest without any delay. After roving the forest for a long time, once again they came to the cave and sat down to eat and to rest. When the adults finished eating, they again hit the rock and once more it judered so violently that Orunmila had to repeat the same incantations.

When he yelled "ORAA", the adults replied "ARAJE". When he pronounced "IGE WOMI", they replied "KUE'RUBO ORA". He followed it up with "IBO OHO" but the adults did not know the key to those words.

When Orunmila asked who they were, they replied that they were the able-bodied adults of Otu-Ife. In reply to the next question of what they were doing in the forest, they explained that they were in the forest to hunt for medium-sized animals for sacrifice in the town. Once again, he told them that they would find pigs, deers, antelopes and bush goats, but that if they killed any of them, all the remaining male adults in Ife would die before they returned home. Unfortunately they could not comprehend the significance of the foreboding because they set about the business of killing these animals and returned home with their games with a feeling of accomplishment. To their utter dismay, they got home to meet people crying their eyes out because all the adults of Ife had died. Once again, the sacrifice was abandoned.

In the ensuing state of utter confussion, they made yet another divination, which advised that the elders of Ife should go to the forest to fetch over-aged animals for sacrifice. They subsequently left for the forest with their hunting instruments. Once again they saw the mysterious cave and stopped at its base to rest. When they again hit the cave, it shook Orunmila and he started the incantational dialogue by saying "ORAA" and they replied with "ARAJE". At that moment Orunmila was doing a festival as a result of which all his inmates in the cave had been fetching water for the ceremony. For that reason, there was already plenty of water in the cave. When he next said "IGE WOMI", they replied "KUE ERUBO ORA". He followed that with "IBO OHO" and they replied "AA OFIN". Finally, he said "OOTIGBEJI" and they replied with "OOLUMO". When he asked who they were and what their mission was, they replied that they were the elders of Ife out in the forest in search of big animals for sacrifice at home. He told them that they would come across elephants, gorillas, buffalos, pythons, but that if they killed any of them, all the remaining elders in Ife would die before they got home. That was how the elders discovered what had depleted the population of Ife so desolately.

They instantly gave up their hunting expedition and decided to probe the death-dealing occupant of the cave. They collected plenty of dried leaves from the forest and stuffed them into the cave after which they set it ablaze. As the fire was blazing, Orunmila was at the point of his ritual when he was pouring water into the shrine of the divinity of the ground (Oriole) whose festival he was making. At that point, he said:

Legbe Legbe eye, Legbe Legbe eye,
Oda omo le ufe, olu agba ufe,
Oma domi boo, kpere gun ese
Domi boo, kpere gun ese.

He was not aware of what was happening outside the cave, but the water he was pouring into the shrine was passing through the entrance of the cave and inadvertently extinguishing the blazing inferno. When he completed the water pouring ceremony, he decided to come outside the cave to see how far the water flowed. He came out to see a heavy smoke oozing out of the cave and he began to wonder who was trying to roast him alive inside the cave. At the same time the elders of Ife who had meanwhile concealed themselves were emerging to find out whether the fire had killed the fiendish demon of the cave.

When they got to the mouth of the cave, they saw Orunmila and by reflex action, all of them went on their knees to sing his praise. They said that they never knew that he was the one in the cave, because they had been searching for him for a long time. They told him that the town of Ife was almost desolate and that they had been trying to make sacrifice to procure his return to his home, people and family, and to help them rescue the town from total destruction. In reply, he reminded them that he was hounded out of the town and they even pursued him to the cave where he took refuge. They all begged him to forgive and forget. He told them that if they wanted him to return home, they should bring a goat, a hen, a rat, a fish, a bundle of yam tubers and a gourd of oil.

The elders gave up their hunting expedition and returned home to bring the materials demanded by Orunmila. After receiving the materials, he assured them that he would return home in seven days time and that before then he was going to use the materials to offer a thanksgiving feast to the hosts who gave him hospitality during his exile. He subsequently used the materials to feast the animals of the cave. That cave has since become a shrine where the people of Ife serve Ifa annually, after Orunmila named it ODU, after the name of his mother. On his return to Ife, all the tribulations came to an end and peace and prosperity returned to the town. That cave is where initiation ceremony into IFISM is done in Ife.

Divination Made for Orunmila When He Was Touring for IFISM:

Inu ni gbe inu, abe ni ki jeni. Eyanmu yanmu egberu ku oda,
Ina jeni jeni, Uja je eniyan je eniyan. Arina kpaa. Arina
kpaa A i ri uya kpaa. Adiye ote tina nbo, ofi erun ni ale
kuye kuye. Iferi fe Ogun ori oroke. Ofan oye ude feere fe.
Adifa fun Orunmila baba shawo lo si ono jinjin gbon gbon gbon.
lo'de ibile re.

Those were the Awos who made divination for Orunmila when he was advised during his tour to return to his ancestral home to make sacrifice. He was at that time very poor, having only just returned from exile. He was told to give a he-goat to Esu before going to his home town, and to add the cutlass he inherited from his father. He was also to serve Ifa with rolled dried fish, akara, eko, beans and a boa, and to serve his head with an unsplit kolanut fruit (odidi-obi aila in yoruba and Ohia-evbee in Bini). He was to serve his late father with a goat in his home town.

He made all the sacrifices but refused to part with his cutlass. His wife, who knew that prosperity would be the result of the sacrifice, arranged to steal the cutlass from where he kept it, and gave it to the Awos for the sacrifice. On the other hand, he could not find an unsplit kolanut fruit to serve his head, nor the Boa for his Ifa. When he discovered later that his wife had parted with the only cutlass he had, he had her thoroughly beaten for parting with his priceless possession.

The following morning he left with his wife for the land of his birth, since he had no other cutlass the only instrument he travelled with was his Uranke - divination staff, adding the remnant of the eko and beans with which he served his Ifa. As they were going, his wife looked up and saw a single kolanut fruit on top of the kola tree and drew his attention to it. Instead of congratulating his wife for her vigilance, he snapped at her, by asking what he was going to use to pluck the kolanut fruit when she had already parted with his only cutlass. In anger, the wife told him not to worry because the kolanut was required for serving his head and not her own. However, in desperation, he threw his uranke at the kolanut fruit and since it was already ripe, it fell to the ground as soon as the uranke impacted on it. It was the only fruit left at the top of the tree.

As he moved to pick up the kolanut fruit he was shocked to see that it fell on a boa which was resting on the ground. Once more, he turned round to query his wife for dispensing with his cutlass because there was no instrument with which to kill the boa. The wife retorted that he was at liberty to leave the snake alone since he could not think of any improvisation without his much cherished cutlass. Again, she reminded him that the boa was required for serving his guardian angel and not her own. At that stage, he told her to put down the bag she was carrying on her head and he rolled the live snake into it, while tying the mouth of the bag. After tying the mouth of the bag, he gave it once more to the wife to carry.

Meanwhile, they were approaching a no-go forest which was known to be the operational base of three armed bandits. One of the bandits lived in Ado (now Ado-Ekiti), the other lived in Ijero while the third lived in Ilara. They had earlier met the same Awos who divined for Orunmila and they advised them to serve Esu with he-goats to avert the risk of apprehending a victim much stronger than themselves, who would kill them. They felt so insulted by the prediction of the Awos, that they totally refused to make the sacrifice since they could not imagine how any victim could defy the powers of the three of them.

As Orunmila and his wife were passing through the much dreaded bandit-infested forest, they were accosted by the three bandits. They apprehended Akpetebi on account of the bag she was carrying. When they were taking her away, Orunmila tried to follow them, but they commanded him to disappear if he did not wish to be killed. Since he was totally defenseless, he went to hide behind a big tree. Asked what she was carrying, Orunmila's wife told them she was carrying the food they wanted to eat during their journey. They tried to rape her, but since the food was more in need at that time, they decided that the love-making could wait.

When the first bandit opened the bag, the boa who was already charged for action, bit him. He then complained to the others that something in the bag had stung his fingers. The second bandit also tried to bring out what was in the bag and the boa also bit him. As the third bandit was doubting the intentions of his two commrades, he took the bag from them and dipped his hand into it, only to be stung again by the boa. Thereafter, they tied up the bag and ordered the woman to carry it and follow them to their staging post in the heart of the forest. Orunmila was however behind them trailing their footsteps stealthily .

As soon as they got to their camp they blindfolded Orunmila's wife and bound up her hands and feet. Thereafter, they took up the bag once more to open it. Incidentally, at that point the noxious effect of the snake's bite had overwhelmed them. One after the other, they fell to the ground, stone dead, without being able to see the contents of the bag. Orunmila's wife heard the sound of their falling to the ground, followed by what sounded like total silence. After failing to hear any sound from them for a long time, she imagined that the venom of the boa in her bag had taken its toll on them. All three of them were stone dead.

She subsequently began to sing in praise of Ifa and of the Awos who made divination and sacrifice for her husband. When Orunmila heard Akpetebi's song, he realized that his sacrifice had manifested and ran hurriedly to meet her. His first inclination was to remove her blindfold and unblind her. It was thereafter that they saw the treasures of the camp. It contained all items of value that the bandits had been robbing from people for a long time. When Orunmila discovered that the bandits were all dead, he decided to embark on instant divination to seek directions. His own odu appeared telling him that that was the end of his journey to his home base and that he should move forward further away from the camp. He did as he was directed and he came to a second camp containing men and women previously captured by the bandits and tied up awaiting being sold into slavery. Orunmila quickly untied them and in return, they proclaimed allegiance to him as their new lord and master.

Meanwhile, since there was no other way of compensating the boa for the good job it did for him, he decided to set it free to return to the freedom of its bush habitat. At the same time, he used his ASE to proclaim that anybody for whom this odu appears at initiation (Ugbodu) should from that day forbid killing or eating the boa or indeed any snake.

In accordance with Ifa's advice, he told the human captives to carry the loot and accompany him back to Ife. On second thought, he stopped short of making a direct entry into Ife, because he knew that Olofin would ask for a share of his windfall if he entered the town in broad day-light to the full view of everybody. He decided to ask his entourage to hide in the bush on the precincts of Ife, while he went to bargin with the Oba and his friend, the Oliwo (chief priest) of the Oro cult that a curfew should be declared that night because he was going to make a special ceremony to mark the anniversary of his mother's death. His request was granted.

From about 8.00 pm on that night, the Oro cult heralded a curfew throughout the town of Ife and all and sundry had to stay indoors. Under cover of the curfew and darkness, Orunmila was able to bring his human and material treasures into his house without the knowledge of anyone in the town. As Orunmila was moving in his loot, he sang a song which has since become part of Ifa tradition. ORO LO, ORO LO SO SO several times. When people asked him the following morning how he came by the human and material possessions in his house, he explained that it was his share of his parents' legacy that he brought from his home town. Even the Olofin wondered that Orunmila must have come from a prosperous family in his home town. Not long afterwards, the Oba appointed Orunmila to the position of a high chief and to become his right hand man.

Three months later, he feasted the whole town with a cow, goat, ram and fowls and invited the two Awos who made divination and sacrifice for him. At the height of the feast, he sang in praise of the Awos who divined for him.

When this Ifa appears at Ugbodu, the person will be advised to make sacrifice with materials purchased either on credit or with borrowed money because that was what Orunmila did on that day. He should serve the new Ifa with a goat, a hen, pigeon, fish and rat, and to serve Esu with a he-goat. After completing the Ifa initiation ceremony, he should proceed to his home town, that is, his ancestral home, and make sacrifice there with a goat. If he serves Ifa well, he will become prosperous.

When it appears at divination, the person should be told to have his own Ifa and to serve

Esu with a he-goat and the head of a boa.

He Made Divination for the Snail in Heaven

*Aba she kere mu legun, Odifa fun ibikunle to ma nu kon
kunle ara le*

The umbrella tree is short when young, but a little later, it will become taller than the roof of the house. That was the name of the Awo who made divination for Ibikunle, when she was single-handedly going to populate her house by herself. Ibikunle is the heavenly name of the snail and it means the one who produced enough children to fill his or her house. She was advised to make sacrifice with hen, rat and fish. She made the sacrifice and began to produce children to fill her house.

When it appears at divination for a woman anxious to have children, she will be advised to make sacrifice because she will have so many children that she will eventually be tired of having more.

He Later Divined for his Friend Oro

*Okon kpoki, Erigidi kpii, adifa fun Oro nijo ti Oro wo
orun kenge kenge.*

One sharp sound (Okpa kpoi in Bini) and one loud sound (Okpa gbii in Bini) are the names of the Awos who made divination for Oro when he was so ill that he thought he was going to die, (that is figure of speech, "when he was looking obliquely at heaven"). He was advised to make sacrifice with eko, akara, rat fish and a chicken. After preparing the sacrifice, the Ifa priests told him to carry it on his head to Esu shrine. He was further told that on getting to the shrine, he was to back it and incline his head backwards in such a way that the sacrifice would drop on the shrine.

As soon as he allowed the sacrifice to drop on Esu shrine, while still backing Esu, a voice instructed him to stretch his hands and feet forward. First, he stretched out his left limbs and next his right limbs. The moment he did that, the disease that had afflicted his body to the point of incapacitation suddenly disappeared. From the shrine, he began to dance and sing towards the house:

*Ijo logo ji jo, erigidi kpii, erigidi.
Ijo logo ji jo, erigidi kpi-kpi-kpi, erigidi.*

He was singing in praise of Orunmila and his two surrogates for the miraculous healing he had just experienced.

When this odu appears at divination as AYEO (that is, foreboding danger) the divinee will be told that he/she is suffering from a disease which he or she is concealing, but will be advised to make sacrifice to get rid of it. If the indication is UREE (which means that there is no danger to worry about) the person will be told to be expecting some gift or favor.

He Made Divination for the Stingy Hunter

Ogunda-so-Orire made divination for the hunter who was so niggardly that he never shared his game are with his neighbors. He was told to serve Esu with a he-goat to avoid embarrassment. He did not do it. One day, he returned from the forest with a single dove. His next door neighbor, an elderly woman, begged him for the dove because she needed it for a special sacrifice. Characteristically, he bluntly refused on the pretext that since the dove was his only game on that day, he could not part with it at any price.

The following night robbers went to burglarize a house on the next street. When the robbers discovered that their victims were in hot pursuit of them, they entreated the hunter to allow them to off-load their loot in his house and he agreed. Incidentally, the old woman was watching all the developments. The robbers escaped all right, but as the victims of the robbery were returning home dejectedly after failing to catch up with the burglars, the old lady beckoned to them and they went into her house. Thereafter, she intimated to them that their stolen property were concealed in the hunter's house.

When the people subsequently gate-crashed into the hunter's house, they found all their stolen property in his parlor. He was accused of being a thief and he was about to be lynched, but for the timely intervention of the palace police who arrested him for arraignment before the royal court. He was in detention, when he remembered the sacrifice he failed to make. He was under custody when he told his wife to implore Orunmila to do the sacrifice for him. The sacrifice was duly made.

At his subsequent court trial, he explained that he merely obliged some people who were passing by and besought him to take custody of those materials before they returned to collect them. Esu influenced the trial judge to reason that since the goods were found in his living room, it was an indication that he had no reason to believe that they were stolen. If he had knowingly agreed to take custody of stolen goods, he would have hidden them away instead of leaving them in his sitting room. Besides, Esu had meanwhile suborned a high chief to testify to the erswhile impeccable integrity and the law-abiding disposition of the hunter.

In his verdict, the judge, who was already under the influence of Esu, decided that the hunter was only a victim of circumstances and not a thief. He was accordingly discharged and acquitted.

When this Ifa appears at Ugbodu, the person will be advised to serve: his head with a cock: Ifa with another goat; and Esu with a he-goat, to avert the risk of losing an imminent windfall. He should be advised never to allow anyone to keep any goods under his custody. Moreover, he should serve his own head before honoring an invitation, to obviate the risk of losing his luck to other people.

When it appears at divination, the person should be advised to serve Esu with a he-goat, one snail and seven needles, on account of an impending robbery.

He Made Divination for Tella-Roko, When He Was Poor

Leke Leke ko ye didu. Ogbigbo lila fo raba ribi.
Adifa fun Tella Roko nijo ti won ni tie titon.
The cattle eaglet (Leke Leke in yoruba and Enibokun in Bini)
does not lay dark eggs.
The tiokam (ogbigbo in yoruba and Owonwon in Bini) is the
bird that flies with large wings.

Those were the two Awos who made divination for Tella-roko, when people wrote him off as a hard-luck case, and that he was already finished, in simple words, when he was languishing in abject poverty. The Awos confirmed that fortune had eluded him for good unless he was able to make sacrifice. He was required to make sacrifice with a cock, rat, fish, six bitter kolas, kolanuts, and snails. He made the sacrifice without delay.

After the sacrifice, the Awos gave him the six bitter kolas, predicting that his prosperity would arrive during the yam planting season. Meanwhile, he brushed his farm, felled the trees, burnt the shrubs, cleared the stumps and began planting his crops. He became rather restive and jittery when it was time to plant yams, as he began digging the ridges for planting seed yams. After digging three ridges, he was on the fourth one when his hoe stuck a hole containing a pot ostensibly buried there a long time ago. When he opened the pot, he discovered that it contained money, beads and jewels. The excitement so overwhelmed him that instinctively, he began to sing and rejoice with the words:

"Tella Roko, mojin showo loko, Tella Roko."
"I have hit a pot of wealth in my farm".

He chanted the song for so long and so repeatedly that the neighbor with whom he shared the same farm boundary, overheard him. After ensuring, by listening attentively to Tella Roko's song of joy, that he had hit a pot of money buried in the ground of his farm, the neighbor left at once for the Oba's palace. When he got to the palace, he reported that his farm neighbor with whom he had a common border, was rejoicing because he had discovered a pot of wealth buried in the ground, he suggested that the Oba should send policemen to go and collect the pot from Tella Roko, because according to the tradition of the land, anything discovered from beneath the ground belongs to the Oba. Accordingly, the Oba dispatched a contingent of policemen to go and bring Tella Roko and the pot of wealth.

Incidentally, before the royal policemen arrived at his farm, Esu transfigured into a benevolent passer-by, to advise him to change the motif and theme of his song because the Oba had sent policemen to come for him and the pot of wealth he had avowedly discovered in his farm. Esu advised him to change the tune of his song and to leave for home at once. Esu asked him for the bitter kola with which he had made sacrifice and he showed all six of them to him, tied to his loin cloth. Esu told him to start eating them on his way home, after showing him a bitter-kola tree with ripe fruits near his farm which he had not erstwhile discovered. Before leaving him, Esu taught him the words to sing with:

"Woni te mi ti ton,
Te mi oo tii ton
Tella Roko ti ri igi orogbo loko.
Moti ri igi orogbo to ma fun mi lowo.
Tella Roko, temi o tii ton".
"People say that I am finished,
But I am not finished because,
I have discovered a tree full of bitter-kola,
which will give me plenty of money."

Thereafter, he immediately left for home chewing his bitter-kola and singing with the bitter kola tree he had just discovered near his farm.

That was the situation in which the royal policemen met him on their way to his farm. The policemen were satisfied that he was not rejoicing for discovering a pot of wealth in his farm as his neighbor spuriously alleged, but that the poor man was excited over the tree of bitter kola he discovered near his farm. They told him to take them to the bitter kola tree and he did so willingly. Thereafter, they told him to follow them to the palace to tell his story by himself to the Oba.

When he got to the palace, the Oba asked him for the pot of wealth he had discovered in his farm and he feigned total bewilderment. When he was able to calm down to make an intelligible reply, he said that he was dumbfounded because he had never before heard of any pot of wealth, let alone discovered one on his farm. Asked whether he did not sing to rejoice over the discovery of a pot of money in his farm, he replied that he only sang and rejoiced over his discovery of a tree full of bitter kola in his farm. To substantiate his assertion, he produced the bitter kola fruits he plucked from the tree and cited the royal policemen as his witnesses because they saw the tree with their own eyes. He became exceedingly happy because the sale of the fruits was going to give him plenty of money.

The royal policemen who went to his farm confirmed that before they met him on his way home from the farm they had overheard him singing joyfully about the bitter kola tree he had discovered in his farm. They added that he was still chanting the bitter kola song when they met him and he was in fact chewing some of the fruits at the time. They also confirmed that to test the veracity of his story, they made him to take them to the tree which they actually saw on the periphery of his farm.

At that point the Oba invited his farm neighbor to substantiate his story. He explained rather dejectedly and deflatedly that he must have misconstrued what he overheard from Tella-Roko's song. He apologized that he never knew that the man was singing with the bitter kola tree and that he thought he was singing about money. On that note, after rebuking him for bearing false tales, the Oba decided summarily that he was to be executed for lying against his farm neighbor.

Subsequently, Tella-Roko began by plucking the fruits from the bitter kola tree and preparing them for sale. It was after selling all the fruits that he bought another he-goat to thank Esu and invited and feasted his two Ifa priests sumptuously for the efficacious divination and sacrifice they made for him. That was the point at which he went to his farm to remove the contents of the pot to his house. He became so wealthy that the Oba eventually conferred a high chieftaincy title on him. He easily became the wealthiest man in the community, without anyone knowing the secret of his prosperity, apart from Esu and his guardian angel.

When this Odu appears at divination, the person will be advised not to disclose his secrets to anyone and not to be loquacious about his fortune, especially in his dealings with close friends who can easily betray him. He should make sacrifice because prosperity is on its way to him.

The Divination Made for Orunmila When His Prosperity Came

Okete gun ori ebe, O ho ra kuye kuye.
Adifa fun Orunmila ni jo ti uwa re she she mbo.
The rabbit climbed the ridge of a planted yam and
used its fingers to scratch its body gently.

That was the name of the Awo who made divination for Orunmila when his prosperity began to blossom. That was when the appurtenances of prosperity left heaven on their journey to his house. He rejoiced when they got to him and began to sing:

"Okete gun ori o gerere,
Ni uwa idu she ibo o gerere.

He was thanking the Ifa priest who predicted that prosperity was on its way to him. He thanked; his Ifa with a goat, and Esu with a he-goat for piloting prosperity to his house.

When it appears at divination for a man, he should be advised to have his own Ifa so that his prosperity hitherto held up in heaven, might be liberated to come to him. If it appears for an unmarried woman, she should be advised to marry a man having his own Ifa. If she is a married woman, she should be advised to tell her husband to have his own Ifa so they might prosper.

The Divination for Orunmila When He Bought a Slave

Ushe ti'nshe awo, kii she ashe ku.
Iya ti onje awo, aje la'ni.
Adafa fun Orunmila nijo ti onlo ra Igbira le eru.
The deprivations and sufferings of a divine priest do not
end his life.
More often than not, such setbacks are a
prelude to his prosperity.

Those were the names of the Awos who made divination for Orunmila when he travelled to the land of Igbiras (now the Kwara State of Nigeria) to buy a slave. He was advised to make sacrifice with a cock and a hen before travelling. He made the sacrifice and eventually bought three slaves from the place and brought them home to serve him. They served him so well that they made him become rich, after which he proclaimed that the Igbiras were endowed with good heads and guardian angels, that is, that they are harbingers of good fortune and prosperity.

When it appears at divination, the person will be advised that some servants, if he does not already have them, will come to live with him. He should treat them humanely, because their stars would bring him good luck.

He Made Divination for Aban, the Slave of Oni-Taaji

Ibembe oku bi ojo. Odifa fun Aban, Aban Ioni kerun oro.
Aban ni ke run ode. Erun de, adifa fun Onitaji ni jo to
ma kpa ire lo mi re.

The big drum sounds like rain drops, was the name of the Awo who made divination for Aban, the slave of the father of Oni-Taji who in turn, made divination for the Oba of Itaji. The traditional idol worshipped by the people of Itaji was the boa constrictor or python (Ere in yoruba and Ikpin in Bini).

The Ifa priest advised Oni-taji to make sacrifice with one of the boa constrictors in order to live to a ripe old age. The Oba made the sacrifice by killing one of the sacred boa constrictors. Traditionally, the Oba never gave any gifts to Aban after making divination and sacrifice for him because he always derided him, being his own slave. After the Oba had used the boa constrictor for the sacrifice, Aban decided to watch out for subsequent developments. In the night, Aban left the house stealthily after people had gone to sleep, and began to beat the bembe drum, through-out the town, singing that the bembe drum was sounding like rain-drops because the Oba had killed one of the sacred boa constrictors for making sacrifice (Oni-taji ti kpa ere je).

The announcement so infuriated the entire citizenry of Itaji that they trooped out in a popular uprising to demand the dethronement of Oni-Taji. When the Oba saw the sour turn of events, he called a conference of diviners and invited Orunmila who blamed him for undermining Aban for so long. The unanimous advice of the conference was that he was to invite Aban and pacify him by giving him food, dresses and money. Accordingly, the Oba invited Aban and pacified him passionately. After giving him adequate compensation in cash and kind, he sought his opinion on what to do to defuse the charged political and social atmosphere in the town.

After expressing his grievances against the way the Oba had been treating him, he advised him to cook beans to feast all his chiefs and members of the palace societies. After the Oba had made the feast, Aban took the bembe drum once more after midnight, and he began singing and drumming with the words, (Oni-taji ti se ere je) the Oba has cooked beans to eat. Aban's latest announcement puzzled the populace so much that they began to wonder whether Aban was changing his earlier story. That was why he explained with drumming and singing that his first announcement was "Oni-Taji se ere je" and not "Oni-Taji kpa ere je". Incidentally, the beans and python mean the same word "Ere" in yoruba. The chiefs apologized to Oni-taji for daring to plot his banishment. Thereafter, the people and Oba of Itaji lived in peace ever after.

When this Odu appears at divination, the person should be told to make sacrifice to avert the danger of undermining any of his dependents. He should bring his dependents closer to himself, and treat him or them more humanely in order to avoid their nuisance value.

He Made Divination for Ataparapa and His Friend Ole

*Ogunda bede babalawo Ole odifa fun Ole, obufun Oluku meji re
ti'anpe Ataparapa olori ole, nijo ti won ti kole orun bowa si
kole aiye.*

He made divination for Ole, and his friend Ataparapa, the pioneer and king of robbery in heaven, before they came to the world.

They went for divination because they wanted to know what to do to thrive as robbers on earth. He told them to feast the policemen of heaven so that they may thrive through stealing on earth. he also advised them to serve; their guardian angels with a goat, chain, matchete, clubs and needles, and Esu with a he-goat, gun powder and fire flames, before leaving heaven, and also to serve Esu with the same materials as soon as they got to the world, so that the evening of their lives might be blissful. They made all the sacrifices before leaving heaven.

They were born of different parents on earth but were raised in the same locality. They were so successful as robbers that others began to emulate them. They were never apprehended during all their expeditions. They also developed such diabolical powers that rather than getting caught after any robbery, one would transfigure into a cat and the other into a rat, and whenever they found themselves in tight situations, the cat would grip the rat and both would escape. They became outrageously prosperous through stealing and people in their community began to wonder whether there was any virtue in living honestly and righteously. Their success was so remarkable that they did not have any cause to go for divination, let alone make any sacrifices which was contrary to the advice given to them in heaven..

They lived through middle age to the beginning of old age. That was the point at which Esu got up to ask his friend Ighoroko whether the two notorious robbers made any sacrifice. When Ighoroko replied that they failed to make sacrifice, Esu set out on their trail. One night, Ataparapa slept and died in his sleep. The members of his household discovered his death in the morning and immediately began to make arrangements for his burial.

As soon as he died on earth however, he appeared before his guardian angel in heaven, who directed him to a roofless and dilapidated building, as his heavenly house. At this point, it is necessary to explain that any asset one acquires honestly on earth is replicated in heaven, whilst assets stolen or unscrupulously acquired from their bonafide owners on earth, return to enrich the rightful owners in heaven. When Ataparapa discovered that his heavenly house was empty and uninhabitable, he asked his guardian angel, the reason for its desolate condition. He got the depressing reply that, the condition of the house was a reflection of his genuinely acquired possessions on earth because the fradulently acquired belongings had returned to their bonafide owners in heaven. It had no roof, no furniture and no household equipment and utensils, because he stole them for his house on earth. His greatest puzzle was when he discovered that two of his children who had previously died before him were living as homeless layabouts in heaven because of the uninhabitable condition of his house.

When he came to realize that depriving other people of their possessions to enrich one's self on earth, served no useful purpose in heaven, he appealed to his guardian angel to allow him to return momentarily to earth to warn members of his family of the consequences of stealing.

His request was granted, but Esu stopped him to demand a he-goat, but since he had nothing to offer, he promised to abide by Esu's request upon his return from earth. The members of his family stopped weeping and mourning, when his heartbeat resumed and he regained conciousness. As soon as he opened his eyes, he directed that all his wives and children should be assembled for a special meeting.

When they were all gathered, he warned them not to utilize money and materials in his house for his burial. He advised them if possible to borrow money to fund his funeral because that was the only way he could derive any benefit from them in heaven. He narrated the horror of his brief experience in heaven and strongly advised his people to refrain from stealing. As his family was getting acquainted with the realities of his resurrection, he lapsed once more into a coma and eventually died. His burial was subsequently financed with honest money and all the materials used, went to provide a new start for him in heaven.

The experience of his bosom friend was slightly different. When he was told about the resurrection advice of his friend, he dismissed it as a paranoid mannerism. He reiterated his characteristic philosophy that whether the money or property belonged to devil, divinity, death, or any mortal, he was free to steal it to live a full life here on earth, because he could not be bothered with the hereafter, because he would cross that bridge when he got there. Little did he realise that his own nemesis was in the offing.

Three months after the death of his friend, Ole was taken ill with a fever. Two days later, the fever became so high that he had a stroke which not only paralysed one half of his body but rendered him speechless. He remained in that helpless condition for the better part of six months. The period of his illness however enabled his children to firm up adequate arrangement for his inevitable death and burial. In addition to preparing a lavishly equipped vault for his remains, a brass coffin was provided for his interment. Cannons and gun-powder were stored in the cellar of his palatial house for use during the funeral ceremonies.

Finding himself living like a vegetable for so long became an unbearable suffering for him. Since he was too helpless to physically take his life, he decided to fast to death. Six days after he stopped eating and drinking, he eventually died. His death was a great relief to his family and soon afterwards, the exigency arrangement for his burial was set in motion. After giving his corpse a clean bath, he was dressed up gorgeously and laid in state. During the day, friends relations and sympathisers filed in to pay their last respects. In the evening, it was time for a family ritual which was to be followed by cannon salutes to the memory of the dead. By tradition the ritual marks the commencement of the funeral ceremonies and it is exclusive to the members of the deceased's family.

As arrangements were being made to load the cannons with explosives, one of the children went to the cellar with a naked lantern to remove some kegs of gun-powder. All of a sudden, there was a massive explosion from the cellar followed by secondary explosions of the entire arsenal of gun powder and explosives which in a matter of minutes set the whole house in total conflagration. All the members of Ole's family, his corpse, and the entire building was burnt to ashes. The spectators who were watching the events outside the house were the only people who escaped unscathed.

Some of the spectators remarked that the notorious Ole had an ignoble end to his life. Others concluded that retribution had caught up with the bandit at the end of his life. The general consensus was that indeed retribution has settled scores with Ole in the evening of his life. That was how the adage began that "Retribution awaits a thief (ole) at the evening of his life."

When this Odu therefore appears at Ugbodu, the person will be advised to refrain from all fraudulent and evil practices in order to have a blissful end to his life. When it appears at divination, the Ifa priest will immediately snap out his third finger with his thumb, to say "Ale kpa osika lojo kon" or (ota ihen khe ole in Bini) that is, "retribution will one day catch up with the evil doer." The divinee should be advised to make sacrifice to avert the danger of an imminent robbery.

Chapter 2

OGUNDA-OYEKU
OGUNDA-ARIKU

He Made Divination for the Bird Called Oge

Agbonrin lo'nfi oju kan efun. Lo tu fi ese kun efun
Orisa oge lo oko de si ose oge. Mejeji lo fi ese oge
mejeji da ojuju. Adafa fun yeye oge. Ebo ni ki oru tori
arun ese.
The deer painted his face with white chalk, and also rubbed his
Two legs with white chalk. God created the bird called Oge
(Ahiamwen-osa in Bini) with two brass bangles to wear on her legs.

These are the names of the Awos who made divination for the mother of the bird called Oge. She was told to make sacrifice with a he-goat on account of the child she was expecting. She did not perform the sacrifice. The child was born and developed sores on the two legs, because of the sacrifice the mother failed to make.

When it appears at divination, the person will be advised to make sacrifice to avert the risk of developing problems with the legs. When the divination forebodes danger (Ayeo), the divinee will be warned to perform sacrifice to avoid being poisoned on the legs.

He Made Divination for the Palm Wine and the Deer

Ogunda-Ariku, babalawo Adokpe, odifa fun Adokpe, nijo ti on
fi omi oju shubere aje turuutu. Abufun Agbonrin.

He made divination for the palm wine tapper when he was anxious to become prosperous. He also made divination for the deer when he wanted to start stealing.

The palm wine tapper was not prospering from his business and he went to Orunmila to find out what to do to make better progress. He was told to make sacrifice with four pigeons, two cocks, two hens, and two snails. He refused to make the sacrifice on the ground that if he had the amount required for funding such an elaborate sacrifice, he would not have regarded himself as poor.

Meanwhile, the deer went to Orunmila for divination on what to do before he embarked on a robbery programe. The deer was advised to make sacrifice to Esu with baby he-goat, which he was told not to eat with Esu, and a gourd of palm oil. He made the sacrifice but contrary to Orunmila's advice, he ate of the meat of the he-goat with which he served Esu.

Meanwhile he got a sharp pointed piece of long iron pipe (Okpakata in yoruba and Oha in Bini) prepared for piercing into and siphoning palm wine from a gourd. He decided to use the pointed iron pipe because his hands could not reach the location of the palm wine gourd. He was thus able to collect palm wine by puncturing the gourds with the sharp pointed iron pipe. Incidentally, the palm wine tapper borrowed the gourds for collecting tapped palm wine. When the palm wine tapper discovered that his palm wine was not only being stolen, but that the gourds he borrowed were also being vandalized, he decided to go to Orunmila for another divination. Orunmila told him that his double jeopardy was a function of his refusal to make sacrifice.

In the ensuing divination, Orunmila advised him to make sacrifice with a baby he-goat to Esu and not to eat of it. This time, he borrowed money to make the sacrifice. Thereafter, Orunmila advised him to go early in the morning to hide near his palm trees to apprehend who was stealing his palm wine and puncturing his borrowed gourds. The following morning he went to the bush to find out who the culprit was. Eventually, he discovered that the culprit was the deer. When he came out of hiding to confront the deer, the latter ran away and the palm wine tapper pursued him right up to the venue of the meeting of all the animals.

As soon as the animals saw the palm wine tapper, they arrested him for intrusion and spying. When he however explained that he had no intention of interrupting or spying on their conference, and that he was only pursuing the deer who had been stealing his palm wine and destroying the gourds he borrowed, the animals explained to him that the deer was in fact a thief because they were always giving him money to buy and not to steal palm wine. On that note, the animals decided to pay for all the palm wine that the deer had been stealing and for the gourds he had been puncturing. Additionally, they gratuitously agreed to teach him the language of birds and animals, after which he returned home happily.

In his characteristic parsimony, instead of using part of the money paid by the animals to defray the value of the gourds he borrowed, he offered to give indentured service to his lender as recompence for the damaged gourds. Paradoxically, as he was working one day in the house of the gourds' owner, he heard one hen saying to her chickens not to use their toe nails to dig a particular spot so that their master might not see the treasures hidden there, because he was not only selfish but also given to starving them. Since the palm wine tapper already understood the language of the birds, he quickly marked the spot. He procurred corn immediately to lure the hen and her chickens away from that spot. He subsequently dug up the place and discovered a small iron casket containing plenty of money and beads. He later took the casket to his house.

A few days later, he overheard the mother goat ordering her kids to leave a particular spot because their "stupid master" was going to be buried there in five days time. Their lord and master actually died on the fifth day and the palm wine tapper inherited all his possessions, thus eventually coming into the prosperity for which he made sacrifice.

When this Ifa appears at Ugbodu, the person will be advised to serve: the new Ifa with the meat of a deer, two hens and four pigeons; and Ogun with a cock. At divination, the divinee should be advised to serve;- Esu with a baby he-goat to achieve his ambitions in life, and Ogun with a tortoise to thwart the nefarious plans of a trick associate.

Divination for Him When He Travelled to Ikimi for Ifa Practice

Aki ka ragba koje ki olodo teri. Odifa fun Orunmila nijo
ti on shawo lo si ode Ikimi.

A piece of calabash does not drown in the river. That was the name of the Awo who made divination for Orunmila when he was going to perform Ifism in the town of Ikimi. The Oba of Ikimi had been hearing about the fame of Orunmila and decided to invite him to help his town. Before leaving for Ikimi, the Awo told Orunmila to make sacrifice with a he-goat, rat and fish. He made the sacifices. He was also advised to make a feast with akara (bean buns) on the morning following the day of his arrival at Ikimi.

Accordingly, on the morning after the day he arrived at Ikimi, he gave out the beans he brought from home for use in frying akara. On the same morning, the Oba who invited Orunmila sent three messengers to deliver poisioned akara to welcome him. Orunmila took the akara from the three messengers only to return them to the messengers because he was also making a feast with akara. The messengers ate the akara because they were not aware that they were poisioned.

As soon as the messengers returned to the palace, one of them died from the effect of the poison. No long afterwards, the second messenger became comatose and also died, while the third messenger was also reeling and groaning with pains. Seeing the condition of the third messenger, the Oba asked him whether they ate akara in Orunmila's house. He just managed to scuffle an affirmative nod before he died. When people began to wonder why three palace messengers died in such mysterious circumstances the Oba made a metaphoric observation "Ejeki oro Ikimi ko maa gbe Ikimi" meaning "let the story be consigned to everlasting silence".

When this Odu therefore appears at divination for someone who is proposing to travel on a business or official trip, he or she should be advised to make sacrifice on account of a test to which he or she is likely to be subjected at his or her destination.

This Odu's Special Sacrifice for Long Life

Orunmila says that if one lives long enough one will enjoy all the good things of life. He went on to disclose that the sacrifice for long life is made with an ewe (female sheep), a piece of: iron, lead, bronze and silver.

When the materials were produced, he made the sacrifice with the following incantation:-

A ki gbo ikuide.
A ki gbo iku oje.
A ki gbo iku ibaba.
A ki gbo iku irin-dudu.

Gbogbo ara ni agutan fi nse ewu gbu gbu.

Meaning:

No one hears of dead bronze.
No one hears of dead lead.
No one hears of dead silver.
No one hears of dead iron.
The skin of an ewe is lined with grey hairs.

When this Ifa appears at Ugbodu, the person will be advised to make this special sacrifice (ono-Ifa or Odiha) for long life in good health and prosperity.

How Orunmila Knew the Secret of Long Life

Bi omi ba kpe l'enu omi yio da ito.
Bi egbo ba si kpe ni ese, yio wu gan gan.
Bi iroko ba gbo ju ninu ikpakpa, yio da ashorin.

Meaning:

If water is retained for too long in the mouth,
it will become saliva.
If a sore remains for too long on the leg, the leg will
become swollen.
If an iroko tree becomes old in the forest, it will
become stronger.

Those were the three Awos who made divination for Orunmila when he went to God to seek the secret of longevity - Aiku. God revealed to him that there was someone at the gate who is the arch enemy of longevity, whose name is Aworomogoin.

Chapter 3

OGUNDA-IWORI

OGUNDA-LEEDO
OGUNDA-ODO

He Made Divination for Two Women in Heaven

Ogunda Awo agba, Iwori Awo adase. They made sacrifice for the mother of infant children in heaven. They also made sacrifice for her mate Akpo, (infant's mortality). The two women had seven children each, and they were mates married to the same husband. After divination they were advised to make sacrifice each with a he-goat to Esu and to serve the ground divinity with tortoise and snail, but they did not heed the advice. They were also told to serve their guardian angels with fish, but they failed to do it.

Meanwhile, the children of infants went to the market of oja-ajigbomekon, leaving her seven children under the care of her mate. Akpo, or infants' mortality, took such great care of her mates' children that her mate expressed her gratitude when she returned from the market.

Not long afterwards, it was the mother of Akpo's turn to go to the market, leaving her seven children to the care of her mate. As soon as she left for the market, her mate sent one of her mate's children to fetch plantain from the farm. On getting to the farm the boy was seized and mauled by a tiger. After waiting in vain for the boy to return, their mother's mate sent another of Akpo's children to go and look for his brother. On his way to the farm, the second boy fell into a python's trap and he was swallowed by the giant serpent. When the two children failed to turn up, the woman sent another of her mate's children to fetch water from the river. As she was trying to fetch the water with a gourd, she was apprehended by an Alligator and dragged into the depth of the river and swallowed by the reptile. At the same time without sending any of her own children, she dispatched another of her mate's daughters to buy okro from the market. On her way from the market, the girl treaded on the tail of a boa and she was bitten by the serpent. She came home in pain only to die as soon as she got home.

In the meantime, Akpo began to have foreboding signs that something drastic was happening at home. As if the fates of the four children meant nothing to her, the woman sent two others of her mate's children on different errands from which they did not return. There was only one left of Akpo's seven children, when she hurriedly returned home. When Akpo asked for the whereabouts of her children, her mate nonchalantly replied that she did not know what happened to them. In the ensuing polemic, the two women began to fight.

Akpo however told her mate that it was not a matter to be resolved by physical fight, because she was going to exchange tit for tat. One after the other, Akpo attacked each of her mate's children until they were all dead. When the elders intervened, Akpo explained how she took proper care of her mate's seven children before she returned from the market, but that when she left her own children to her care, she returned to meet only one of them. She was vindicated. From then on the disease called Akpo has been attacking small infants without any remedy. Once Akpo attacks an infant, it must die because the mother of the infants was the first to agress her.

He Made Divination for Sango

> Ogunda ki l'akpo, Iwori ko l'ofa. Ofa kan ofa kaan, t'onshe
> oju akpo yoro yoro. Odifa fun ori na, okonbi omo olodumare
> (sango) nijo t'oma gba ashe lowo olodumare. Oni ko lo gba
> Ifa.

Ogun does not have a bow, Iwori does not have arrow. One shot of the arrow does not miss its target. Those were the Awos who made divination for Sango, the only son of God (there being no other Sango created by God). Sango was advised to have his own Ifa and he did. It was after having his own Ifa that Sango began to command dignity and authority.

When this Ifa therefore appears at divination for a man, he will be advised to have his own Ifa. When it appears for a spinster, she will be advised to marry a man having his own Ifa. If it appears for a married woman, she should be advised to persuade her husband to have his own Ifa so that they might both prosper. When this Odu appears at divination, there is no argument with him because whatever he says must come true.

He Made Divination for the Majority

> Eji welu ni gba oju ale. Ojo gidi gidi ni gba
> owuro. Odifa fun oyigbo t'inshe oko aiye.
> Light showers of rain disrupt the evening chores.
> Heavy showers of rain disrupt the morning chores.

These are the names of the Awos who made divination for the majority of people to become the husband of the world. The world often moves and reacts in accordance with the whims and will of the majority.

When it appears at divination, the person should be advised to have his own Ifa in order to command universal honor and respect. If he is not in a position to have his own Ifa, he or she should be advised to make sacrifice with he-goat and rabbit.

He Made Divination for Orunmila When Death was Gunning for Him

> Atanrere tanrere. Odifa fun Orunmila nijo ti onu orun nishu
> meta tan iku je.

When Orunmila made his morning divination, Ifa revealed to him that Death was sending messengers to invite him to heaven. When he sounded Ifa on what to do to ward off the danger of death, he was told to make sacrifice with a cock, rat, fish, a bag containing his wearing apparels, the Ikin of his Ifa, three pieces of yam, a new cooking pot and a gourd of water. After preparing the sacrifice, he was to deposit it by the side of the road leading to his house. He was also required to give a he-goat to Esu before making the sacrifice.

After giving the he-goat to Esu, he took the sacrifice to the roadside where he prepared a tripod with firewood under it while igniting fire on it. He placed the three pieces of yam inside the cooking pot. The yam was cooking when he hung up the bag containing his wearing apparel and after tying the live cock to a stick, he returned home. Having eaten his he-goat, Esu went to the spot where Orunmila deposited his sacrifice and hid behind a thicket.

When the messengers of Death got to the spot where the sacrifice lay, they cooked the yam, killed and roasted the cock and helped themselves to food. Esu allowed the three of them to finish eating before coming out to challenge them. When he asked them where they were coming from, they explained that they were sent by Death from heaven to bring Orunmila with them. After accusing them of stealing, he reminded them of the heavenly rule that a divinity does not kill a person after eating his food, he disclosed to them that Orunmila was already on his way to heaven and that they would have met him on the spot but for the fact that he returned home to collect his divnation instruments. He told them that the food they had just stolen was being prepared by Orunmila for his journey to heaven. Esu told them to return to heaven to tell the divinity of death that they had inadvertently eaten Orunmila's food and hence, could not bring him to heaven. They were much relieved to return to heaven, thus obviating the risk of courting the death penalty for stealing. Orunmila was subsequently left in peace on earth to live to a ripe old age.

When it appears at divination, the person will be told to make a similar sacrifice to forestall the danger of death. He should however be fore-warned that he is likely to be a victim of robbery as an atonement for saving his life.

He Made Divination for the Rats

(When this Odu appears at divination, a kolanut should be provided and split instantly)

It is a good word that brings out kolanut from the pocket. It is a bad word that invites a slap to the face. That was the proverb with which Orunmila made divination for the rats when they were being plundered by the cat. The cat had always succeeded in stopping relief from coming to the rats by shooting any divine priest coming to the land of rats. Anyone going to the home of the rats had to pass through the fortress of the cat.

Orunmila had been invited by the king of rats (Ukpere in Yoruba and Uyenghen in Bini), to come and assist them in solving their problem of sudden deaths and loss of children as a result of the menace of the cat.

When Ogunda-Iwori was travelling to the land of the rats, he was suddenly accosted by the cat who was armed with his sword strapped to his waist. When he asked Ogunda-Iwori where he was going, he lied that the king of the rats (Ukpere in Yoruba and Uyenghen in Bini) had for long been indebted to him and that he was going to demand re-payment. The cat also lied to him that he was appointed as the watch-dog of the rats to stop intruders from coming to disturb them because they were celebrating their annual festival.

Ogunda-Iwori however coaxed the cat with the proposal to accompany him to the land of the rats in order to reassure them that he was not a dangerous intruder. The cat reiterated by clearing Ogunda-Iwori to proceed on his journey, because if he accompanied him the rats would be scared. On that note, the cat brought out a kolanut from his pocket for Ogunda-Iwori to split for libation. That was how Orunmila concluded that it is a good word that brings kolanut from the pocket, while a bad word bring out the sword from its case.

When Orunmila got to the town of rats, they were happy to receive him, for successfully getting through the cat's barricade. At the subsequent divination he made for them he advised them to serve their heads together with melon sauce (Iru in Yoruba and Evbarhie in Bini). He added that they were not to eat out of the melon sauce with which they served their heads and that all of them were to stay at home for seven days after the sacrifice without venturing out. He also used a bell to make sacrifice for them after which he positioned it at the entrance to the town. He told them that if they could stay home after the sacrifice for seven days without going out, Esu would ring a bell to alert them whenever the cat was approaching.

After leaving for home, the rats got together to reason among themselves, wondering whether they would not starve themselves to death, if they had to remain at home for seven days. They agreed among themselves in concluding that Orunmila did not know his job. Since they could not resist the urge to eat from the melon sauce with which they had served their heads, they had thwarted the manifestation of the sacrifice. Besides, they could not stay at home for even a full day. Three days after the departure of Orunmila, they held another conference at which they decided not to wait for Esu to ring the bell to warn them of the approach of the cat, but to tie it by themselves to the waist of the cat. After removing the bell from the gate where Orunmila had positioned it, their king called for volunteers to tie the bell to the waist of the cat.

That is the origin of the saying "Who will bell the cat?" since no one volunteered to bell the cat. That is why the cat has continued to plunder the rats at will ever since.

When this Ifa appears at ugbodu, the person will be advised to serve; the new Ifa with an aged mother-goat and ukpere or uyenghen rat; Ogun with a snail to be smashed on its shrine; and a baby he-goat for Esu to eat alone, in order to overcome the evil machinations of a powerful enemy.

At divination, the person should be advised to make sacrifice with a he-goat to Esu to frustrate the plans of an enemy and to forestall the risk of saying the wrong things at a meeting.

Contest Between two Competing Ifa Priests

Ogunda Awo Ashe, Iwori abose. They were two brothers who were proficient Ifa priests and often competing for supremacy. One day, they gave their mother money to buy a goat for them to make sacrifice. After their mother left for the market, an argument ensued between them as to whether their mother would misconstrue their instructions and buy two goats instead of one. One of them predicted that their mother was going to buy one goat while the other predicted that she was going to come home with two goats.

Meanwhile, their mother got to the market and bought one goat, but unknown to her, it was in its last stage of pregnancy. She had assumed that since no live-stock breeder would knowingly sell a pregnant goat, she concluded that its robust physique was a function of excessive fatty cholesterol. However, before the last bend to their house, the goat suddenly stopped moving and began to groan in pain. As the old woman was still trying to find out what was wrong with it, the goat delivered a kid. She quickly ran home to call her children to take the mother goat and its kid to the house.

Later in the day, when they were assessing the manifestations of their predictions, their mother decided the matter by declaring both of them right, because she actually bought one goat from the market but arrived home with the two goats. She put it in the following words:- Ogunda se -Iwori ase.

When it appears at divination, the person will be advised to serve Esu with crushed yam, roasted yam, a spoonful of palm oil and a he-goat in order to win a contest in the offing.

Divination for Asese-Lagodo, the Head Server

Ogunda ko Lapo, Iwori ko ni ofa.
Omo olofa raja, Omo olofa rajo.
Adifa fun Ase se lagodo.

Those were the awos who made divination for Asese Lagodo who was going to be serving the heads of kings. The literary translation of his name was "wherever the head is destinated to go, the feet wil carry him there." He was advised to make sacrifice with 16 pigeons, 16 kolanuts and a big he-goat. He made the sacrifice and the necessary medicine (Ayajo) was prepared for him. He was given two of the kolanuts to serve his head and another two to serve his feet while serving his head and feet, he was to pray as follows:-

"Ibi ori ngbe mi re,
Ki ese ma sin mi lo."

Meaning:

Wherever my head takes me to,
my feet will get me there.

When some friends heard his prayers as he was serving his head, they reported him to the Oba, who ordered that the man should be arraigned before him. When he got to the palace, the Oba asked him to mention the kind of work he wanted to do, he replied that he was specialized in serving his head. The Oba asked the palace orderlies to provide a room for him in the palace.

The following morning, the Oba invited him and gave him kolanuts to serve his (the Oba's) head. He prayed for the Oba, the kingdom and himself. While praying for himself, he repeated his usual prayers "for his feet to carry him wherever his head was destined to go." His prayers so infuriated the Oba that he ordered him to be sold into slavery. For that same reason, he found himself serving as a head-serving slave in the palaces of the sixteen Obas of the known world of the time, ending up with the Oba of Benin. His prayers also annoyed the Oba of Benin who ordered that he should be put live into a coffin and used to make sacrifice to Olokun, the water divinity. He was accordingly interned into a coffin and jettisoned into the sea. On account of the sacrifice he had made originally, Esu made sure that he did not suffocate inside the coffin.

Meanwhile, king Asawori of Iwori, an island on the sea, had died and after the funeral ceremonies, the king-makers invited traditional diviners to make divination for the appointment of a new Oba. The diviners arrived at a unanimous revelation that the next king was going to come from the water and not from the land. That was interpreted by the elders to refer to the mariners and divers. The diviners dismissed the interpretation and insisted that the next king was not going to come from the town of Iwori but from a distant land through the sea.

After the predictions, the elders positioned some people to man an over-head light-house tower in order to keep a twenty-four hour vigil on the sea's embankment. One morning the watchmen at the tower sighted a coffin flowing towards the beach of the sea. The divers were immediately invited to retrieve the coffin from the water. As they were about to use the axe to break the coffin, Asese Lagodo cried from within the coffin "Ema-kpa-mi-o", since he spoke in Yoruba, the people did not understand what he said, but his words were enough to alert them that a human being was inside the coffin. When they eventually carefully opened the coffin, they found a pale-looking male adult, and took him to the elders. When the diviners were once more assembled to make divination on the significance of the strange development, they all confirmed that the strange man was their new king. He was treated for three days to recover from his sea ordeal. Three days after his arrival, he was crowned as the new Asawori of iwori. His enthronement ushered in a epoch of peace and prosperity to the island kingdom of Iwori. It is the sea kingdom of Iwori that the Portuguese explorers later changed to the town of Warri in the Delta State of Nigeria.

On the third anniversary of his coronation, he decided to visit the Oba of Ado. After the exchange of pleasantries, he asked the Oba of Benin whether he recognized him. The Oba replied that he did not, although he had been informed that a new king had been crowned in Iwori. The Oba was dumbfounded when Asawori disclosed that he was the slave he consigned to the water divinity in a coffin for praying that his feet should carry him to where his head was destined to go. The Oba concluded that indeed, his feet had carried him to his destination, adding that truly, "No one can kill anyone unless the head agrees to kill one."

When it appears at divination, the person will be advised to make the above-mentioned sacrifices and serve his head in order to position his feet on the path of his destiny.

He Divined for the Catapult

> Ogunda ko la kpo, Iwori ko lo fa. Ifon kan ni o nse
> inu akpo rojo rojo.

Those were the Awos who made divination for the catapult, who gave birth to a child she was going to send on a long journey. She was advised to make sacrifice so that the child might not die during the journey. She failed to make the sacrifice. Nonetheless, she sent her child on a distant journey from which he did not return home.

When she was asked for the whereabouts of her son, she replied that he had gone on a long journey ("olo si ode i jan") which is the noise made by the catapult to this day.

At divination, the person should be advised not to send his children on any long journey without making sacrifice to avoid the risk of sudden death during the tour. The sacrifice is made with a he-goat to Esu.

Chapter 4

OGUNDA-IDI
OGUNDA-DI-UGBIN

The Divination for Him Before Leaving Heaven

*Ogunda du gbin, Agele dadi okoko, obere jaki ra udi yo
se se.
Kiki ki moki ogbe, kaba ti ki ogbe m'eta, Ara osule ni
ta. Odifa fun oja oluo ojomo.*

When this Odu was coming from heaven, he went for divination on what to do to improve the lives of people in the world. He was told to make sacrifice in order to be able to lead the people of the world with the crown he was bringing from heaven. He was required to serve Esu with a he-goat in order to avoid being killed by the beneficiaries of his benevolence, through ingratitude. He was also to make special sacrifice with white chalk, cowries and parrot's feathers, rabbit, pigeon, white cloth, snail and a gourd of palm oil, in order to be sexually potent right up to the evening of his life. He made all of the sacrifices and the Awos prepared a bath for him on an ant-hill with an open top. It was a bottom disease that troubled the ant-hill that made it to open its top. After making the sacrifices, he came to the world.

He was confronted with all kinds of problems from various sources when he got to the world. Charms were used against him and the club of witchcraft marked him out for destruction to stop him from carrying out his good intentions in the world. The mark on his head called "kill a snake when young because he will do wonders if allowed to grow into adulthood". The mark on his head was an identification signal to alert witches everywhere he went that he was slated for elimination.

After experiencing several problems at different stages of his life, he suddenly discovered that he was sexually impotent. He then went for divination at which he was told to give a he-goat to Esu and to have a bath inside the river with the appropriate Ifa leaves mixed with the blood a castrated he-goat, cock and pigeon. He made the sacrifice, after which he regained his potency, and his prosperity left heaven to meet him on earth. He began to make remarkable progress in his work. He also married more wives and had several children. Any man for whom this Odu appears at Ugbodu will have many children if he makes this special sacrifice, following a spate of transcient impotence.

Meanwhile he was told to forbid snail because it was the snail that accompanied him from heaven. He was told to make another special sacrifice with his own sputum, white cloth, the snail's special leaf called ewe-ugbin which grows one leaf a year, in order to achieve a position of honor and dignity. It is with its salive (the Ase given to him by God) that the snail climbs trees and moves and to tread on the ground.

Divination Made for Orunmila in Heaven to Forestall Enemies' Plans to Shorten His Life

Ogunda-di-igbin, Igbin ku, ori ni iku olobahun.
Iru gan-gan ni ija ejo, Eni ke ni ti o ba te ejo-oka ni iru,
ija ni on wa.
Adifa fun Orunmila ba'de orun. ifa sowipe o nyio lo gbe
igba odun l'aiye. Awon ota sowipe ko'saye. Orunmila bere
lowo okeponrin wipe kini ebo? Oso wi pe odidi oka kon,
Odidi ekun kon, odidi ki niun. Orunmila ru ebo.

Orunmila fried the snail and it died. The tortoise dies through its head. The tail is the untouchable part of the boa's body. If one touches the boa's tail, one is inviting its indignation. Anyone who molests dada-akuja, the daughter of Sango will see the reaction of Sango. If Ogunda is beaten, one will see the reaction of Idi. If an Ifa priest is molested, one will realise the efficacy of sacrifice. If I am beaten, the aggressor will see the reaction of the powerful forces behind me.

These were the Awos who made divination for Ogunda-Idi when he told God in heaven that he was coming to spend two hundred years in the world in order to make it more habitable. His enemies mocked him that he was joking because they were neither going to give him a chance to live that long, nor to allow him to embark on his reformatory designs. He was advised to make sacrifice with a whole boa, a whole tiger and a whole lion. He made the sacrifice after which the Ifa priest prepared a special black powder for him to mark on his head once a year on earth, while repeating the following incantation:

It is impossible for 200 hoes to overcome a mountain.
It is impossible for 200 cutlasses to cut and bring down the sky.
It is impossible for 200 flies to defeat the cow.
It is impossible for 200 dogs to defeat the tiger.
It is impossible for 200 animals to defeat the lion, and
It is impossible for 200 trees to defeat the Asori tree in the forest.

After the preparations, Orunmila came to the world and although he was badgered and tormented by his several enemies on earth, he did not only outlive all of them but also lived to a ripe old age before returning at will to heaven.

When this Ifa appears for anyone at Ugbodu, this special sacrifice (Ono-Ifa) will be prepared for him. In addition to parts of the above-mentioned plants and animals, an animal called Ikoko will be added, something will be taken from seven hills / mountains, and the bark of Asori tree. They will all be burnt or ground together for the person to mark on his head once a year and when he has stiff opposition resulting from enemy action.

How His Prosperity Came From Heaven

Aiyele 'ekpo, Aiye lo oun, Aiye lu ma ba dongbongbon
Aiye han owo otun, Aiye ro owo osi. Adaghin da ko, Ama me
hin mona, adafa fun Asikolokolo. Ogbe no reshi yun bo.

After calling Ogunda dugbin, say, the world that has palm oil, the world that has salt, the world of the town of Umoba, is very sweet. The world that endowed the right hand with prosperity without remembering the left hand. It made divination for Asikkolokolo (the heavenly name of this Odu). When he got to the earth, he was very poor, having no wife, no children and no house. He then went for divination to the above-mentioned Awos, who advised him to make sacrifice with a single snail to his head, and to cook the snail to eat with ewe-ugbin. That was to be the last snail he was to eat for the rest of his life. He was also advised to give he-goat to Esu and to send gifts to the water divinity. Finally, he was told that he would soon have enough money to build a house of sixteen rooms. He served his head but forgot to serve Esu, which he was required to do in order to enjoy his wealth to a ripe old age. Not long afterwards, he was able to build a house of sixteen rooms. He had been advised to make fire in his house every day, so that smoke would come out all day from the chimney of his house. He was doing so every day.

Meanwhile, Iya-Alaje (the mother of wealth) went in heaven to Orunmila for divination on what to do before going to earth and in order to come across the right husband on earth. Orunmila told her to serve Esu with two he-goats, one big one and another small one for Esu to eat alone.

Orunmila told her to return to him after three days to tell him the dream she had, (that is why when this Odu appears at divination, the person will be asked to narrate the dream he/she had within the last three days). She made the sacrifice and three days later, she returned to report the dream she had to Orunmila. She explained that she saw the three strongest men on earth called, Ogun, Sango and Sankpana, and she was determined to marry one of them on getting to earth. Orunmila however warned her not to allow herself to be misled by outward appearances. With that advice she left for a temporary visit to earth.

On getting to the world, she first met Sango. When she got to his house, she demanded to see Sango. When he appeared to introduce himself, a ball of flames gushed out of his mouth, which scared her so much that she could not look at his eyes. She subsequently lied that she was in fact looking for a man called Ogun, and Sango showed her the direction of Ogun's house. Whe she got to Ogun's hut, she met him pacing restlessly back and forth. When Ogun was sufficiently at ease to see his vistor, he brought out a red-hot iron from his blast furnace and faced her. When she wanted him to take her to his house, Ogun confirmed that was his house, she lied once again that she was in fact looking for Sankpana. Ogun also directed her to Sankpana's house. On getting to Sankpana's house, she found that only one part of the house was built. On the side that was not built up she saw the corpses of hundreds of human beings recently killed by Sankpana with small pox, she met him spreading epidemics by throwing corn about. She was so thoroughly perplexed that she began to wonder why she saw such dangerous men in her dream and why they were so popular in heaven.

Having been scared by Sankpana, she asked for the name of the owner of the house from which smoke was coming out in front. Sankpana told her that the house belonged to a hard luck nonentity called Asikolokolo who lived alone in a big house without any family or dependants. It was very late in the evening when she got to Asikolokolo's house, she met him at home, and exchanged greetings. On account of his meek disposition she asked to see the owner of the house. Asikolokolo lied that the landlord had travelled. One particular characteristic of the children of this odu is that they are generally unassuming, humble and self effacing. She however asked whether he would be kind enough to give her a place in the house just for the night, because it was already too late for her to return home.

He then took her through the rooms in the house to see which of them was going to be suitable for her to stay. She chose one of the rooms, and Asikolokolo opened the room for her to enter. When she entered the room, she brought out the small stick (Okpa oje in yoruba and Uwenriontan in Bini) she brought from heaven, hit the floor of the room with it, and all the necessary requirements she needed to use, appeared from heaven. They included money, goods and beddings. When she was leaving the following morning, she told Asikolokolo that she was going to the market of oja-Ajigbo mekon akira and would return in five days time. Before leaving, she promised to buy him gifts from the market for being so obliging to her, and told him to tell the landlord to take everything found in the room she lodged in, when he returned from wherever he went. After departure, Asikolokolo opened the room and he was astonished to find the money and wealth the woman left behind. He was able to have money to furnish the rooms in the house to make them more habitable. He however began to wonder who the woman was.

As she promised, she returned after five days and gave Asikolokolo the gifts she bought for him. He thanked her immensely. When she asked him whether the owner of the house had still not returned from his tour, it was then that Asikolokolo replied that the house belonged to him, and he expressed his profound gratitude for the elaborate gifts she left in the room during her last visit. At that point, Iya-Alaje offered to marry him and he agreed. She then invited the men and women that accompanied her from heaven, telling him to choose six out of the women to marry him along with her. That is why cirumstances will always make children of this odu to marry seven wives. Iya-Alaje brought in wealth and prosperity and bought him a horse because she did not want her husband to walk about on foot. From then on, Iya-Alaje was travelling back and forth to heaven. She did not have a child for him, but the other wives had plenty of children.

One day, he was riding on his horse when he met one of the Awos who made divination and sacrifice for him before he became prosperous. Instead of coming down from the horse to greet him, he waved his fly-whisk (horse tail) to greet him. The man was annoyed. At the same time, it was at that point that Esu decided to punish him for the he-goat he failed to give him. Esu blinked his eyes to him and he fell down from the horse and became unconscious. Esu however, again appeared to him in the guise of a philanthropist and revived him into consciousness. He also advised him to go back to his Awos for divination on what to do so that all his prosperity might return from heaven. When he got to the Ifa priest, he told him that after his wife left for the market, he should renovate his house with human wastes.

Unknown to him, Iya-Alaje forbade to see human wastes. When she returned from heaven to see the abominable face-lift he gave to his house, the woman was annoyed and left him for good. That is why the children of Odu are told to be prosperous enough to ride in cars, but should always come out of their car to greet their Ifa partrons (the Ifa priest who gave Ifa to him). They should never wave their hands to greet their Ifa priests, or show any form of disrespect to them.

When this Ifa appears at Ugbodu, the person should be warned never to show ingratitude or disprespect to his Ifa father or patron. He should serve Ifa with 16 snails, by knocking them against one another, (one of them for Ogun) on the Ifa shrine. He should get 201 wallnut leaves (ewe asala in yoruba and Ebe-okhue in Bini) 201 leaves of ewe agban (Urua in Bini) and a whole boa (oka in yoruba and Arumwoto in Bini). Squeeze all the leaves in a basin of water and use the water to wash his ikin. Serve the Ifa with the boa and a hen, and serve the head while backing the Ifa shrine with a guinea-fowl. He should beseech Orunmila to send his prosperity to him without demanding it. In other words, he should not demand bribes but should not reject gratuitous gratifications. He should; never rear a dog, and not eat the fruits of african sherry (Osan agbalumo in yoruba and otien in Bini.) He should also forbid the meat of all snakes and the meats of he-goat and castrated he-goat. He should forbid plaintains cooked or roasted with its skin.

He Made Divination for Shaaki When Going to Make Divination for Olokun

Ogunda-di-igbin, akpere ja di araro. Odifa fun Shaaki, oron
Ogun odidi, ni jo to'nshe awo fun Olokun sherin ade. Ani ki ofi
ewure ati eyele merin, ru ebo.

Ogun cut the tail of the snail. The basket had peace of mind after losing its base or bottom. Those were the Awos who made divination for Shaaki with the help of Ogun when he was going to make divination and sacrifice for Olokun, the water divinity. He was told to make sacrifice with a goat and four pigeons. He made the sacrifice with a goat and four pigeons. He made the sacrifice, after which he became wealthy. Thereafter, Olokun compensated him for the efficacy of the work he did for him.

When this odu appears at Ugbodu, the person should be advised that his prosperity will come from living and working near the sea.

He Made Divination for Ekiri, the King of Antelopes

Ogunda-di-igbin, agba ojadi oda lowo ara re, okusu dadi
agere, agere odadi arawon. Adafa fun Ekiri nijo ti ofe lo
je oye olowo njo.

The iron cut the tail of the snail. The basket removed its bottom to achieve independece. The case dye cut the bottom of the pot, and its remains was used to make another dyestuff. Those were the Awos who made divination for the king of bush goats when he was about to ascend to the throne of his father. He was told to make sacrifice with the dark apparel he had. He refused to part with the dress, because he earmarked it for his coronation ceremonies.

On the coronation day, Esu transfigured into an elderly man, who asked whether Ekiri had performed the pre-coronation ritual in the forest. When it was confirmed that he had not performed the ceremony the elderly man (Esu) directed Ekiri to go to the tree located on the right of the gateway to the town and that on getting there he would find a thicket to the right of the tree. Just after the thicket, the man directed, he would find a lane, which he was to follow, until he came to a heap of white sand. He was to touch the heap of white sand with his head three times before returning home for the coronation ceremonies to take the crown.

Ekiri succeeded in locating the heap of white sand, but after touching it with his head, three times, he raised up his head to return home. Thereafter, he found himself surrounded by a thick forest which led to nowhere. He wandered in the forest without being able to find his way back home.

After the king-makers had waited in vain for Ekiri to return home, the crown was given to someone else. Ekiri remained in the thicket where he is often found by hunters and killed to this day.

When this Odu appears at divination for a man, he should be advised to have his own Ifa without delay to avoid doing things in half measure or unconsummated fortune (Amubo in yoruba and Osobonomasunu in Bini). He should make sacrifice with a he-goat and a black cloth or dress which he has at home, in order to succeed in achieving his objectives. If it appears for a woman she should either marry a man having his own Orunmila or advise her spouse to have his own Ifa in order to prosper in life. She should also serve Esu with her black dress and a he-goat.

He Made Divination for Idaho and the Daughter of Olokun

*Kpata riko abawo mono mono. Adifa fun Idaho t'onlo fe omo
Olokin sherun-ade shaya. Ani ki omo Olokun fi abo adiye bo
ori. Atun ni ki Idaho fi abo adiye bo ori.*

The branches of the royal palm with a smooth shining body was the name of the Awo who made divination for Idahor when he was poor and had no wife, children, or money. He was advised to serve his head with a hen, and to make sacrifice with a cock and a guinea fowl. At the same time, the daughter of Olokun was advised to serve her head with a hen in order to come across her destined husband.

When she subsequently went to the market to buy the hen to serve her head, she only came across a single hen in the market. While she was pricing it, Idahor pre-empted her by putting down more money than the asking price. The daughter of Olokun was annoyed and a quarrel ensued between herself and Idahor. In spite of the premium paid by Idahor, she held on indomitably to the hen. Since both of them were required to serve their heads with a hen on that day, none of them was prepared to concede to the other.

Meanwhile, Esu emerged from nowhere to play the role of an elderly arbiter. Since both of them had to defer to the elderly man, he took the hen from them while asking them to state their cases. After listening to them he settled the dispute by advising Idahor to pay for the hen, while the girl held it, and following the former to his house so that both of them could serve their heads together with the single hen. They willingly acceded to the advice.

When they got to Idahor's house, they sat together and served their heads with the hen. Thereafter, the girl went to the kitchen to cook the hen and to prepare pounded yam with tubers provided by Idahor. The night was far gone by the time they completed eating the sacrifical meal. Consequently, they had to spend the night together. As they were making love during the night, the girl disclosed that she had just completed her menstration.

In the morning, the girl got ready to return home, but Idahor stopped her on the ground that he was told at divination that any woman who joined him when serving his head should be made to stay a minimum of seven days. The daughter of Olokun agreed to his injunction. At the end of the seven days, she had made up her mind to live perpetualy with him as man and wife. Idahor soon became wealthy in the wake of the prosperity which the daughter of Olokun brought in her train.

At the height of his prosperity, Idahor bought a horse. He had been warned at divination never to wave a fly-whisk to the Awos who made divination for him, while riding a horse. He observed the injunction for a while, but after his prosperity became multi-facetted, he became delirious with affluence. One day he was on top of his horse when he saw his Awos. He did not dismount from his horse to greet them as he used to do. He merely waved his horse-tail (Oroke) to them.

The Awos were offended for doing what he was warned never to do. They decided to invite him to make another sacrifice, after which he was deceived into believing that it would make him even wealthier. He was told to make a feast with a cow and to request his invitees to pass excreta (human waste) in front of his house. He was to make the feast when his wife was away to the market. The daughter of Olokun forbade living in the same place with excreta, but Idahor did not know that. When the woman returned from the house to see the front of the house decorated with human waste, she left for good with all the prosperity she brought into his life, thus returning him to penury.

He Made Divination for the Snail to Marry Uke, the Daughter of God

Tedimale, Awo Ugbin, odo
ifa fun Ugbin nijo t'onfe gba uke omo
Olodumare shaya.

The snail was a servant in the divine household of God. He was very friendly with the dog. God had a daughter called Uke who was ripe for marriage and many suitors had been seeking her hands in marriage. The snail was also interested in the girl, although he was often derided. Meanwhile the snail obtained his freedom, as a result of which he left Gods house to be on his own and he began to practice as a traditional doctor. The snail confided in the dog, his friend that he was interested in marrying Uke. The dog subsequently betrayed the trust and confidence of the snail by declaring his candidature for the hands of Uke in marriage. The dog even went to the extent of denouncing the snail to the girl. He also suggested to God that since many suitors were contesting for the marriage of Uke, He should stipulate a condition that the first of them to see him having his bath would be given the first refusal option to marry her. That was a contrivance for out foxing the snail who could neither move fast nor run. God however accepted the dog's suggestion by inviting all the suitors contending for Uke to meet Him the following morning promising that the first to do so would be given the girl in marriage.

On his way home from the briefing, the snail decided to go to Tedimale Awo lode Ilara for divination. It was Ogunda-Idi which appeared at divination. He was advised to serve Esu at once and to rub his body with white chalk. After the sacrifice, Ifa advised him not to return home but to return at once to God's bathroom, and to conceal himself from view there.

The following morning, as soon as the cock crowed, God went into the bathroom. As soon as God entered the bathroom, the snail greeted Him with the heavenly greeting of Salauku-Babao. God answered him and told him to go and wait for Him in the inner chamber. All the other contenders, including the dog came later to meet the snail in the inner chamber. Uke had been given to him in marriage before the dog arrived. Subsequently, God announced to the others that the snail was the first contender to see Him in the bathroom, and He had consequently given Uke to him.

From then on, the envy against the snail began. When he got home with the girl, he could not make love to her. After repeatedly trying in vain to mate with her, Uke went to God to report that the snail could not make love to her. Subsequently, God invited the snail to embed Uke within his shell. He was told to look for the barks of trees called gbaingbain, oshunshun (Asuen in Bini) and egbeda, and to cut them into pieces and put them inside Oten (plantain wine), to be drinking. He prepared and was thereafter able to have normal sexual cohabitation with his wife.

Thereafter, the dog contrived another problem for the snail and his wife. The dog led a delegation of mammals to God to promulgate a decree banning animals with no ears from procreating through pregnancy and to limit them to procreation through the laying of eggs. God agreed to the suggestion and made a divine proclamation accordingly. Incidentally, Uke, the wife of the snail was fair in complexion and she has the same color as the snails eggs. That was how this odu earned the nickname of Ogunda-di-ugbin.

When this Ifa appears at Ugbodu, the person should serve the new Ifa with sixteen snails. He should also serve Ogun with a dog, after which it would be buried on the ground outside his house, adding the following leaves: seven ewe-efan, seven ewe-irosun, seven ewe-agbigbara (Osan in Bini) and seven ewe-tete (Ebi-tete in Bini). All the leaves should be used to under-lay the grave before burying the dog in it. The special sacrifice is done to prevent bad women from entering his life. At a convenient period in his life, he should serve Ifa with a ram and use the meat to cook for Ifa over a three day period consecutively, adding pounded yam.

When it appears at divination, the person will be advised to serve Ifa with a he-goat to avoid having problems because of women.

He Made Divination for Yeye-Oja to Save Her Only Son's Life

Ki ki ki moki ogbe. Ki aba ti ki ogbe me eta,
Ara osule ni'ta. Odifa fun Oja oluo ojomo.

He made divination for Yeye-Oja, who gave her only son to chief Ojomo as a servant. Overtime, the service of the young man satisfied him so much that he was put in charge of Ojomo's farm with the sobriquet of Ojomo-oko. Once upon a time chief Ojomo sent for Orunmila to come and make divination for him.

When Orunmila was travelling to answer chief Ojomo's invitation, he passed through a farm where he plucked some Ifa leaves for his work. In the hut of his farm was the meat of a bush goat which was being dried on the fire-place. As soon as Ojomo-oko saw Orunmila, he asked him who gave him the authority to pluck leaves in the farm. Orunmila replied that they were the leaves of plants freely endowed by God and not the leaves of farm crops. Ojomo-oko retorted by giving Orunmila a slap.

After the shabby treatment, Orunmila proceeded on his journey to chief Ojomo's house. On getting to chief Ojomo's house, he proceeded to make divination and it was Ogunda-Idi that appeared. He told chief Ojomo that there was turmoil in his household and that his prosperity was not consolidated. He advised him to make sacrifice with a goat, hen, fish, rat, the meat of bush goat, and Ojomo-oko tied up for the sacrifice, in order to alleviate his problems. After making the divination, Orunmila decided to attend the meeting of the divine priests which was being held on that day.

Meanwhile, chief Ojomo issued instructions that Ojomo-oko should be bound in chains and brought from the farm for the sacrifice. Incidentally, Yeye-oja, Ojomo-oko's mother was a lover to Orunmila. She was visiting chief Ojomo's house on that day to look up her son. She was present when her son was brought from the farm with hands, feet and mouth tied up. When she asked what the matter was, Chief Ojomo, explained that Orunmila prescribed sacrifice to be made with him. When she asked who the Ifa priest was, she heaved a sigh of relief when she heard that it was Ogunda-Idi. She asked for his whereabouts and was told that he was attending a meeting of divine priests.

She quickly raced to the venue of the meeting, where she demanded private audience with Ogunda-Idi. Whe he came out to meet her, she went on her knees to beg him to spare the life of her only son, who had been tied up in Ojomo's palace for sacrifice on his recommendation. He told her to stand up and return to wait for him in chief Ojomo's palace. When the conference dispersed, Orunmila returned to chief Ojomo's house, where he found Ojomo-oko tied up for sacrifice. He wondered and demanded an explaination, and chief Ojomo explained that it was he who recommended that the man (Ojomo-oko) should be used among other things, because God forbode human sacrifice for sacrifice.

Orunmila laughed hilariously exclaiming that he did not recommend human sacrifice. He went on to explain that what he meant by Ojomo-oko was any yam tuber in the farm that was too huge to be barned. It was that kind of yam that he meant should be tied up for the sacrifice together with the meat of a bush goat from the farm. Chief Ojomo's servants went to fetch such yam tuber, and all the meat of bush goat being dried in the farm. Meanwhile, Ojomo-oko was untied and Orunmila told him to wait for the sacrifice to be made.

When the yam and the meat were brought from the farm, Orunmila prepared the sacrifice by cutting pieces of the yam and the meat putting them together with the rat and fish on Esu's plate. He slaughtered the goat for Ifa and told the two Ojomos to kneel down. Thereafter, he touched their heads with the skull of the goat and Esu's plate while singing:

Ki Ki KI mo ki Ogbe. Aba ti ki Ogbe meta,
Lere meta, Ara osule ni ita. Odifa fun Yeye oja,
Oluo ojomo, Ogbo oru, otu lu Esu etu.

Oja orire du siseo oja,
Isu koni, oko jomo oko,
Oja orire du sise o oja,
Ke soja ba ni ma so jomo oko,
Oja orire du sise o oja.

Meaning that he had forgiven Ojomo oko because of his mother. The sacrifice manifested and peace and prosperity returned to chief Ojomo and he compensated Orunmila for the assistance.

When this Ifa appears at divination, the person will be advised to make sacrifice with a he-goat, the meat of bush goat, rat and fish to Esu to deter the risk of offending a higher authority that could either lead to death or imprisonment. The person should also be advised to have his own Ifa.

Another Special Sacrifice (Ono-Ifa or Odifa) of This Odu so That Good Fortune Will Always Come to Him

The son of this Odu is always highly principled to the point of becoming fanatically didactic and perfectionistic. Since he is not likely to make money by corrupt and unscrupulous behavior, he will require this sacrifice so that the good things of life (Ofe in yoruba and Ohe in Bini) will always come to meet him at home. The following materials are required for the sacrifice: the head of birds called eye-igun (vulture), eye-akala awo-ewiri and the heads of a boa, a boa constictor, (ori-oka and ori-ere) and okuru-kuru-aso-afon. After burning and grinding them together, the Ifa priest will add the iyerson of this odu and repeat the following incantation:

Ofe ni igun ma nje ebo.
Ofe ni akala ma nje oku.
Tofe tofe ni ewiri ma nfe ina.
Ojukan ibi ti oka ba joko si, ni ire re mba.
Ojukan ibi ti ere ba joko si, ni ire re mba.
nfi ire re mba.

Meaning:

The vulture eats sacrifices freely.
Akala bird feed on corpses freely.
The wind fans the flames of fire freely.
Food comes to meet the boa in a torpid position.
Food comes to meet the python in a torpid position.
Patronage comes to meet the cloth seller in a
sedentary position.

After repeating the incantation, the black powder should be put in a small calabash and kept at his Ifa shrine and to rub it on his head from time to time. Thereafter, prosperity will gradually travel to meet him at home.

The Divination Made for Okusu When He Travelled to Ila for Divination

Ogunda-idi-igbin, igbin ku, agere jadi okusu, agbon ja idi
o jingiri.

Those were the Awos who made divination for Okusu when he was travelling to the town of Illa-Orangun for Ifa practice. He was advised to make sacrifice to prevent his benevolence from being rewarded with ingratitude. He was required to make sacrifice with a he-goat, his knife and a cock. He made the sacrifice but failed to add his knife because of its significance to him. He then left for Illa Orangun.

On getting to the place he did a lot of impressive work. He was able to make; barren women to become pregnant, becalmed pregnancies to be delivered, the poor to become affluent, and make social mayhem and carnage to be replaced by peace and amity. The people of Illa were generally satisified with his performance. After completing his sojourn, he told the Orangun of Illa that it was time for him to return home.

That was the point at which Esu decided to punish him for the half hearted sacrifice he made. Esu made himself a harbinger to spread the false rumor that Okusu made love to all the barren women that became pregnant through his treatment. When the gossip got to the palace grapevine, the Orangun of Illa convened a conference of elders to deliberate on the veracity or lack of it, of the tittle-tattle. At the same time Esu went as a benevolent informant to warn Okusu that the conference convened by the Oba was to diliberate on how he was going to be executed for the false information that he pregnated all the barren women he helped to become pregnant. Without collecting the reward and gifts earmarked for him for his miracles, he absconded from the town in the night empty-handed, forgetting his cherished knife behind.

As soon as he realised that he had left his knife behind, he decided to brave the consequence of returning to collect it. The moment Esu sighted him in the town, the divinity of evil made the following announcement throughout the town:- "eko igi oti n pada bo wa ja" - by which he instigated the populace to rise up in revolt to use clubs and matchetes to lynch Okusu because he was returning to the town to wage war. He succeeded in retrieving his knife, but as soon as the citizenry noticed his presence, they pursued him and he only saved his life by taking refuge inside the river. From the depths of the river he was able to use his knife to invoke malediction against his assailants. Esu, the ambivalent and duplicitous double-dealer, meanwhile warned those pursuing Okusu to refrain from trying to kill him because "anyone who kills Okusu will die with him." When they got back home, they began to die one after the other. He eventually returned home safely but without realizing any recompense for all the good work he did for the people of Illa Orangun, for failing to part with his knife.

That is why when Ogunda-idi appears for anyone at ugbodu, the person should be warned never to travel to the town of Illa-orangun throughout his life. He should be advised to make sacrifices fully.

Special Sacrifice (Ono-ifa or Odiha) Against Deadly Enemies

He made divination for the white yam (called Egbenehi-khuere in Bini) with a smooth stem.

When he was going to the farm, he was told to make sacrifice because he was going to sink or swim among enemies from all sides, especially members of his family. He was advised to make sacrifice with the blast furnace used by blacksmiths (Ekue agbede) head of vulture, head of akala, heads of boa and boa constrictor, together with the heads of any snake he could obtain, fingers of witches, cloth used by witches, sand from the sea (Olokun) 201 leaves of iroko tree, tortoise, cock, camwood (Osun in Yoruba and Ume in Bini) something taken from the cooking tripod and rubbish dump, head of lion and parts of tiger's head, red, white and black pieces of cloth, sand taken from the palace, and something taken from the canoe. This is the special (madarikan) sacrifice of this Odu, to be able to fight his enemies effectively. The white yam made the sacrifice. When he got to the farm, his elder brother the thorny yam tuber (Ogigban in Bini) went to build a mountain of hooks and thorns round his house, challenging him to see how he could move from his house without being caught mortally injured by the web of danger woven round it.

The white smooth bodied yam began to struggle for existence amidst a wave of bruises, wounds and injuries, until he was able to tower over the wall of hooks and thorns surrounding him. Eventually , when it was time to harvest the white yam, Esu invited the farmer to destroy the wall of dangers surrounding him.

The children of this odu should therefore expect problems from their close relations and from people who have enjoyed their magnanimity. With sacrifices and forebearance, they will tower over their enemies towards the evening of their lives. Among the things they should forbid are:he-goat, tortoise, rabbit, dog and eggs. The person should not mix up, sleep on the same bed with, or eat food prepared by a woman under menstruation. He should also refrain from day time love-making. He should not wear black and red clothes. He should also refrain from swim-ming in the sea or big rivers. In addition to Orunmila, he should have his own Ogun, Olokun, Sango and Osun shrines.

Chapter 5

OGUNDA-OBARA

He Made Divination for the Ostrich When He Was Indebted

*Ogunda shawo, Obara shawo, Awon mejeji l'on difa fun Ako Lololo
nijo ti onje gbese lowo eniyan meta.*

Ogunda-Obara made divination for the Ostrich (Ako lololo in Yoruba and Eringoin in Bini), when he was indebted to three lenders. He owed debts to the farmer, the trader and the hunter. The three lenders met in his house one morning to demand the payment of their debts. He told them that he had no money to pay them. As the three lenders were tearing him to pieces, Orunmila begged them to spare his life. They refused to let go their hold on the Ostrich insisting that if Orunmila truly sympathized with him, he should defray the debt from his own pocket. Accordingly, Orunmila paid all three of them and it was then that they left the Ostrich alone.

When it appears at divination for a man, he should be advised to have his own Ifa. If he already has Ifa, he should be advised to make sacrifice so that someone else will pay a debt he owes. If it appears for a spinster, she will be advised to marry a man having his own Ifa. If it appears for a married woman, she will be advised to pursuade her husband to have his own Ifa.

He Made Divination for the Deer and the Farmer

Latanbo lo le bo, awo ogbe odifa fun Ogbe, abufun agbonrin.

Ogunda - Obara made divination for the farmer and the deer, when the latter was eating up the crops in the farmer's farm. The farmer had tried desparately to apprehend the deer who was ravaging his farm crops, but the deer proved to be very elusive.

Meanwhile, the farmer went to Orunmila for divination on what to do to end the menace of the deer. He was advised to serve his head with a cock, to spread palm frond at the entrance of his farm, and to bore a hole at that point. As the farmer was being advised by Orunmila, the deer also came in for divination. When Orunmila saw that the deer was coming to his house, he told the farmer to hide behind the mat.

When the deer got inside, she wanted to know through divination, what to do to avoid being caught by the owner of the farm from which she used to steal. She too was advised to serve Ogun with a cock. After making the sacrifice, Orunmila advised the deer never to go to the farm with her son Sifonren and to refrain from going where the palm found was spread.

The following day, the deer went again to the farm but avoided the direction of the palm frond. Before she returned, her son Sifonren was crying that he was hungry. He therefore insisted on accompanying his mother to the farm for supper in the evening.

Since the mother was too supple to stop him from going with her, they both went to the farm. The mother however forgot that she was told never to go to the farm with her son. In the same vein, she failed to brief her son not to go near the palm frond.

As soon as they got to the farm, Sifonren found the okro near the palm frond to be very alluring, not having previously been touched. He dashed straight for them and ended up in the hole dug by the farmer. The mother subsequently escaped leaving the son in the hole to the mercy of the farmer the following morning.

When this Ifa appears at Ugbodu, the person will be advised to make sacrifice with the meat of a deer, and to serve his Ogun with a cock after spreading palm frond on the shrine. He should also serve Esu with a he-goat. He should avoid match-making any woman to anyone for marriage, and he should not allow people to avenge an aggression or insult. At divination, the person should serve Esu with a small chicken and six bags of money to avoid losing something for failing to heed advice.

The Divination He Made Before Leaving Heaven

Ogunda o fo da'kpawo, Obara fo da ba awo ku. Ogunda recommended the death of a divine priest, Obara objected because it is forbidden for a divine priest to be killed in any town.

Those were the names of the Awos who made divination for Orunmila when he was coming to the world. He was told to make sacrifice because he was going to be very vindictive on earth. He was to make sacrifices with: a goat to his guardian angel, a he-goat to Esu, and tortoise to Ogun. He did all the sacrifices.

On getting to the world, he was so effective and efficient as an Ifa priest that people were prepared to pay his exhorbitant fees and charges. He became very prosperous in the process.

When it appears at Ugbodu, the person should prepare his Esu and Ogun without delay so that his work might bring him satisfaction and advancement.

He Made Divination for the Oludaren of Idanren

He made divination for the Oba of Idanren at his invitation. He disclosed that his predecessors never used to live long on the throne because there was a secondary divinity called Oro-run in the town which the Oludanren was required to be worshipping. He advised the reigning Oludanren to; clear and regenerate the shrine, and thereafter to serve the Orisa with fourteen different sacrificial animals and birds. He also prescribed that the reanimation festival was to span over a fourteen day period and that thereafter, the ceremony should be solemnized as an annual festival.

The Olodanren heeded the advice of Orunmila and he lived to a very ripe old age. When he became too senile to function at a very old age, another Oludanren was appointed in his place. That is why it is often said that the Oludanren never dies, because a dying one is replaced by a new one before his death. "Aigbo uku Oludaren birin. Aja se mii ngbinrin."

He Made Divination for the Olobahun

Egitan Obara, awo Olobahun, odifa fun Olobahun nijo ti ire
meta nbo wa ba. Oni ki oru ebo. Sugbon ko ru ebo na.

He made divination for a proficient divine priest called Olobahun when three favors were coming to him. He was advised to make sacrifice to Esu in the bush with a he-goat, a make-shift drum prepared with cocoyam leaves, crushed yam, fried corn and groundnuts to avert the risk of unconsumated fortune, (Amubo in Yoruba and Osobonomasunu in Bini). He often relied on his wits and proficiency to see him through any difficulties, and hence he refused to make the sacrifice.

Three days later, Alara-isa, Omo ajigbolu, the Alara of Ilara sent for him to show his appreciation for the successful manifestation of the work previously done for him. The thanks-giving ceremony was scheduled for seven days' time. On the same day the Owa-bokun of Ijesha and Olowo of Owo also sent for him for similiar reasons all on the same day.

Olobahun then wondered whether sacrifice was not going to be superfluous when the three favors had virtually fructified. It only remained for him to go and receive them.

Three days to the appointed day, he got dressed and left for the journey since he had many places to visit. As a divine priest, he often divined by possession, and it only required the beating of drums and the appropriate songs for him to be hynotized into a feat of enchantment and augury.

Meanwhile, Esu fried corn and groundnuts and organized an ensemble of drummers accompanied by small musical instruments and took position behind a thicket on the road through which Olobahun was going to travel. After travelling for about half a day he was getting hungry and tired. Meanwhile, he oveheard someone singing with the following words:

Kperi umogbon mogbon,
Ogunda gbain Obara gbain.

As he approached the spot, the music was amplified into what sounded like an enchanting allegro., accompanied by small musical instruments. He had to stop to find out who the musicians were. At that point, Esu released the fried corn and the groundnuts to him and after eating to his heart's content, he drank water. Thereafter, he could not account for what transpired. The melody of the music soon moved into crescendo and it allured him into a delirium, followed by total possession and he began to sing and dance.

At nightfall, he swooned into a heavy honey dew of slumber. The following morning, Esu resumed the music and Olobahun again got possessed. Not long afterwards, men going to their farms and women on their way to the market, saw him singing and dancing alone in the forest. First they thought he had gone out of his senses, until he began to divine for them. When the spectators realized that he was a possessed divine priest, they led him to their village and brought out drums, gongs, maracas and trumpets to provide the music. He began a spate of sooth-saying and divining in the village which lasted for five days, during which he remained perpetually possessed, feeding only on white chalk as possessed divine priests are wont to do.

Five days after he got to the village, Esu realized that the three Obas who invited Olobahun had given up the idea of compensating him, having failed to turn up, and so, decided to return him to the reality of mortal reasoning. The three Obas, who incidentally wanted to betroth their daughters to him, gave them to more deserving spouses. That was the state of affairs when Olobahun resumed his journey. As if they were acting in concert, the three Obas politely ignored him for failing to turn up when they lined out red carpet treatments for him. He was dismissed with token gifts and he had to return home almost empty-handed.

Since the disappointment was too embarrassing to report, he decided not to return home. He decided instead to settle down to a new life in the village where he had spent five days.

When this Odu appears at divination, the person should be advised to make the sacrifice that Olobahun refused to make to avert the risk of unconsummated fortune (Amubo in Yoruba and Osobonomasunu in Bini).

He Made Divination for the Snake Catcher and the Farmer

*Ogunda-gbon, Obara-gbon. Poporo eka, gbonrongondon ni ori
eda. Oda eda gborongondon ni poroko.*

Those were the Awos who made divination for the snake-catcher appointed by Orisa to wipe out the snake-kindred when they began to use the authority (Ase) given to them for killing human beings and animals. The snake-catcher went to Orunmila for divination and he was told to make sacrifice in order to succeed in his mission. He did not make the sacrifice. The same Awos also made divination for the farmer, advising him to make sacrifice to avert the risk of becoming the victim of his own generosity. He too failed to make the sacrifice. He was to make the sacrifice with his farm-dress, hoe, cutlass and a he-goat.

Meanwhile, the snake-hunter set out on his job of searching and destroying the snake. He soon saw the cobra and pursued him until he ran into a farm. The snake begged the farmer to accomodate him, because the hunter was hotly pursing him. The farmer told the snake to hide in his rubbish dump, but the latter appealed that his assailant would trace him there. Even when the farmer agreed to open the door to his farm house for the snake to take refuge therein, he still insisted that the hunter would comb the house for him. When the farmer asked the refuge-seeking snake precisely what he wanted him to do, he proposed that the only safe haven for him would be inside his bowels. He asked the farmer to open his mouth for him to hide inside his stomach. The farmer acquised to the snake's request and accommodated him inside his stomach.

When the hunter eventually trailed the movement of the snake to the farm, he turned the place inside out while the farmer reassured him that he had refused to accommodate the snake as a result of which he passed by. The hunter, realising that he had come to a dead-end, returned home completely dejected.

When the hunter was out of sight, the farmer gave the snake the all-clear to come out of his stomach, the snake refused to come out because the farmer's stomach was the only long-term bolthole for him. In spite of all the farmer's appeals, the cobra refused to budge.

The farmer abandoned his farm and began to run for help. As he was running, he came across the hen and asked her whether benevolence begets ingratitude. To the farmer's surprise, the hen gave an affirmative reply, by narrating her own experience. She explained that after laying and hatching eggs, producing children and nurturing them to adulthood, they were all rounded up and sold in the market. The proceeds of the sale were used to buy corn from the market. When the corn was brought home, and she tried to have a taste of it, she was beaten and driven away with a broom. She ended up by asking the farmer whether her experience was not sufficient to illustrate that generosity begets ingratitude. Realizing that the hen was in fact mirroring his own experience to him, he left her alone.

Wherever the farmer went, he was given the same answer and accused of being naive for not knowing that such was the hard reality of existence. Eventually, the farmer came across a bird called Ako, who had just been for divination to an Awo called "Bi ore ba kpo ni akpoju, ibi ni won nfi nsan" - meaning, "over-generosity is rewarded with crass ingratitude". Ako had been advised to make sacrifice with a cock and a club, but refused to do it.

When the farmer eventually came across Ako, he put the same question whether it was true that magnanimity begot ungratefulness. Ako was the first to aswer the question negatively. The farmer narrated his experience with the snake and the snake stated his own case from within the stomach of the farmer. Ako, now acting as an impartial adjudicator, told the snake to show up his face while narrating his case. As soon as the snake brought out his head, Ako gripped the former's head and a scuffle ensued between the two of them. As Ako and the snake were fighting, the farmer picked up a club and hit Ako on the neck. Ako then shouted, "Ori re di'bi o" meaning "charity has begotten ingratitude".

That is Why Ifa Priests Sing the Poem

Bi ore ba po ni a poju,
Ibi ni won fi n san.
Odifa fun oun ako ni ojo ti oun
yio lo yo ejo ni ikun ogbe
Esu ai ko ru Egba aikoteru,
Ifa wa se bi ala.

Meaning:

Over-generosity is invariably repaid with ingratitude.
Is the name of the Awo who made divination for Ako,
when he went to rescue the farmer from the snake
Inside his stomach. For refusing to make sacrifice,
Esu had taught him the lesson of his life.

The headless remains of the snake's body is the worm present in the bowels of every human being to this day. When this Odu appears at divination, the person will be advised to make sacrifice to forestall the danger of becoming over-generous, because it will be repaid with boorish ingratitude.

Special Sacrifice Against Death by this Odu

When this Odu appears at divination and it forebodes the danger of death (Ayeo), the person will be advised to take a kolanut, pass it round the windows of his house, before passing it through the main entrance of the house. Thereafter he will sit down in his room to use the same kolanut to serve his head. Thereafter, he will serve Esu with a small chicken, a piece of cloth and a he-goat to expel death from his house.

If it appears as Uree at divination, the person will be told that he has been having a dream recently. He/she should make sacrifice to remove the danger posed by the dream.

Chapter 6

OGUNDA-OKONRON

Divined for the Alligator When He Seduced Sango's Wife

Ogunda rankan ko'ton. Osare igbo koro. Odifa fun Onne
waka waka t'onlo gba aya oni'le oroke.

Ogun instigated a crisis and without resolving it, he escaped into the forest of Igbo ' koro. That was the Awo who made divination for the Alligator when he seduced the wife of the divinity who lives in the sky (otherwise known as Sango). He was advised to make sacrifice with a snail and a he-goat to Esu. Instead of making the sacrifice he began to hide in the hole, to hinder the wrath of Sango.

Sango however decided to give the Alligator a wide berth as if he was indifferent to the offence. For a long time, Sango did not react, which lured the Alligator to become euphoric. After ensuing that the Alligator had taken safety for granted, he decided to strike. Sango took position near the mouth of the hole in which the Alligator was taking refuge. As soon as the latter ventured out of the hole one bright morning, the cloud suddenly gathered and Oya targeted the Alligator with lightening while at the same time, Sango threw his missile at his victim and struck him dead.

When it appears at divination for a man, especially if it forebodes death or dispute (Iku or Ija) under Ayeo, he should be told that if he is flirting with a married woman and that the husband is stealithy planning to react violently. He should serve Esu with a he-goat and a snail to assuage the danger of sudden death.

He Made Divination for the Vulture When He Married Egherun

Bi Ogunda ba konron, bi Ogunda ko konron. Adifa fun Igun
ni jo t'oma mu Egherun shaya. Abufun Egherun.

This Odu made divination for the Vulture when he was going to marry a girl called Egherun. Several suitors had been wooing the girl without success. She was a very pretty woman and made a point of cold-shouldering any man who made amorous overtures to her.

Meanwhile Igun went to Orunmila for divination and he was advised to make sacrifice with a bunch of palm fruits. He made the sacrifice. After preparing the sacrifice, Orunmila told Igun to deposit it on the main market highway. Thereafter, in conformity with the advice of Orunmila, Igun hid himself at a vantage point from where he was not only able to see whoever was coming and going, but also to watch the sacrifice he had deposited.

When Egherun was returning from the market, Esu focussed her eyes on the attractive palm fruits. She could not resist the yen to go for them. She moved the bunch and began to pluck the fruits into her bag.

As she was plucking the palm fruits, Igun came out of hiding to accuse her of stealing, an offence which carried the death penalty. She pleaded passionately with Igun for forgiveness, but he bluntly refused. After imploring him to no avail, she demanded to know precisely what prize she had to pay and Igun replied that the only atonement acceptable to him was for her to agree to marry him right away. Since she had no other option, she agreed to become Igun's wife, and subsequently followed him to his house.

When the news got aroung that Egherun had married Igun, those who previously sought her hands unsuccessfully, began to make jest of her for condescending to marry the antediluvian and ugly vulture. When the humiliation became unbearable, she went to Orunmila for divination, and he advised her to make sacrifice with two cocks. She lost no time in making the sacrifice. Orunmila prepared the sacrifice by splitting one of the two cocks, adding the iyerosun and spread-eagled it for her to deposit it at the road junction. She was advised to conceal herself from view at a point from which she could observe what was going to happen to the sacrifice.

After depositing the sacrifice, she camouflaged herself behind a nearby thicket. Not long afterwards, Igun was returning from his daily chores in search of food, when he sighted the spread-eagled cock. He settled down to feed on the cock. While he was still enjoying the meal, Egherun came out of hiding to accuse him of stealing. Igun argued that he was only helping himself to a sacrifice made by someone. When Egherun disclosed that she was the one who kept the cock there, Igun reminded her of the convention that a spouse could not be accused of stealing from the marriage partner. On the other hand, Egherun contened that the convention only held good for transactions within the marital home of a married couple and that apart from the fact that she kept the spread-eagled cock for a specific purpose, the road junction was not part of their marital residence.

At that point Igun conceded and demanded to know her price. Egherun demanded to be absolved from the marriage. Just as he blackmailed her into the marriage, she traded him with the same coin by intimidating him into absolving her from it. Igun had no choice but to grant her an instant divorce, after which Egherun returned to the house to remove her belongings.

When people began to wonder why she left Igun as swiftly as she married him, she re-marked that she did not obtain clearance from anyone before marrying him and needed no clearance from anyone before divorcing him.

At divination for a man, he will be told that a woman is coming to experiment a transient marriage with him and that it will terminate soon afterwards. If it appears for a woman, she will be told that she is not happily married and that if she makes sacrifice with palm fruits and cock, she will end the marriage successfully and happily.

He Made Divination for the Parrot to Marry Jimi

*Bi Ogunda ba konron, bi ogunda ko konron, adifa fun
ayekoto ni jo t'onfe gba Jimi omo Orisa sh'aya.*

He made divination for the Parrot when she was vying for the hands of Jimi, the daughter of Orisa, in marriage. Jimi, a very attractive spinster was being chased by many suitors, and when Orisa saw the crowd of admirers flocking around her, he invited all of them for a contest in his farm.

As soon as he returned home from the briefing, Aiyekoto went to Orunmila for divination. After divination, Orunmila told him to serve; Esu with a he-goat, and his head with white kolanut. Furthermore, Orunmila advised him that when going to the farm on the appointed day, he was to plug his anus with a ripe palm fruit and to make sure that he was the first to get to the farm.

On the appointed day, he was the first to get to the farm and he was given a portion of grass weed, which was equi-distant to those of other contestants. Before setting out to work, he plugged his anus with a palm fruit. As the others were coming to the farm, Esu made the palm fruit on the anus of Aiyekoto, the cynosure of their eyes, whilst infecting them with a feat of endless laughter. While the rest were laughing out their senses, Aiyekoto was clearing away his portion.

Meanwhile, Orisa got Jimi dressed up to go and deliver food to her suitors in the farm. She met everybody giggling away hysterically at the parrot, who was the only one working. When she saw the palm fruit protruding from the anus of the parrot, Jimi too began to chuckle unwittingly, in the wake of which she moved to cover the exposed anus of the parrot, to prevent her father from coming to meet him in that condition. As she was about to touch the anus of the parrot, Esu blinked his eyes to her and her two hands got glued to the anus of the parrot.

When Orisa eventually came to meet the others frenzied up in an endless chuckle. He asked them what the matter was, and they told him what the parrot did. He retorted by reminding them that he invited them to work and not to laugh. When he asked for Jimi, they told him that she was holding on to the anus of the parrot. Orisa reacted by proclaiming that Jimi had thus chosen her husband, which is signified by the red feathers on the anus of the parrot, and from that day, anyone who wanted to address him was to do so through the parrot.

As soon as this odu appears at Ugbodu, the person should be advised to serve: Esu with a he-goat, Ogun with a cock, and his head on account of a test that would come to him before the completion of the Ifa ceremonies. At divination, the person will be advised to serve Esu with a he-goat because of something for which other people are going to compete with him.

He Made Divination for Orisa-Nla, Oshere-igbo when He Was Coming to the World

*Ogunda ka kan ko'tan. Odifa fun Orisa-Nla Oshere-igbo
nijo ti on kole orun bo wa si ko le aiye.*

Ogun caused trouble for Orisa-Nla Oshere-igbo (God's own representative on earth) when he was leaving heaven for earth. He was advised to make sacrifice in order to subdue the evil artifices of Esu on earth. He however felt that as God's own proxy on earth, there was no necessity for him to make sacrifice to anyone. He was to have served Esu with a He-goat.

He left for the world afterwards without making the sacrifice. Esu was equally determined to make Orisa-Nla realize the consequence of under-mining him. In the interim, Esu went to the route through which Orisa-Nla was travelling and caused a fight between two people. When Orisa-Nla met the two combatants, he tried to intervene to stop them from fighting. At the same time Esu blinked his eyes to the two of them and they transferred their fury to Orisa-Nla and they both had him throughly beaten up. After the incident, the servant travelling with Orisa-Nla re-minded him of the sacrifice he refused to make.

Thereafter, Orisa-Nla decided to return to heaven to make the sacrifice. When he got back to the Awo, he was advised to make the sacrifice to Esu with a he-goat, adding akara, eko, rat, fish, pigeon, white cloth and a snail. He made the sacrifice and returned to earth where he began to command eternal honor and respect. Wherever he went on earth. Esu would herald his approach as the surrogate of the creator of heaven and earth, and people were acknowledging his divine glory with the exclamation "Obata la o"!

When this Odu appears at divination, the divinee will be advised not to ignore one divinity that followed him/her to the world, apart from Orunmila. If the person is proposing to travel, he will be advised to make sacrifice before embarking on the journey to avert the risk of embarrass-ment. The sacrifice to the divinity will be made with white cloth, pigeon and a snail, in addition to serving Esu with a he-goat, akara and eko.

The Divination Made for Him When He Was Coming to the World

O ma kpa de - re, amubogunale, omu aluko mu la rin oja.
O ya gbo di ako ko joru ako.

Those were the Awos who made divination for this odu when he was leaving heaven for earth. He was advised to make sacrifice in order to avoid the danger of death through his wife or children. He was required to serve Esu with two he-goats, his guardian angel with an electric fish and a castrated he-goat, and Ogun with a dog, tortoise and cock. After making the sacrifice Ogun decided to accompany him to the world.

On getting to the world, he became an Ogun priest as well as operating as an iron-smith. He was doing well as iron-monger and was soon able to marry and to have children. After having several children, his wife began to create problems for him. As his children were growing up, they too began to create additional problems for him. He subsequently went for divination and was told to serve Esu, Ifa and Ogun. He wasted no time in making the prescribed sacrifices.

One day, he was preparing to go to the market to sell his wares. Previously, he often trav-elled to the market with two other traditional diviners called Ipadere and Aluko. On that particular occasion, they learnt that the king of the market town had joined his ancestors and that the search for a new successor had begun after the completion of the funeral rights. The tradition of the town was to look for a king from outside because the native born were forbidden to be made king. The kingmakers of the town had invited diviners to find out from where the new king was to come.

After divination, the kingmakers were told that three non-indigenous diviners used to visit the market regularly. They were advised to apprehend the three of them and to make use of them as follows:- one was to be used to make sacrifice to the iroko tree over-looking the market; the second one was to be offered as sacrifice to the Ogun shrine of the town; while the third one was to be made the new Oba of the town.

On the eve of the day he was to leave for the market, Ogunda-Okonron had a petrifying dream. The following morning he sounded Ifa on the significance of the dream and his own Odu appeared. Ifa advised him to delay his departure for the market and to make sacrifice before going. He was required to serve; his Ifa with a castrated he-goat and an electric fish, Esu with he-goat, and Ogun with a dog, cock and tortoise. He was to do the sacrifices that morning and to leave for the market in the evening. He made the sacrifices accordingly. While the food for the sacrifice was being cooked, his two fellow-travellers came to join him for their journey to the market, but he told them that he had served his Ifa and that the food was still being cooked. Since they could not wait for him, Ipadere and Aluko both left for the market.

As soon as they landed on the market, they were both apprehended and used for sacrifice respectively to the market's iroko tree and the traditional Ogun shrine of the town. In the evening, Orunmila arrived at the market and he was carried shoulder high and hailed as the new Oba of the town. He was carried on a chariot to lead a procession through the main streets of the town, before being crowned as the new Oba of Oja Ajigbomekon akira. After settling down, he en-quired after his two friends. When he was told of what happened to them, he realized how narrowly he too escaped death. He then sang in praise of Orunmila and Ogun.

When this Odu appears at Ifa initiation ceremony, the person will be told to have his Esu and Ogun shrines prepared without any delay to avoid sudden death, and in order to live to occupy a high position of authority destined for him.

He Made Divination for Ako, the Fisherman

He made divination for the fisherman called Ako when he was very poor. After divination, he told Ako to make sacrifice with: he-goat to Esu; hen to Ifa and cock to Ogun. Much as he was prepared to make the sacrifice, he lamented that he was too poor to fund it. Akpetebi, Orunmila's wife took pity on him and appealed to her husband to borrow the cost of the sacrifice to Ako. Orunmila gave the money to Akpetebi to buy the materials from the market, on the condition that he was to repay the loan when his situation improved.

In the wake of the sacrifice, Ako began to catch more fishes and he was realizing a lot of money in the process. Even though he was making a lot of money, he neither remembered; to thank Orunmila, nor to repay the loan. One day, Orunmila reminded Akpetebi of Ako's ingratitude and she decided to look for him. After waiting in vain for him to show up, Orunmila lost his patience and told Esu about Ako's ingratitude. In no time Ako was back into abject penury. One day, Akpetebi found him looking dejected and wretched, but held on to him. He agreed that he was ungrateful to Orunmila, but had lost all his money. He promised however to repay Orunmila in some other way. He promised to create a havoc in Alara-Isa's palace, which would make him to invite Orunmila for assistance.

A few days later, he caught a giant electric fish and dumped it into the well from which the royal household fetched drinking water. Subsequently, all those who drank water from the well developed stomach trouble. That gave rise to a pandemonium in the Oba's palace, and being the chief diviner of the Oba, an invitation was sent immediately to Orunmila. When Orunmila got to the palace, he made divination after which he told the Oba that the cause of the problem was in his private well. Following a search, an electric fish was found in the well. Orunmila prepared the appropriate leaves, added iyerosun and gave it to all those afflicted with stomach upset to drink. They all became well instantly. The Alara-Isa rewarded Orunmila with gifts comprising a man and a woman in addition to a goat, a ram, a cock and plenty of money.

Afterwards, Ako visited Orunmila to verify the manifestation on his devious gimmick. When he was told of its resounding success, Ako subsequently repeated the experiment in the palace of the Owa-Obokun of Ijesha. Orunmila was again invited to solve the problem after which he was given four men, four women, a cow and six bags of money.

Ako repeated the experiment at the palaces of the Olowo of Owo and the Orongun of Illa, all having salutary consequences for the fortunes of Orunmila. Eventually, Orunmila became very wealthy and he gave a he-goat to Esu to undo the problems he had generated for Ako. Not long afterwards, Ako visited Orunmila and he was given two men, two women and a goat. That marked the beginning of his return to opulence.

When this Odu appears at divination, the person will be advised not to repay benevolence with ingratitude. In any event, he should make sacrfice in order to derive benefit from unscrupulous behavior.

He Made Divination for Ogun When He Was Going to Wage War on the Town of Egba-ruku-Esido

Ogunda Kanbu, Okonron Kongbon made divination for Ogun-oniju, when he waged war on the people of Egba-ruku-Esido. He was advised to serve his guardian angel with a big dog, a roasted tuber of yam and palm wine. He made the sacrifice after which he embarked on, fought and won the war. He returned home with a crown, many war captives and treasures which made him to become very prosperous. He went to thank Orunmila with gifts after returning home triumphantly.

When it appears at divination, the person will be told to serve Ogun with dog, roasted yam and palm wine in order to succeed in achieving an objective that will involve travelling away from home.

He Divined for Two Bosom Friends to Avoid Quarrelling

Ogunda fo si Olokonron fo si Oloye.

A o kilo wi pe ki ole ma wo ishu eba ona mo.
A o so fun ishu eba ona wi pe ki o ma ma ta, ata ajade.
A o so fun ore meji ki won maja, ki ashiri ara won ma ba tuu.
A o so fun babalawo meji ki won she imule po ki won ma ba she
oro ai ko sun won.
Adafa fun Arogundade, omo ' kunrin omukpo, abufun Dosumu,
omo 'kunrin idere mo awise.

Ogunda chatted with okonron, Okonron chatted with a chief;
Advising the Chief not to tread on the yam growing by the road-side
While advising the yam to check its stem and branches not to
over-shoot the roadway.
Two robbers were advised to avoid altercation, to obviate the
risk of exposing their mutual secrets.
Two Ifa priests were advised to take mutual oaths, to avoid
deceptive divination.

These were the Ifa priests who made divination for two bosom friends, Arogundade and Dosumu. They were advised to make sacrifice to prevent their friendship from going sour. They ignored the advice because they could not imagine what could generate any misunderstanding between them. They did not stop at refusing to make sacrifice to Esu, but also vilified him, and concluded that the Ifa priests were talking nonsense.

They affirmed that nothing was capable of upsetting their friendship. Experience was soon to demonstrate that they had underestimated the limitless disruptive capabilities of Esu. It was not long before Esu tempted them into developing seductive impulses for each other's wife, resulting in sensual cohabitation. After the wife-swapping exercise had been going on for some-time, Esu brought it out to the knowledge of their two wives, thus instigating a fight between the two women. Their two husbands at the same time became wise to their mutual dishonesty and a fight also ensued between them.

The intensity of the fighting attracted neighbors who intervened to stop the pandemonium. The matter was brought before the elders and after narrating their sides of the story, they were all found guilty not only of societal moral depravity, but also of polluting the traditions of and morés of the community. Since the friends were divine priests, they were also found guilty of debasing and desecrating the dignity and imagery of divine priesthood. They were each fined a goat, a he-goat, a cock, a hen, a gourd of palm wine and six bags of money to annoint and consecrate the profaned land. What a high price to pay for refusing to give a single he-goat to Esu as sacrifice.

When this Odu appears at divination, the person will be advised not to deceive or abuse the confidence of his friend, that is, if it is uree. If it is ayeo, he or she will be told that he/she is the victim and offender in the act of mutual deception with a friend. He should not delay sacrifice.

Orunmila's injunction to his priests and children

Ki ogunda ma kon-karan, ki okonron ma nkan olile
Ki ogbigbo meji ma je oso igi kon,

Ki omo fi ibi kpalaba ori kan arawon,
Ki agbo meji ma mo mi la akoto,
Ki a ma fi tu lu kan tuutu,
Adifa fun won ni ilode, abufun won ni Ijebu iremo
tori oron la akpa mu eru. La akpa merun oruko
ti anpe obo.

Ogunda was advised not to undermine Okonron,
So that Okonron might not fall victim to misfortune.
Two tiokams were advised not to eat the same fruit,
To avoid knocking their heads against each other.
Two rams were advised not to drink water from the same gourd
To avoid locking horns.

These were the Ifa priest who made divination for the people of Ilode and Ijebu-Remo. They were advised to make sacrifice to avert the danger of carrying a mortal burden capable of killing the carrier. The "mortal burden" is the heavenly name of the female genitals.

When it appears at divination for a man, he should be told that he is flirting with a married woman, whose husband is stronger than himself. He should be told to enquire from Orunmila whether to continue or to discontinue with the immoral relationship because one of the men could lose his life in the process. In any case, he should ask Ifa for the requisite sacrifice to prevent the danger.

Chapter **7**

OGUNDA-IROSUN

The Divination Made for Him Before Leaving Heaven

Akiko idi ko, yin gbe re nu. A cock cannot crow without growing its long tail feather. That was the name of the Ifa priest who made divination for this odu when he was coming from heaven. He was forewarned that a difficult time awaited him on earth because he was going to be the spokesman of his people. To forestall the risk of becoming the victim of falsehood, he was advised to serve Esu with two he-goats; Ogun with the fourteen traditional instruments for preparing one's Ogun, including a dog, cock, tortoise, snail and fish; and Olokun with a white cock. After performing all the sacrifices, he was warned never to marry a light-skinned woman. Thereafter, he left for the world.

He became very popular on earth because he was quick in assuming the role of peacemaker in settling disputes. His leadership qualities were quickly recognized and he was made a chief at a very early age. He was also the blue-eyed boy of all the divine priests and meetings were often held in his house. Not long afterwards, the yellow-complexioned daughter of Olokun fell in love with him. The light skinned daughter of Sango also fell in love with him. The dark-skinned daughter of Ogun also fell in love with him and he ended up marrying all three of them. He became known by the nickname of Olugotun.

One day, Ogun's daughter offended him and he hit her and she fell down unconscious. When the father heard about it, he threatened to kill him, but for the fact that his daughter regained consciousness. The incident scared him into going for divination where he was told to give a he-goat to Esu, and to fry the meat and share it with everybody around. He was also to serve Ogun with a dog and fry the meat for those who could eat dog's meat. He was also advised to serve his Ifa with a goat and to treat the meat the same way.

He started by serving his Ifa with the goat and he invited the priests of the 200 divinities to feast on the meat after frying it.

While the feasting was going on, his wives got hold of the maracas and began to sing and dance. They sang that there was no other divine priest as good as their husband, the Olugotun. Ogun got infuriated by the song and he went in hot pursuit of Olugotun and everybody he could apprehend in the house. When Ogun pursued Olugotun he was able to escape. Ogun was being assisted by Esu who had not been given his he-goat.

In this connection, it is important to emphasize that if one is asked to make sacrifices to divinities including Esu, it is often advisable to begin with the sacrifice to Esu. He eventually took refuge in a big stone inside the river. Incidentally, Esu had pre-empted him by positioning a shark inside the hole in the stone. As soon as he entered the stone, the shark swallowed him up.

When this Ifa appears at Ugbodu, the person will be advised never to marry any light-complexioned woman. He should immediately prepare his Ogun, Olokun and Esu.

He Made Divination for the Two Pages of the Oba in Benin

Ogunda roro bi aro, Irosun roro bi eje, won difa fun Onita-agba, abufun onita-kekere, awon mejeji she wole wode ni'le Oba ado ajuwaleke.

He made divination for the senior and junior pages in the palace of the Oba of Benin. They were advised to make sacrifice and not to get needlessly embroiled in futile arguments. As the senior page was getting old, the junior one (Olotu-odibo in Bini) was told to understudy his aging superior. That was when they both went to Orunmila for divination. He advised each of them to serve Esu with a he-goat and to serve their heads with a cock. The senior page made his sacrifice but his junior colleague did not. They were advised to make sacrifice to impede the risk of becoming the victim of an undeniable falsehood.

Two days later, the senior page was taking his junior colleague through the main shrines of the palace. When they got to Ogun shrine; they saw the skulls of beheaded victims. The senior page observed rather emotively that "those were the heads of both guilty and innocent victims". The younger page retorted contentiously that "the Oba does not kill innocent and law-abiding citizens and that the skulls belonged to villains and those who ran foul of the law."

The Oba of Benin had a cock which used to crow in the morning before the king woke up. After the younger page had argued on three occasions that the king and the law were too infallible to condemn law abiding and innocent persons, the much more experienced page contrived a strategy for teaching him a veritable lesson on the indubitable realities of human existence.

One night, the senior page captured the Oba's favorite cock, and hid it far away from the vicinity of the palace. At the same time, he got hold of another cock having a similar color scheme as the palace cock. After removing the feathers of the cock, he spread them from the palace wall to the house of the junior page to charm him (Ikanse in Bini) and mesmerise him into a hypnotic sleep. As soon as he was dead asleep, the senior page, rubbed his head with white chalk, slaughtered the cock and dubbed his head with the bood of the cock, to give the appearance of having just served his head with the cock. In accordance with tradition, he made a circle with white chalk and deposited it in pieces of the kolanut, coconut and the head of the cock inside the circle before covering it up with a basket. He also took pains to fry the meat of the cock and to use the oil of the cock's stew to rub the mouth of the junior page.

At dawn, the Oba did not come out to begin his daily chores because the cock did not crow. When the senior page went into the king's chamber to find out why he had not woken up, the king ordered him to find out why the cock had not crowed. The senior page (Olotu-odibo) convened an emergency meeting of all the palace pages, orderlies and the policemen and instructed them to find out what happened to the cock. Incidentally, the junior page was conspicuously absent from the meeting. The search for the cock eventually took the searchers to the feathers that lined the route from the palace to the junior page's house.

When the searchers got to his house, they met him still fast asleep, but found all the evidence that he was the culprit who used the palace cock to serve his head. That was the point at which the senior page undid the charm with which he hypnotised his argumentative junior colleague into a deep sleep. He was awakened by the palace policemen and bound in chains and gagged in his mouth for summary trial at the palace. With all the evidence produced against him, he was not only dumb-founded but also without benefit of defense. He was condemmned to instant execution, and the royal executioner was invited to perform his assignment. As the condemned page was taken to the Ogun shrine for execution, the senior page sought permission to speak. His request was granted.

He started by asking the junior page to confirm or deny in his own words whether he killed the palace cock. He could only nod his head to indicate a negative answer. The senior page then confirmed that the palace cock was alive and well. He sent police orderlies to go and fetch it from where he kept it. As soon as the cock was released, it crowed and they all went before the Oba. The senior page narrated the arguments between them which culminated in his decision to teach his junior colleage to appreciate that it is possible for an innocent person to be executed and beheaded for an offense he or she did not commit. That was the point at which Onita-kekere remembered the sacrifice he did not make. He was accordingly given the white chalk of innocence and released.

When it appears at divination, the person will be advised to refrain from being argumentative, presumptuous and audaciously forward, when dealing with his superiors in his place of work. Nonetheless, he should give a he-goat to Esu and serve his head with a cock.

When it appears at Ugbodu, the person should be told to prepare his Esu with a he-goat the following day, and to serve his head with a cock while backing his Ifa shrine.

He Made Divination for Two Friends

Ori ari'se Ori ari're ki iyu umagun.
adifa fun Irosun t'in she ore Olofin. Irosun lo ngba akun
Oba da ni. On lo to ju re. Ore ni Irosun ati egitan.
Egitan omo ibiti, irosun gbe ugba akun Oba si, Egitan o
ba mso irosun titi oba yo ikon ni be. Oyo okan ninu akan
na. O lo ju si omi.

Irosun was friendly with king Olofin. He was the custodian of the container of the king's beads. At the same time Egitan was friendly with Irosun and knew that the chest of royal beads was being kept by him. Egitan also knew where Irosun kept the chest of beads. Meanwhile, to create a problem for his friend, Egitan went to the Oba to report that Irosun had removed one of the beads under his custody and sold it for money.

The king reacted by calling on Irosun to produce the chest of beads. On getting home, Irosun discovered that one of the beads was missing. After searching in vain for it, he went to Orunmila for divination. He was advised to make sacrifice after which he was told to serve his head with a freshly caught live fish. He made the sacrifice with a cock and a hen, after which he went in search of fishermen at the bank of the river to buy a fish for serving his head. The first fisherman he saw, had only one fish and Irosun bought it from him.

On getting home, he served his head with the fish, praying not to be killed by the Oba for the loss of the bead. After killing the fish, his wife split it open and found the missing bead inside its intestines. It was a happy moment when she took the bead to the husband and it proved to be the missing one. Soon afterwards, he carried the entire chest of beads to the Oba, who inspected them and found them to be correct. The Oba subsequently admonished Egitan for bearing false information. That was how Irosun's head saved him from the evil contrivance of his friend, Egitan.

When it appears at divination, the person should be warned to beware of a friend who is plotting to get him into trouble. He should make sacrifice in order to neutralise the plot.

He Made Divination For Shede, Advising Him Not To Go To The Farm On New year's Day

Kikan edun kpaa. Arikan edun kpaa.
Adifa fun Shede ti ani ko ma lo si oko ni
ojo odun. Shede ko gbo.

Whatever part of an axe hits the ground, it makes the same sound. That was the name of the Ifa priest who made divination for Shede who was told not to go to the farm on New Year's Day. In spite of the advice, he insisted on going to the farm on the first day of the year.

On his way to the farm he came to the bank of a river where he saw a bird on top of a tree. He put a missile on his catapult, took aim at the bird and released the shot. When the missile hit the bird, it picked up the weapon and threw it back at Shede. The missile hit Shede and he fell to the ground, dead. Later in the day, his friends and relations noticed that Shede had not returned from the farm. A search party was organized to look for him. When his mother began to call him in the bush, the bird was replying as follows:-

Tani kpe Shede ni be yen Shede.
Won sho'dun ni'le, awa na nshoro loko Shede.
Shede ti aun lo fa kan mi, emi na mo ta Shede na
san, Shede.
Bo ya oku wara mi o ma Shede.
Ariku wara mi o ma Shede.
Ki ani ka e ku majo gboro.

Meaning:

Who is calling on Shede?
The New Year was being celebrated at home,
And we were celebrating it in the forest.

Shede threw a missile at me, and I threw it back at him.
Whether he resultantly died, I do not know.
Whether he did not die, I do not know.
Whatever is done at home is replicated concurrently
in the forest

The duet between Shede's mother and the bird continued until she came across the corpse of her son. There was weeping from the forest to the house.

When this Odu appears at divination, the person should be warned to heed advice and not to be foolhardy and impetuous.

Special Sacrifice for Child-Bearing

Mi o ta saara, Emi na ni o ta suuru.
Eyi ti o ta saara shi ku omo eku.
Oyun lo fi she, omo lo fi bi.

Meaning:

It oozed into the genitals of the rat,
And it became pregnant, giving birth eventually
to a child.
It oozed into the vulva of the fish, and it became
pregnant, Giving birth in the fullness of time to
several children.
It oozed into the vagina of a woman, and she
became pregnant. And in the fullness of time, gave
birth to a child.
It also oozed into the womb of Akpetebi, and she
became pregnant, Eventually giving birth to a child.
This calls for sacrifice for child-bearing,
comprising of two hens, two pigeons and a rabbit.

If this Odu appears at divination for a woman who is anxious to have a child, she will be advised to make sacrifice and she will surely have a child.

Chapter 8

OGUNDA-OWANRIN
OGUNDA-MI-LERIN
OGUNDA-DERIN

Made Divination for the Seed-Yam

Ada Kasha, Arin kasha, O tete de idi iroko de elebo.
Adifa fun omo titun, ishu ti o mo araye she ika binu re.
The vainglorious swagger got to the foot of the iroko tree
before the sacrifice was deposited there.

That was the name of the Awo who made divination for the seed yam when human beings got a matchete and slaughtered the yam tuber into pieces and buried the pieces on the ground. The yam had been told to make sacrifice with a hen to forestall that eventuality and to ensure that whatever was done to undo her would turn out to be a blessing in disguise. She made the sacrifice. After the pieces of yam were buried beneath the ground, they germinated and grew. At the end of six months, the yam which went into the ground in pieces emerged as a complete and whole adult yam tubers, and her enemies eventually rejoiced with her over the children she brought forth.

At divination, the person will be told that he/she has several enemies, but that with sacrifice, he/she will derive a benefit from whatever was done unto him/her.

The Divination Made for Him Before Leaving Heaven

Okiki ba ba ba ni me run okpokpo was the Awo who made divination for this Odu when he was coming to the world. He was told that he was coming to trade in the world and that he should make sacrifice with corn, yam, plantain, cocoyam, tortoise, snails, hen and cowries to the ground divinity. He was also told to obtain the blessing of God with a piece of white cloth, white kolanut and cowries. He was going to practice Ifism as his main profession. He was therefore advised to serve Esu with a he-goat. He made the sacrifice before leaving for the world.

He was accompanied by Sango and Olokun to the world. On getting to the world, he took to trading, but he did not make much progress. When he subsequently went for divination, he was told that he had strayed away from the path of his destiny. He was told to take to the practice of Ifa as his main vocation while trading on the side-line. He was told to serve; Esu with a he-goat and Ifa with a multi-colored goat.

After the sacrifice, he took to itinerant Ifa practice together with trading which involved frequent travelling. His eldest brother was an Ogun priest, while the next one was a Sango priest. His eldest sister was a Sango priestess. Each of them used to send gifts to their father from time to time and he used to treasure the gifts from his children separately. Orunmila was away from home when their father died and the Ogun priest, took charge of their father's estate and divided it as he saw fit.

When Orunmila subsequently returned home from his tour, he lamented that his father died in his absence. When he asked for his share of their father's estate, he was told that his share was the ground occupied by their father. He had lots of problems from his half brothers and sisters.

As the torture became unbearable, he went once more for divination. The Awo told him to give another he-goat to Esu and to approach the young servant of their father, who would tell him where their father kept his important belongings.

On getting back home, he served Esu with a he-goat. Three days later, the favorite servant of their late father paid Orunmila a visit. The young man told him that he was earmarked by their father to inherit the whole place. The man took him to the shrine of their father's guardian angel and showed him where his things were kept. Eventually, he solicited the help of Esu in asserting his rightful ownership. He began to sing on Esu shrine "Maa gba ile baba mi, Ogun de lo ni," that is, I am ready to fight to assert my right of ownership of my father's estate.

Thereafter, things began to happen amidst total confusion stimulated by Esu. He ordered his other brothers and sisters to remove their property because the ground on which they stood belonged to him. They were all compelled to acknowledge his right of ownership and he made them give an undertaking to pay homage to him annually. That is why all other divinities pay annual obeissance to Orunmila to this day. He became very prosperous in the process.

When this Ifa appears at Ugbodu, the person should be advised to expect lots of problems from his half brothers, but with perseverance and sacrifice he would truimph eventually.

He Divined for the Wife of Ogun

> Ogun da mi le rin. Ori buruku ko bu tu lu tuulu.
> Adifa fun Omo-boni ti'nshaya Ogun, ni ojo to fe ko Ogun.
> Gbogbo aye so fun Omo-boni ko ma ko Ogun. Sugbon ko gbo.
> O ba ko Ogun si le.

Ogun aroused my laughter. Hard luck or a bad head cannot be determined by looking at the face. These were the Awos who made divination for Omoboni, the wife of Ogun, when she wanted to leave her husband. In spite of everybody's advice to the contrary, she insisted on carrying out her wish, and eventually left Ogun.

After she left, Ogun used his instrument of command (Ase) to curse her, by proclaiming that she would remain listless and baseless for the rest of her life. Three days later, she went beserk, stripped herself naked and ran mad. Thereafter, people began to make jest of her with the words

"Ogun lo fi Omoboni derin," that is, it was Ogun who transformed Omoboni to become an object of ridicule. That is how this Odu got the sobriquet of "Ogun derin."

When the odu appears at divination for a man and it declares uree (that is, there is not much to worry about) he should be advised not to curse anyone. If it is Ayeo (when it forebodes danger), he should be told that one of his wives is proposing to leave him and that if he curses her, it will manifest. If it appears for a woman, she will be advised not to leave her husband because she will not only regret it but also suffer the consequences immensely to the point of having to pick things from the ground or rubbish dump to eat.

He Made Divination for Ogun and His Wife

Ona kan ti yi wa. Ona kan ti ohun wa. Ikpade ona meji ni o
ma nje eso genge.
One road came from one side and one road came from the other side. Their intersection was the truth or the way it was expected.

Those were the Awos who made divination for Ogun and his wife. Ogun was advised to make sacrifice with his sword and a he-goat to avoid doing damage under a feat of uncontrollable temper. His wife was also advised to make sacrifice with the clothes she was wearing and a cock to prevent the danger of being beheaded by her husband. Since it was a sacrifice to Esu, Ogun refused to do it because he habitually looks down on Esu. The wife however made her own sacrifice.

As Ogun was drinking palm wine one day, his wife was trying to rescue a child who fell to the ground when she too slipped to the ground and inadvertently overturned the gourd from which Ogun was drinking the palm wine. Overwhelmed by frenzy, he went into tantrum and got his sword to behead the wife. She narrowly missed death, although wounded on the mouth. The injury did not respond to treatment and it led to the exposure of the woman's teeth. People soon began to taunt her with her exposed teeth especially whenever she went to the market. She often retorted by saying that she did not blame those who were making jest of her and that if Ogun had not inflicted the injury on her, she would not have become the object of ridicule. That again is how this Odu became known as "Ogun damikrin" - meaning it was Ogun who made me an object of ridicule."

When it appears at divination, the person will be told to make the above-mentioned sacrifice to avoid accidental injury or to prevent the risk of inflicting serious injury on someone as a result of uncontrollable temper. He/she should make the sacrifice without delay.

He Made Divination for all Divinities on Earth

Elerin moro aron orongun maja loko. Owa lomo sanda
ajegbin. Adifa fun egberin aworo tionbu ikin le okuro.
Ifa yio kpa oluwa reje. Egberin aworo t'onbi ikin lo okuro,
Ifa yio kpa gbogbo won je.

Three Awos made divination for the divinities on earth, when they were deriding Orunmila as mere palm nuts. They were warned that whoever called him mere palm nut would be killed and eaten by Orunmila, even if it was the whole lot of them. That is why it is said that anyone who despises Orunmila as mere palm nuts will be destroyed or crushed.

He Made Divination for the Farmers and People of Kosoko Town

Ogunda-da-won tan arin - made divination for the farmers and the entire people of the town of Kosoko. They were told to make sacrifice with all edible foods adding hoe and cutlass. The people made the sacrifice, but the farmers refused to join the other people in making the sacrifice. Thereafter, the people gave up farming on the ground that they lacked the equipment for farming. However, they began to flourish through trading, and other vocations. The people became rich generally from whatever they did.

In the town to this day, farming is marginalized, although poverty is a rarity in the place. That was the result of the command given by Esu in the following incantation:

Ota bota, Ore bo re
Ana mu mi ti oga
O ni ibi ti eru ba ni eru mo.
E ko gbo do lo si oko mo.
E ma rin igboro kiri.
Ibe nii onje yi o ma de ba yin
Awon ti o lo se ishe ni oko, ile ni e o,
ma wa ti won yi o ma ko onje wa.

Enemy knows how to get enemies.
Friends know how to get friends.
The chameleon turns its color to whatever it sees.
Whenever the slave ends his servitude and gains freedom.
He does not go anymore to the farm.
When you go out to walk about,
That is where food will meet you.
Those who go to work in the farm,
Will come home with the harvests.

Thereafter, the Ifa priest told Orunmila that he did not know the town he called Kosoko and he replied that it was Ilorin.

When the odu appears at divination, the person will be advised not to engage himself in any enervating profession that requires physical exertion, because he cannot become wealthy by so doing. If he makes sacrifice, his means of sustenance and opulence will come to him by sitting in one place. If it appears at a naming ceremony divination, the parents will be told that the child should not be allowed to engage in any hard labor and that the above-mentioned sacrifice should be made for him. He will become prosperous in life without physically debilitating in energy and effort.

How This Odu Became Known as Ogunda-Mi-Lerin

Oni bu ma ni igba. Oni igba ma ni ibu. Awon mejeji niwon
jojo she ore.
The pond owner had no instrument for bailing out water.
The bail owner had no pond in which to use his bailer.

They were two friends who agreed to establish a partnership to undertake an enterprise in fish farming. Whenever the fish pond was ripe for harvesting, they shared the harvests equally. The partnership thrived successfully for many years until they both died. After their demise, their children continued the partnership. One year, as a result of their failure to make the sacrifice that was usually done by their parents, only one fish survived. An argument arose as to who was entitled to keep the single fish. The son of the pond owner argued that without his father's pond, there would have been no way of nursing fishes. On the other hand, the son of the bail owner argued, that without the use of the father's bailer, there would have been no way of reaching the fish. The dispute became dead-locked.

They were at daggers-drawn when Ogun came by to intervene. After narrating their cases to Ogun, he told the partners to close their eyes. Thereafter, he used his matchete to cut the fish into two pieces. When they opened their eyes, he collected the two halves and blew into them and the two halves became two whole fishes. Ogun subsequently gave one fish to each of them and they thanked him with a broad smile. That is how this odu got the name of "Ogun-da-mi-lerin" - meaning "It was Ogun who made me smile at the point of a fight."

When it appears at divination, the person will be advised to make sacrifice to avert the risk of a dispute in a partnership he has with another person.

Orunmila's Eulogy on the Efficacy of a Smile

Orunmila asked his followers to smile, because;
One smiles when counting plenty of money,
One smiles when playing games,
One smiles during marriage,
One smiles at the birth of a new child, and
One smiles when sitting on top of prosperity.

He subsequently prescribed sacrifice with white kolanut and salt to serve one's head and pray to God to bestow the good things of life on the divinee.

When it appears at divination, the person will be advised not to worry because God has endowed him with happiness and prosperity.

Chapter 9

OGUNDA-OSA

OGUNDA-MAA-SAA

He Made Divination for the Frogs and the Toads in Heaven

Ogunda Maa Saa Ijarayin aya re ma ma soju.
Adifa fun akere, abufun Kounko, nijo won fi omi shubere omo
turutu.
Ogunda do not run away. Ijarayin, his wife should not be worried.

Those were the two Ifa priests who made divination for the frogs and the toads when they were anxious to have children. They were advised to make sacrifice with two hens and four eggs. After making the sacrifice, they were told to go to God to promise what they would use to show their appreciation after having children. Eventually, they went to the divine altar of God, promising to produce two hundred elephants (ugba erin) when they started having children.

After the sacrifice, they began to produce children in hundreds at a time, and not long afterwards, their children and grandchildren also began to have children in multiples of hundreds at a time. That was the point at which God reminded them of the promise they had made to produce 200 elephants when they started having children, since it appeared that they reneged on it. They were astonished, or so feigned, to hear about 200 elephants because, they lacked the physical means of attacking or capturing a single elephant, let alone 200 of them. They corrected that what they had promised to give as recompense for having children was to sing two hundred songs in praise of God, which they been doing since becoming productive.

To Put It In Yoruba They Recalled That What They Said Was

"Waan ko igba erin fun Olodumare" and not
"Waan gba igba erin fun Olodumare"

Since "erin" means both songs and elephant in Yoruba, God could not fault them. The Almighty Father in that case, told them to sing the song they had been singing. All the frogs in a concert ensemble started singing:

"Ba a ta la she re ba ri sha, oohen oohen." and the sound was so melodious that God expressed deep satisfaction. Those words have become the songs of the frogs and the toads to this day.

When it appears at divination, for anyone anxious to have children, the person should be advised to make sacrifice to a divinity in his family, promising to pay a recompense he/she will not be able to afford, and he/she will definitely start having children

He Also Made Divination In Heaven For Ekunkun

Ogunda ma saa o. Ijaranyin aya re maa soju o.
Akere ari kounko lo'mbe le'ti odo ti'nsunkun,
omo winyin winyin. Adifa fun Ekunkun, nijo
ti ofe gba aya erin.

The same Ifa priests made divination for Ekunkun, (Ebo in Bini), the plant whose leaves are used for sewing bags, when he was going to seduce Irin, the wife of the elephant. He did not know that irin was a married woman when they fell in love with each other. He only knew that fact after the woman have moved into his house to live with him, following a threatening ultimatum from the elephant that he was coming to eat him raw, for daring to seduce his wife.

He was so scared that he ran to Orunmila for divination. He was told to make sacrifice with two cocks and 201 needles. After making the sacrifice, the Ifa priests advised him to change his abode to live on the swamps of the river. He was also told to serve his head with a hen after changing residence, on the banks of the river. He heeded the advice to the minutest detail, and his new abode was right inside the swamps of the river.

Meanwhile, the Elephant sent a final intimidating message to Ekunkun, warning him to consume whatever he had because he was coming to feast on him in seven day's time. After enjoying the sacrifice made by Ekunkun, Esu reassured him not to be unduly disturbed by the threat from the Elephant.

At the end of the grace period given to Ekunkun, the Elephant went to the former residence of his wife's seducer only to be told that he had moved to the embankment of the river. The Elephant headed at once for Ekunkun's new residence. On getting there, the Elephant bellowed whether that was how far Ekunkun could run. That was how he alerted the seducer and the seduced that he had come to settle scores with them, as he promised to do.

Thereafter, he moved one fore-limb into the swamp and it sank through. He tried to support the movement with the second fore-limb and it also sank. In an attempt to maintian balance, he moved his hind limbs and they too sank. With his four feet embedded in the swamp, his abdomen rested on the swamp. In a desperate move to launch a long-range attack on the couple, he stretched the full length of his trunk. At the same time Esu brought out the 201 needles with which Ekunkun made sacrifice and they pierced into the sensitive trunk of the Elephant and he breathed his last and kicked the bucket. Those 201 needles are the sharp thorns lining the leaves of Ekunkun to this day. After the demise of the Elephant, Ekunkun and Irin enjoyed a blissful matrimony ever after.

When it appears at divination for a proposed marriage or love affair, the man should be told that the husband of the woman is a strong, big and over-bearing man and that unless he makes sacrifice the man will destroy him. On the other hand, if it appears for a woman, she will be warned that her flirtation will cause a fatal affray between her lover and her husband and that without making sacrifice, she too can become a casualty.

The Divination Made for Him Before Leaving Heaven

Uroke mi lawo li gon rin, Oroke mi la'wo le turuye, were the Awos who made divination for this Odu when he was coming from heaven. He was advised to make sacrifice so that his good gestures on earth might not be repaid with ingratitude. He was also advised to make sacrifice in order to live long on earth and not to lose his life on account of a woman. He was required to serve: Ogun with a cock and tortoise; the ground divinity with tortoise; his guardian angel with a guinea fowl; and Esu with a he-goat. He made all the sacrifices and came to the world with his wife.

When he got to the world, he found life very difficult. He subsequently met Orisa-Nla who agreed to house him. Himself, Sango and his wife Oya, together with Erinle were all staying with Orisa-Nla. He was quick in establishing himself as a proficient Ifa priest. Sango also proved to be a very powerful divintiy and both of them became very friendly. Sango's mother had a thrallish ancestry. She was called Torosi-Iya ngbodo and the daughter of King Kariba. During the war she was taken away as a war captive, sold into slavery, and eventually bought by Elenkpe-Adodo. The other members of Orisa-Nla's household used to taunt Sango by asking him to name the place from where his mother hailed. Incidentally, Sango neither knew his mother nor the name, although he was told that she came from Takpa. This incident accounts for the aggressive and ferocious behavior of Sango.

He Divined For Sango to Up-root the Obiri Tree

Sango lived and operated for most of his life in the town of Oyo-koro. There was a tree called Obiri (black Afa) in the town where the cult of witchcraft held their nocturnal meetings, and from where they used to cause havoc in the town. That tree or its branch is normally used for preparing Sango shrine. In view of the danger which the tree posed for the citizens of Oyo-koro, the king made a proclamation, offering a handsome reward to anyone who succeeded in cutting it down. Sango volunteered to destroy the tree and asked for the reward to be specified. The king promised to give him a ram, 201 bags of money, 200 goats, a barn of yams, a bundle of red cloth and 200 fowls.

That was the point at which he approached his friend, Orunmila for divination and he was advised to give a he-goat to Esu and a rabbit to the Night. He did not make the sacrifice. The following morning, Sango got dressed in his battle outfit and invited his wife Oya to ignite light-ning for him to locate the target. Sango cannot see his target unless his wife flashes lightning. Meanwhile, as soon as he was stimulated for action, the cloud gathered and there was almost total darkness in broad day-light. Oya then flashed lightning and Ekun-o-ke the tiger of the sky (as Sango is called), roared as if there was an earthquake and used his axe to tear down the Obiri tree right up to its taproot. He eventually up-rooted and removed it to a different location. Sango was given a rousing applause as he retired to his house to rest.

Later in the day, he went to the palace to report mission accomplished and to collect his reward. He was disappointed to see that the compensation was not forth-coming in spite of the resounding success with which he performed his side of the bargain. He went back to Orunmila to inform him that he was going to generate a cataclysm in the town. Orunmila advised him that if he caused mayhem in the town, no one might survive to give him his reward. Orunmila told him to tie a chicken to his waist and to prepare a special wand to wear on a basket-cap and to sit in front of his house. Thereafter his reward would be delivered to him.

He did as he was advised by Orunmila. The sight of him in the outfit caused a stampede which reverberated in the palace. The warning signals scared the king into ordering that Sango's reward should immediately be assembled and delivered to him. Thereafter, it was the turn of Esu Awon-Iyami-Oshoronga to fight back. Esu went round to instigate the Elders of the Night that the son of a slave who did not even know his mother dared to destroy their conference hall with brazen affrontery.

The instigations of Esu incited the Elders of the Night into deciding to destabilze Sango. They launched their attack by formenting a misunderstanding between his wife and himself over who was to take the head of the ram. Oya insisted that the head of the ram belonged to her, because Sango could not have accomplished the task without her active support in showing the way. On his part, Sango was determined to establish his authority as the Lord and master of the house and everyone under his command including Oya. A fight subsequently ensued between then.

An old woman called Oji-fefe, herself a witch who was their neighbor, fanned the embers of the dissension between the couple by singing an aggravating song: "Oya o ma je ori agbo. Bu oje woje eghi gho." When Oya heard the song, she vowed that rather than concede the head of the ram to Sango, she would prefer to leave his house for good. When Sango remembered how he seduced Oya from Ogun, he agreed to surrender the head of the ram to her. It will be remembered that Oya was originally Ogun's wife. Ugbo-oro was the private latrine of Oya when she was married to Ogun. Sango was going there stealthily to make love to Oya. It was when the secret leaked out that the divine council ruled that women should no longer have access to Ugboro or secret conclave.

It was on account of the surrender of the head of the ram to Oya that her shrine is traditionally prepared on the head of a ram while the shrine of Sango is customarily prepared on a mortar prepared from the stem of Obiri or black afa tree. The dust of that upheaval had scarcely settled when the Elders of the Night released their next salvo. Sango suddenly became ill with lunacy. That was the stage at which his wife arranged to pay the debt of sacrifice he owed to Esu with he-goat and the Night with a rabbit and a hen, both of which were fried to feast the club of witchcraft. When he became well again, he insisted on sitting on a mortar prepared from the stem of the tree he uprooted.

When this Ifa appears at Ugbodu, the person will be advised to prepare his own Sango immediately; serve Esu with a big he-goat; and serve the new Ifa with two hens, two guinea-fowls, two pigeons and a bundle of five tubers of yam tied together.

At divination, the person will be advised to serve:- Sango with a cock; Esu with he-goat; and a family divinity with a cock, to remove obstacles from the path of his destiny. He should beware of an old woman living with or close to him.

He Made Divination for the Ajero for His Favorite Wife to Have a Child

With the passing of time his fame and fortune spread to the four winds of the known world. The Ajero of Ijero heard of his proficiency and sent for him. He became popularly known as Awodi-Orisa. The Ajero had no children and all the Awos of the known world had tried but failed to solve the problem.

When he received the invitation from the Ajero, he went to two Awos for divination. He was advised to make sacrifice to Ifa, Esu, Ogun and the ground divinity and he did all the sacrifices before leaving for Ijero. He was fair in complexion and was born with a protruded navel.

On getting to the Ajero's palace, he made divination and advised the Oba to make the following sacrifices: a big he-goat to Esu; dog, cock and tortoise to Ogun; female sheep to the ground divinity and a goat to the elders of the night through Ifa. After making the sacrifice, he began to prepare medicines for the Oba and his wives to be using. He was cleared to move freely about in the palace. The following month, the Oba's favorite wife became pregnant. That was quickly followed by the pregnancies of several other wives in the royal harem. The Oba's favorite wife was three months pregnant when he left for home. The Oba promised to give him half of his kingdom when his wives safely put to bed.

In the fullness of time, the Oba's favorite wife gave birth to a male child, followed quickly by several other births by the other wives in the harem. Coincidentally, all the children had protruded navels like that of Orunmila. The coincidence, meanwhile sent tongues wagging with the tittle tattle that Orunmila might easily have been responsible for the pregnancies of the Oba's wives, since the children had his type of navel.

It was in that scenario that Orunmila was invited to Ijero to come and collect his compensation. When he received the invitation, he went to his Awos for divination. After divination he was told that the invitation had a hazardous foreboding, and that he had to make sacrifice in order to return alive. The sacrifice involved giving a he-goat to Esu, and serving Ogun in a wasteland with a big scissors, a cock and a tortoise. After preparing the sacrifice, he was given the scissors to travel with for his journey. Inspite of the sacrifice, he was apprised that the journey remained fraught with ominous expectations, but that he would survive the inevitable ordeal.

Eventually, he left for Ijero to honor the invitation, holding the scissors in hand. As soon as the people of Ijero saw him, he was given a rousing applause. After the usual exchange of pleasantries, he was told that there were strong suspicions that he might have been responsible for the pregnancies of the Oba's wives. Although he was not being formally charged with the offence of cheating, it was necessary for him to go for trial by ordeal in order to establish his innocence. The trial was fixed for the following morning.

When he came out for the trial in the morning, he saw a giant-fire burning in front of the palace. He was told to enter the blazing inferno to remove a brass object with the caveat that if he was innocent he would accomplish the task unscathed, but that if he was guilty of the charge, the fire would consume him. After thanking them for giving him the opportunity of establishing his innocence, he walked into the ball of flames in search of the brass object. He made three attempts and it was on the third attempt that he picked up the brass bangle. He was given a rousing plaudit by everyone present, but he neither considered the situation funny, nor warranting any celebration. He told the Oba, that he got a worthy price for his magnanimity and proclaimed that if his treatment was their way of expressing gratitiude to their benefactors, that would remain the tradition of the town from generation to generation.

He left immediately for home without collecting or demanding his reward. When this Odu appears at divination, the person will be advised to be selective in his magnanimity to avert the risk of crass ingratitude. He should however make sacrifice to avoid losing his life on account of his benevolence.

He Made Divination for Ogun and His Wife Before Going to War

Ogunda maa saa, Ijaranyin aya re maa ma so ju

That was the Awo who made divination for Ogun when he was going to wage war on the town of Inomu odo. He was told that his journey to the war front would be trouble-free and that he was going to be victorious in the war, but that he should make sacrifice to return home triumphantly and without problems. He refused to make the sacrifice because he could not imagine any problems that could confront him. He was to serve his guardian angel with a guinea-fowl, roasted yam, a gourd of palm wine and a gourd of oil and to give a he-goat to Esu. While bluntly refusing to serve Esu, he promised to serve his guardian angel after returning from the battlefield.

On the other hand, his wife Ijarayin (Elaghalogho in Bini) was told to make sacrifice so that her good gestures might not be rewarded with ingratitude. She made the sacrifice with the wooden instruments used for weaving cloth, and a cock. Ogun subsequently left for the battlefield with his wife and troops. He fought gallantly at the war front and lost no time in defeating the enemy. On his return journey, he dispatched his troops to move forward as an advance party before he left for home with his wife. That was the time when Esu rose up to punish Ogun for failing to make sacrifice.

When they got to the big river on the way, Esu had assembled all the available frogs to be singing a war song. Ogun had given all his fighting weapons to his troops to carry home and he was totally defenseless. Suddenly, he heard battle cries of:

"Ogun ma de o, Ho Ho Ho Ho, Ho Ho,
A A'kpa o Ho Ho Ho Ho, Ho Ho."

Meaning:

"Ogun has come and we are going to kill him."

Apprehensive of who these unexpected enemies were, Ogun began to run backwards until he fell flat on his face, exhausted. After waiting for three days for her husband to return to meet her, Ijarayin decided to venture to the bank of the river to spy on the "enemy." She was astonished to see a huge constellation of frogs jumping into the river singing:

Aya Ogun ma de o
Ho Ho Ho Ho.

Thereafter, she began to hail on her husband to return to meet her. There was no response from him because he had passed out into a coma. She combed the bush looking for him without any sign of him. She then travelled home to consult Orunmila on the fate of her husband. She was told after divination that her husband was still alive, but that he owed Esu a sacrifice, which he had refused to perform before going to war. Ijarayin decided to make the sacrifice on behalf of her husband. After preparing the sacrifice, she was told to deposit it on the bank of the river.

She subsequently took the sacrifice to the river where they were previously held up by the cries of frogs. As she began to pray to Esu to make it possible for her to see Ogun, her husband, Ogun overheard someone mentioning his name and asked who it was, and she replied that it was Ijararyin, the wife of Ogun. Ogun soon met her and complained that the war-cry from the bank of the river continued and that was why he had to hide away. After meeting him, the wife told him that she subseqently discovered that what they regarded as a war cry was merely the squeal of a large number of frogs. Ogun suddenly felt humiliated and deflated.

As they were leaving for home, Ogun warned his wife not to let anyone know that he was held up for three days by the cry of frogs. Incidentally, he was soon to discover that women are not the best keepers of secrets. Meanwhile, Ogun was obviously very hungry and tired. He fell quickly asleep while the wife was cooking yams on the fire. Ogun woke up terribly hungry and enquired angrily whether the food was still not ready. The wife replied that she was pounding the yam. A little later Ogun again yelled iracibly whether the yams were stones for taking so long to prepare. The question infuriated Ijarayin and she replied in an equally irritable manner by wondering why he was so impatient with her, adding, "after all frogs kept you waiting in the forest for the last three days." Her remarks overwhelmed Ogun with uncontrollable anger and he got his sword to attack the wife, who succeeded in escaping his wrath. When Ogun could not see his wife, he began to yell the following words: "Ijarayin ni emi yio ma kpe sa."

These are the spoken words by the people of Iworo when serving Ogun, to this day. From that day, Ogun stopped eating pounded yam.

When this Odu appears for a woman at divination, she will be advised never to shout insolently on her husband to avoid unpleasant consequences. She should however be advised to make sacrifice. If it appears for a man, he should be advised to serve Esu with a he-goat and Ogun with a cock, to obviate the risk of being humiliated and of committing felony in the process.

He Made Divination for the Olowo of Owo When a Rat Made Him to Get Lost in the Forest

Erinrin gun sin, Odifa fun Olowo omo aji gbolu, ni jo ti odan eku
kon soso ti oma ku ni'bo.

That was the Awo who made divination for the Olowo of Owo when a single rat made him to get lost in the forest. The Olowo had been advised to make sacrifice with a single rat to avoid getting lost. He not only wondered how he, an Oba, should make sacrifice with a small rat, but wondered how to imagine the possibility of getting lost in the forest. He refused to perform the sacrifice.

Early the next morning, he was urinating at the back of his palace when he observed that a rat was moving under his legs. The rat was moving so sluggishly that he decided to catch it. As he tried to hold it, the rat was moving forward. He began to wonder what kind of mysterious rat it was, as he became determined to catch and kill it. The rat continued to move a little distance outside his reach at a time, while he continued to pursue it. When the rat subsequently entered the bush, he followed it. As soon as Olowo entered the bush, Esu blew ashes into the air and the Oba lost contact with the rat. He soon found himself in the heart of the forest without the slighted clue on how to find his way home.

The Oba spent the night in the forest. The following morning, he heard the monkeys shouting on the top of the tree at the foot of which he spent the night "Olowo ora sham" (here is Olowo wandering in the forest). He replied that the monkeys should not laugh at him and that what he required was sympathy and not ridicule, because he was unable to find his way home. The monkeys asked him how he would reward them if they sent one of them to take him home. The Olowo paused to reflect on the question before promising that if they showed him his way home, he would promulgate a decree banning his subjects from ever killing or eating them to eternity. On that note, the monkeys sent one of them to pilot him to the back of the house.

As soon as he sighted the garden at the back of his palace, the monkey bade him good-bye, and returned to the forest. His subjects were relieved to see the return of their Oba, and when they were curious to know where he had been during the last twenty-four hours, he replied gleefully that he went into a retreat in the forest to probe what was responsible for the high incidence of deaths in the kingdom of Owo. After relaxing for some time, he instructed the royal herald to convene a conference of chiefs, consellors and elders for that evening.

When the conference was assembled, he announced the admonition he was given by the king of the forest during his day-long retreat in the forest. He reported that his ancestors had told him why the kingdom was experiencing such an unprecedented death rate. He retired to the forest the previous day, as he was told to do, without any aides. In the night, the king of the forest met him and told him that his people were dying in their thousands because of doing what their ancestor forbade them to do, that is, the killing and eating the meat of monkeys. That is why the people of Owo forbid monkeys to this day.

If this odu appears as ayeo at divination, the person should be told to make sacrifice with a single rat immediately.

Chapter 10

OGUNDA-ETURA
OGUNDA-TE-TURA-LA

He Made Divination in Heaven for the Parasite Plant

Oro gba gede gba. Odifa fun Afuma.

That was the Ifa priest who made divination for the four hundred and eighty plants in the forest when they were contesting for leadership. Each of them was told to make sacrifice with a he-goat, parrot's feather and white cloth. None of them made the sacrifice except the parasite plant (Afuma in Yoruba and Ose in Bini). The plants in the forest had been arrogating leadership roles to themselves all along, culminating in a dispute which had to be remitted to God for resolution. The Creator told all 480 of them to assemble at the divine chamber in seven days time.

Three days to the appointed day, Esu caused Afuma to develop severe injury and pains on his two legs, which prevented him from being able to walk. On the appointed day, his colleagues came to invite him for the conference, but he complained that he was too ill to walk and that in any event, he did not regard himself as standing a chance in a contest with towering giants like the iroko, oak, asori, akobrishi kolanut, obeche etc. The others then left without him. When Iroko also came to call, Afuma declined to go to the conference. Realizing that God would order them to return to fetch Afuma, he decided to carry him on his head, with a parrot's feather on his head.

When all the plants were assembled, God asked them whether everybody was present and they replied that the only absentee was the Iroko and the inconsequential Afuma who was too ill to come. They had scarcely finished giving the reply when they saw the over-bearing Iroko, in the distance dressed in his full regalia. When God saw Iroko carrying someone wearing a parrot's feather (which Esu had just placed on his head), He asked him who he was carrying, dressed in immaculate white, and Iroko replied that it was Afuma.

When Iroko wanted to put Afuma down, God told him to wait for a while. The Creator asked all the plants to explain how they came to the conference and they answered that they came on their feet. After observing that it was only Afuma who came on someone else's head, God proclaimed that the force of circumstance had confirmed Afuma as the king of all of them, and that from then on he would always sit and be carried on the heads of other plants. That is why the parasite plant grows on the heads and shoulders of other plants to this day.

When it appears at divination, the person will be told to make sacrifice in order to come across someone who will lift him up to greatness, provided he arranges also to have his own Ifa.

He Made Divination for the Bush Fowl

Okiti kpuke, awo eba ono odifa fun Oyele, abufun Adaba.

The road-site hill was the name of Awo who made divination for the bush fowl (Oyele or Okorebajo in Yoruba and Ukorobozo in Bini). He also divined for another bird of the pigeon and dove kindred, called Adaba in Yoruba and Erekhue in Bini. Oyele and Adaba were bosom friends living in the same house. Each of them had a child; Oyele's child being called Ura, while Adaba's child was called Urojo

When Adaba was going on tour, she left her son to the care of her friend Oyele. Meanwhile, when Oyele and her son became hungry, they arranged to sell the son of Adaba into slavery, using the proceeds to buy food to eat. On the return of Adaba from her tour, she asked for her son and Oyele replied that she had sold him into slavery. Adaba reacted to the incident with stoical equanimity, without allowing it to affect their friendship.

Long after they had put the incident behind them, Oyele travelled and left her son to the care of Adaba, who eventually paid her friend in her own coin by selling her son into slavery. When Oyele returned to discover that her son had been sold into slavery, she became so furious that she began to yell:- "wo tu ra wo tu ra" which is the call sign of the bush fowl to this day meaning why have you sold my son into slavery?.

Adaba retorted by reminding her of her placidity when she sold her own son into slavery "Ijo wo tu rojo ki me'she", which has also remained the call sign of Adaba to this day.

When this Odu appears at divination, the person will be advised never to keep his or her son or daughter under the care or guardianship of anyone, to avoid getting lost.

He Made Divination for the Dove When She Had Many Lovers

Ogunda te-tura-la made divination for the dove when she was flirting with umpteen lovers. She was simultaneously befriending inter alios, the tortoise, the tiger, the lion and the boa. When she became apprehensive that her action was fraught with danger, she went for divination, to find out what to do to avoid getting into trouble with her lovers. After divination, she was advised to serve her head on the eve of the market day with white kolanut and coconut. She was warned to serve her head, and to say amen to her prayers alone, without the presence of anyone else. Before serving her head, she was told to visit each of her lovers to invite them to spend the night with her in order for them to accompany her to the market the following day. She acted accordingly.

The tortoise was the first lover to arrive at the dove's house. On getting there he overheard her praying to her head while apparently someone else was interjecting her prayers with "Amen". The tortoise began to suspect the dove had another man with her. He decided to wait and see who the intruder was. Not long afterwards, the tiger arrived, stepping his foot on the tortoise, who immediately asked who the hell was treading on him. When they discovered that they both came to see the same lover, the tortoise told the tiger that there was already another man with her in the room. Eventually, the lion and the boa joined the other two lovers.

After making sacrifice to her head, the dove went into her bedroom to sleep. All the lovers kept vigil until the cock crowed in the morning, and they all resolved that whoever her lover was, he was bound to accompany her to the market. All four of them decided to go and wait for the dove and her unknown lover on the way to the market. After taking position on the way to the market, the tortoise proposed and others agreed, that in order to reduce the margin of friction, each of them should disclose what they forbade, in case they had to fight with the dove's lover. The tortoise began by saying that he forbade being eyed askance or scornfully. The lion revealed that no one should ever startle him by hitting anything on the ground. On his part, the Boa disclosed that it was forbidden for anyone to tread on his tail.

On that note, the tiger decided to take position on the top of a tree to await the arrival of the dove and her lover, as a vantage point from which to launch an attack. Incidentally, he climbed the dead branch of the tree and it suddenly broke and as it fell to the ground, it made a disturbing noise that startled the lion into turning his eyes upwards to find out from where the sound sourced. Instantly, the tiger accused the lion of eyeing him contumeliously, while the lion accused the tiger of causing a noise that jolted him. In a gesture designed to defuse the charged atmosphere, the tortoise appealed for an armistice. They retorted by asking him to keep his mouth shut since he lacked the strength and vigor to do battle. A fight subsequently ensued between the tiger and the lion.

During the fracas between the two giant combattants, one of them inadvertently trod on the tail of the boa, which action gave rise to the spontaneous release of the deadly arrows of the boa, impacting on the two fighters. Realising that the Boa's venom was sooner than later, going to kill them, the lion trod on the head of the boa and trampled him to death. As the lion and the tiger were dying, they fell on the tortoise, who was also choked to death. All the four lovers died without seeing their common girlfriend and their supposed rival.

When the Dove subsequently got to the spot where the battle took place, she met all her four lovers dead and she began to dance and sing on the road:

"Temi to tijo jijo. Temi to tege yiye"
My fortune is enough to be happy about, I am dancing with joy.

That has since remained the song of the Dove when dancing on one spot. Eventually, she got happily married to an innocuous bird called Atata in Yoruba and Ogbodu in Bini. On account of the self awareness of her beauty, she became too vainglorious to submit to her husband. She eventually left Atata after having two children for him. That explains why the Dove does not lay more than two eggs at a time, to this day.

When this Ifa appears at Ugbodu, the person will be advised to serve his/her head with a pigeon, white kolanuts and coconut; Ifa with a goat; and Esu with a he-goat, the bones of Boa, Lion, Tiger, shell of Tortoise and the feathers or skull of a Dove, to avoid losing his life on account of a woman.

At ordinary divination, the person will be advised that he is competing with at least three other men for the love of a woman. He should serve, Esu with a he-goat, and his head with a pigeon to avert the danger of locking horns with his rivals.

The Divination for this Odu When He Was Leaving Heaven

Ono ni mo ko jo, Ono ni mo ko oyo, ono ni mo oriri-biri toun tege yiye.

Those were the Awos who made divination for Orunmila when he was coming to the world. He was advised to serve his head with a tiger, a lion and a boa. They also advised him to serve Esu with a he-goat, a tortoise and an insect that raises sand from the ground (called hook up the draft for the Yoruba name in Yoruba and Izeruru in Bini). He had no clue on how he was to get hold of the lion, tiger and boa, since they are not ordinarily available for sale in the market and can only be obtained fortuitously and infrequently. He however decided to serve Esu without any delay.

After eating his he-goat, Esu firmed up a strategy for wheedling the lion, the tiger, and the boa into a noose, by inviting them to follow him to the spot where he saw the eyes of the ground. In other words, he was whetting their appetites by telling them metaphorically that he was inviting them to help themselves to a goldmine of fortune. They agreed to follow him immediately. On their way to the supposed gold-mine, Esu stopped in his tracks to put a suggestion to them. He proposed that in order to minimise or eliminate the risk of offending one another, each of them should disclose his sorepoint.

The Lion began by saying that he would consider it as derisive if anyone threw sand at him. The Tiger followed by disclosing that it was an abomination for anyone to look askance at him. The boa concluded the exercise in candour and forthrightness by unfolding that inescapable death was the price of touching his tail because he paid a high premium before God gave it to him.

After the heart-to-heart disclosures, Esu led the way, after surrepticiously inserting white divination sand and the sand raising insect in the Tiger's bag. As the journey proceeded in earnest, the sand raising insect in the tiger's bag began to throw the divination sand upwards and it was falling on the Lion who was behind the Tiger. The Lion subsequently challenged the Tiger with a contemptuous look, a fight presently ensued between the Lion and the Tiger. While Esu was intervening to stop the fight, both the Lion and the Tiger inadvertently stepped on the tail of the Boa, who instinctively reacted by releasing his noxious arrows to bite them. As the Tiger and the Lion began to feel the toxic effect of the Boa's bite, they finished off the Boa in their death throes by shredding him into pieces.

Following the deaths of the three victims of his sacrifice, Esu raced to Orunmila's house to tell him that his sacrifice had manifested, because the sacrificial victims he had been looking for, were ready for collection. Orunmila followed him to collect the corpses of the Lion, Tiger and Boa, using them to serve his head that evening after thanking Esu with another he-goat. In consonance with the prescriptions during divination he went to God to obtain his blessing for a successful sojourn on earth.

His Experience on Earth and Why the Children Forbid Alcoholic Drinks

When he got to the world, he soon became the beneficiary of fame and fortune, but he was to run into difficulties with his three elder brothers who were divine priests. He had been warned at divination not to reveal the secret of his prosperity to anyone, and to make sacrifice to the obstacle divinity, but he forgot all about it.

In the course of his Ifa practice, he came across the daughter of the divinity of prosperity (Aje) who fell in love with him at first sight. Before meeting him however, three other men had been courting her. They were an Ogun priest, a Sango priest and a priest of Obaluwaye. The daughter of Aje however did not requite their advances. When Orunmila met the daughter of Aje, he went for divination to find out whether to requite her love for him. He was told that he was destined to become prosperous through the woman, provided he could refrain from taking alcoholic drinks and revealing the secret of his success to anyone. He was told to make sacrifice to Esu with the meat or bones of Lion, Tiger, the head of a Boa and He-goat in order to win the contest for the hands of the woman. He made the sacrifice.

Thereafter, the daughter of Aje encouraged Orunmila to visit her. One day the lady told Orunmila to visit her the following day to meet her father. Unknown to anyone the divinity of prosperity was coming from heaven on that day to give his daughter away in marriage to a suitable spouse. After enjoying his sacrifice, Esu persuaded the three unsuccessful suitors to rendezvous in the woman's place on the eve of her father's visit from heaven. Meanwhile, Orunmila sounded Ifa for directions and he was told to make a special sacrifice the following morning on the way to the woman's house and to hide and watch what was going to happen to the sacrifice.

After inviting the three suitors to meet at the girl's place on the eve of her father's visit, Esu also told them that the girl's heart had been stolen by Orunmila and that they would meet him on the way to the woman's house that night. Since the girl was totally unaware of the upcoming visit of her three suitors, she went to sleep early that night in order to wake up early in the morning to prepare for her father's visit. When the three lovers met in her place, Esu instigated a fight between them which culminated in their killing one another. She woke up the following morning to see that her admirers had killed one another. She then began to sing the following song:-

Ekini te kini kpa ra
Ere bele kpe kpe kpe erebele.
Tekeji te keju kpa,
Ere bele kpe kpe kpe Erebele.
Teketa Teketa kpa
Ere bele kpe kpe kpe ere bele.
Ekun to ri Orunmila ya se abe mewa,
Omu kpa ara re ku,
Ere bele kpe kpe kpe ere bele
Ikariko to ri Orunmila ya so omimi,
Omu kpa ara re ku.
Erebele kpe kpe kpe ere bele.
Oka tori Orunmila ya so oro meta,
Omu kpa ara re ku,
Erebele kpe kpe kpe ere bele.

The daughter of Aje was rejoicing that the three rivals of her beloved Orunmila had killed themselves with the weapons with which they intended to fight him.

While she was expecting her father, Orunmila had meanwhile prepared his sacrifice and deposited it on the approach road to the lady's house, while concealing himself from view to see what was going to happen to it.

Not long afterwards, the divinity of wealth (Aje) was on his way from heaven, hungry and tired. He was relieved to see the sacrifice deposited by Orunmila which comprised roasted yam, vegetable soup prepared with ewedu leaves, a gourd of palm wine and red and white kolanuts. After looking round to see that no one was looking at him, (because apart from forbidding roasted yam and palm wine, Aje does not eat in the presence of anyone) he sat down to help himself to the food and drink.

As soon as he finished eating and drinking, Orunmila came out to confront the divinity, accusing him of eating the food and drinking the wine he was sending to the people helping him in his farm. Aje told Orunmila not to reveal what had happened to anyone, in return for which he gave Orunmila a small gourd with which he was to command all the good things of life to come to him in his house. Orunmila raced to his house to test the efficacy of the gift he had just been given.

On getting to his house, he met all items of wealth waiting for him. He met a large settlement encircling his own house, complete with servants. He was so confused that he decided to race back to meet his loved one. His cycle of bewilderment was complete when he found that the man who gave him the instrument that translated him into instant prosperity was the father of the woman who had fallen in love with him. Aje subsequently bethrothed his daughter to Orunmila with the advice never to release his secret to anyone and not to drink any intoxicating wine from that day. Thereafter, Aje returned to heaven, after promising to visit them at the end of the year.

In the meantime, Orunmila was wallowing in unlimited affluence. At the same time his eldest brother called Ogbigbo became curious and was determined to find out the secret of Orunmila's sudden oppulence. Ogbigbo subsequently went for divination to find out the secret of his junior brother's wealth. He was advised to serve his mother with rolled dry fish a gourd of palm wine and a gourd of water and to invite his most junior brother, Orunmila to the ceremony excluding his two other brothers, Awawa and Atirala. Earlier on, Orunmila had been warned at divination never to join any of his brothers in serving his mother. Unfortunatly, on account of the sacrifice he failed to make to Elenini, the obstacle divinity, the latter made him to forget the warning.

Meanwhile, when Orunmila was invited by Ogbigbo, he readily agreed to honor the invitation. The ceremony was to take place three days later. After serving their mother, it was time to pour drinks for libation. Ogbigbo gave the gourd of palm wine to Orunmila, while he kept the gourd of water. They soon began to drink and before Orunmila could realize what was happening, he was already drunk and tipsy. In his *delirium tremens*, he blared out the detail of the sacrifice he made to Aje whose daughter he married, adding that his father-in-law was due to visit them in a couple of weeks, he even mentioned the exact date of the expected visit of Aje.

After obtaining his brother's secret, Ogbigbo prepared the same food and drinks in anticipation of the return of Aje to visit his daughter and her husband. On the day Aje was visiting, Ogbigbo went into hiding after depositing the shabby and dirty sacrifice he made. This time, Aje was accompanied by several followers. As he was passing he ignored the sacrifice. When

Obigo saw that Aje took no notice of his sacrifice, he confronted the divinity to ask why he did not take his sacrifice. His followers told him that those were materials forbidden by Aje. Ogbigbo however fouled the air by recalling that Aje had previously eaten and drank similar material prepared by Orunmila.

Thereafter, Aje cursed Ogbigbo that peace of mind would always elude him forever and a day. That is why Ogbigbo lives a restless life to this day. On getting to Orunmila's house, Aje asked him for the result of what he gave to him on his previous visit, and he replied that it made him exceedingly wealthy. Aje then asked him whether he had taken any alcoholic drinks and revealed the secret of his prosperity to anyone since then. He confessed that his brother got him drunk when he joined him to serve their mother. Aje asked for the small gourd he gave to Orunmila and cursed that he would return to a state of penury for revealing his secrets to his brother and for drinking intoxicating wine, contrary to his advice. He left after proclaiming that Orunmila was not going to get more properous than he already was because he was totally unreliable.

When this odu appears at divination, the person will be advised to make sacrifice because of a woman for which he would have to compete with three other rivals. He should refrain from drinking entirely if he wishes to enjoy enduring prosperity. After becoming prosperous he should not reveal the secret to anyone. When it appears at Ugbodu, the person should make sacrifice to the obstacle divinity, and have his own Ogun, Sango and Olokun.

Sacrifice for Mutual Understanding and Amity

Orunmila said that rats do not understand rats, fishes, birds and animals do not understand themselves, just as human beings do not understand one another. He added that the sacrifice is done with a rat called Akosi and an egg-laying hen. When it appears at divination, the person will be told to make sacrifice in order to achieve his objectives. He should also be advised not to be rude to his parents.

Chapter 11

OGUNDA-IRETE
OGUNDA-KETE

He Made Divination in Heaven for Ukubi, the Son of Orisa Gbuwuji

Ogunda Ke te, Odura ni nkponkpo.
O she agada iku ranje ranje.
Adifa fun Ukubi, okonbi omo Orisa Gbuwuji. Iku ki
kpa ofo, omo Orisa.

Ogunda Kete stood on a straight road,
Brandishing the matchete of death in hand.
That was the name of the Awo who made divination for Ukubi,
the only son of Orisa gbuwuji. Death does not kill Emptiness
(ofo in Yoruba and ihoi in Bini) the son of God.

When this odu appears at divination, the person will be advised to make sacrifice with three empty parcels to one divinity with which he or she is connected. He should also make sacrifice with cock, snail, rat and fish.

He Divined for Adibo, the Son of Orunmila

Ku ku du ku she'we geru geru.
Okpolokpo Ogun sh'omo gale gale.
Bi a ba ni Ogun egbe rin dilogun,
Bi a ba ni eke si, ko'ni je.
Adifa fun Adibo t'inshe omobibi ina agbon iregun
nijo ti iku fi ojojumo de ode re, A ni ki Adibo ru ebo.
Oru ebo. Iku ki kpa Adibo, uku to ba fe kpaa Adibo, oko ni shaa

The sweet potato endowed with rich foliage.
Too many diabolical charms stimulate a youth.
Even if he owns sixteen deadly charms,
Unless he has a humane disposition,
They will not work efficaciously.

These are the names of the Ifa priests who made divination for Adibo, the lot casting son of Orunmila when he was being targeted daily by Death. He was advised to make sacrifice with a he-goat and he did it. Thereafter, Esu sacked Death from his trail.

When it foretells the danger of death (Ayeo) at divination, the person will be told that Death is gunning for him. He should therefore make sacrifice to avert the danger.

He Made Divination for Orunmila When He Seduced the Wife of Ogoronigara

Ogunda Kete Oduro ni kponkpo. Adifa fun Orunmila baba on
lo gbe aya Ogoronigara.

He made divination for Orunmila when he was going to seduce the wife of Ogoronigara. When he saw the woman, he took fancy to her, but she warned him that her husband was a very powerful man. He reassured the woman that he was equal to the task. Thereafter, he invited her to his house and made love to her. The woman however told him that her husband had the esoteric power of seeing and knowing what he had done to her.

Before the woman returned to her marital home, Ogoro nigara gathered all her belongings and kept them at the gate. On getting home, he asked her what she went to do in Orunmila's house. He went on to add that after profaning herself by submitting to making love with Orunmila, she had to return to him. He however sent her to tell Orunmila that he should be prepared to pay the price of seducing his wife, and that he was going to visit the two of them to destroy them in seven days time. When Orunmila got the message, he underestimated the threat by telling her that they would at least continue to enjoy themselves until the appointed day.

On the fourth day, Orunmila sounded Ifa who reassured him that the man could not do anything, because he only depended on charms and witchcraft. Ifa told him to give a he-goat to Esu and a rabbit to the Elders of the Night. He made the sacrifice quickly. On the seventh day, Ogoronigara left home with two bags loaded with charms, carrying them on both shoulders, while holding a gun in hand. He also went in the company of his dog. Very early that morning, Esu and an Elder of the Night had visited Orunmila and told him to put his divination powder on their palms. He marked the Iyerosun of this odu on the Ifa tray with the incantation that:

Ashe follow those who sweep them
The cow puts its tongue into its nose after
stretching it out.
The mucus discharged by a tree drops on its own body,
When a pig digs a grave, it puts its head into it.

After repeating the incantation, Orunmila gave the iyerosun to his two visitors and they left to await the arrival of Ogoronigara. As soon as they sited him in the distance, the witch told Esu to pluck Ogoronigara's left eye, leaving his right eye for her to pluck. When he met his assailants, they blew the divination powder into his two eyes and he instantaneously became blind. As he was unable to find his way thereafter, he strayed into the forest. As soon as he stepped into the bush, Esu blew the remaining divination powder to command him to live in the forest for good. That is why Babaji or Eziza lives in the forest to this day, blind. Orunmila lived happily with the woman ever after.

When it appears at divination for a man, he should be told that he is flirting with a married woman having broad chest, plump buttocks, stout physique and good looking, but fairly short. That was the stature of the woman that Orunmila seduced. He should be advised to serve Esu and the night in order to go scot free with the woman if he wants to marry her.

He Made Divination for Igun When He Went for Ifa Practice to Ilode

Ogun Kete, Oku lo ku. Ara orun o shunkun.
Eniya lo bi mo ti en yo she she. Osan lo ru ebora.
Adifa fun Igun ni igun nijo ti o nshawo lo si Ilode.
Death on earth does not generate grief and weeping in heaven.
Birth generates happiness in both heaven and earth.
Daylight on earth is night time in heaven.

Those were the Awos who made divination for Igun when he was travelling for Awo practice to the town of Ilode. He made sacrifice before going. On getting to Ilode, he met two women who were weeping because they had no children. He told them to stop crying and to meet him at his lodging, while assuring them that they would have children.

They subsequently met him and he made divination for them. He told each of them to make sacrifice with a hen, a rabbit, eko, akara, fish and rat. One of them made the sacrifice, and the other did not. The following month, the one who made sacrifice became pregnant. It was only then that the second woman decided to make her own sacrifice, after which, she too, became pregnant. In the fullness of time they both gave birth to healthy babies, and they began to rejoice and to sing in praise of the Awo:

The people of Ilode saw an Ifa priest,
But did not recognise him.
Igun is a true Ifa priest.

When this odu appears for a woman who is anxious to have a child, she will be advised to make a similar sacrifice.

He Made Divination for Ogun in a Contest for Seniority

When all the divinities were arguing about supremacy, they decided to go to God to declare who was the most supreme among them. God directed them to go to the earth, where their efforts would determine which of them was endowed with leadership qualities.

Sango was the first to set out, but he could not find a route to the earth, so he gave up. All others tried and equally failed. When it was Ogun's turn to go, he went to Orunmila for divination, and Ogunda Kete appeared. He was advised to make sacrifice with sixteen snails. He made sacrifice, and set out for the world.

He succeeded in tracing a route up to Odo mimipo the river separating heaven and earth.

On getting to the river he met the boa constrictor, who attacked him as he tried to cross the river. He gave his foot to the python and he swallowed it up to Ogun's waist after which he brought out his dagger to tear its mouth open. Thereafter, the python died, and he crossed over to the earth to establish a habitation.

Ogun however suffered a temporary paralysis of his legs as a result of the mauling of his legs by the python. Seven days later, Ogun went back to heaven to report mission accomplished to God. When all of the divinities subsequently appeared before God to report the results of their efforts, it became clear that Ogun, otherwise a junior but powerful divinity, was the only one who succeeded in establishing a route to the earth and building a dwelling there. In consequence, God proclaimed, that no one would ever be able to exist and eat without the help of Ogun, thus promoting him to the status of a supreme and indispensable divinity, which he remains to this day.

When this odu appears during initiation into Ifism, the person should be advised to prepare his own Ogun shrine without delay to avert the danger of leg pains or even paralysis. He should also prepare his own Esu shrine with a he-goat, and serve the new Ifa with the meat of python, two pigeons, two hens and sixteen snails. At divination, the person will be told to give a he-goat to Esu and serve his head with a cock.

The Divination He Made Before Leaving Heaven

Igbodogi okpe ara re Iono meji - was the Awo who made divination for this odu when he was coming from heaven. He was advised to make sacrifice because he was going to fish in troubled waters on earth. To be able to live long on earth, he was advised to serve:- Ogun with cock, dog, tortoise, gourd of palm wine, roasted yam and palm oil; Esu with a he-goat, the elders, of the night with a rabbit; and to seek and obtain God's blessing with white cloth, white chalk and white kolanut. He left for the world after making all the sacrifices.

He became a very popular Ifa priest on earth. He had been hearing about the town of Imure which was totally inhabited by witches and wizards. Any lay visitor to the place was often used to make a feast. One day, he decided to visit Imure, but made divination before going. Ifa advised him to serve; Esu with a he-goat, as well as white, black and red pieces of cloth; Ogun with a dog, cock and tortoise and to make special sacrifice with two pigeons with which he was to travel in order to return alive. He made the sacrifices after which he travelled.

He met the people of Imure celebrating their annual festival and the people were happy to receive a stranger who was to serve as meat for their festival. He was lodged in a secluded part of the town awaiting the time he would be used as a sacrificial victim. Meanwhile, Esu infiltrated their ranks and proposed that before daring to touch the visitor, they should try him first because he could prove to be a strong man. He proposed that on the following day all the inhabitants of Imure should dress in; white apparels in the morning, red dresses in the afternoon, and black dresses in the evening. He added that if the visitor could not match the changes in dressing, it would confirm that he was going to be an easy prey.

Thereafter, Esu appeared to Orunmila to give him the white, red and black clothes to wear the following day, having prepared the dresses with the ones with the cloth which he made sacrifice before embarking on the tour. The following day, he was able to come out with the color of dresses that all and sundry wore. In fact his dresses were more gorgeous than those of the indigenes of Imure. The fact that he was able to match the color scheme of their dressing drove the point home to them that he was not going to be an easy prey to handle.

The following day, the people dispatched two persons to go and welcome him with kolanuts, with an apology that their festival had not given them a chance to receive him formally. He received his visitors by presenting them his own kolanuts and drinks from his bag. As the visitors were about to split the kolanuts, the two pigeons inside his bag flew out and he gave them the kolanut seeds to eat. The visitors were frightened after which they left without splitting the kolanut. On getting home they reported that the man was himself a witch and that he had two witches capable of flying in the presence of visitors. When the two messengers refused to go back to invite him to meet the elders, two other men were sent to deliver the invitation.

When the new visitors got to his house, they heard the two pigeons making noise inside his bag (akpo minijekun), which made them run away. He subsequently went with his bag to visit the elders. When they saw him, they all admitted that they were all witches and wizards belonging to Awon Iyami Oshoronga. He challenged them that if they could truly fly, they should demonstrate eight eyes while his pigeons were making noise from within the bag. With that, the people conceded that he was a tougher witch than themselves. He was instantly made their Oloja to stay to hold the town for them.

After staying in the town for sometime, he decided to return home. When he sounded Ifa for directions, he was told that the people would give him the last test by trying to arrest, and prevent him from leaving. Ifa therefore advised him to leave the town in the outfit of Orisa-Nla, by; dressing in immaculate white, wearing a red parrot's feather on his head, rubbing his entire body with white chalk, and holding in his right hand, the traditional staff of divinity (okpa oje or okpa atori in Yoruba and Uwenriontan in Bini). When he was eventually leaving the town in Orisa-Nla's outfit, Esu played the fore-runner by heralding his approach as that of God's own representative on earth. The people lined his route and were glorifying him with cheers of "Bata la o". Even the people who were subborned to waylay him, also greeted him as Orisa-Nla. That was his ploy for a safe journey home. On getting home, he gratified his Awo, his Ifa and Esu, with thanks-giving sacrifices.

When this Odu appears at divination, the person should be told to put his mind at rest because he is worried about a task he is about to embark upon. He should use his hand to touch the ground and his chest three times, but should also make sacrifice.

The Divination Made for Orunmila to Buy a Corpse for Sacrifice

Ojo batarigi batarigi, Ojo natarigi, adifa fun Ira-lum-oye
abufun Orunmila

When Orunmila ran short of money, he went to the Awos for divination. They advised him to buy a human corpse for sacrifice to his Ifa, adding four snails and a rat. He went to the market to buy a mummified human corpse, four snails and a rat. On his way home, he stopped at the river to have a swim, leaving the materials he brought on the bank of the river. By the time he finished swimming, he did not find the materials he left on the bank of the river. Unknown to him, the mummified corpse had resurrected into a full blown man and collected the materials Orunmila had left behind and went with them to his house to wait for him.

On getting to Orunmila's house, he met Akpetebi and told her to prepare pounded yam for her husband. While Orunmila was fidgetting about what might have happened to the materials he left by the side of the river, one woman who saw what happened, told him that the man he left on the ground had walked away with the things he kept with him. The woman did not know that the man was supposed to be a corpse. Overwhelmed with curiousity, Orunmila went home, only to see the man waiting for him. He asked the man what happened, and he explained that he came to live with Orunmila as his servant, and that his name was Arira Lumoye.

From then on, the man began to pre-empt Orunmila by revealing the cause and cure of the problems of clients coming to Orunmila for divination. His own style of divination became so effective that no one bothered to consult Orunmila anymore. Orunmila began to wonder about the efficacy of the sacrifice he was advised to make, since he had run short of clientele and was becoming poorer than he was before he went for divination. Arira Lumoye became more popular than Orunmila and words soon reached Olofin that the slaves bought by Orunmila was more proficient as a diviner and seer, than himself.

Meanwhile, the Oba invited the two of them for a contest. He kept 14 sheep in his stable and asked each of them to declare what he had kept in the stable and to mention their number. Before leaving for the contest, Orunmila had given a he-goat to Esu. While Orunmila was still preparing for divination, Arira Lumooye mentioned without any ceremonies that Olofin kept 14 sheep in his stable. Nonetheless, Orunmila went ahead to perform his divination and the odu which appeared was Ose-Etura, which revealed how Orunmila appointed his sixteen Olodus, after making sacrifice with an ewe (Aguntan). After divination, Orunmila confirmed that indeed what Olofin kept in his stable were agutan (sheep or ewe) but that far from being sixteen in number, they were sixteen.

The Oba was already wondering why Orunmila missed the number and surmising that probably as the tittle-tattle has prattled, his slave was probably more proficient than himself. Meanwhile, the stable keeper was told to open the gate for the sheep to come out. Thirteen sheep came out, while the fourteenth one was canoodling the two young lambs it had delivered overnight, which meant indeed that although the Oba kept fourteen sheep in the stable the previous evening as affirmed by Arira-Lumoye, one of them had given birth to two lambs overnight bringing the number to sixteen, in consonance with the declaration of Orunmila.

The Olofin then praised the two of them for being right and compensated them accordingly, giving slightly more gifts to Orunmila for being able to reveal what no one else including himself (Olofin) knew. Thereafter, Orunmila and his mysterious slave left for home. Orunmila was beginning to wonder what to do about Arira Lumoye, who had by all intents and purposes, stolen the show from him. He subsequently decided to consult his Okeponrin (ikin divination). His own odu came out directing him to serve Esu with another he-goat, adding three u-bolts, three akara, the skulls of three different animals and 3 eko. He got the materials together and made the sacrifice.

In the meantime, Arira Lumoye decided to mark the first anniversary of his coming to Orunmila's house. He had become immensely wealthy in his own right. The ceremony was well attended.

There was plenty to eat and drink. After the feasting, there was dancing at which he was able to sever his head from the rest of his body and both parts were dancing separately to a tunderous applause from the crowd. That was the point at which Esu discovered that Arira Lumoye made no sacrifice. To punish him for failing to make sacrifice, Esu seized his head in the air and used the u-bolt with which Orunmila had made sacrifice to nail it to the stem of an Iroko tree.

After dancing for a long time, the rest of his body, not finding his head to link up with, fell to the ground dead. The spectators alerted Orunmila to what had happened and he told them to throw the headless corpse into the river where he turned from a corpse to a living being. The headless corpse subsequently turned into a crab, which explains why the crab has no head.

When this odu appears at divination, the person will be told that he has a subordinate in his place of work who is making charms to outshine him. He should make sacrifice to call off his bluff.

He Made Divination for Osanyin When Death Was Trailing Him

Arikeshe ni o nshe omo ile iku.
Arigogo ni o nshe omo ile iku.
Arigidi ni o nshe omo ile iku.

These are the names of the messengers of Death whom he uses to kill human victims.

Ogunsimo Lakete, o gbe owo agada je je je je was the Awo who made divination for Osanyin when death was gunning for him. He was told to make sacrifice with a tortoise and a cock and pebbles. He was to cook the meat together with the pebbles and the yam pottage and to put the clay pot at the centre of his living room and to light sixteen open oil lamps round it. Thereafter, the members of his family and himself were to be eating from the pot while throwing the pebbles away through the window.

At the same time, Death sent his first messenger called Arikeshe to bring Osanyin to heaven. When Arikeshe got to Osanyin's house, he saw him and his family eating from fire and throwing part of the food (stones) away through the window. As Arikeshe tried to taste the 'food' they were throwing away, he found it too hard to crack. He suddenly heard Osanyin boasting:-

"Bi ma ba ri Arikeshe,
Emi yo kpa Arikeshe"

Osanyin was boasting that if he set his eyes on Arikeshe, who was coincidentally watching them through the window, he would kill him. Arikeshe, after hearing the intimidating words of his supposed victim, ran back to report mission impossible to Death. He explained that from the kind of food the man and his family were eating, and the proclamations he was making, he would squeeze him with his fingers.

Death next sent Arigogo and he had the same experience because he met Osanyin and his household still eating from the fire and boasting

"Bi ma ba ri Arigogo,

Emi yo kpa Arigogo"

When Arigogo was frightened away from daing Osanyin, Death sent Arigidi to fetch him. Once more, Arigidi met Osanyin boasting:-

"Bi ma ba ri Arigidi,
Emi yo kpa Arigidi",

The failure of his messengers annoyed Death so much that he decided to accomplish the task by himself. When he got to Osanyin's house, he saw him and his family still eating from burning fire and throwing part of what they were eating away. When Death tasted what they were throwing away, he concluded that Osanyin must truly be too strong for anyone to dare, since he (Death) could not eat what they were eating. Osanyin eventually stood up and began to sing:

"Bi ma ri'ku ma baja.
Omi wowoji, OMi wowoji wowo"

As soon as Death heard the song, he ran away. That was how Osanyin used the special sacrifice to fend off Death from his trail.

When this odu appears at divination especially if it is Ayeo, the person will be told to perform the same sacrifice to ward off the threat of death. Orunmila says that when Death and sickness are declared to be one's trail after divination, the person should be told to crack three palm kernels, grind them and mix them with pap or porridge, adding the divination powder of this odu, and the danger would be abated.

Chapter 12

OGUNDA-EKA

The Divination Made for Him Before Coming to the World

Adiyika Lere, Adiyika. That was the name of the Awo who made divination for this odu when he was coming to the world. He was advised to make sacrifice to neutralize the threat of enmity on earth. He was to present a goat, hen, rat, fish and a gourd of palm wine to his guardian angel; serve Ogun with ram, dog, cock, tortoise and a gourd of palm wine; and serve Esu with two he-goats. He was advised that trading was going to be his main vocation on earth and that he was going to derive benefit from the problems created for him by a woman.

On getting to the world, he began to trade in beads, corals and other jewels. He was trading to all the markets around including Oja-Ajigbomekon. He met the girl who was to become his wife in the market. She was a princess of the royal house of the Oba of Orita-Ijaloko. They fell in love with each other and the girl agreed to marry him. She eventually followed Orunmila home to live with him. She turned out to be a spoiled brat, who neither knew how to keep a home nor how to go to the farm. The only thing she knew how to do well was to glamorize herself and sit in front of the house everyday while the husband was away to do his daily chores. Incidentally, she was the only child of her parents.

As if to aid and abet his wife's cosmetic tendencies, he adorned her with beads and the other jewels he was selling. The wife's ornamentation not only made her the cynosure of all passers-by but also attracted a host of male admirers around her, a situation which she enjoyed and encouraged, since her husband was away from home for most of the time anyway. Meanwhile, to be able to seduce her from Orunmila, some of her more ardent admirers were plotting against him as a result of which, his fortunes began to ebb.

At that point, he invited his Awos to make divination for him. During divination his own odu appeared. He was told that his problems arose from his failure to consult his Ifa before marrying his wife, and that his guardian angel did not approve of the woman as his wife. He was told to make a special sacrifice to his Ifa with a ram, a hen, rat and fish; serve Esu with a he-goat; serve Ogun with dog, cock, tortoise and a gourd of palm wine; and to feast the people around him with a goat. He lost no time in making all the sacrifices.

After eating his he-goat, Esu came to him in the guise of a well-wisher to inform him of the promiscuous infidelity of his wife whenever he travelled to the market. To test the veracity of his information, Esu advised him to return from the market well ahead of his schedule the next time he travelled to the market. When he was leaving home for the next market trip, he told his wife that he was going to be away for two weeks because he was going to Oja-Ajigbomekon akira. The wife was only too happy at the prospect of being left alone to do her thing for as long as two weeks.

There was an elderly woman who was Orunmila's next-door neighbor and who used to observe the flirtatious behavior of his wife. A week after he travelled away from home, he returned home without notice and took temporary accomodation with his elderly woman neighbor. After wondering why Orunmila sought refuge in her house, she briefed him on the recurrent extra-marital cohabitations of his wife during his absence. While Orunmila was being briefed by the old woman she told him that the only son of the Oba of the town was at that moment in bed with his wife. Orunmila stealthily entered his house through the back entrance only to catch his wife in flagrante delicto. They were both startled to see Orunmila. His first reaction was to tell the young prince that the inescapable price for seducing his wife was death. Thereafter, he invoked Esu and Ogun to be prepared to do battle on his behalf.

Almost immediately afterwards, Esu sounded the war cry and there was turmoil in the town, as a result of which people were dying in large numbers giving rise to stampede and pandemonium. The Oba was soon told that his son was responsible for the cataclysm in the town, for having insulted the masculine pride of Orunmila. The Oba who knew from experience, the consequences of offending Orunmila lost no time in inviting him for a chat on the commotion in the town.

As he was going to honor the invitation of the Oba, he used the appropriate incantation to request Esu and Ogun to up-hold a temporary cease-fire. When he got to the palace, he told the Oba that his son had to die for profaning his masculinity and defying his manhood. The Oba besought him to name the atonement for the offence and he declared that it would cost him 200 men, 200 women, 200 cows, 200 goats, 200 rams, 200 he-goats, 200 cocks, 200 hens, 200 bags of money and 200 pieces of white cloth, warning that there would be total confusion in the town unless these requirements were produced. The Oba tried his utmost to assemble the requirements but could not succeed, while Orunmila insisted on getting everything. The Oba eventually invited Orunmila to take over the throne. The deal was agreed.

Thereafter the Oba called a conference of the town's chiefs and elders to inform them of his decision to surrender the throne to Orunmila, while at the same time, agreeing to serve under him. Orunmila thus became the Oba, and upon ascending the throne, he made a feast for his diviners and the divinities, at which he sang in praise of them.

When this Ifa appears at Ugbodu, the person will be advised to make sacrifice in order to avoid coming across a woman who will generate unhappiness for him. If he however has his own Ogun and makes the special sacrifice which this odu made, he will rise to the pinnacle of his vocation.

Special Significance of this Odu

Ogbomudu Lere, miogbomudu yi soro.
Orangun Illa soro, Ogbomudu ba unshe.

Owa ijesha soro, Ogbomudu ba unshe.
Orunmila soro, Ogbomudu ba unshe
Ijo ti Ogbomudu soro re, oun ni kon l'onshe.

Orunmila says that Ogbomudu enjoys the best of many worlds. When the Orangun of Illa, Owa of Ijesha and Orunmila performed their annual festivals, they invited Ogbomudu. But when Ogbomudu does his own festival, he does not invite anyone. He does it alone. When Orunmila was asked why the situation was like that, he explained that it was because Ogbomudu is Esu himself, who enjoys the sacrifices made by all and sundry, but he himself makes sacrifice to no one, because he owes no allegiance to anybody.

When this Ifa therefore appears at Ugbodu, the person should prepare two Esu shrines; one by the side of Ifa shrine inside the house, and the second one outside the house in the usual way.

He Made Divination for the People of Ofa

Ogunda-monu-aka, Ija aka ko le ba aka ja.

He made divination for the people of Ofa to avert the danger of enslavement and subjugation. When enemy forces were threatening them, they invited Orunmila for divination. After divination, he advised them to make sacrifice with dog, tortoise, cock and snail to Ogun and to serve Esu with a he-goat, a drum and gun powder at the last junction before getting to the town.

When the army of Imole (Muslims) was coming to invade the town, Esu took the drum with which the people of Ofa made sacrifice and danced round the encampment of the Muslim forces in the night, threatening that none of their soldiers would return home alive if they invaded Ofa. As if to demonstrate that he was not bluffing, he caused an explosion in their camp which set all their own amunitions ablaze, giving rise to secondary explosions which killed and injured many of their soldiers. Those who survived the explosion took to their heels and returned to their base in Takpa.

He Made Divination for the Farmer Against the Risk of Robbery

Ogunda-mo-le-Eka made divination for the groundnut farmer when he was going to begin his farming year. He was told to serve; Esu with a he-goat and Ogun with a cock. He did not consider the sacrifice necessary.

When his groundnuts were due for harvesting, Esu alerted the hare, the rodent like, the grass-cutter and the rats to the presence of food in the farm. Meanwhile, these animals invaded the farm and they had successfully made three raids before the farmer discovered that his crops were being plundered. He accused Esu of being responsible for his plight. He got a cudgel to beat Esu on the head. Esu then told him that it was going to be a fight to finish.

Apprehensive of what Esu was going to do next, he ran back to Orunmila who told him after divination that a total war was being planned against him by a superior power that he had offended. At that point he admitted that he had gone to hit Esu on the head for inviting animals to plunder his farm. Orunmila told him that it was better to bribe Esu with sacrifice than to engage him in combat because, not even God, the Creator of heaven and earth, has won a fight against Esu. Orunmila then advised the farmer that the sacrifice had doubled. He was then required to appease Esu with two he-goats, two cocks and two pigeons.

When Orunmila got to Esu's place to appease him, he agreed to accept the sacrifice, but insisted that the farmer had to hit him once again on the head before he ate the sacrifice. That ceremony has been signified since then by the Orofa (divination staff) with which Ifa priests hit the protruding stone(iyangi) Esu shrine before making sacrifices to him.

After enjoying the sacrifice, Esu advised Ogun to look out for the rodents plundering the farmer's groundnuts. Ogun in turn invited the hunter, who killed several of these animals with weapons and traps after which they stopped going to the farm. The farmer enjoyed a good harvest thereafter.

At Ugbodu, the person should serve; Ogun with a cock, his head with a pigeon, and Esu with he-goat to impede trouble from close relations. At divination, the person will be told that problems are imminent at his place of work. He should serve; Esu with a he-goat, Ogun with a cock, and his head with a pigeon.

He Made Divination for Orisa-Nla

Gbegidi na'boshu kitikpa. Odifa fun Orisa-Nla, oshere-igbo
ni jo ti onlo si ono jinjin gbongbongbon.

That was the Awo who made divination for Orisa-Nla, God's own representative on earth, when he travelled to a distant destination. After travelling for a long distance, he became very hungry, but could not find food to buy or eat.

At dusk, he sought accommodation in the house of Okpe tiri-Eluju, who surprisingly extended elaborate hospitality to him. When he was taking leave of his host, he brought out his divine staff and prayed for him, proclaiming prosperity would always come to him throughout his life, and that all parts of his body would be money. That is why every part of the palm tree provides money to this day.

When this odu appears at divination, the person will be advised to have his own Ifa in order to prosper in life.

The Divination Made for Him When He Traveled on a Long Trip

Ogunda ka Ijaforo ma mu eko. Adifa fun Orunmila baba she awo
lo si ono jinjin gbongbongbon bi ojo.

That was the Awo who made divination for Orunmila when he was going on a long trip. He was advised to make sacrifice with a cock, hen, pigeon and rabbit in order to realease plenty of gifts from his divination trip. He made the sacrifice and set out on his journey. He was however told that he was going to realize the reward of his trip from his third port of call.

He stopped at the first town, but had no encouragement. He therefore left for a second town, but still had no satisfaction. He subsequently left for a third town where he had plenty of gifts which made him to return home a rich man.

At divination for a person travelling, he will be told that he will only achieve his objective on a third trip or at a third stop. For a person arranging for a wife, he will only succeed on a third attempt. If it is for a woman, she will be told that she is going to settle down with a third husband.

Chapter 13

OGUNDA-BA-ETURUKPON

He Made Divination for the Cow

Gidi gidi guo, babalawo elila, odifa fun elila ni tori onje.

He made divination for the cow when he was not able to procure enough food to feed himself and his family. He was advised to make sacrifice with four guinea fowls and four hens, and warned to refrain from greediness and contemptuous behavior because that was why people tended to hate him at sight. He only made sacrifice with two guinea fowls and two hens.

The next day, he left for the farm, ate to his heart's content, leaving very little for the owner of the farm. When the owner of the farm subsequently saw the plunder, he made a fence to block the route used by the cow. When the cow went on a subsequent occasion, he could not enter the farm. He then went to Orunmila to protest that the sacrifice did not manifest, because the route he took to fetch food had been closed. Orunmila reminded him of the warning against greediness, because he surmised that it was the greediness of the cow that made the farmer to close the route.

Orunmila however made divination for him, advising him to make sacrifice with a chicken and a trumpet. After making the sacrifice, he was given the trumpet to use on his approach to the farm, assuring him that whoever heard the sound of the trumpet would run away. When he got to the farm the following morning, the farmer was in the farm. As soon as the cow blew the trumpet, Esu amplified the sound and excited the cow to start digging the ground with his left foot while his tail stretching out as if charged for combat. On seeing the cow in a fighting mood, the farmer ran away for safety, thus clearing the way for the cow to enter the farm to eat.

When this Ifa appears at Ugbodu, the person should serve the new Ifa with four hens, four guinea-fowls, four snails and four pigeons, five days after going to Ugbodu. He should add cow's meat to the sacrifice. After divination, the person should serve Ifa with a hen and cow meat, his head with a guinea fowl, and Esu with he-goat in order to succeed in his job.

He Made Divination for Oluweri to Become Prosperous

Ayinyan oji, oro asho mu aya. Erira ji, ogbaja ijokun
kanle. Esin kan rin lo lu akpesi babare kpin rimbiti.
Adafa fun Oluweri ni jo ti ono ifaa ono ere se.

The cockroach woke up wearing a dress up to his chest.
The ant woke up and tied a piece of cloth up to the ground.
The black ant woke up to beat the father's drum to give a
heavy sound.

These were the three Ifa priests who made divination for Oluweri when all roads to prosperity were closed to him. He was told to make sacrifice with a sheep and he did it. Thereafter, all routes to prosperity opened once more for him and he sang in praise of his Ifa priests.

At divination, the person will be advised never to use strong charms. He should serve the water divinity with whatever he can afford. Any child born after this divination, should be named Awopetu.

He Made Divination For Ogidi-Olu, Otherwise Called Ajayi

Egutan omo aboshun, Eturukpon omo abo Orisha.
Aa ki bo Baatala ka ba bo Orisa, ki erumole ma gbeni.

Ogunda served the water divinity (Osun in yoruba and Olokun in Bini) while Eturukpon served Baatala divinty. One cannot serve Orisa and Baatala without obtaining the protection of the divinities.

These were the Awos who made divination for Ogidi-Olu, otherwise called Ajayi who derived benefit from serving God. He was advised to make sacrifice with guinea-fowl and pigeon. He made the sacrifice and told the Ifa priests that anyone going to the sea (Okun) and the big river near it (Osa) should serve Ifa for salvation in the house of his father, where he was born. When this odu appears for a pregnant woman, the child when born, should be named Ajayi.

He Made Divination For Oluloko When He Was Going to Marry

Osa ka ni soko, omi ko she isa re ki afi oju kponmi wa le.
Odifa fun Oluloko ti on lo mu omo Alake shaya.

It is neither possible to run inside the river, nor to fetch water from it with the face or eyes. That was the name of the Ifa priest who made divination for Oluloko when he was going to marry the daughter of the Alake of Abeokuta. He was told to buy a goat and a hen to give to the girl to rear, before marrying her. He did as he was told and the marriage was very successful.

When it appears at divination for a man seeking to marry a woman, he should be advised to buy two domestic animals for the girl to rear before marrying her so that the marriage would flourish.

He Made Divination For The Market Woman

Iran ni idi ahun. Eji doro ni idi agbo. Adafa fun Yeye
oloja ti ani ko ru ebo tori omo araye.

One pointed knife is the anus of the tortoise.
Two long testacles constitute the anus of the ram.

Those were the Ifa priests who made divination for the market woman. She was told to make sacrifice to neutralize the evil designs of her enemies, when they were planning either to kill her or to sit on her trade or steal all her wares. She was advised to make the sacrifice with 4 hens, four rabbits, four pigeons, four rats, four fishes and four bags of money. She made the sacrifice and the danger was averted.

When it appears at divination, the person should be advised to make a similar sacrifice in order to avert the risks of loss of life or job, and the destruction of whatever he or she does.

The Divination He Made Before Coming to the World

Iginda Eginyo se se re re/ igi ba ti da, eye fo lo.
When the branch of a tree breaks off, it is happy.
When the branch of the tree on which a bird stands breaks, the
bird flies away.

Those were the names of the Ifa priests who made divination for Orunmila when he was leaving heaven for the earth. He was advised to make sacrifice in order to forestall the risk of unconsumated fortunes (amubo in Yoruba and Osobonomasunu in Bini). He was told to serve Osanyin (Osun) with a dog, tortoise, and palm frond. He was to serve his guardian angel with a piece of white cloth, white chalk and cowries. He was also to serve Esu with a collection of rotten foods and meats in addition to a he-goat. After making the sacrifices, he sought and obtained the blessing of God for a happy sojourn on earth. God however advised him to live on earth in accordance with His will as it is done in heaven.

He was accompanied to the world by Osanyin and Esu and they did not live in the town but built their abode in the forest. They got to the world at a time when it was in a state of turmoil. After trying their utmost to put things right, the people sought the assistance of the men in the forest who were presumed to be from heaven. When the errand-men saw Orunmila in the forest, they told him that they were sent by the elders to solicit their assistance in solving the problems besetting the earth. He advised them to feed his two associates first and they did so, accordingly.

Thereafter, he made divination for them and disclosed that the unsettled condition of the earth was a function of the wickedness of mankind. He advised them to change their ways so that conditions might improve for the better. He however told them to serve:- Osanyin (Osun) with cock and tortoise, and Esu with he-goat because they would help them to put things right on earth. When the delegates reported the findings of Orunmila to their people, they made arrangements to perform the sacrifices without delay. Thereafter peace and concord returned to earth.

Long afterwards, the people had forgotten the help rendered to them by Orunmila, and they began to create problems for him. After concluding arrangements to kill him, they successfully persuaded Orunmila to leave the forest to live in their midst in the town. He decided to embark on divination before going and Ifa advised him to serve Osun, Esu and to look for the branch of a tree that got broken and fell to the ground when a bird was standing on it and to add the appropriate leaves to prepare a soap with which to bathe. It took him a long time to get the branch of the tree that got broken when a bird was standing on it. That was Ifa's ploy for delaying his movement from the forest to the town. He eventually moved to the town.

One day, the Oba decided to invite all his subjects to the town's ancestral shrine of the elders for a special sacrifice. Meanwhile, assassins had been suborned to lynch Orunmila on his way to the shrine. When the assassins saw him, they came out from hiding to attack him, but he disappeared before they could touch him. After that brush with death in the hands of the beneficiaries of his benevolence, he decided to return to heaven. On getting to heaven, he reported to God that the earth was beyond redemption because evil had taken deep roots in it. God however wondered whether there was any point in encouraging other righteous reformers to go to the world. It was after that experience of Orunmila that Jewesun (Jesus) came to the world and also lost his life to his good deeds because he made no sacrifice.

When this odu appears at Ugbodu, the person will be told that he is a benevolent reformer, but should be advised to make special sacrifice to avert the risk of being killed for doing good. The world of evil has no place for benevolent reformers, so warned Orunmila.

Chapter 14
OGUNDA-OSE

He Made Divination For The Penis

Ogunda-se-se babalawo oko, odifa fun oko.
He made divination for the penis when he was going to play with
the vulva.

The penis was advised to make sacrifice to avert the danger of suffering from transient power failure. He was also advised not to eat in his friend's house. He was required to make sacrifice with okro and pap, but he did not do it.

When he subsequently visited the vulva, he began to eat in her house by having fun with her. After eating, he began to vomit the mixture of okro and pap with which he failed to make sacrifice. As soon as he finished vomiting, he lost his strength as a result of dehydration and he became flabby. It was then that the penis remembered the sacrifice prescribed for him by Ogunda-se-se, which is the noise the penis makes after having fun with the vulva.

When this odu appears at divination, the person should be advised not to eat in anybody's house.

The Divination He Made Before Coming To The World

Ise kpe igi aworo - was the Awo who made divination for this Odu when he was coming from heaven. He was advised to make sacrifice in order to succeed in the trading business he was going to do on earth, with farming on the side. He was required to make sacrifice with; dog, cock, tortoise and snail to Ogun; monkey or its meat and okin bird or its meat to his guardian angel; and he-goat to Esu. He did all the sacirifices before leaving for the world.

On getting to the world, he built his house near the market of Oja-Ajigbomekon. Osanyin and Ogun accompanied him to the world. In addition to trading, he was also making divination for people. He was doing well initially, but the problems from close relations soon caused his fortune to decline. His wives subsequently left him with their children and he was left alone.

At the height of his problems, he decided to go for divination, at which he was advised to serve his Ifa with monkey and eye-okin (bird); and Esu with he-goat. Since he could not get hold of the bird and the monkey he got a big pot and positioned it at the foot of a big tree. After putting a number of things into the pot, Esu filled it with water. Meanwhile, there was drought in the world and there was a shortage of water everywhere. Okin, the friend of the monkey, was a carnivorous bird, who fed on other birds. Meanwhile, they went in search of water until they met Esu who directed them to the giant pot of water he had deposited at the foot of the tree. When they saw the pot, they bathed inside it and drank from it.

Thereafter, it became their regular source of water supply and Esu made sure that the pot was always filled with water. After ensuring that the water pot had become a second habitat for the monkey and Okin, Esu alerted Orunmila that he had positioned a big water pot in the forest on his behalf and offered to take him there to catch those who were unauthorizedly using it. When Orunmila and Esu got to the foot of the tree where the pot was located they decided to hide in order to apprehend the intruders.

No sooner did they hide themselves than the monkey and Okin came to the pot. After having their bath and drinking, they began to pray for whoever it was that positioned the pot there and who was refilling it every day. They professed that if they had met the benevolent person, they would have offered to live with him to serve him. At that point Orunmila and Esu came out to accuse them of stealing, which offense carried the death penalty. After identifying himself as the owner of the pot they admitted their guilt to Orunmila but made passionate appeals for forgiveness because the prevailing drought had left them with no other option. They begged to be allowed to serve Orunmila the best way they knew in order to atone for their offense. They assured Orunmila that they would make him rich if he spared their lives by giving them an opportunity to serve him. Orunmila agreed to take them home to live with him.

However, faced with the problem of whether or not to kill them to serve his Ifa or to spare them to serve him as they proposed, he decided to sound Ifa once more for directions. Ifa advised him to spare their lives because they would help him to live an oppulent life once more. Meanwhile, Okin asked Orunmila whether he would like to make a farm, and he agreed to the suggestion. Thereafter, Okin and the monkey followed Orunmila to the location of the pot and brushed a farm there.

After brushing and firing the farm, they cleared the stumps and it was ready for planting crops. Okin planted grasses, his other staple food aside from the flesh of other birds. Orunmila planted yams and corn on the farm. On his part, the monkey fetched palm fronds from the forest to make a circle round the pot of water in the forest. Thereafter, Esu blurred Ogun's vision making him to think that the encircled palm frond was his forest shrine. Besides, when he saw the footprints of animals round the water pot, Ogun concluded that it was an auspicious spot for hunting. He therefore concealed himself from the view of animals coming from the pot. He succeeded in killing several animals. As soon as Esu discovered that Ogun was using the pot as a decoy for hunting birds and animals, he decided to humiliate him. Ogun incidentally, was one of the relations of Orunmila who had created problems for him.

While Ogun was waiting to shoot birds and animals using the pot, Esu had hidden to catch Ogun *flagrante delcto*, stealing. After waiting for Ogun to shoot three birds and an animal, he came out to accuse him of stealing. Ogun explained that he thought that the pot was his own forest shrine. When Esu took the veil from his eyes, Ogun realized the mistake he had made and fervently appealed to become a servant of the owner instead of risking the death penalty for stealing. When he eventually knew that Orunmila was the owner, of the pot, Ogun offered to assist him in his farming chores and promised never to create any more problems for him.

Soon afterwards, Esu also caught Osanyin (Osun) peeling the back of the tree encircled with the palm frond, accusing him of stealing and profaning the shrine where Orunmila served his guardian angel. He too begged for forgiveness, offering to serve Orunmila by fetching the leaves and materials for his work and to stop bothering him since he was one of the relations who formented problems for him.

Meanwhile, the crops on Orunmila's farm were due for harvesting. A precious bird which was endowed with the fortune of excreting beads and corals (Akon and Ileke in Yoruba and Ekan and Ivie in Bini) flew into the farm in the company of other birds while Okin was watching the farm. As they settled down to feed on the maize, Okin apprehended the precious bird, while the others flew away. The bird entreated Okin to spare his life, while offering to enrich the owner of the farm as his servant. Okin took the bird to Orunmila who agreed to the deal proposed by it.

When the bird was told to excrete corals and beads, it actually did so and Orunmila rejoiced, after thanking Esu with another he-goat. Within a matter of days, Orunmila become rich in jewels. After making a beaded outfit for himself, he was able to sell beaded dresses, shoes and crowns to all the Obas of the known world, which made Orunmila to become exceedingly wealthy. At the same time, Ogun and Osanyin (Osun) remained permanently at his beck and call instead of being adversaries.

At that point, he invited his Ifa priests for a thankgiving feast at which he gave them plenty of money and other gifts. When this Ifa comes out at Ugbodu, the person will be advised that his prosperity will come from trading and farming. He should be told that he has two brothers who are plotting against him, but that with perseverance and sacrifice, they would be compelled to transform their enmity to his servitude.

He Made Divination For Orsemi-Lere

Iwu ni ori arugbo, ka shan orun ajewa. Takuta-kpa, okete.
Irun .... gangan ni'di imodo

Those are the Awos who made divination for Orisemi-Lere before he achieved fame and fortune. They advised him to make sacrifice to his head with beans and corn, and he did it. Thereafter all the good things of life began to come to him. He thanked his Ifa priests and began to rejoice and to sing in praise of Ifa.

When it appears at divination, the person will be told to serve his head with cooked beans and corn in order to enjoy the good things of life.

He Made Divination For Ogun When He Was Going To War

Ti a ba to ogun de, ohun ti a ba ri ki a fun baba eni
ti bi ni lo'mo. Won difa fun Ogun nijo ti onlo si ogun
aja gbe ire bo.

When one returns from war, whatever one brings there from as spoils should be surrendered to one's father. Those were the Ifa priests who made divination for Ogun when he was going to war. He was told to serve his guardian angel with a dog, cock, and to serve Esu with a he-goat. He made sacrifice to his guardian angel but refused to serve Esu.

He went to war and was victorious, but he did not have the spoils of war to bring home. He only came home with one pretty girl, who had just completed her menstrual period. He took fancy to the girl and made love to her. The following day, his father the Olofin of Ife, called him to explain why he had not reported to him with the spoils he brought from the war front. He said that he did not bring any loot from the war front, except a girl whom he wanted to keep to himself. The father told him that tradition was not on his side and so prevailed on him to surrender the girl. The father subsequently made love to the girl, and retained her as a bride in his harem.

The girl became pregnant at the end of her menstrual cycle and in the fullness time gave birth to a male child. She also became pregnant soon after delivery and gave birth to another male child. At a ripe old age, the Olofin joined his ancestors and in accordance with tradition the first male child born after becoming Oba, had to take the throne. He happened to be the child born with Ogun's sperm.

While on the throne, he turned out to be a very autocratic ruler, and became notorious for settling disputes by condemning the guilty party to death by execution. The elders of the kingdom became so curious about his paternity that they went back to his mother to find out how he was conceived. The woman made a clean breast of the story by confirming that Ogun, the son of the Olofin was the first to make love to her after her menstruation, before his father took her over. She thus confirmed that the new Olofin was the son of Ogun and not the son of the late Olofin. The next problem however was how to replace him with his junior brother on the throne.

The king-makers and counsellors succeeded in resolving the problem by cajoling him to accept the honorific title of the Elemo of Ife, which meant, the father of the Oba. His junior brother subsequently became the Olofin which returned peace and tranquility to the kingdom.

When this odu appears at divination for a man, he will be told that a woman is coming into his life whose first pregnancy will be of doubtful paternity. The woman had sex with another man before she slept with him in the month she became pregnant. If it appears for a woman, she will be told that a strange man who did not seek her consent will make love to her and she will become pregnant and give birth to a male child. She is likely to be under mentruation at the time of the divination, and is subsequently likely to be raped by a strange man.

Divination For The Eldest Son Of Ogunda-Alashe

Iwu lori arugbo. Kasha Kasha lorun aje ewa. Takuta kpa

*okete. Irun gan gan ni idi imodo. Adifa fun Ikudamiloju
arimo Ogunda alashe. Ebo oriku ni ki oru.
Grey hairs signal the beginning of old age.
Cooked beans are sampled in a hurry.
The trap caught the rabbit. There are strong hairs on
the anus of the lion.*

They were the Ifa priests who made divination for Ikudamiloju, the eldest son of Ogunda-Alashe when death was gunning for him. He was told to make sacrifice with a he-goat. He made sacrifice and he did not die.

When death is portended under ayeo at divination, the person will be told to make sacrifice to Esu with a he-goat.

Chapter 15
OGUNDA-OFUN

He Made Divination for the Male Sperm

Ogunda fifun ru ru ru, babalawo ato, odifa fun ato.

He made divination for the male sperm when he was relatively unknown. He was told to make sacrifice with palm wine and pap. After making the sacrifice, he went to live with the divinity of child-birth (Olugbodo in Yoruba and Akobie in Bini). Whoever wanted children went to the divinity of childbirth for help. After going to live with Olugbado, Ato advised the divinity to tell anyone who wanted a child to make sacrifice, after which he (sperm) would follow them home. Nonetheless, he remained ineffectual.

Subsequently, the sperm went to Ose-Etura for divination, who advised him to make sacrifice with okro and a kind of edible clay called Eko in Yoruba and Eko in Bini. Ose-Etura made the sacrifice for Ato by burning up the two materials and grinding them into powder, After giving him the Ase, he was told to be taking the powder with pap every morning. Thereafter, he was able to become effective in bringing forth a new life in mankind and animals by fertilizing the female egg. That was how and when the sperm became famous and indispensable.

When this Ifa appears at Ugbodu, the person will be told to serve the new Ifa with another goat. The breast of the goat will be used to prepare a special okro (Edure in Yoruba and Ohukpo in Bini) soup for him or her to eat so that the Elders of the Night might not make his/her reproductive organs barren and ineffective.

At ordinary divination, the person if a man, should be advised to serve Esu with a he-goat to prevent his wife from deserting him as a result of delayed child-birth. If it appears for a woman, she will leave her present husband for a second one.

He Made Divination for the Father of all Snakes

Pelebi abidi soro - was the Awo who made divination for Ojola-gidigba when he was about to become the father of all snakes in the forest. He was advised to make sacrifice to prevent his children from becoming ill. He was required to make sacrifice with the clothes he was wearing, a cock and palm kernel oil (adin in Yoruba and uden in Bini). He made the sacrifice after which he was given a special Ifa medicine which he was told to share among his children, in other to make them live naturally. Instead of becoming ill, they shed off their scale skins and get rejuvenated, because of the cloth their father used to make sacrifice.

When this odu appears at divination, the person will be told to make sacrifice to deter the risk of becoming ill.

Orunmila Advises Cleanliness at all Times

Orunmila ni oga se se. Oni ki o mu nkan ebo oga se se wa.
Moni emi ko mo nkan ebo oga se se.
Orunmila advises absolute cleanliness in all that one does.
Before speaking to Ifa or serving him, the worshipper should
clean his/her feet, hands, and wear clean white dress, have a
clean heart and wash kolanuts before using them to talk to him
or serve him. Anyone who serves Orunmila in that way will surely
receive the reward.

When this odu appears at divination, the person will be advised to wear clothes with light colors throughout the days of his life, and should neither dress nor behave untidily, because goodness dwells in clean environments.

He Made Divination for the Pig to Have Children

Ogunda fun fun fun, awo ema olo ikin fun ema ati esi.

He made divination for both domestic, and the bush, pigs to have children. They were advised to make sacrifice with a hen and a pigeon, six akara, six eko, and six kolanuts. They made the sacrifices and hence became very productive. That is why pigs produce many children at a time.

At divination, the person will be advised to make sacrifice in order to have children. If it appears for a woman and she makes the sacrifice, she will begin by having twins or triplets. If the divinee is a man, he will be told that he will come across a woman who is not very pretty, but that if he makes sacrifice, she will give birth to many children.

He Made Divination for the Mother of Alajunare

The same Awo made divination for the mother of Alajunare to have children. She was required to make sacrifice with guinea-fowl, hen, pigeon, beans and corn. She did the sacrifice, after which she became pregnant. Her first delivery was a pair of twins. Yeye Olojunare is the colloquial name for the mother of twins.

At divination, for a woman, she will be advised to make sacrifice and be told that she is likely to have twins sometime in her life.

He Made Divination for Ogun During his Dispute with Akin

Ogunda fun fun fun, odifa fun Ogun ni jo ti Akin le kpa re.

He made divination for Ogun when he was being pursued by Akin, the agressive one. Ogun was advised to make sacrifice to be able to subdue his assailant. He made the sacrifice with a hen and three maize combs.

When Akin eventually accosted Ogun, a fight ensued between them. In the process, Esu placed the maize comb with which Ogun made sacrifice behind Akin. As soon as Akin stepped on the comb, he slipped and fell to the ground and Ogun would have beheaded him with his sword but for the fact that Akin conceded superiority to Ogun.

At divination, the person should be told to make sacrifice in order to overcome an enemy who is threatening to undo him or her.

The Divination He Made Before Leaving Heaven

Owo ale e ba to'wuro jo. Owo ale o rein owuro.

Those were the two Awos who made divination for Orunmila before he left heaven for the world. He was advised to make sacrifice to forestall the nefarious plans of enemies. He was required to make sacrifice with a bag containing all edible food-stuffs, sixty-five thousand dollars, crushed yam, small chicken, and a three-piece kolanut. He was also told to serve his guardian angel with a ram, cock and tortoise. He was also told to serve Ogun with cock, tortoise, roasted yam, palm wine and palm frond. Immediately before leaving for earth, he was required to obtain God's blessings with white pigeon, white cloth, white kolanuts, coconut and red parrot's feather. After making all the sacrifices, he left for earth.

During his journey to the earth, he met Esu on the way, who queried him for daring to leave for earth without obtaining clearance from him. He replied that he was not told at divination to serve him. Esu however insisted that he was not going to allow him to proceed on his earth-bound journey without getting a he-goat from him. Ogunda-Ofun eventually returned to heaven to Esu, after narrating his experience to the two Awos who made divination for him. They apologized to him for not telling him to serve Esu in the first instance. He eventually served Esu with a he-goat, white cloth, palm oil, rat, fish and a new pot.

After eating his food, Esu offered to escort him to earth, during which Esu told him that he was going to be a proficient and famous Ifa priest, but warned that his success was going to generate tremendous animosity against him unless he joined other Awos to be holding meetings in order to understand and emulate their methodology.

On getting to the world, he started with initial success, but his fame and fortune soon began to generate envy and the Awos he met on earth started using the power of witchcraft to obstruct his work. One day, Esu reminded him that he had made no sacrifice since coming to earth. He advised him to make a feast for people with a goat. He made the feast at which some of his invitees expressed appreciation by telling him that they thought his success would endure by ignoring them. Before dispersing, the invitees told him to be present at their meeting that night. Incidentally, his sworn enemies did not participate in the feast. Also absent was his own wife who, unknown to him, belonged to the club of witchcraft.

It was Esu who again directed him to do something about his principal enemies who were obstructing his work. Esu however asked for his own he-goat at that point and it was given to him. Thereafter, Esu disclosed the identities of his principal enemies as comprising: the handmaid of Orisa; the handmaid of Oshun/Olokun; and the handmaid of the divinity of death. Esu advised him to produce a big gourd of palm wine for him to use, which he quickly made available.

Ogunda-Ofun attended that night's meeting of the club of withcraft where he discovered his wife to be a prominent member. Orisa, Olokun and Death all forbid wine. As soon as the meeting was fully gathered, Esu pretended to have inadvertently broken the gourd of palm wine and the smell drove away the three divinities from the meeting. Thereafter, Orunmila was formally initiated as a member of the club and he was told that the meeting would be held in his house on every eighth day. Thereafter, his prosperity began to blossom and he lived to a ripe old age. At the height of his prosperity, he made a large feast with a cow, goat and rams to which he invited his Awos and sang in their praise. At that stage, he served his Ifa with a cock, since he was already a witch himself. It will be mentioned that only witches serve their Ifa with cock.

When this Ifa appears at Ugbodu, immediate steps should be taken to prepare the Esu shine of the Ifa. The person will be told that his wife is a witch and that circumstances are likely to make him become one himself. He should make sacrifice to be able to withstand and overcome the evil machinations of his enemies, who are not happy about his fame and fortune.

Chapter 1

OSA-OGBE
OSA-LO-GBE-JO

He Came to the World to Live in the Midst of Enemies

Ota'ra ta awo emi na'le, odifa fun Orunmila ni igba t'o
ma mba awon ota re jeun nkpo. Ebo ishegun ota lo'nru o.

That was the Awo who made divination for Orunmila when he came to the world to live in the midst of enemies. He was told to serve Ifa with a ram, and Esu with a he-goat, and the Elders of the Night with a hen and all pieces of edible foodstuffs. He was required to perform the sacrifices because he was going to live and thrive on earth in the midst of enemies.

He came to the world and he was very poor. He could not afford to marry a wife and so had no children. He was then operating as an unknown Ifa priest at Ife. One night, his guardian angel appeared to him, giving him the marching orders to travel to the land of Ilu-eleye, that is, the town of witches. He travelled almost immediately to the place, where he was warmly received.

Being the only Ifa priest who had the courage to live in the town, his importance was soon acknowledged. Incidentally, every inhabitant of the town was either a witch or a wizard. As the only lay odd-one-out, he was immediately slated for use in a feast at the appropriate time. Meanwhile, the people of the town joined hands to build a house for him through mutual effort.

After building the house for him, he occupied it alone since he had no dependants. As soon as he occupied the house, he formally became a citizen of the town. Meanwhile, he was given an invitation to attend the meeting of the council of witchcraft. He had no option but to accept the invitation. When he eventually got to the meeting, he saw two goats tied up to be slaughtered. When the goats were slaughtered, he told the meeting that he was only interested in two parts of the goats; the hearts and their blood. Nonetheless, in addition to the blood and the heart of the goats, he was also given his own share of meat.

When he got home with the parts given to him, he went without delay to Esu shrine, where by special incantation, he beseeched Esu that he should consume the blood and heart of the goats, if indeed they were created as goats by God. On the other hand, if they were originally created as human beings, and were only turned to goats by the cult of witchcraft, Esu should revert them to their original forms. Two full blown human beings, a man and a woman, emerged from the shrine of Esu.

He did not eat the goat meat given to him as his share. He dried it up in his fire place. That was what he did on every occasion in which goats and other animals were slaughtered. Within a very short time, his house was booming with the presence and activities of several dependents. He married the women and the men began to work for him. The people of the town were wondering over the source of the people occupying Orunmila's house, since it was common knowledge that he came to the town and that they were the products of his Ifa practice outside the town.

Meanwhile, he was told at the council meeting that it was his turn to feast all the members. He told them that he was ready provided they agreed to have the feast in his house. When he sounded Ifa on what to do, he was told to give a he-goat to Esu and to add the meat to the ones he had been drying up since he was enlisted to the club of witchcraft. Ifa also told him to add sasswood powder (Obo in Yoruba and Iyin in Bini) to the drinks with which he was going to entertain them.

After the eating and drinking, all the members started dropping dead one after the other, with the exception of the Ojugbona and his wife who did not partake in the feast. When Orunmila observed the absence of the Ojugbona and his wife at the feast, he sent for them. They were astonished to see the colossal carnage that had taken place in and around Orunmila's house. As he ordered them to eat and drink their share of the feast. they went on their knees to beg for their lives to be spared. Orunmila reacted by making them to take an eternal oath on the ground that they would never harm or disrupt the affair of his family and followers. Thereafter, Orunmila lived a peaceful and prosperous life.

When this odu appears at Ugbodu, the person will be told that circumstances will compel him to become an esoteric witch, but that he will have to make sacrifice to overcome his multitudinous enemies. At divination, the person will be told that he is surrounded by enemies who are mostly witches, without being a member. He should refrain from belonging to any meeting, but if he cannot avoid it, he should not eat or drink at such meetings, because he would not be able to abide by the rules.

The Divination Made for Him When Three Favors Were Coming to Him Simultaneously

Osalogbejo showo gede molo mude ni
She orun sale degua.
Kpako ko no ko ba ra ta'ye she.
Adifa fun Orunmila nijo ti won ni ure meta bo fun lo no.
Prepare both hands to receive prosperity.
Prepare your neck to support superlative beauty.
Prepare your vulva properly to receive the saviour.

These were the Awos who made divination for Orunmila, on the day that three agents of prosperity were coming to visit him. They advised him to make sacrifice immediately with a single rat. Incidentally, he had no rat at home and could not get any to buy. Meanwhile, Esu agreed to lend one to him. He added the divination powder (iyerosun) of the sacrifice and shouted on Esu to receive it (Esu gbaa) and Esu received it from him and ate it.

After eating the rat, Esu turned round to demand another rat to pay for the one he borrowed to Orunmila. Orunmila retorted by saying that if he had a rat immediately available, he would not have had cause to borrow one from him. Esu reacted by threatening to block the three fortunes coming to him from reaching him. Orunmila begged Esu to exercise patience and to bear with him. Since it is not the tradition of Esu to hold brief for anyone, he left at once to actualise his threat, by taking position at the heaven and earth junction. (Orita ijaloko).

Knowing that Esu is not known for making empty threats, Orunmila left for the forest in search of a rat. He quickly prepared an Ebiti trap for catching a rat. With the appropriate incantation, he lured a rat to the trap and it was caught. Thereafter, Orunmila raced after Esu to repay his debt.

Meanwhile, Esu met the three agents of prosperity bringing wealth to Orunmila from heaven. When he asked them where they were bound for, they told him that they were sent by the divinity of prosperity to send gifts to Orunmila. Esu lamented that they had come too late to help Orunmila, because he had gone mad and escaped into the forest.

The three agents turned back to return to heaven. They had scarcely left when Orunmila came panting with a rat in hand. After receiving the rat from him, Esu told him that he had already told three agents bringing the fortune to him to return to heaven but that he could bellow on them because they were still within hailing distance, and they had not reached Ogun's residence.

When Esu asked him whether he knew their names, he began to call on the names of the three Awos who made divination for him.

Showo gede molo mudeni
Shorun jege sale degua
Kpako ko no ko bara taye she.

Orunmila then hailed on Ogun to stop them from going beyond his house because he was on his way to meet them. He did so in the following words:

Ogun mo la du gbere
Da u dan rode mi dugbere
Ogun mo la du gbere.

As soon as Ogun heard Orunmila's voice, he came out of his house and not long afterwards, he met the three agents. When Ogun asked them for their mission, they replied that they were sent by Ala to send gifts to Orunmila, but that they met a short man on the way who told them to return to heaven because he had gone mad and run into the forest. Ogun told them that Orunmila was hale and hearty, and that he was already racing to meet them. On that reassuring note, they agreed to wait at Ogun's house for Orunmila to meet them.

When Orunmila eventually met them, he returned home with them and the event translated him into immense fame and fortune.

When this odu appears at divination, the person should be told that some benefits are on the way to him, but that he should immediately after the divination, make sacrifice with a single rat to avert the misfortune of losing them. If it is ayeo, the person should be told that a close associate who is very short, has already turned back the favors coming to him. He should immediately serve Esu with a rat, and Ogun with tortoise, roasted yam and palm wine so that they might return to him.

He Made Divnation for the Crown Prince of Ife

Emune mune mudi reyi. Adifa fun Ajebaye omo olofen
nijo t'oma fe aya Esu.

He made divination for Ajebaye, the crown prince of Olofin when he made love to the wife of Esu. He was advised to serve Esu with a he-goat to avoid the danger of being killed by his own son, but he failed to do it. He was in the habit of waking up every morning to sit on an easy chair in front of his house to see who was coming and going.

A few days after the divination, he was sitting on his easy chair in the morning, when he saw an attractive young girl going to the river to fetch water. Ajegbaye invited the girl into the house. The girl herself, who was overwhelmed by the elation of being invited by the crown prince of the kingdom, readily accepted the invitation and went into the bedroom with him without any hesitation. He made love to the girl, after which, she continued her journey to the river. Unknown to anyone however, the girl was the impish wife of Esu, and she had just gone through her menstrual period. While the girl resumed her journey to the river, Ajegbaye left for the forest to cut palm fruits.

When the girl got to the river, she was surprised to hear the voice of a child from her womb warning her to move softly because he was preparing to come down from her womb. On getting home she began to experience labor pains and before she could ask for help, a male child jumped out from her womb, and stood firmly on his feet. He came out with his placenta in hand and put it over his shoulder as a bag and asked for the whereabouts of his father.

While the mother was still trying to find her bearing from her bewilderment on the speed at which events were unfolding, the child left the house and headed alone for the forest in search of his father. Before leaving the house, he said that he knew his father was going to fetch palm fruits in the forest, and promised to rendezvous with him there.

When he got to the foot of the palm tree on which his father was cutting his way to the bunch of palm fruits, he greeted him as his son. While he was wondering where and when he had such a child, he challenged the father to a throw and catch contest. Bemused, Ajegbaye swore at the imp as an abominable *bete-noire*" (wo so fi or wo'diro in yoruba or udiyi in Bini). As if to demonstrate his seriousness, he told the father that he was the product of the love affair he had earlier on that day with a girl who was on her way to the river. He then told the father that there were two ripe bunches of palm fruits on the tree. He told the father to cut one of them and throw it to ground for him to catch.

After cutting his way clear to the bunch of palm fruits, the father threw it down with a view to smashing him with it, but the demon of a child held it with his left hand. Thereafter, he told the father to climb down. Without the aid of the palm tree climber, he climbed his way like a squirrel to the top of the tree. Ajegbaye was now trembling not knowing what to expect. Before he figured out whether to run or to wait, the imp had the bunch of palm fruits in hand to throw to his father. When Ajegbaye saw the imp holding the bunch of palm fruits, he took to his heels. Nonetheless, as he was running, the demon threw it at him, smashing him to death.

Thereafter, he jumped to the ground and headed for the town, where he challenged anyone he found to a wrestling match. He killed whoever wrestled with him, seizing their belongings and storing them in his bag that was never filled up. He destroyed every man he came across with the exception of those who escaped into the forest. After ravaging Ife, he left for the next town where he performed the same feat. After dealing with six towns in a similar manner, he left for the seventh town called Ijelu.

Before getting to Ijelu, the Oba of the town had been alerted to what had been happening in the other towns and he quickly invited his diviners to go into action. After divination, they told him to make sacrifice quickly to Esu with a he-goat, net, sticks, maize comb and a number of slippery objects. The sacrifice was made without any delay. The Oba of Ijelu had one pretty daughter who was ripe for marriage. The diviners advised the Oba that when the mysterious war-monger arrived, he should invite him for entertainment and ask the girl to present kola and wine to him in the nude, as was the practice in those days.

The sacrifice had scarcely been completed when tumultuous yells were heard throughout the town as the invader was killing everyone on sight. When he got to the palace, he challenged the Oba to a wrestling match, but the Oba told him that much as he was prepared to accept the challenge, he should come for a formal reception. He heaved a sigh of relief at the prospect of formal hospitality. He went into the palace where the Oba's beautiful daughter presented kolanuts and palm wine to him in the nude. He offered at once to marry the girl and she agreed to marry him.

Without any ceremonies, he went into the visitor's apartment with the girl and he made love to her while hanging his bag on a hanger nailed to the wall. After the lover making, he began to drink until he became throughly drunk. That was when the girl asked him what was responsible for his invincible power, while coaxing him with the adulation that she had long been looking for a strong man like himself to marry. In a state of *delirum tremens*, he disclosed that he was Eseku the son of Esu himself and that his strength lay in the fact that he had not seen and should never see unripe palm fruits, punch, and a newly born child whose hair had not been shaved. Thereafter, he fell asleep. While arrangements were being made to collect all his taboos, a child spoke out from the girl's womb.

The girl went to her father and told him that she was having severe pains in the area of her pelvis. Before any one could diagnose what was wrong with her, a baby boy jumped out of her womb. It was the bawl generated by the astonishment of the arrival of the mysterious baby that woke up Eseku. Before then, in addition to the new baby whose hair had not been shaved, all the other things he forbade were lined out conspicuously for him to see. That was the scene against the background of which the king of Ijelu accepted his earlier invitation to a wrestling contest.

As they began to wrestle, the king threw Eseku in the direction of the Esu Shrine, and Esu got him to tread on the maize-comb, which slipped him into the other slippery objects, and he ended up in a net and was tightly held in place. After conceding defeat to the Oba of Ijelu, he aked to be beheaded. The Oba then cut his neck with his sword and his head jumped up to the Oba's Ogun shrine. His body was buried at the Esu shrine.

Three months after the eventful fairy-tale, there was an earth tremor in the town of Ijelu, which killed 200 men, women and children. After three such occurences at three monthly intervals, the king invited Orunmila for divination and he was told that the calamity was being caused by the unburied corpse of Eseku. He was told to exume the body and to bury it properly with a cow, 200 goats, 200 baskets of Eko, 200 packets of ekuru and 200 cowries. After the burial, the Oba was told to offer sacrifice to the grave annually.

Three days after the formal burial, Eseku spoke from the grave, confirming that he had accepted the sacrifice made to him and promised from then on to help them in protecting the town, and that he should be notified with the traditional rituals if there were any problems to be solved in the town. That is the origin of esu-jelu which the people of Ijelu serve to this day.

When this odu appears at ugbodu, the person should be advised to prepare carved or moulded effigy of Esu-jelu to be kept on the Ifa shrine and to eat out of whatever is given to Ifa and the traditional Esu-Obadara. The two Esus; Esu Obadara and Esu-jelu should be prepared for the Ifa within seven days, failing which, either the Ifa patron or the father of the person, will not live long thereafter. On the other hand, the mother of the person will live to a ripe old age.

When it appears at divination, the person will be advised to have his own Ifa and to serve Esu with a he-goat in order to avoid producing a child who is an imp through a hit-and-run love making, and whose birth will presage his own demise.

He Made Divination for the Oloba of Obaa to Survive the Onset of Several Dangers

The fame of Osalogbejo had echoed throughout the known world of the time, which was the setting in which the Oloba of Obaa invited him for divination when he was having problems. He was accompanied to Obaa by one of his surrogates called Sawo-sigi. After divination, he told the Oba that gunning for him were six deaths, six illnesses and six cases. To prevent them from manifesting, he was advised to make sacrifice with a cow, six rats (Eku-eda) six cocks, six fishes, 6 he-goats and six bags of money. The Oba arranged for the sacrifice without any delay.

After preparing the sacrifice, a grave was dug on the floor of his palace and the heads of the cow, the cocks, rats fishes, etc. were buried there. Thereafter, six deaths, six illnesses and six case visited him in turns and they were all driven away by Esu. He then ruled the town of Obaa in peace and tranquility to a ripe old age.

When this odu appears as ayeo at divination the person will be advised to make sacrifice to ward off the approach of death, illness and dispute.

He Made Divination for Two Anonymous Friends of Contrasting Orientations

When two friend were leaving heaven, they made two conflicting vows. The miser (Awin in Yoruba and Ukhienkuen in Bini) promised never to sell anything on credit when he got to the world where he was going to trade. His friend, the chronic debtor (Onigbese in Yoruba and Akaruosa in Bini) vowed never to pay for whatever he bought in the world. For the purpose of this passage, the one shall be referred to as the Miser while the other shall be the Debtor. On getting to the world, they went their separate ways.

When the Debtor got to the world, he developed the habit of sitting in front of his house every morning to buy things on credit without ever paying for them. He had a chewing stick which he always chewed in his mouth, which had the effect of charming people into selling goods to him on credit, without remembering to ask for payment.

One day, the Miser was hawking his wares of palm oil when the Debtor requested to buy from him. He bought the equivalent of three bags of money and told the seller to return later in the day to collect the money. When the Miser returned to demand the payment, the Debtor replied that it was not his tradition to pay for anything he bought, because he was so ordained by God. On his part, the Miser laughed scornfully while retorting that the Miser was joking, because he was himself notorious for not selling anything on credit because he was so ordained by God.

Their polarised stances generated a heated altercation culminating in a physical exchange of blows. Eventually, they were both arraigned before the Oba, accused of disturbing the peace. The Debtor bluntly denied buying anything from the Miser, who swore that he sold palm oil to him for three bags of money. The judge who was appointed to determine the case, invited each of them to carry the "witness box" (Akpoti eri in Yoruba and Ekpetin-ose in Bini) over a distance of seven hills, at the end of which the truth would emerge. The pad for carrying the box was a chain. Unknown to each of them, the box contained a talking parrot who could hear and report any comments made by the carrier during the journey.

The Miser was the first to carry the "witness box". By the time he got to the fourth hill he was already very tired but he vowed that he would insist on having his money, and even if he had to die in the process, he would yet go and demand it in heaven. He however survived the ordeal by completing the seven hills after which he put down the box.

It was the turn of the Debtor to carry the box. By the time he got to the third hill, he was in such great pain from fatigue that he regretted that it would have been easier for him to admit the indebtedness and beg to repay it gradually instead of risking death over a mere three bags of money. He however survived the ordeal by completing the seven hills.

At the end of the exploits, the judge opened the box and the parrot confirmed that the first man to carry the box had told the truth. After recalling the comments made under severe stress by the two of them, the Debtor was ordered by the court to pay his debt to the Miser.

On getting home the Debtor resolved that it was better to die than to break his eternal vows never to pay for whatever he bought. He got himself into a coffin loaded with food and drinks to last for a long time, and it was buried in a tomb. When the Miser subsequently came to demand the payment of his debt, the Debtor was nowhere to be found. Three months later, the Miser returned to demand the payment of his money. When he was told that the Debtor had died three months earlier, he decided to ask to verify from the grave where he was buried. On getting to the tomb, he opened the coffin and found the Debtor still alive. Eventually, the Debtor had no option but to pay the money. He died in the night after repaying the debt.

When this Ifa appears at Ugbodu, the person should be told that five days later he should go and steal a hen and to buy kolanuts on credit, to serve the new Ifa. Three months after coming out of the secret conclave (Ugbodu) he should serve the Ifa with a goat in order to live long and prosper on earth, because he came from heaven with a hard-luck head. When it appears at divination, the person will be advised to serve Esu with a he-goat bought on credit in order to prosper in his work. He should buy the he-goat on credit, even if he has the money to pay for it.

He Made Divination for the Rat Called Eku-Eda

Osa lu lu - Odifa fun Eku-Eda to ntori tomo difa nigba
ti oju omo mkpan.

He made divination for the rat called Eda when she was afraid, not only of not having children, but also of death. She was told to make sacrifice with a hen. She did the sacrifice, after which she began to have children.

When the odu appears at divination for a person who is anxious to have a child, he or she should be advised to make sacrifice with with two hens.

Divination and Sacrifice for Checkmating Death

O te kpa ko de orun ese. Odifa fun Odumibaku, oma mu
ekuru ko iku je.

One who supported himself with a walking stick, but did not pay the debt of premature death. That was the Awo who made divination for Odumibaku when death was on his trail. He was advised to make a feast with bean pudding (Ekuru or Emieki). Thereafter, he survived the onset of death.

When this odu portends the danger of death at divination, the person will be advised to make sacrifice with a duck, rat, fish, eko, akara and ekuru, to avoid dying during the year.

The Divination Made for Him to Prosper

Oni ima ima. Amo koko komo a ka. Odifa fun Osa to'nle
oweriola ni osa.

The sculptor may know how to cast or mould a pot, but not how to mould the rack. That was the name of the Awo who made divination for Osalogbejo when he was going to wash with four hens, four pigeons and four bags of money.

At divination, the person should be advised to have his own Ifa and that he will prosper immensely if he lives and works in Lagos, the source of the Osa river.

Orunmila's Advice to the Wives of Ifa Adherents

Iki shimi so'de. Winrin winrin mi sedin.
Akpetebi kpale ta bi ko kpale?
Moni akpetebi kpale o,
Bi akpetebi ba ti kpale,
A ni ganaku iwaju.
Bi akpetebi ba ti kpale,
A ni gunrun kan leyin
A ni omo yoyo leyin ose.
A ni sho sho owo.

This is when Orunmila advises the wife of an Ifa man to sweep, clean and scrub the house in order to become pregnant, back her own child, and to have money in hand.

When it appears at divination for a woman, she will be told that she is the wife of Orunmila, and should therefore marry an Ifa man. An Ifa-Ude (bangle) will be prepared for her to wear. If it appears for man, he will be told to have his own Ifa if he does not already have one. If he already has Ifa, he should be told to learn to become an Ifa priest.

Divination and Sacrifice for Alleviating Problems

Orunmila ni Osa-ogbe, Moni Osa-ogbe.
Oni omo eku ti o ba mora, mosa ni osa ma ngbe.
Oni omo eja ti o ba mora, mosa ni osa ngbe.
Orunmila ni osa ogbe, Moni osagbe,
Oni omo eye ti o ba mora, mosa ni osa ngbe.
Oni omo eni ti o ba mora, mosa ni osa ngbe.
Orunmila says water has blessing. The Ifa priest agreed.
He said that if the rat, fish, bird or human being,
is as clean as water, it will attract blessing.

When asked for the appropriate sacrifice, he enumerated them as; two kolanuts wrapped in the leaves called ewe igi asa, two live fishes kept in a pot filled with water, to serve Esu-alajogun or Ifa with the following prayers:

Orunmila gba wa o-o-o,
Omi ti o ba le la ni o ngba.

Meaning

Orunmila save us because,
It is the big river that contains a big fish.

When it appears at divination, the person will be advised to make a similar sacrifice while kneeling down for Ifa. After adding the relevant iyerosun, the person will go and bathe with the water, and all his problems will abate.

He Made Divination for Chief Elemure When Esu Blocked His Fortunes

Ki a so oko akara lu esu. He made divination for Chief Elemure when Esu dammed the flow of his fortunes. He was advised to make sacrifice so that Esu might remove the dam and allow prosperity to reach him. He made sacrifice with akara or bean buns. When he presented the sacrifice in the morning, Esu rejected it. He represented it at noon and Esu still refused to budge. Later in the evening Orunmila intervened with a passionate appeal to Esu. As soon as Esu got up to receive the sacrifice, the fortune of chief Elemure on which he had been sitting, moved into his house. At divination, the person should make a similar sacrifice.

Chapter 2

OSA-OYEKU

He Made Divination for Orisa-Nla When Coming to the World

Osa yeku yeku o kpa erin sinu'gbo.
Osa yeku yeku o kpa efon si eluju odan.
Oni ohun ki i sa yeku yeku te un shere o.
Adafa fun Orisa-Nla Oshereigbo ni ojo ti oun ti'ko le
orun bo wa si'ole aiye. Ebo uyi ni won ni ki Orisa-Nla ru o.

He ran swiftly and shot to kill an elephant in the forest.
He ran swiftly and killed a buffalo in the grass-land.
But no one runs swiftly for the fun of it.

These were the Ifa priests who made divination for God's own representative, when he was leaving heaven for the earth. He was advised to make sacrifice in order to command universal and eternal honor and respect in the world. He was required to make sacrifice with a sheep, four pigeons, eight snails, and white cloth. He made the sacrifice which earned him everlasting sovereignty over the earth.

When it appears at divination, the person should be advised to make sacrifice in order to prosper in life. He should however refrain from drinking. He should fence his house round to avert the risk of luring robbers to share their loot in his compound. He should warn members of his household not to venture out at night to obviate the danger of coming in contact with night marauders.

He Made Divination for a Man Who Was Having Diarrhea

Osa oyeku efunfun lele bale gbale oja toun toun.
Adifa fun Ashumi Agbale ti yi o ri ere ole je.

The wind which swept the grounds of the market clean, was the name of the Awo who made divination for the man who was having frequent stool in the night. When he developed diarrhea, he went for divination when he became so dehydrated that he thought he was going to die. He was reassured after divination that far from taking his life, the sickness was going to bring him a windfall, provided he made sacrifice with a basket of beans. In spite of the fact that he made the sacrifice, the diarrhea did not stop because he continued to move his bowels.

At nightfall, he was still going to the toilet frequently. Meanwhile, some thieves had gone on a robbery expedition and brought their loot to the back of his house for sharing among themselves. When he subsequently came out of his house to go to the latrine, his emergence startled the robbers and they escaped in fright abandoning all the goods they had stolen. He immediately removed them into his house which made him become wealthy because the thieves were meanwhile, apprehended and executed.

When this odu appears at divination, if it is ayeo, it which case it forebodes danger, the person should be advised not to go out in the night to prevent the danger of being killed by armed robbers. If it comes out as Ure, which foretells goods tidings, he will be told that he is going to have a stomach upset which will become a blessing in disguise.

The Divination Made for the Hunter Who Saved His Father From Witches

Osa yeku yeku okpa erin si nu'gbo.
Osa yeku yeku okpa efon si eluju odan.
Odifa fun ode nijo to ma gba babare lowo awon iyami osoronga.

Those were the Awos who made divination for the hunter who delivered his father from the wrath of the club of witchcraft. He was told to serve Esu with a he-goat and he did it. The following morning he left for the forest where he shot and killed an elephant, a buffalo, and a lion. While the animals were still bleeding, he ran home to call for help to butcher and carry the meat home. He met his father playing the Ayo game and told him about the three games he shot in the forest.

Meanwhile, the Elders of the Night trooped to his father's house to eliminate him. When he saw that the witches were poised to attack his father, he intervened and took aim warning them to desist from their morbid intentions because having succeeded on that day in killing a lion, buffalo and an elephant, the witches would be easy targets for him if they provoked him into combat.

The leader of the witches' delegation called Ifayemi pleaded for an armistice after seeing the bellicose mood of the son of their proposed vicitim. They offered to come to terms with him, by telling him to advise his father to feast them. When he promised to feast them out out of the meat of the three animals he had killed in the forest, they agreed to relent and asked for a goat, eggs and crushed yam, which they were instantly given.

Thereafter, they initiated the son into their club and he became one of them. That was how he helped to save his father's life.

When it appears at Ugbodu, the person should be advised to make sacrifice to the Elders of the Night after serving Ifa with a goat, adding the meats of elephant, buffalo and lion, including crushed yam and eggs. At ordinary divination, the person should serve Esu with a he-goat, the night with rabbit, and Ogun with cock and tortoise.

He Made Divination for the Oloja of Ado and a Lunatic

Osa yekutu yekete lo'ndifa fun Oloja ule ado, abufun asi iwere.

He made divination for the Head chief of the town of Ado who was told to make sacrifice in order to live and occupy his throne up to a ripe old age. He also divined for the lunatic to make sacrifice in order to get well. The Oloja was told to serve; God, the Night, and Esu with a he-goat. He was also advised to change his habit of praying for his kingdom without praying for himself. He was told to pray first for himself before praying for the state. On his part, the mad man was told to serve Esu with a he-goat. Neither the Oloja nor the lunatic made the prescribed sacrifices.

The following morning, the nutcase prayed to God to let him see the feces discharged by the python (Iyin esumare in Yoruba and isan Oghi'kpin in Bini). When God heard his prayers, he wondered why the lunatic prayed for something that was bound to be useless to him instead of praying to get well. On his part, the Oloja prayed for the peace and prosperity of his subjects and not for himself.

Not long afterwards, the Oloja died and another one was appointed in his place. When this odu appears at divination, the person should be told that he cares more for others than for himself. He should make sacrifice in order to live and prosper to a ripe old age. He should also be told that he has a madman in his family, who should also make sacrifice to get well.

Orunmila's Care for His Children

Orunmila said that he heard the sound of a rat running up and down in the bush, but insisted that before looking for it, he would save his own children first. He also said that he saw the fish swimming back and forth in the river, but decided to give salvation to his children before looking for it. He also heard the goat crying that the house was full, but that before listening to the tidings of the goat, he would save his own son first. That was when Orunmila's son was sick and dying.

Orunmila subsequently went to heaven to appeal to God, Esu, and the divinity of Death to spare the life of his son. Eventually the sobriquet of Akpe ojo iku da (one who can alter the appointed date of death) was given to Orunmila, because of the length he went to save the life of his son who was already slated to die.

When this odu appears at divination the person should be told that death is hard on his trail and that he should make sacrifice hurriedly with fish, rat and goat. The person should also use eko, akara, and a chicken to promise a he-goat to Esu if he survives the wrath of death.

He Made Divination for Jogbo, the Hunter

Osa yereku - okpa erin si'nu igbo.
Osa yereku - okpa efon si odan.
Enia sheku yi wo igbo.
Egigun asheku jade
Ta ni ko mo wi kpe enia asheku ti o yi wo.
Igbo ni o gbe egigun asheku jade.

They made divination for Jogbo before he left for hunting in the forest. He was advised to make sacrifice in order to return safely from the expedition. He was required to make sacrifice with a big he-goat, and 200 bags of money (igba-oke-owo). Without performing the sacrifice, he left for hunting, promising to do it on his return from the forest.

When he got to the forest, he saw an elephant and shot it. Although the bullet hit the elephant, nonetheless before feeling its toxic effect, the elephant turned round and pursued Jogbo, and trampled him to death. The elephant subsequently also fell down and died.

After waiting in vain for Jogbo to return from the forest, his family became worried and were arranging for a search party to look for him. Meanwhile, his friend Ilu volunteered to go in search of him. On getting to the forest, Ilu found the corpse of Jogbo and the elephant he shot.

He came home to report that Jogbo had killed an elephant in the forest, but that in turn, the elephant also killed him. When this odu appears at divination, the person should be advised to make sacrifice before embarking on a journey he is contemplating, in order to return home safely.

Special Sacrifice for Prosperity

Orunmila ni osa yereku. Moni o rin yereku.
Oni egigun ashe kude. Oni ojo ti o nwo ile alara
oni ojo na ni alara di eni nla.
Oni egigun ashe kude. Oni ojo ti o wo ajero ni ajero
di eni nla.
Oni ojo o wo ile Orongun ile-ila ni o di eni nla.
Oni ojo o wo ile loja-loja, ti o si wo ile loba-loba.
Ojo na ni gbogbo won si di eni nla.
Oni ojo ti o wo ile akakpo, meji awise ni akakpo di eni nla.

Orunmila is saying that a person becomes wealthy when prosperity moves into his or her house, because; Alara, Ajero, Orongun-Illa, other Obas and head chiefs and his adherents, became rich on the day that prosperity moved to their respective home.

He presribed that sacrifice should be made with eight pigeons, white bean pudding or ekuru fifun, banana, ewe-aje, ewe-ego and black soap. The sacrifice is prepared by grinding the leaves with the blood of two of the pigeons and the other materials and mixing them with the black soap. After adding the divination powder of this odu (iyerosun) the person will be using the soap to bath all from time to time while rearing the remaining pigeons in the house. The pigeons will use their wings to fly prosperity into the house.

When the Ifa appears at divination, the person will be told that prosperity is poised to move into his house, provided he makes the above-mentioned sacrifice.

Chapter **3**

OSA-IWORI
OSA-AWURE
OSA-OLAWURE

He Made Divination for the River When Coming to Earth

Abudi, babalawo omi, odifa fun omi nijo ti ounti kole
orun bo wa si'kole aiye.

Cut and heal up, was the name of Ifa priest who made divination for the river when he was coming to the world. He was advised to make sacrifice so that no one will ever be able to discover the secret of his source and origin, to avoid being in want, and to have honor and dignity. He made all the sacrifices.

That is why, the secret of the river is not known to anyone. He has so many children who are never lacking in food and sustenance.

When it appears at divination, the person will be told to make sacrifice with he-goat to Esu including all edible foodstuffs, in order to gain universal honor and respect, and so that the myth surrounding him remains a mystery.

He Made Divination for the Dog and the Ewe (Sheep)

Ki ato Kete si eti omi, ki ato kisi si be be le re.
Adifa fun aja abufun agutan.

Jump by the side of the river, and stand at the river's head, were the names of the two Awos who made divination for the dog and the sheep (ewe) when they were going to the river for waterbail fishing. They were told to make sacrifice with a he-goat and a cock. They made the sacrifice.

On getting to the river, they isolated a portion of it and began to bail out the water in order to remove the fishes. Meanwhile, the dog saw a tiger on top of a tree by the side of the river and he began to shout to draw the attention of the sheep by yelling wo! wo! wo!, that is, Look! look! look!. As soon as they both saw the tiger, they quietly sneaked away.

At divination, the person should be advised to make sacrifice in order to survive a sudden confrontation with death.

He Made Divination for the Dog and the He-goat

Osa ya, Iwori ya, made divination for two friends, the dog and the he-goat. He advised them to make sacrifice in order to succeed in a common venture without losing their lives. They were required to make sacrifice with broken calabash, dried granulated pepper and cock. It was only the he-goat that made the sacrifice. The dog preferred to rely on his agility and alacrity for surviving any calamity.

One day, as the dog was strolling in search of food, he came across a river, where he saw many fishes moving up and down. After the discovery, the dog ran home to inform his friend, the he-goat, that he had found an eternal source of food. Unknown to them, the river belonged to the tiger.

The following day, they went with bowls of calabash to begin water-bail fishing. Not long afterwards, they heard the unmistakable growl of the tiger. When they looked up, they saw the tiger gloating contemptuously at them. The dog however suggested that they should mind their business while ignoring the tiger to mind his own, because of the aphorism that it is the one who minds his business that succeeds in any combat. On his part, the he-goat retorted that it was not enough to concentrate on their fishing business because it is the use of one's brain that gives rise to success. While the two friends were still arguing between themselves, Esu went under the water to snatch the bowls of calabash from the he-goat's hand flinging it farther away from him. As the he-goat swam to retrieve the bowl, Esu threw it to the other end of the embankment. That provided the he-goat an opportunity to escape from the scene.

When the tiger saw that the he-goat had escaped to safety, he pounced on the dog to devour him. When the he-goat got home, he went to thank the Ifa priest for the pleasant manifestation of the sacrifice he made for him. However, the Ifa priest told him that there was yet another hurdle to scale, which required a second sacrifice, involving serving his head with a kolanut each consecutive day over a six day period.

On getting home, he bought a kolanut and proceeded to serve his head with it, while praying as follows:

Iwo ori mi, e kun mefa ni won ni ki
Emi fi bo ori mi. Sugbon eyo kon so so
Ti mo ti ri niyi.
Jowo jeki mi ri marun ti o ku.

Meaning

My head, I was told to serve you with six
kolanuts (which he mistakenly called Ekun,

meaning tigers). But I have so far seen only
one. Please let me find the remaining five
to serve you with.

Unknown to the he-goat, the tiger had taken a vantage position at the back of his house from which to launch an attack. When the tiger therefore overheard the prayers of the he-goat to his head to serve it with one tiger while looking to find the remaining five, the tiger thought that the he-goat was referring to him as the sacrifical victim for serving his head. Since he did not know the strategy of the he-goat, he decided to escape to prevent the he-goat from using him to serve his head.

Thereafter, Esu used his wand of authority to command the tiger never to hunt for the he-goat, while proclaiming that the day the tiger prepares to kill the he-goat, he (the tiger) shall die on that day. That is why to this day, the tiger does not dare the he-goat.

When it appears at divination, the person will be advised to make sacrifice with a cock to Esu and to serve his head with six kolanuts in order to survive the death awaiting him in a venture to which a friend will invite him.

He Made Divination for the Gorilla

Osa ge ge ge. Iwori ge ge ge - made divination for Elegbede (the gorilla) advising him to make sacrifice to avert the danger of losing a soul to Ogun. He was told to serve Esu with a he-goat, and to serve Ogun with a dog and a cock. He did not make the sacrifice.

The following morning Alazi, the head of the gorillas took out members of his family for a promenade. After touring the forest for some time, he came across a tree with a hole in it and he held on to it and began to make jest of the Ifa priest by drumming:

Ora ge-ge-ge. Iwori ge-ge-ge
Ere mi ke mi - Ere mi ke mi.

He was thus boasting that in spite of the predictions of the Ifa priest, he could not imagine any danger to worry about. Meanwhile, the hunter's wife had just delivered a baby and he went into the forest in search of meat with which to feed his family.

As soon as he entered the forest, Esu directed the hunter to a portion of the forest where he over-heard the familiar drumming of the gorillas. When the hunter trailed the direction from which the apes' sound was coming, he saw the entire herd dancing to the drumbeat of their leader, the Alazi. The hunter took aim at one of them and pulled the trigger. The giant ape fell to the ground, dead while the others ran away. When they got to base, the Alazi took stock and discovered that one of them was missing. That was when he remembered the words of the diviner. He later made the sacrifice.

When this odu appears at divination, the person should be told to serve Ogun in order to avoid losing a member of his family to an accident.

The Divination Made for Him Before Leaving Heaven

Uroke mi lawo li gonrin. Oroke mi la awo le'turuye,
awon lo'ndifa fun Orunmila nijo ti o ounti kole orun bo
wa si kole aiye.

Those were the Awos who made divination for this Odu, when he was coming to the world. He was advised to make sacrifice to forestall the risk of destroying himself on earth. He was required to serve Esu with a he-goat, Ogun with a cock and a tortoise, his guardian angel with a guinea-fowl, and Osanyin (Osun) with a dog. He left for earth after making all the sacrifices. He was warned not to get involved in any association or meeting while on earth.

He turned out to be a highly proficient priest on earth. Whatever he predicted came to pass. He did so well that the other divine priests proposed to him that he was to be their leader in an association of all divine priests, and the venue of the meetings was to be his house. He was flattered by the proposal and he readily acquiesed to it. Unknown to him, the establishment of the association was the strategy of his enemies for emasculating him. His enemies were the other divine priests who were not as effective as himself and who were envious of his unparalleled competence.

He had two wives. Since the enemies realised that the easiest way of destablizing a powerful man is by dishonoring his marriage, they began to seduce his wives. Meanwhile, he had a dream in which his guardian angel admonished him for doing what he was advised not to do before leaving heaven, - getting involved in an association of his rivals. The following morning, he made divination and Ifa told him to prepare a feast of eating and drinking for all the members of his association after giving a he-goat to Esu. After preparing the food and drinks, he was to use granulated sass-wood (Obo in Yoruba and Iyin in Bini) as the divination powder of the feast. He accordingly prepared the feast.

After eating to their heart's content, they began to drink in earnest. Soon afterwards, the divination powder began to take its toll on those who had offended him by profaning his masculine dignity. An Ogun priest was the first to start confessing openly. He disclosed sarcastically that Orunmila no longer had any wife because his two wives used to visit him regularly for love making. The Osanyin (Osun) priest was the next to confirm that he too was sleeping with his wives regularly. He also enumerated the names of the members of the association who conspired to unsettle him by alluring his wives into becoming unfaithful to him. One after the other all his enemies confessed their stratagem for destabilizing him. Thereafter they all fell asleep.

As soon as they all woke up from their delirium, he announced his withdrawal from the association after using the appropriate incantation to curse all those who conspired to destabilize him. That marked the end of the association.

When this Ifa appears at Ugbodu, the person should be advised not to join any meeting to avoid exposing his wife to the risk of infidelity. He should however make the necessary sacrifices. He should refrain from becoming pompous on account of his wealth, because he will prosper immensely. Sacrifices are to be made with a he-goat to Esu; a guinea fowl and sixteen snails and gorilla meat to Ifa; cock to Sango; tortoise to Ogun; dog to Osanyin (Osun); and rabbit and three eggs to the Elders of the Night.

The Divination He Made When He Was Travelling to an Unknown Destination

*Osa wo, Iwori wo odifa fun Orunmila baba shawo losi ilu
Aima. Ani ki ofi okete kpelu ewu orunre ru ebo nitori uyi
ati gbogbo ire. Oru ebo na, ofi agrikpa obuko bo esu, ofi
ewure bo ori re.*

When he made divination before traveling to an unknown destination, he was advised to make sacrifice with a rabbit not to get involved in someone else's problem. He was also required to serve his head with a goat. He made all the sacrifices before setting out for the journey.

When he got to the place, his first client was a fairly elderly barren woman who was still hoping to have a child. After divination he told the woman that although she had reached menopause, she had a slightly better than ever chance of having a child if she was able to make sacrifice with the meat of bush pig, ewe ekunkun leaves (ebe ebo in Bini) guinea-fowl and the leaves of sogun-osegen. She lost no time in producing them and Orunmila used them to prepare Ifa soup for her to eat. At the end of the following month, she observed changes in her breast and body.

When it subsequently became obvious that she was pregnant, her husband could not believe it because all previous divinations had declared her to be permanently barren, and incapable of producing a child. He was so overwhelmed with joy that he began to wonder how to show his appreciation to the Awo who made it possible. Eventually, he made a gorgeous dress for Orunmila in addition to a parcel of fish because he was a fisherman. The woman gave birth to a female child who was forbidden to eat electric fish.

The husband went to announce the miracle to the Oba, who was happy to know that such an Awo existed because the wives in his own harem had no children. Try as he did, the Oba's wives did not become pregnant and he subsequently returned home.

On his way home, he noticed that his canoe was leaking. When he examined it carefully, he discovered that the leakage was caused by a giant electric fish. He dived into the water and killed it. On getting home, he used the fish to serve his Osun.

When this Ifa appears at Ugbodu, the person will settle near a sea or river, where he will prepare one Osun to be serving, with electric fish. He should also serve his head with a cock and serve the Ifa with a big bat to avoid vomiting what he has eaten because he will be an Ifa priest.

At divination, the person will be advised to serve Esu with a he-goat in order to gain advancement in his work, and to avoid any problems involving women.

He Divined for Two Babalawos

Ikun awo loju ido, Ifa lawo ewi la'do. - Were two Ifa priests who operated together in partnership. When they met Osa-Olawure, he told them to make sacrifice with a he-goat and a club to avoid being clubbed to death. They did not make the sacrifice.

Meanwhile, there was no rain in the town of Ilu-Ido. Ikun was invited to procure rain, and he did it so successfully that it rained non-stop for three days. Ikun was rewarded with two rams, two he-goats and various precious gifts including money. Nonetheless, he still did not consider it necessary to make the sacrifice he was told to do. When it was time for him to return home, Esu transfigured into a rabble-rouser and incited some local thugs to mug him, seize his gifts and club him to death.

When his friend Ifalawo heard of the death of Igun, he remembered the prediction for which they were advised at divination to make preemptive sacrifice. He quickly went to make his own sacrifice. On hearing about Igun's death, the Ewi of Ado sent a six man vigil to watch over the grave to prevent his killers from exhuming it. The Oba of Ilu-Ido also sent six representatives for the same purpose. The two delegations remained at the three road-junction cemetery until it developed into a full blown town which became known as Ifaki (or Ilu-Ifaki) to mark where an Ifa priest was murdered.

When it appears at divination, the person will be advised to beware of getting involved in any partnership business with any friend or indeed, anyone. He should also make sacrifice to forestall the danger of becoming the victim of an armed robbery attack, which could cost him his life.

He Made Divination for the Man Whose Fortune Was Not Consolidated

Iwori Lere moni jijo lojo. Oni ki nlo fi ma'jo?
Moni eku, eja ati eyele meji, ati abo adiye meji, ati
agba merindilogun, ati ekpo, ati obi. Eyi ni aofi ru ebo
kii oro eni ko ni akojo.

He made divination for the man whose life was undulating between opulence and penury. The pendulum of his life was oscillating between two extremes of satisfaction and destitution, because his fortunes were not consolidated. That was why he went for divination at which he was told to make sacrifice with rat, fish, two pigeons, two hens and eight or sixteen bags of money. He made the sacrifice and his life became more stable.

Chapter 4

OSA-IDI

He Made Divination for the Grass-Hopper

She she murele. Odifa fun Lamu foto, nigbo ti on lo si oko aloro odun. No one goes on a journey without returning home, was the name of the Awo who made divination for the grass hopper when he was going to the farm at the beginning of the farming year, after his enemies had threatened that he would not return home alive. He was advised to make sacrifice with a cock and a pigeon. He did the sacrifice after which he left for the farm.

He did so well in the farm that year that he recorded a bumper harvest and returned home alive with his gains from the farm. When this odu appears at divination, the person should be advised to make sacrifice before travelling anywhere in order to return home alive.

He Divined for Arawo the Mother of the Hawk

Osa di, oru, Oru la agbalagba jo mu lele'di, adifa fun
Arawo ti'nshe yeye Asa. Ani ki Asa gba ifa.

Osa and the Night should tie it, because the battle of the waist is fought in the night. That was the name of the Awo who made divination for Arawo, the mother of the hawk when the fortunes of the hawk were flagging. The hawk was advised to have his own Ifa and he did so. Thereafter, his life became prosperous again. After taking his Ifa, the Awo told him to make another sacrifice with a pigeon and he did it, after which he had no difficulty in feeding himself.

When it appears at divination, the person should be told that his life is not full. If he is to prosper, he should have his own Ifa and serve his head with a pigeon after completing the initiation ceremony.

He Made Divination for the Father of Orofo

Osa di, Orudi, adifa fun baba eye orofo to'nlo fe Tiku
shaya. Won ni ki oru ebo tori omo to'ma bifun Tiku.

He made divination for the father of a bird called Orofo when he was going to marry a wife called Tiku. He was told to make sacrifice on account of a child the woman was going to bear for him. Baba Orofo did not make the sacrifice. The woman Tiku gave birth to Asa (hawk). When the hawk grew up, he began to feed on his elder brothers and sisters who were born before him.

When this odu portends danger at divination, before marriage the man should be advised not to marry the woman because she is a witch who would give birth to a witch who would be destroying the other children born before him or her. When it appears for an invalid, he or she should be told to make sacrifice because his or her sickness was caused by a brother or sister who is a witch.

The Divination He Made Before Leaving Heaven

> *Osa Kandi, Ori kandi, oro mi lere bodi ola. Awon ni won*
> *lo'ndifa fun Orunmila nijo ti outi kole orun bo wa si kole*
> *aiye. Won niki oru ebo nitori obrinrin yio ma kpaa kaiye.*
> *Oru ebo na.*

When he was leaving heaven, he was advised to make sacrifice with a he-goat and spoilt and rotten materials. He made the sacrifice before coming to the world. He became a success story on earth as an Ifa priest. At the height of his popularity, the Olofin invited him for divination when his household was in turmoil.

After making divination he told the Olofin that the problem in his household was being caused by one of his wives who was at that time away to her home town, and that Esu had driven the woman out of his house because she was a destructive witch. As soon as the Olofin heard the revelation, he gave orders for the woman to be bundled back from her home town. When she was brought in she confronted Orunmila who confirmed not only that she was responsible through witchcraft for upsetting the peace and tranquility of her husband's home, but that she had also cohabited with another man in her home town. She denied the charges and vowed to destroy Orunmila for daring to level false accusations against her. Meanwhile, Orunmila served Esu with a he-goat to checkmate the evil intentions of the woman.

Following her denial, the Olofin decided to put her on trial by ordeal at the instance of Esu. She however failed at the trial because in a state of delirum as if possessed, she confessed that she was responsible for all the problems in Olofin's palace and that she left for her home town after foementing the havoc. She also confirmed that without any thought of returning to Ife she had gotten a lover in her home town. After cursing her, the Olofin compelled her under torture to undo the havoc she had done.

When the Olofin refused to take her back as his wife, he used his Ase to proclaim that never again would she be able to have sex with any man. She was expelled from the kingdom of Ife and she subsequently developed piles in her genitals which closed her vagina for good. Olofin gave a handsome reward to Orunmila.

When this odu appears at divination for a man, he should be told that his wife is responsible for his problems, and that the wife in question is not only a witch but also an infidel.

The Divination He Made Before Performing His Annual Festival

When Orunmila was proposing to perform his annual festival, he sounded his okeponrin (Ikin divination) and his own odu appeared as ayeo. He was told to serve Esu with a he-goat and to go to the market to buy the materials by himself. He made the sacrifice but had no time to go to the market by himself to buy the materials required for the festival.

Meanwhile, he sent one of his servants to the market with money to buy the materials. Unknown to Orunmila, Death and his wife, Illness (Aron) had come from heaven in search of food on earth, and they had taken different positions on the main road to the market. When death saw the messenger sent by Orunmila to the market, Orunmila sent a second servant to look for the first one. He too met (Aron) illness on the way. She attacked him in his chest and he suffered a heart attack which killed him right away and left with his corpse for heaven.

When the two men failed to return home, Orunmila sounded Ifa once more, and he was reminded of his earlier injunction to go by himself to the market. He was advised to hold a parcel of kolanuts when going to the market. Before dawn, Death and his wife Aron had again taken positions on the way to the market. Later in the morning, Orunmila left for the market.

As soon as he met Death, Orunmila greeted him familiarly by calling him: eku aro o - uku omo alugbogbo. Death wondered who it was that greeted him with his heavenly name. Orunmila answered that it was his friend, Orunmila. Death returned the greeting with Eku abo eleri ukpin while embracing Orunmila which he does not do traditionally. Asked where he was going, Orunmila presented Death with kolanuts after replying that he came to pay his respects when he was told that he was in town. After spliting the kolanuts, Death ate piece of it while Orunmila continued his journey to the market. Soon afterwards, Orunmila met Aron shivering at a point very close to the market.

Once again Orunmila greeted her with a familiar air by saying: Eku aro o Aron onigbo yeghe. When asked who it was that knew her by her nickname, he replied that it was her friend Orunmila, and that he came to greet her. When she retorted that it was not an auspicious moment for greeting anyone because she was hungry. He again gave her kolanuts and she cleared him to proceed. Orunmila subsequently entered the market and bought all his requirements for the festival.

On his way home from the market, he greeted the husband and wife and each of them proclaimed that from that day, the presentation of kolanuts would save any son or daughter of Orunmila from the cold hands of Death and Illness. It was then that Orunmila appreciated why Ifa advised him to go by himself to the market while surmising that the two servants he sent the previous day must have fallen victims to the two divinities. He was able to perform his festival successfully with a white ram.

When it appears at Ugbodu, the person should make sacrifice with: rotten meat and kolanuts to Death; and rotten yams and kolanuts to Illness on the market road and serve the new Ifa with a white ram.

At ordinary divination, the person will be advised to serve Esu with a he-goat to prevent any disruption to his business.

He Made Divination for Lakola, the Friend of Orisa

Asa-ka-di, arin-da-di ko she fere fere wo inu odi ilu.

That was the Awo who made divination for Lakola when he was befriending Orisa. He was advised to serve Esu with a he-goat to allay the danger of embarrassing a powerful friend that could give rise to an eternal calamity. Since he was hands-in-glove with Orisa, he could not imagine how he could ever embarrass him.

When Esu was told the following morning by Ighoroko that Lakola refused to make the sacrifice prescribed for him, he decided to teach him a lesson. Meanwhile, Orisa invited Lakola to enjoy dinner with him. As they were eating, Esu tickled the alimentary canal of Lakola and he suddenly developed nausea. Before he could do anything about it he began to vomit and the substance he vomitted entered Orisa's food and mouth. Orisa was so annoyed that he proclaimed that from that day, nothing eaten or taken by Lakola would ever settle in his stomach. He would always vomit whatever he ate and drank, and that he would respirate through his mouth while his anus would remain closed. He eventually became a bat.

At divination, the person will be advised to make sacrifice to avert the risk of an embarrassing abdominal upset. If he already has stomach trouble, he will be told to produce shea-butter (ori-oyo) and palm oil to which the Ifa priest will add sand scraped from the door and the iyerosun of this odu, for him to be leaking from time to time and the sickness will abate. The incantation which the Ifa priest will use to prepare the medicine is:

Aikiti enu ya igbe,
Aiko gbodo ti ide kpo.

Special Sacrifice for Producing Children

Orunmila ni osa ga a ra. Moni owo idi.
Oni eyi ti o wo idi eku, ni ofi ni oyun.
Oun ni ofi bi omo
Oni eyi ti owo idi eja, ni ofi ni oyun ti o fi bi omo.
Orunmila ni osa gaara. Moni owo idi.
Oni eyi ti owo idi eye, ni o fi ni oyun ti o fi bi omo.
Oni eyi ti owo idi eronko, ni ofi ni oyun ti o fi bi omo.
Oni eyi ti owo idi omo eni, ni omo eni yio fi she oyun ti o
fi bi omo.

Orunmila said that the spermatozoa that entered the productive organs of female rats, fish, birds, animals, and a woman, fertilized their ova, made them pregnant, and gave birth to their young ones or offsprings.

When he was asked for the requisite sacrifice for productivity, he enumerated them as snails, bat, fish and rat. At divination, the person will be told that his wife is due to become pregnant provided the foregoing sacrifice is made.

Chapter **5**

OSA-OBARA

Divined for the Water Divinity to Become Great

Orunmila oni ka bere bere. Emina ni ka bere bere.
Oni ka bere ni owo omo eku, kini oun fi she won? Woni kosi.
Oni ka bere lowo omo eja, kini oun fi she won? Oni kosi.
Orunmila ni ka bere lowo omo eronko, kini oun fi she won? Oni kosi.
Orunmila ni ka bere lowo omo araye, kini oun fi she won? Oni kosi o
Orunmila oni omi omo 'olokun oun lo di ore re lo lo kan osa,
Oni ebo lo ma ru o, ni tori kpukpo ni eniyan.

When Orunmila was having problems, he enquired to know what he did to offend the rat, fish, animals and mankind. That was the poem with which Orunmila made divination for the water divinity when he was going to make the sea and the lagoon great. He was told to make sacrifice with he-goat to Esu. After making the sacrifice, Esu proceeded to make all the smaller rivers to be paying homage to the sea (Okun) and the lagoon (Osa).

When the odu appears at divination, the person will be told to make sacrifice in order to prosper in life.

He Made Divination for Fire When his Life Was Ebbing

Osa bala bala, babalawo una, odifa fun una nijo ti aye relo
si ale, ti ko dara mo.

He made divination for Fire when his fortunes were ebbing. He was told to make sacrifice with dried palm leaves. He did the sacrifice and his life was rekindled. At divination, the person will be told that his/her life is weak. He/she should make sacrifice to become rejuvenated.

He Divined for 76 Different Animals

Osa kpaa, Obara kpaa, made divination for seventy-six animals when they went up the hill to play. They were advised to make sacrifice. They all refused, with the exception of the horse who made the sacrifice with a he-goat and his wearing apparel.

When the animals were moving up to the top of the hill, Esu made the trip so enervating that none of them succeeded in reaching the top of the hill, let alone taking advantage of the goodies which God had provided on the hill top. When it was the turn of the horse to move up the hill, Esu assisted him in obtaining the speed and vigor to get to its top, where he alone collected all the good things lined out there.

As the horse was rejoicing, the cow (Elila) and the other animals regreted their failure to make sacrifice. That is why mankind is more at home with the horse than his brothers, the ox and the buffalo.

Special Sacrifice For The Birth of Twins

Aja lafi sisara koja ule. Agaban lofi ogban wiwo she oran.
Adifa fun okomuba bi aji wo le to mi wa.
The day ran with so much speed that it ran beyond its house.
The sheep solved its problems by overlooking the house.

These were the awos who made divination for the expectant mother who looked forward to giving birth to one child but delivered a pair of twins. She was told to make sacrifice with a brown cock to Sankpana, because Sankpana and Sango are the patron divinities of twins. If it appears for a pregnant woman, she will be advised to make sacirifce in anticipation of a twin birth.

They Also Made Divination for Orunmila to Receive Two Favors

Aja lofi sisa ra koja ule. Agutan lofi ogban wimo she oran.
Adifa fun Orunmila ti y o ri ifaa meji je ni ogbegbe ile re.
Eyele lofi ru ebo

They made divination for Orunmila when he was going to obtain two benefits near his house. He was told to make sacrifice with a pigeon.

At divination as Ure, the person should be told to make sacrifice in order to receive two favors at the same time.

He Made Divination for a Man With a Deformed Leg

Osa ti Onsa ni kponkpo. Ebara ni o sa ture, ni bere ono.
Odifa fun omo atira to ni oun yio ba ile aduje.
Osa ran on the straight road. Ebara ran by the side of the road.

They made divination for the man with a deformed leg who vowed to destroy Orunmila's house. However, Orunmila told him that, he was joking. After failing to make sacrifice, he also failed to heed the advice not to carry out his threat. He was throughly disgraced and deflated after trying and failing.

When it appears at divination, the person will be told to make sacrifice to prevent a person with a deformed leg from damaging his house and to avert problems sourcing from a curse in his previous incarnation. The sacrifice is made with a cock and a hen.

Special Sacrifice for Peace and Prosperity

Osa bere, Orunmila ni Osa emi ni ni oba.
Ikari bi o oba si emi ni oba leri eguogun.
Orunmila ni a ti ba ri're Oba leri uroko.
Karibi ti oba si emi ni oba leri uroko.
Orunmila ni e ti ba rire o. Orunmila lo'ri onsa.
Emi ni o baa. Orunmila ni ki a ri bi oba si.

In answer to my question, Orunmila declared that he stood on the oak tree. I put the question a second time and he replied that he stood on the iroko tree. But Ifa told him that he was not standing properly. When I put the question a third time, he replied that he stood on the Ejire tree. To a fourth question he replied that he stood on the Osan agbalumo (otien) tree, the leaves, bark and fruits of that tree generate prosperity. He went on to declare that pigeons are used to make sacrifice for money; guinea-fowl is used to make sacrifice for victory over enemies, and he-goat is used to make sacrifice to solve problems, while a goat is used to make sacrifice for prosperity.

The Sacrifice He Made Before Leaving Heaven

Osa bara bara ba, agbara okoro, Ogbiye lo'gun Okara la'lade
Orun Ogbiye ni otito okoro.

Ogun, Osanyin and Orunmila, left heaven for earth at the same time. Before leaving, they were advised at divination to serve their heads with a cock, their guardian angel with a hen; Orisa with a pigeon; and Esu with a he-goat in order to succeed on earth. Orunmila was the only one who made the sacrifice.

On getting to the earth, they were invited to assist in solving a problem that had defied the capabilities of the awos of the known world of the time. Olofin's wife had been in labor for seven days and she was very close to death. Ogun and Osanyin, looking as impressionistic as ever, were invited to help the woman to deliver. Try as they did, the woman became even weaker. Orunmila did not look as impressive because he never interacted with anyone. He was known for putting on his loin cloth and sitting in front of the house every morning. After Ogun and Osanyin had tried and failed, the chiefs of Ifa sent a delegation to invite Orunmila to the palace.

Before leaving home with the errandmen, he consulted Ifa after which he directed them to tell the woman that she had cohabited with three men and that she would deliver only after confessing the acts. When they got home to the palace, they told the woman what Orunmila said, and the woman made a clean breast of the matter. By the time she mentioned the name of the third man with whom she had an affair, she delivered safely. Orunmila was given a rousing applause, and a standing ovation. He received gifts from all and sundry.

Thereafter, there was an influx of callers on Orunmila for divination. He realised a lot of money in the process. In the wake of his prosperity, he got married and began to have children. Ogun and Osanyin continued to wander from one place to another without any success. People who sympathised with Ogun and Osanyin subsequently went to enquire from Orunmila why his two brothers were not doing well. He retorted by declaring that success would continue to elude them until they returned home to make the sacrifice prescribed before leaving heaven.

Ogun and Osanyin eventually returned to heaven to make the sacrifices. When they returned to earth, they began to divine by possession and all the work they did began to succeed so much that they became prosperous.

His Experience on Earth - When He Seduced Sokoti's Wife

Orunmila subsequently took to farming at the instance of his guardian angel in addition to his Ifa practice. One woman was always coming to buy vegetables from him. Unknown to him, the woman used to come from heaven and she was the wife of Sokoti, the famous blacksmith.

One day, Orunmila begged the woman to buy him a hoe from wherever she came. She subsequently brought a hoe from heaven which she sold to Orunmila at the price of one bag of money. He paid her for it in kind, with yams. The woman sold the yams on getting to heaven but failed to give the money to her husband. When he asked her for the money realised from the sale of his hoe, she lied that the buyer had not paid her. After demanding the money after four subsequent visits to the earth, her husband became annoyed and decided to go by himself to draw the debt. She however succeeded in dissuading him from following her.

On his part, Orunmila had developed a fancy for the woman. After one visit to her farm, he offered to follow her home, but she refused bluntly on the ground that her husband was too strong for him to challenge. When she was returning home, he decided to trail her. He followed her up to the bank of Odo-Aro (the black river). After the woman had crossed to the other side, he discovered that he could not cross it. He subsequently returned home for divination at which he was told to serve his head with a cock and Esu with a he-goat and to back the river because it was forbidden to approach it frontally.

During the woman's subsequent visit, he trailed her once more and succeeded in crossing the Aro river. When the woman got to a second river called Odo-eke, or the blood river, she crossed it but not knowing the pass-word he had to return home once more for yet another divination. This time around, he was told to give another he-goat to Esu, serve Ogun with a dog, and to touch his palms with the water from the river in order to cross it.

When the woman next visited his farm, he was able to trail her successfully to her marital home in heaven. On seeing a stranger with his wife, Sokoti asked her about his mission and she replied that although she had no idea that the man was following her, he nonetheless was the man who bought the hoe without paying her. Sokoti then turned to Osa-Obara to ask him why he followed his wife to his house. He replied that in addition to coming to confirm that he had previously paid for the hoe in kind with yams, he added that he had fallen in love with the woman because she never told him that she was married.

Without putting up any resistance, Sokoti asked his wife whether she was willing to leave him to marry the man. She replied that although she had remained faithful to her husband right up to that point in time, she was ready to go with the man if he (her husband) had no objections.

Sokoti there and then cleared his own wife to return to earth with the man to become his wife.

When this Ifa appears at Ugbodu, the person will be advised to be cautious in matters affecting women. He should serve Esu with he-goat, Ogun with dog, and his head with a cock. At divination the person should serve his head with a cock and Esu with a he-goat to avert a fight over a woman.

The Divination He Made Before Going to Oshogbo

Osa kpa, Obara kpa, Ogunfun kani, Ojibamu, bamu babara, was the awo who made divination for Orunmila when he was traveling for Ifa practice to the town of Oshogbo. He was advised to make sacrifice to avert the risk of ingratitude. He did not make the sacrifice.

He got to Oshogbo where he found that the people had been afflicted by all kinds of diseases. On getting to the farm, he was taken to the Oba who asked him whether he could do anything to cure the town of the afflictions besetting the people. He promised to do his best. Within a very short time, he was able to make all the people well, but in spite of the fact that he remained in Oshogbo for three years, he did not receive any of the compensation promised to him.

When he was about to leave the town he went round to demand the compensation promised to him, but nobody responded favorably. He therefore decided to leave the town in anger. Before leaving however, he sounded Ifa who told him that his shabby treatment was the prize he had to pay for failing to give a he-goat to Esu before leaving home. Rather belatedly, he gave the he-goat to Esu. Thereafter, Esu invited Sankpana and Songo to visit Orunmila. When he told them of the ingratitude shown to him by the people of Oshogbo, the two became annoyed, and decided to intervene to bring the ingrates to their knees.

On getting to Oshogbo, Sankpana threw about his corn indiscriminately, and people in their thousands were afflicted by small pox. Sango made the Oba and all the chiefs to suffer from all kinds of cardiac diseases and attacks. At a subsequent divination, they were told that they were being punished for the ingratitude with which they reacted to the magnanimity of Orunmila. Orunmila was having a brief stop-over in the nearby town Ikirun while Sankpana and Songo were ravaging the town of Oshogbo. Meanwhile, the Oba, chiefs and elders of Oshogbo dispatched a high-powered delegation to meet Orunmila to apologise to him. On meeting him, members of the delegation went on their knees to apologize and persuade Orunmila to return to Oshogbo. He subsequently agreed to return with them.

On getting back to Oshogbo, he asked for a he-goat to serve Esu, a goat and fried corn to gratify Sankpana and a ram, bitter kola and yam flour pudding (Amala) to appeased Songo. After making the sacrifices, the people became well again. Although they besought Orunmila to remain for good with them, he refused on the ground that their ingratitude would have been final but for the timely intervention of Esu and his colleagues. He finally left Oshogbo to settle down at Ikirun. On their parts, Sankpana and Songo were successfully persuaded to remain in the town of Oshogbo.

That explains why to this day, the shrines of Songo and Sankpana are a common feature at

Oshogbo, while Ifa shrine (Okpe-Ikin) are few and far between. The presence of Ifa in Oshogbo is limited to the three-dimensional shrines (Ikin-loju-meta). Whoever is desirous of having the traditional four-dimensioned-Ifa (Ikin-loju-merin) has to go to the nearby Ikirun town.

When this odu appears at divination, the person will be told that he is about to show ingratitude to a benefactor and that unless he or she makes amends, he or she runs the risk of losing the benefit bestowed on him.

Chapter 6

OSA-OKONRON
OSA-KUNRIN

He Made Divination to Save the Guinea-Fowl from the Tiger

*Osa Kanranranranran Okonron Kanron, Babalawo ago. Odifa
fun ago ti o tori tomo dafa.*

He made divination for the guinea-fowl when she was concerned over the security of herself and her children, at the time when the tiger pretended to be her relation. As soon as the guinea-fowl hatched her young ones, the tiger went to her to feign a blood relationship with her as a pretext for getting close enough to feed her children. When the guinea fowl retorted that her parents did not give her any intimation of a blood connection with the tiger, the latter disarmed her by drawing attention to the semblance in their color schemes. After being effectively conciliated, the guinea-fowl allowed the tiger free access to her roost. Meanwhile, the tiger used the opportunity to capture one of the guinea-fowl's children for food any time she was away from home.

Realizing the dilemma into which she had been cornered, she went to Orunmila for divination, where she was advised to make sacrifice with fallen leaves and charcoal. She quickly made the sacrifice. Thereafter, on the next occasion in which the tiger came on his nefarious mission, as he moved to strike, Esu covered up the children of the guinea fowl with leaves while startling them into flying to the top of a nearby tree. From the safety of the tree-top, the guinea-fowl shouted "Moti she bo Osa kanranranranran, Okonron Kanran" which has remained her call-cry ever since.

When this odu appears at divination, the person will be warned that a strong person will emerge to profess blood relationship with him or her. He/She should make sacrifice to forestall the danger of the person using the leverage to attack him/her or the children.

Another Variation of the Same Divination

Osa kooonron, Okonron-konron was the Awo who made divination for the guinea -fowl when she was anxious to have children. She was told that she would have plenty of children, but should make sacrifice to checkmate the problems she was going to have from her relations after having children. She was required to make sacrifice with a he-goat and two types of yams called Shuru or Esuru in Yoruba and Erhuru in Bini and another one called Ulo in Yoruba and Emile in

Bini. After making the sacrifice; she was advised to lay her eggs at a secret spot, and to conceal them from an everyone, no matter how closely connected.

Incidentally, the guinea-fowl had one sister called Okparo and a brother called Okoko. Contrary to the advice given to her not to reveal her egg-laying secrets to anyone, the guinea-fowl out of excitement, disclosed to Okparo that she laid thirty eggs, which information immediately evoked the sister's envy, because she (Okparo) only laid three eggs. As soon as Okparo left her, she went right away to inform the egg-eating Okoko (Areken in Bini) that the guinea-fowl had prepared a prolific feast for him by laying thirty eggs. Thereafter, Okoko began to pick the guinea-fowl's eggs one after the other. When she discovered the rate at which her eggs were being stolen, she went to Orunmila who reminded her of the injunction given to her at divination not to reveal the secrets of her eggs to anyone especially to her relations. Orunmila told her that she was responsible for her own undoing because it was her relations who were responsible for her problems.

Eventually, the guinea-fowl went into the forest to lay her eggs in the cave without telling anyone about them, after which she began to hatch all the eggs she laid. She came to have many children.

When this Ifa appears at Ugbodu, the person will be advised to serve Esu with he-goat, and his head with guinea-fowl to avert the danger of his children being bewitched by his relations. When it appears at divination, the person should serve his/her head with guinea-fowl, and Ogun with cock to neutralize any danger from close relatives.

Yet Another Variation of the Same Revelation

The same awo made divination for Aworogbo when she had three friends called Ekun, Amo and Ologbo. Aworogbo regarded her three friends as true and faithful, but unknown to her, they were responsible for the frequent death of her children. On a subsequent occasion when she became expectant, she went to Orunmila for divination and Osa-konron appeared to advise her. She was advised to make sacrifice with palm kernels, cotton wool and a cock. She made the sacrifice and it was prepared for her to keep beside her whenever she retired in the night to sleep. She was also advised to keep her children in a secret place where no one could have access to them. She did as she was advised.

At about midnight, Ekun (tiger) moved stealthily into Aworogbo's house, but before he could do any damage, the sacrifice incapacitated him and he fell down, dead. Not long afterwards, Amo sneaked in toAworogbo's house, but as soon as he saw the corpse of Ekun, he took to his heels and escaped. Ologbo also ran away in fright as soon as he saw the dead body of Ekun.

At dawn, when Aworogbo saw the corpse of Ekun, it was then she realized the duplicity with which her friends had been dealing with her all along. She suddenly burst into tears as she sang:

Itan ekun, itan osho,
Itan amo, itan osho,
Itan Ologbo, itan osho,
Itan rede rede, itan oso.

That is the cry of Aworogbo to this day.

When it appears at divination, the person will be advised to keep his/her secrets from friends, and not to rely on outward appearances in his/her dealings with people, especially friends. He/she would make sacrifice to prevent friends and relations from damaging his possessions.

He Made Divination for Ikon, The King of Termites

Ikon, the king of termites went to Osa-konron for divination on what to do in order to prosper. He was told to make sacrifice with a guinea-fowl to her guardian angel, and a he-goat to Esu. After making the sacrifice, he came to have more followers than any other king. Far from being allowed to walk on his feet, his subjects preferred to carry him from place to place. When the king of human beings heard about the majestic splendor of Ikon's life-style, he sent for him.

On getting to the human king, he accused Ikon of immitating him by his regal behavior. Ikon retorted that much as he denied any immitation of the king, no one could deny him the right to enjoy his prosperity. After saying that, he challenged the king to two contesting exercises in sovereignty. He told the king to build an apartment with 201 rooms not with water but with sputum. He invited the king to begin the exercise.

The following morning the king made a royal proclaimation inviting his subjects to spit into several calabashes preparatory to using it to build a palace of 201 apartments. The entire citizenry of the kingdom could not fill one calabash with their sputum. After conceding his inability to continue that first contest, the king invited Ikon to take up the challenge.

Within a space of a few days, the subjects of Ikon had built a multi-storied building containing 201 apartments completely adorned, furnished and decorated. When the king's verifiers saw the massive building, they were astonished.

After that first exercise, Ikon announced that he was about to begin his annual festival and that it was going to last for three months. During the span of the festival he promised to liberate 200 subjects daily never to return to his domain. The king however boasted to be able to match him on that score. Once again, Ikon asked the king to begin the contest. The following morning the king dispatched 200 of subjects into exile never to return to the kingdom. The following day, the king could not assemble another 200 volunteers or conscripts. He therefore admitted his inability to continue with the exercise. It was the turn of Ikon to perform the feat.

The following morning, after releasing 200 termites to fly out he ordered the closure of their gates. He repeated the exercise daily for two months after which the king invited Ikon for another chat. The king conceded that Ikon was by far richer than himself, to which Ikon retorted that in spite of his opulence, he was nonetheless under the soverigity of the king. Eventually, the king confirmed Ikon as the king of the underground. Thereafter, Ikon began to pay annual homage to Orunmila, who divined and made sacrifice for him.

When this odu appears at divination, the person will be advised to serve his head with a guinea-fowl and a termite, and to serve Esu with a he-goat so that he might truimph in an upcoming contest. When it appears at Ugbodu, the person will be advised to make the same sacrifice adding Ikon to the sacrifice to Esu, because he is destined to become very wealthy.

The Divination He Made Before Leaving Heaven

Okonron kamu kamu was the awo who made divination for him before leaving heaven. He was advised to serve his guardian angel with a guinea-fowl and Ikon the termites' king; to serve Esu with a he-goat; to serve the ground divinity with a tortoise; and to serve Orisa with a piece of white cloth; white chalk and a red parrot's feather mounted on a stick called Opa-atori. He made all the sacrifices and left for earth after obtaining the blessing of God.

He started his life on earth with farming. When he did not make it, he went for divination and he was advised to repeat much the same sacrifice as he made in heaven. After the sacrifice, he was advised to take to the full-time practice of Ifism. Not long afterwards, he became very famous and prosperous. He was able to buy several slaves who continued with his farming. He had many wives and children.

Special Sacrifice for Fighting Enemies

Ki Osa mu ita junkun, ki ola Okonron mu obi kunkun.
Ohun kunkun ni a fi ishegun eni kunkun ile eni, Moni ta ni je
eni kunkun ile eni? Oni ile enikin kun. Orisa ile eni leni
Kunkun ile eni. Ebo ni ka ru o, ki a ni ishegun ile eni kunkun.
Osa took pepper and Okonron took kolanut.
Pepper and kolanuts are the things used to fight the war at home.

The kolanut is used to appeal to one's head to assist one in fighting the enemy at home. The kolanut is also used to beseech the divinity at home to fight the enemy in one's house. The head and the patron-divinity are the two forces that can conquer the enemy in one's home, in addition to making sacrifice to Esu.

At divination, the person will be told that his enemy lives with him in his house, and that he should serve his head, the divinity in his house, and Esu, to help to give him victory over the enemy.

He Divined for Lemikan of Ijesha

He told Lemikan to make sacrifice with a he-goat and a cock to avert the risk of losing his son who was ill. He made the sacrifice and the son did not die.

When it appears at divination for a sick person, the person will be advised to make a sacrifice in order to get well.

Orunmila Advised His Adherents Against Abandoning Their Ifa

Orunmila nio Asamorikan, Moni Osamorikan.
Oni ile aro Bini asamorikan agbo alagbede.

Oni inu oko ni asamorikan agbo.
Oni igbo ni asamorikan ode.
Oni inu oja n asamorikan anishowo.
Oni idi okekponrin ni asamorikan babalawo.
Oni ki a so fun Akakpo wi kpe ki o mama
Kuro ni idi mi. Oni ibe ni rere yi o to ma ba.
Oni inu oja ni rere yi oti ma ba onishowo.
Oni inu igba ni ode yi o ti ma ri rere wa si ile.
Oni ile aro ni rere yi o ti ma ba alagbeded.

Meaning:

Orunmila pronounced business. I also said business.
He explained that:
The smelting shop is the business of the iron-smith;
The bush is the business of the farmer;
The forest is the business of the hunter;
The market is the business of the trader; just as
Orunmila's altar is the business of the Ifa priest.
He went on to emphasise that anybody having his own Ifa
should not abandon it for any reason whatsoever, for
there lies his prosperity. Just as:
Prosperity comes to the trader in the market place;
Prosperity comes to the farmer through the farm;
Prosperity comes to the hunter through the forest; and
Prosperity comes to the iron-monger for his workshop.

When this odu appears for an Ifa man, he should be advised never to discard his Ifa because he might be tempted to do so. His fortune is in the offing. For a non-Ifa person, he should be advised to make sacrifice against the danger of frequent loss of jobs in order to consolidate his fortune. he should stay on his job.

Chapter 7

OSA-IROSUN

He Made Divination for the Camwood and the Rat

Osa roro bi ekpo, Irosun roro bi eje
Osala, Otala, Adifa fun Akponjulosun eyi ti onshe iyawo Ebiti.
Abufun eku niojo ti nse ale Akponjulosun obinrin Ebiti.

They made divination for the Camwood, the wife of the Palm Fruit. They also made divination for the Rat when he was befriending the Camwood (Akponjurosun), the wife of the Palm Fruit. The Rat was advised to make sacrifice in order to obviate the risk of getting into trouble for his adulterous relationship with a married woman. He refused to make the sacrifice because she had been in love with him for a long time and could not see the relevance for sacrifice at that point in time.

When Esu discovered the contempt with which the Rat treated the advice, he went to alert the Palm Fruit to the illicit love affair between the Rat and his wife. The Palm Fruit had doubts on the veracity of the allegation because he trusted his wife. Esu told him to lie low to watch developments around mid-day. The Palm Fruit accordingly concealed himself at a vantage point on the roof of his house from where he could see whatever was happening below.

Subsequently, the Rat came stealthily into the Palm Fruit's house and made straight for the room of Camwood. As he was preparing to make love to the camwood, her husband descended from the roof-top and smashed the Rat to death.

When this Odu therefore appears at divination, the person should be warned not to have any love affair with a light complexioned person. If the divinee is a man, he should be advised to resist the temptation to have any love affair with a married woman to avert the danger of sudden death. If he is already involved, he should make sacrifice to save his life and advised to refrain from it.

He Made Divination for the Ear When He Seduced the Wife of the Mosquito

Osalesun Osaleji was the awo who made divination for the Ear when he seduced the wife of the mosquito. He was advised to make sacrifice to ward off the nuisance effect of seducing the wife of a helpless creature. He was also told that if he could give up the woman, he should refund to the mosquito the dowry he paid on the woman. The ear brushed the advice aside after boasting that the Mosquito was not worth the trouble of making sacrifice.

When Esu discovered that the Ear had treated Orunmila's advice and warnings with disdain, he advised the mosquito to be visiting the Ear anytime he wanted to sleep in the night.

That is why the mosquito goes to the Ear at night-time to demand the refund of his dowry in the following war-cry.

Itama ro, Obinrin un, Erin run.

At divination, the person will be advised not to seduce the wife of a seemingly harmless and inconsequential man because he is capable of generating termendous nuisance affect. If he had already done it, he should make sacrifice with brown and red cock, red cloth and a he-goat to minimize the consequences.

He Made Divination for the Goat

Osa roro bi ekpo. Irosun roro bi eje made divination for the goat when she was indebted to many creditors. When she was unable to repay the debts, she went to Orunmila to tell her what to do. After divination, she was advised to serve her head with kolanut and coconut. Moreover, she was told that after serving her head with the two materials, she should conserve them and be chewing them anytime the creditors came to demand payment. She was to tell them to wait for her to finish eating although she was to continue to chew, her teeth in perpetuity. In consonance with Orunmila's advice, she was always chewing the kolanut and the coconut in her mouth. Anytime the creditors visited her and after waiting endlessly, they left her alone. That was how all her debts lapsed.

Incidentally, she did not pay for the divination that Orunmila made for her because she was pregnant at the time and she promised to pay after birth. Long after Orunmila learnt that the goat had delivered, he sent someone to demand the payment of the consultation fees from her, she replied that she was still eating. Orunmila concluded that since he was responsible for advising her to use that ploy on her creditors, he had no cause to expect to be treated differently. He forewent the debt.

When this Ifa appears at Ugbodu, the person should serve his head while backing the Ifa shrine on account of debt he owed in a previous incarnation. He should serve his head with a cock, coconut and kolanut. At divination, the person should be told to serve Ifa with her and his/her head with a pigeon, coconut and kolanut, to avoid falling into indebtedness.

The Divination He Made Before Leaving Heaven

Aa gbo ni ishe eti - Hearing is for the ear.
Aa gbo she ni ishe okon - Hearing and heeding is for the mind.

Those were the two Awos who made divination for this Odu when he was coming to the world. After divination, the Awos asked him whether he was given to heeding advice. Although he answered the question affirmatively, they insisted on testing the veracity of his assertion by requesting him to serve his mind with a tortoise, which he was to cook with fine palm oil and white pounded yam. He was to do the sacrifice so that his mind might not mislead him on getting to earth. Thereafter, he was to serve Esu with a he-goat and a piece of white cloth; his guardian angel with white hen, snail, and fine palm oil; before setting out.

He reacted by querying the Awos for prescribing such triffling sacrifice for him to make, and that unless they made more in depth divination, for him he was not going to make the sacrifice. Nonetheless, they forewarned him that unless he made the sacrifice, he should neither expect to live long on earth, nor to achieve his objectives. He stuck to his point that the sacrifices were too commonplace for him to make. Thereafter, he left for the earth without making any sacrifice.

On getting to the world, he soon established himself as a competent and effective Ifa priest. All his predictions came true. It was at the high point of his popularity that Esu intervened to teach him the inescapable consequences of failing to make sacrifice. The first onset of Esu was to take over his mind. Esu was aware of the vow he made in heaven to operate simultaneously as a good and wicked Awo. After taking over his mind, Esu began to manipulate his thoughts, words and actions.

Meanwhile, he was invited to a conference of divine priests in the kingdom of Ife. During the deliberations, he unwittingly dropped a bombshell, that in contrast to his erstwhile benevolent disposition, he was about to foment a turmoil that would make king and people appreciate his capabilities. As soon as the conference dispersed, Esu instigated a spate of negative events throughout the kingdom. There were epidemics of convulsion among infants, chicken pox among adults and miscarriages and fatal labor among pregnant women. In the light of the correlation between his outburst at the conference and the pandemic calamity, he was accused of being responsible for the afflictions. Although he denied responsibility, nobody believed him. To demonstrate his good faith, he proposed that the culprit should be cursed at the Oba's Ogun shrine.

His proposal was accepted and arrangements were made for the Ogun priest to use an egg and Ase to curse whoever was responsible for stimulating the problems with the special caveat that the curse was to manifest by exposing the culprit within 24 hours. Soon afterwards, he left for the bush to fetch leaves and other materials for his work. As soon as he entered the forest Esu lured him into the path of a hunter, to whom Esu also sent signals to befog his vision. The hunter took Osa-Irosun for a gorilla and shot him. Although he was not killed, the injury he sustained was enough to make everyone to conclude subsequently that Ogun had indeed declared him as the culprit.

Thereafter, he was formally accused of generating chaos in the kingdom since Ogun had declared him guilty. Since Esu had no intention of finishing him off without realizing his mistake, he transfigured into a visiting divine priest from heaven to intervene just before the death verdict was to be passed on him. The Esu-turned-divine-priest, told the Oba and his chiefs that Osa-Irosun was not the culprit, but that the higher powers created the problems in the town to give the appearance that he was responsible for them for two reasons; his failure to make the sacrifice prescribed for him before leaving heaven and the abandonment of his heavenly vow to interlace between good and bad faith on earth, because he had only been doing good works since coming to earth, while forgetting about his wicked side. The 'divine priest' declared that he was required to serve; his mind, Esu, Ifa and Ogun, and from then on to alternate his disposition between good and evil.

Thereafter, the 'divine priest' to the full view of everyone, disappeared from view. It was then generally agreed that heaven had come to declare him innocent and the sacrifices were speedily made. He subsequently regained his sanity and was treated for his gun shot wounds. As soon as he became well, he had to learn to be both good and bad, which enhanced his fame and fortune.

When this Ifa appears at Ugbodu, these special sacrifices (Ono-Ifa or Odiha) must be made before the conclusion of the initiation ceremony, to oviate the danger of committing murder. It is a debt of sacrifice which he owes from heaven and must be made at the appearance of the Odu at the secret conclave. If it appears at divination and it is ayeo, the person will be told to make sacrifice to avoid being arrested and jailed for an offense he did not commit or of becoming the victim of his own words.

The Divination He Made Before Marrying a Yellow Woman

> *Osa roro bi ekpo. Irosun roro bi eje. Adifa fun*
> *Orunmila ti yi o gbe iroro-rara ni yawo. Eje edunje*
> *Irororara. Eje ni ifa nje Iroro ra ra. Ebo ni o ru o.*

Osa is as red as palm oil, while Irosun is as red as blood, were the Awos who made divination for Orunmila when he was going to marry a light complexioned woman called Irororara. Orunmila only eats blood and not meat. The woman ate all the meat. He married her and the marriage was a success.

At divination, for a man, he will be told that a light-complexioned woman who eats plenty of meat is coming to marry him. He should serve Ifa with a goat before marrying her. It will be a success story.

He Made Divination for His Wife When She Was Having Genital Hemorrhage.

> *Osa roro bi ekpo, Irosun roro bi eje. Adifa fun*
> *Akpetebi Orunmila ni ojo ti o fi ojojumo she owo eje.*
> *Ugbin ni ebo ati agbebo adiye ati asho kpikpa.*

Osa is as red as palm oil and Irosun is as red as blood, made divination for Orunmila's wife when she was suffering from genital hemorrhage (issue of blood). She was advised to make sacrifice with snail, hen and red cloth. She made the sacrifice and the affliction abated, after which she became pregnant and gave birth to a child.

When this odu appears for a woman at divination, she will be told to make sacrifice to avert the danger of excessive menstrual bleeding, which can otherwise prevent her from getting pregnant.

Chapter 8

OSA-OWANRIN
OSA-OLUBI

He Made Divination for Aromi, the Son of the River

*Arigbanran san san san Arigbanan. Odifa fun Aromi ni joti
eja konti ile baba Aromi mba shota.*

That was the Awo who made divination for Aromi (Etebe tebe in Bini) the son of the river when the tenants in his father's house, were plotting to kill him. The tenants in the house of Aromi' father were the fishes. He was told to make sacrifice with a special kolanut called Aridan in Yoruba and Ebidan in Bini, Oribaza (or ewe oriboje) leaves, pepper and a he-goat.

After eating the he-goat, Esu advised human beings to grind the other materials (viz, Ewe-oriboje, Aridan and pepper) and put them in the river. Before the following morning, all the fishes had died and their corpses were afloat on the surface of the river. When people fetching water came to see the dead fishes the following morning, they were happy to pick them up. On his part when Aromi discovered that all his enemies were dead, he began to sing and dance in praise of the Awo who made divination and sacrifice for him. That is why Aromi is always seen dancing on the surface of the river.

The use of Oribaza for killing fishes in the river has become a tradition in many places to this day. When the Odu appears at divination, the person should be told that his enemies are in the father's house and that if he would like to destroy them, he should make sacrifice with a he-goat, pepper, Aridan and Oribaza.

He Made Divination for the Iguana

Osa rerere. Owanrin rerere, made divination for the Iguana (Aghanringhan in Yoruba and Omianwenze in Bini) when he was going to receive a visitor. He was told neither to harbor any visitor in his house nor to enter into any partnership business, without serving Esu with a he-goat.

Without making the sacrifice, he proceeded nonetheless to accept a lodging visitor in his house soon afterwards. After worming himself into the confidence of Iguana, the visitor proposed that they should be trading together. Forgetting or ignoring the warning he was given at divination, Iguana went ahead to agree with his visitor's proposal.

Meanwhile, Iguana traveled to the market alone, but before he returned, his visitor made away with all the valuable belongings of his host and set his house on fire. Upon his return from the market, Iguana had no house to enter. He subsequently went to Orunmila who blamed him for neither heeding the advice nor making sacrifice. He eventually moved into the forest which has become his traditional habitat ever since. The incident however dumbfounded him so much that he became partially deaf. He only hears soft-spoken words but not bellowed or sharp sounds. It must be emphasised that it is forbidden to serve Ifa with the Iguana, beause of the contempt with which he treated Orunmila's advice.

When this Ifa appears at Ugbodu, the person will serve the new Ifa with a crocodile, and his head with a cock. At divination, the person should be advised to serve; Esu with a he-goat, and his head with a cock, to thwart all the evil intentions of a visitor he is soon to have.

The Divination Made for Him Before Leaving Heaven

Angbon do ni ogojo was the Awo who made divination for this odu when he was coming to the world. He went to the Awo for divination when the problems he was having from his three brothers became intolerable. He wanted to escape from heaven to seek refuge on earth. His three troublesome brothers were priests of the Ogun, Osanyin and Oshun/Olokun divinities. He was advised that the only way of avoiding a repeat experience of his heavenly problems on earth was to serve Esu with a he-goat; Olokun with a multi-colored goat and the traditional gifts to the water divinity; Osanyin with a black dog; and Ogun with brown cock and brown dog. Thereafter, he was to serve his guardian angel with a guinea fowl and a grey colored goat. It was the cost of making the sacrifices that scared him into deciding to escape to earth, although the Awo fore-warned him that his brothers would sooner than later join him on earth. He made the sacrifices to Esu and his guardian angel before escaping to the world.

He was born into a family where there were already three brothers born before him. He grew up to become a practicing Ifa priest. As he began to show signs of having made it, his elder brothers teamed up against him. Once again, he found himself surrounded by hostile and jealous brothers. Since he had no where else to escape to, he went for divination and he was told to serve Esu with a he-goat; Ifa with grey goat and guinea fowl; Ogun with cock and tortoise; Olokun with white cock and other materials; and Osun with a black dog. This time, he made all the sacrifices.

Thereafter Esu went round to instigate Ogun, Osun and Olokun to wage war against Orunmila's three brothers. The eldest one became incurably ill, the next one became mad, while the third one strayed aimlessly into the world. Orunmila subsequently enjoyed a blissful life in peace and prosperity.

When this Ifa appears at Ugbodu, the person will be asked whether he is one of a foursome. He should make sacrifices by having his own Ogun, Osun and Olokun in addition to Ifa. If it appears at divination, the person should be told to make sacrifice because of the problems he is having from close relations.

He Made Divination for Onirefi When He Was Poor

Angbon odo ni ogojo. Omi ata si eni ni oju,
Omi a ta si eni ni enu. Adifa fun Onirefi tete omo
afi akoloko eja ni oju omi.

When one splashes water in the river, the water enters the face and mouth. Those were the Awos who made divination for Onirefi the fisherman. He was advised to make sacrifice in order to enjoy the fortune destined to come to him from the river. He was required to make the sacrifice with sweet edibles, white cloth and a small plant. He made the sacrifice after preparing the sacrifice, he was told to take it to the bank of a river and to use a canoe to paddle it to the first land mass he came across. He was to deposit the sacrifice there and build a hut to live in as his dwelling house on the same spot.

He collected all his belongings into a canoe and carried the sacrifices with him. He rowed his boat until he came across a landmass. After dropping the sacrifice there, he built a hut where he began to live alone. Meanwhile, he continued his fishing business, but although he made considerable catches, he had no one to buy them in the hermit island. He however began to smoke the fishes he was catching in anticipation of prospective buyers.

When Esu remembered that Onirefi made sacrifice, he went round to alert people in the adjoining villages and hamlets to buy fish from him. As more and more people came to buy fish from him, the place first developed into a market and subsequently into a town. The town became known as Eko and after it had grown in size and population, the people got together and appointed Onirefi as their king. During his coronation, he sang in praise of the Ifa priest who made divination and sacrifice for him.

At divination, the person will be advised to make sacrifice in order to become prosperous. He should be told that prosperity will come to him if he lives and works in Lagos.

Special Sacrifice to Fight Enemies

Olire fun fun tete, Omo akeruru fe eja. Ijobiriki iti ni ore
mijo shu. Oni awon wo lo ko erun le eru ne mo gun osheko
Moni awon omo eku ni. Oni ta ni won ko sibe de.
Moni iwo Orunmila ni. Oni won o ni lo'ri ogbo-Oni won ko
ni lo ri ato. Oni ijo birikiti, ni ire. Moni ijo shu.
Oni ta lo keru leru si mogun odale. Moni awon omo eja ni.
Oni ta ni won ko si mogun odale. Moni iwo Orunmila ni. Oni won
koni lori ogbo. Oni won koni lori ato. Oni ijo birikiti
ni ire. Moni ijo shu. Oni awon lo ko erun le erun si mogun.
Ohehe lerun. Moni awon omo araye ni. Oni tani wonko si be de.
Moni iwo Orunmila ni. Oni won ko lori ogbo. Oni tani won
ko lori ato. Oni abi won ko awon'kpe ewe kan jaju italo. Oni
ikpanri awo oja ju erumole lo. Oni showere kpekpe, ekpe akpale
le kpe showere kpekpe.

People gathered together to assail someone. Orunmila asked who they were flexing muscles for, and I replied that the rats were waiting to confront him. He cursed that they would never live long. He similarly cursed the fishes as well as human beings who conspire to assail him. He disclosed that there is a leaf in the forest which is more spicy than pepper. The head of an Awo is more vengeful than those of the 200 divinities. Anyone who opens his mouth to curse an Awo will have the curse boomeranging on him or her.

When this Odu appears at divination, the person will be told that some enemies are conspiring to bring about his downfalll. The leaves, (ewe lakparada) are added to pepper leaves and ground with the blood of a hen and marked on his head after which his head will scatter the conspirators.

A Special Poem

Orunmila ni inu ibu. Moni inu ola. Oni inu ibu, inu ola labi
Ogun si ki o to di olagbara. Inu ola ni abi. Esu si ode ijelu.
Inu ola ni a bi. Osun si ni ide ikponda. Inu ola ni abi
Orisa-Nla si ni ode Iranje. Inu ola ni abi Orunmila si ni oke
jeti. Inu ola ni a bi Akakpo meji awishe si.

Chapter 9

OSA-OGUNDA
OSA-OGUNLEJA
OSAGUN-ERO

He Made Divination for Osa When He Seduced Ogun's Wife

Kpara gijan, Ibole gijan. Ewe to be she oron okun takpa
ti tamore a re. Odifa fun Osa ti o ma gba aya Ogun.

That was the Awo who made divination for Osa when he was going to seduce Ogun's wife. He was advised to make sacrifice. When he was told that Ogun would fight him; he bluffed that Ogun only had a short cutlass as his weapon, which could not do any harm. He made the sacrifice with a he-goat to Esu after which he successfully retained Ogun's wife without any adverse consequences.

At divination as Ayeo for a man, he will be advised to abandon the woman he is seducing because the husband will fight him to a finish. If it is Ure, he should be told to serve Esu with a he-goat in order to get away with the seduction.

Divined for Orunmila When His Three Wives Deserted Him

Afun rururu, Ore ele oye sogunru jege. Ore onu Oke ijero
Ara gbagba oro otu ife kiri biti. Adifa fun Orunmila nijo
ti awon ayare sa lo. Osanyin o je Orunmila lowo oke kon.

The three wives of Orunmila; Afunruru, Sogunru jege and Asa gbagba ran away from him and went respectively to Oyo, Ijero and Ife. Meanwhile, Osanyin borrowed one bag of money from Orunmila, promising to work for him in lieu of the loan.

The following morning, Orunmila went with Osanyin to his farm and gave him a cutlass to work in brushing his new farm. After Orunmila had left, Osanyin sat down gazing at the leaves without doing any clearing. When Orunmila returned in the evening to discover that Osanyin had done no work, he queried him for not working. In reply, Osanyin replied that since he knew the uses to which the leaves could be applied, he was not inclined to cut down any of them. He explained that some of the leaves could be used for procurring pregnancies, for delivering children, for healing the sick and for protecting one from the incidence of witchcraft. Orunmila retorted by asking him how he was going to repay his loan since he could not repay it in kind. He advised Orunmila to bear with him but advised him to look for the seeds to plant in the farm.

Orunmila however got other people to brush the farm, fell the trees and burn the farm for him. After clearing the shrubs, Orunmila gave Osanyin the seeds to plant in the farm. He planted all the seeds. When the crops germinated, Osanyin advised Orunmila to go to the market to make a proclaimation that anyone with wares to sell should sell them on the next market day because no one was going to enter the market on the following market day because he was going to monopolize the market for the sale of special wares. He also advised Orunmila to enlist the assistance of market women to assist him in carrying his wares to the market on the operative day.

On the appointed market day, Orunmila assembled all the women who were to carry the crops to the market after telling Osanyin to go with them to the farm. Osanyin went with his special charm to the market (Ado afo in Yoruba and Ukokogho in Bini) Osanyin told them to harvest the vegetables which multiplied so much that they filled sixty baskets. Next, he took them to the Okro section of the farm where the harvest also filled sixty baskets. He performed similar feats with yams, plantains, maize, cocoyam and a variety of crops. The market was totally filled up with the crops harvested from Orunmila's farm. When the three estranged wives of Orunmila saw the crops being brought from his farm, they got together in the market to ponder on the salutary change in the fortunes of their husband.

Earlier on, Orunmila had made sacrifice to procure the return of his three wives. The sacrifice manifested when the three women resolved to return to him to enjoy out of his new-found prosperity. When he eventually left the market, the three wives appealed to him to forgive them and to let them return home with him. There was a happy reunion. With the miraculous feat achieved by Osanyin, he not only regained his reprieve from his indebtedness, but also had his fair share of Orunmila's harvest.

At divination, the person should make sacrifice to Osanyin and Ifa so that all his lost fortune might return to him.

Special Sacrifice for a Cool Life and Peace of Mind

Orunmila ni ero. Moni ero. Oni ero ni ki akpa fun Ogun,
Ki Ogun ki o le fi owo ero mu eni. Oni ero ni ki akpa fun
omo erumole. Mokan le logun. Oni ki akpa ero gi Orunmila,
ki o le fi owo ero re mu eni.

At divination the person will be told that his life is very hot. He should make sacrifice to cool it down.

Divined for Songo to Command Universal Fear and Respect

Otun Ian sa Ogun Alara. Osi ni a awo Ogun ajero

Ibi ti a ba wun eni, ni a nsa Ogun eni si. Odifa fun Songo.
Songo wa ni afishere omo enia.
The charms of Alara occupy the right, while
The charms of Ajero occupy the left.
Man uses charms for any purpose he pleases.

These were the Awos who made divination for Songo when he was being derided as harmless, and when people were making jest of him. He was advised to make sacrifice with a ram, red cloth, white cloth and two hundred and one pebbles. He did the sacrifice secretly without the knowledge of anyone. He was given the pebbles to each time he wanted to talk to anyone.

When people began to jeer at him again after the sacrifice he made, he bellowed the following words:
"Moru gba, Moru gba wa".

Thereafter, he threw one of the stones with which he made sacrifice. The noise thundered throughout the length and breath of heaven and earth. By reflex action people shouted:

"Kawo ka bi ye si"

Instinctively, people paid obeisance to him after his thunderous yell. That is why he is called the divinity that scared people. When this Odu appears at divination, the person will be advised to make sacrifice in order to command universal fear, honor and respect.

The Sacrifice He Made Before Leaving Heaven

Ajakpa da, o ma ke me kun. Owawu o gele.

That was the Awo who made divination for Orunmila before coming to the world. He was advised to refrain from boasting and to make sacrifice to prevent death through a woman. He was required to make sacrifices to his guardian angel with a tortoise, his head with the meat of elephant and a guinea-fowl; and Esu with a he-goat. He made all the sacrifices before leaving for earth. Ogun was his principal enemy in heaven and he had to escape to earth without being observed by Ogun. That is why he is called by the nickname of Osa Ogun tan.

He came to the world and began to have problems. Although things turned out well for him, when he went for divination out of desperation, he was told to serve; his head with guinea-fowl and the meat of elephant, his guardian angel with a tortoise, Esu with a he-goat, and the ground divinity with an ewe (sheep). He made the sacrifices. Soon afterwards, he became so popular on account of his effectiveness that the Alara of Ilara invited him and betrothed a wife to him while at the same time making him the royal diviner.

Meanwhile, Awo ajakpada, his heavenly diviner had also come to the world where he began to boast that he was the force behind Osa-Ogunda's success. Osa-Ogunda sounded Ifa who told him to; give a he-goat, cocoyam and his iro dress to Esu and to serve Ogun with cock and dog in order to avoid death through a woman. He was always swaggering and boasting vaingloriously at meetings of the divine priests, until a priestess decided to befriend him in order to find out the secret of his power. After knowing his secret, the woman waited for the next opportunity to call off his bluff.

At a subsequent meeting of the divine priests, as soon as he started boasting, swearing and threatening, the woman told the Olori-Awo, chairman of the Awos to order that Ajakpada should be apprehended for him to do his worst. The Olori-Awo in consonance with the priestess's advice gave order to the orderlies to apprehend him. As he was being apprehended, he pulled out his sword. As he demonstrated and threatened how he was going to use the sword to cut the throat of anyone who dared to touch him, he injured his own throat fatally and fell on the ground into a coma. He died subsequently in his house, thus killing himself and swooning as the price he had to pay for ignoring advice and for failing to make sacrifice.

When this odu appears during Ifa initiation at the secret conclave, the person should be told to make sacrifice to avoid the risk of boasting and behaving vain gloriously, and to avert the danger of dying through the machinations of a woman. At divination, the person should be asked to serve Esu and Ogun to forestall the danger of undoing himself.

Chapter 10

OSA-ETURA
OSA-ALAWURE
OSA-ILEFIRI

He Made Divination for Alajuba When Death Was Hunting for Him

Ebon nbon mi. Emi nbon ebon, babalawo alajugba, Odifa fun
Alajugba ni ojo ti iku nse ode re.

You deceived me and I deceived you, was the name of the Awos who made divination for Alajugba when death was on his trail. He was advised to make sacrifice to checkmate the plans of death against him. He was required to make sacrifice with empty gourd, used clothes and a tuber of yam. He made the sacrifice after which Esu drove death away from his trail.

When this Odu appears as Ayeo at divination, the person will be advised to make the sacrifice to drive death away from lurking around him.

He Made Divination for Osanyinmola When He Was Ill

Eje ki a fi omo igi ro si lle Olodumare
Eje ki a fi omo enia si'le Olodumare
Awon ni o she ifa fun Osanyinmola. Won fi akuko adiye bo ori re.
Let the young tree dwell in the place of its forebears.
Let mankind occupy the house of God.

Those were the two Awos who made divination for Osanyinmola when he was so ill that the disease defied all kinds of medications and sacrifices. He was advised to serve his head with a white cock and Osanyin with a brown cock. He made the sacrifice and survived the illness and lived to a ripe old age.

At divination, the person should be advised not to rely too heavily on diabolical medicines and charms because they would not help him. He should serve his head with a cock and the divinity or Orisa in his family with a brown cock. They will protect him.

The Divination He Made Before Leaving Heaven

Kin ba ni're joni, A ba ba ni're joni, A mo'ta ire joni.

It is better to move with an honest person. That was the name of the Awo who made divination for Orunmila when he was coming to the world. He was told that he was going to practice Ifism in trying circumstances on earth and was therefore advised to arm himself by making the following sacrifices:

(i)   To serve his guardian angel with a goat, hen, tortoise and pigeon;

ii)   To serve Esu with a he-goat, pepper soup and eko;

iii)   To serve the Obstacle divinity (Elenini or Idoboo) with a cock, gourd of water and crushed yam in the forest; and

iv)   To serve Olokun/Oshun with pigeon, white cock, a piece of white cloth and cowries

He made all the sacrifices before leaving for the world, where he became an Ifa priest. He was doing so well that his fame went to all the ruling monarchs of the known world and the divinities.

Meanwhile, Orisa-Nla sent for him along with all other divinities, and told them that he wanted them to accompany him on a tour in seven days time. On getting home he sounded his okeponrin (ikin divination), and Ifa told him to serve him with a goat, hen, tortoise and pigeon and to cook the soup for eating the accompanying pounded yam with Efirin (Ihiri in Bini) leaves; and Esu with a he-goat and eko and pepper soup. He made the sacrifices before setting out for a journey whose destination and purpose were not disclosed.

When Orisa-Nla got to his gate with the other members of the party, they hailed him and he came out to join them. At the outset, Orisa-Nla fore-warned the members of his entourage that it was going to be a non-stop trip without eating, drinking, resting and sleeping until they got to their destination. After walking non-stop for three days. Orunmila sought permission to ease himself. His excuse was granted and as soon as he got into the bush, he sounded Ifa for directions and he was told that help was on its way to him. He was already very weak, tired, hungry and thirsty.

As he was coming out of the bush, he met a woman who was coming to deliver a sacrifice with eko and akara. He stopped the woman and told her that she was coming to make a sacrifice because she had been pregnant for three years without being able to deliver. The woman confirmed the revelation and he told her to surrender the sacrifice to him. He also collected the gourd of water which the woman was holding, and drank to quench his thirst.

While he was still eating, a hunter came along and Orunmila told him that his wife had been in labor for seven days and was at the point of death. He added that it was the physicians who were trying to assist the woman to deliver that told him to come to the forest where he would meet the Awo who was to solve his problem. The hunter confirmed his pronouncements after which he decided to follow the woman and the hunter to their respective homes. Since Orisa-Nla does not traditionally look back when he travels, he did not notice that Orunmila did not rejoin the retinue.

Since the problems of the hunter deserved more urgent attention than that of the woman, he decided to go first to the former's house where he found the woman in labor to be in comatose. On getting there he brought out materials from his bag (Akpominijekun or Agbavboko) and put them in a pot for cooking. After cooking it, he gave part of it to the woman to drink while she was bathed with the rest. As she was being bathed by other women, she delivered a healthy baby. The hunter was so relieved and happy that he presented elaborate gifts to Orunmila.

Thereafter, he went with the pregnant woman to her house, where he prepared another pot for her to drink from and to bathe. He became beknighted in the woman's house and her husband gave him a befitting hospitality. As soon as the cock crowed the following morning, the woman started having labor pains. At divination, he discovered that the baby was due. He brought out his medicinal calabash and put it in the women's mouth. As the cock was crowing a second time, she gave birth to a baby.

The two incidents launched him in to fame and fortune, and the Oba of the town susbsequently persuaded him to settle down with them. When he agreed to remain in the town, the Oba instructed the people to build him a befitting house by communal labor. His place was always streaming with callers and he was able to satisfy everybody who came to him for help. He became so prosperous in the town that he was made the Araba, Olotu-Awo.

Meanwhile, Orisa-Nla and the rest of his retinue continued on the endless and aimless journey. As soon as Orisa-Nla was told that Orunmila had sneaked away from the train, he proclaimed that it was time for them to return home. It was exactly three years since they set out and when they got to the town where Orunmila was living, they went to his house. Before then, he had been told by Ifa to prepare a feast with a cow which he did in the hope that it was meant for entertaining the people of the town.

After cooking the food and setting the table, he was about to send out public heralds to invite people to the feast when Orisa-Nla arrived with his entourage. They all moved into Orunmila's house where they ate and drank to their heart's content. Before leaving, Orisa-Nla brought out his instrument of authority (ASE) and proclaimed that since it was only Orunmila who passed the test he set for the divinities, by having the intelligence to know when to return home to settle down, all the good things of life would always come and meet him at home. That is why he is the only divinity that does not move around to dance or perform. People come to him in his house.

When this odu appears at Ugbodu, the person will be told that his prosperity lies away from his home town. He will travel to another town or country to settle down, but once he gets there, he should stop moving around. He should make sacrifice for a settled life. At divination, the person should be told that his work will take him to a distant place, but should make sacrifice before going so that he might return to a more prosperous life.

He Made Divination For the Royal Musician

Oshunkpa ronron. Odifa fun Olire. That was the Awo who made divination for the royal musician when death was going to visit him. At divination, Osa-Ilefiri appeared and the musician was advised to serve his head with a white cock, white pigeon, and Esu with a he-goat. The Awo also told him to bring a hen, a snail and a white piece of cloth for a special sacrifice to be prepared for him in order to avert the danger of sudden death within three months. He was not inclined to make the sacrifices because he regarded them as common-place. As the royal musician, he was responsible for entertaining the king and the aristocracy on important occasions.

Meanwhile, it was time for the annual festival of Ogun and he had been rehearsing with his troupe. That was exactly two months after the divination he made. While he was preparing for the festival, Esu alerted the heavenly police force that it was time to hijack Olire to come and entertain in heaven. On the eve of the commencement of the festival, six policemen of the heavenly grail arrived at his house and kidnapped him to heaven. Even the members of his household did not know what happened to him. When the Oba sent for him the following morning, his family could only say that he travelled to an unknown destination. He was missed by everybody at the festival on account of the traditional melody and entertainment value of his music.

When this Odu appears as Ayeo at divination, the person will be advised to make sacrifice to avert the danger of sudden death.

He Made Divination for Nanakuana, the Hunter

Ori buruku ko gba oshe. Lale ki mi da ko gba kainkain.
Adifa fun Nanakuana nijo to'nlo she-oko ode.
The hard luck head does not respond to the cleansing effect of soap.
The use of sponge does not beautify an ugly face.

Those were the Awos who made divination for a hunter called Nanakuana when he was going to hunt in the forest. He was advised to make sacrifice with a he-goat before leaving, but he did not make it because he complained that he had no money. The following day he left for the forest. He travelled far and wide in the forest without being able to shoot a single game. As he was returning home, he saw two bush hens (okparo in Yoruba or Ukorobozo in Bini) and shot one of them while the second one flew away. He subsequently put the bird in his hunting bag.

When Esu discovered that Nanakuana failed to make sacrifice, he decided to foment trouble for him. Meanwhile, Esu stole the king's favorite peacock and hid it. While the town was being combed for the whereabouts of the pet fowl, Esu went to inform the king that he saw his pet running into the bush, but that he also subsequently heard a gun-shot indicating that someone had shot it. The king gave orders at once that check-points should be mounted at all the main entrances to the town.

After giving the fabricated information to the king, Esu in the guise of a policeman, proceeded to take a position at the point at which Nankuana was going to emerge from the forest. As he was coming out of the forest Esu accosted him by demanding to see the bird he shot in the forest. He replied that the bird he shot was a bush hen, but Esu told him that he was lying because he shot the king's favorite peacock. When he brought out the dead bird to establish the veracity of his assertion, he was stunned to see that what came out of his bag was a dead peacock. It so bewildered Nanakuana that Esu subsequently marched him to the palace where he was formally arrested for interrogation.

Under cross examination, he told the king that he was the victim of circumstances, because he could not explain how the bush hen he shot in the forest turned into a peacock. After beseeching the king to listen to his hardluck story he recalled that the two Awos who made divination for him before leaving for the forest were called "a hard luck head cannot be cleansed with soap and Ugliness does not succumb to a sponge." He added that although they advised him to make sacrifice, he could not afford the cost of a he-goat. He was convinced that some mysterious force had punished him for not making the sacrifice, adding melodramatically that apart from attributing his plight to hardluck, he had no other explanation or defense. He was now in tears.

At that point, Esu intervened that the king should give the accused the opportunity of making the sacrifice, but that if his story was not substantiated thereafter, he should be executed. He was allowed to return to his house where he quickly arranged to borrow money to buy a he-goat for the sacrifice. After Esu had finally got his he-goat, he immediately released the king's peacock and it went to sit by the side of the king's throne. The king was astonished by the turn of events and he subsequently ordered the acquittal and release of the accused person.

He Divined for Edigban to Become the Oba of Ede

Eni ti ba fun kpa ko fun kpa, Eni ti ba fun yede kofun yede.
Okun ti oni igba owo ta ni igba ese o nrin rin kpele kpele.
Adifa fun Edigban ni jo ti ofe lo je olojo lo'ke Ede oloja owo.

The prosperous man who should be imperious was not vain glorious.
The powerful man who should be authoritative was meek and benign.
The milipede with four hundred limbs who should be fast moving walks
gracefully.

These were the Awos who made divination for a man called Edigban when he was going to become the king of a town called Ede. He was told to make sacrifice with a ram to Ifa and a he-goat to Esu. He made the sacrifices and his reign was blissful and peaceful. He was later given the nicknames of the king of wealth, peace and prosperity because his kingship brought peace and opulence to all and sundry.

When this Odu appears at divination, the person will be told to make sacrifice in order to achieve the nobility, position and prosperity destined for him.

The Divination Made For Him When Witches Were After Him

Asuye suye. Awo ile Orunmila, Odifa fun Orunmila om be ni
irangun ota awon eleye.

Asuye suye was the surrogate who made divination for Orunmila when he had problems with the club of witchcraft. He was told to make sacrifice with eight pigeons. He was advised to rear the pigeons after preparing the sacrifice. As soon as the pigeons got used to their new habitat, they began to scare off the witches any time they tried to come to Orunmila's house. When the witches could not do anything to checkmate the pigeons from disrupting their strategies, they left Orunmila in peace.

When it appears as Ayeo at divination, the person should be told that the club of witchcraft have an axe to grind with him or her. He or she should rear at least four pigeons to be flying about in the house.

The Divination Made For Him When He Was Travelling to Edidi

Ohun eni kii nu eni. Odifa fun Orunmila baba nshawo lo si ilu edidi.

One does not lose fortune as well as the words of one's mouth.

That was the name of the Ifa priest who made divination for Orunmila when he was travelling for Ifa practice to the town of Edidi. He was advised to make sacrifice with two China plates, two hens and two pigeons. He made the sacrifice. After making the sacrifice he left for the town. Orunmila was given the two plates to travel with during his journey.

There was a spinster in the town who had rebuffed all advances and overtures made to her by prospective spouses. Just before entering the town, Orunmila felt like easing himself. He kept the two plates by the side of the road and entered the bush to answer nature's call. At the same time, the girl and her friend were returning through the route after fetching water from the river.

When the girl saw the beautifully decorated plates on the ground, she picked one up, but Esu blinked his eyes to her and the plate fell to the ground breaking into three pieces. While she was fidgetting on what to do about it, Orunmila came out from the bush wearing the cap containing the medicine that had been prepared for him with ewe ijoki. Seeing that his plate had been broken by the girl, he began to chant the poem of the sacrifice made for him. As he was singing, the medicine inside his cap was oozing water into his eyes, thus making it look as if he was truly in tears.

Instinctively, the girl began to cry with him and persuaded him to follow her home to see her father. On getting home, Orunmila continued to cry that the girl had destroyed the secret of his longevity. Seeing that Orunmila was in tears, the father of the girl begged him to accept money, possessions, etc. to atone for the loss of the plate. He retorted that all the money in the town could not atone for his life. The girl's father resolved the quandary by betrothing her in marriage to Orunmila. That was when he stopped crying.

At divination, the person will be told that he has two spinsters ripe for marriage in his house, and that the eldest of the two girls is the wife of Orunmila. It means that she will have to marry a man having Ifa.

He Made Divination for Two Sisters

Osa-Olawure made divination for two sisters, Teete and Moore.

One day their mother left the two of them at home, when she went to the farm. When she was leaving home, she gave her daughters yam to eat during her absence. After their mother's departure, the two girls began to argue whether to cook or roast the yam. As they were arguing between themselves, enemy troops invaded the town, entered their house and seized the two girls into captivity. They were subsequently sold into slavery.

As the two sisters were being separated, Teete, the eldest one told Moore not to forget her if she prospered wherever she went. True to her sister's prediction, Moore became opulent after regaining her freedom. She became so wealthy that she began to buy her own slaves. She was engaged in the palm oil milling business and her slaves used to crack palm kernels for producing palm kernel oil. One particular year, the palm kernel's yield was so rich that it became necessary to engage additional hands to do the cracking. Moore instructed her aides to buy more slaves from the market.

Among the slaves bought from the market was her sister Teete, although she could not recognise her. Subsequently Teete was reconciled to the chore of cracking palm kernels. Any-time her mistress/sister was away from the house, she would begin to sing while cracking palm kernels. She often sang to reminisce on how her sister and herself Teete and Moore were born, how their mother left one day for the farm, leaving a tuber of yam for them to eat. Enemy soldiers invaded their house to capture them and how they were sold into slavery which separated her from her sister Moore.

An elderly woman who lived with Moore used to listen to Teete's song until she began to surmise that the slave girl could be referring to their mistress. It was apparent that the two sisters had not been able to recognise each other. Meanwhile, the old lady alerted her mistress to the significance of the new slave-girl's songs. One day, Moore decided to hide herself to listen to the song of the slave girl. She hid in the old woman's room and listened while her elder sister was once again singing to recall their experiences. As soon as she heard her out, she looked closely at the slave girl and on realizing that it was her elder sister, she burst into tears and went ahead to embrace her while still in tears.

As soon as the two sisters recognised each other, Moore made Teete the head of her house-hold and they lived happily ever after. When this Ifa appears at Ugbodu, the person should serve the new Ifa with a goat, and Esu with a he-goat, adding cooked pieces of yam to avoid becoming the victim of a national cataclysm. The person will be told that he is going to travel to, and prosper in, a distant land, far away from the home of his birth.

At divination, the person should be told to serve Esu with he-goat and Ogun with a cock to avoid being arrested without justification.

Chapter 11

OSA-IRETE
OSA-OLOYAN

He Made Divination for the Water and the Sand of the River

Ugba yeke yeke, Awo omi. Odifa fun omi, abufun iranyin.

That was the Awo who made divination for the water as well as the white sand of the river. The water and the white sand were brothers born of the same parents. Water, the eldest of the two went to Orunmila for divination and he was advised to make sacrifice with a strong he-goat, pigeon, stone and yellow powder in order to have a home of his own. He did not make the sacrifice. Not long afterwards, the white sand, the junior of the two brothers also went to Orunmila for divination and he too was advised to make sacrifice with a strong he-goat, stone, salt, pigeon and tortoise in order to avoid being in want of food to eat. He made the sacrifice.

When Esu was subsequently informed that water failed to make sacrifice, and that it was only his junior brother, the white sand that made sacrifice, he deceived water into sitting on top of his junior brother's head, while advising the white sand to bear the weight of his elder brother. The significance of the advice is that it made the river to be constantly on the move without having a settled life. While on the move the water is never able to carry the white sand below. All the food given to the river go under to feed the white sand below.

At divination, the person will be told to make sacrifice that his loss does not become the gain of his junior brother, subordinate or associate.

The Same Awo Made Divination for the Frog and the Buffalo

Ugba yeke yeke yeke, Odifa fun Okpolo, abufun Efon

He also made divination for the frog and the buffalo, when they were going to have a contest. He advised the frog to make sacrifice to Ogun with a dog, and Esu with a he-goat. The frog made the from made the sacrifice. He advised the buffalo to make a similar sacrifice but he refused to make it, since he could not imagine how the frog would ever be able to beat him in any contest.

At a subsequent meeting of the frog and the buffalo, the frog boasted to be capable of running faster than the buffalo. The buffalo accepted the challenge and a day was appointed for the contest. On the appointed day, the frog lined up his many children on the route of the contest with each of them holding a red parrot's feather in its mouth.

The frog got set with the buffalo, but as soon as the race began, the frog stayed behind to rest by the side of the road close to the finishing line. The buffalo on the other hand ran like he had never run before, until he was totally enervated. Thinking that he had already out-paced the frog, he decided to stop briefly to rest. As soon as he stopped to rest, the frog in front of him hailed on him not to stop because he was already ahead of him and waiting for him to continue the race.

For fear of being beaten in the race, the buffalo continued to run. The same process was repeated several times by the medley of frogs which made the buffalo to continue to run without resting until he became absolutely exhausted, after which he fell down dead, at which point, the frog announced his arrival at the finishing line. He was declared the winner.

When this Ifa appears at Ugbodu, the person will be advised to make sacrifice with the meat of elephant and buffalo and a ram to the new Ifa and he-goat to Esu. He should be told to look out in his family for a woman having ten children and advised to be friendly with her, and not to alienate her.

At divination, the person will be told to serve Esu with a he-goat, and Ogun with a cock, to avoid being disgraced by an inconsequential colleague.

He Made Divination for Orisa-Nla When His Three Servants Ran Out on Him

Osa rete, Orin rete, Isa riro ko jo ri ogun. Osa okpolo ki
ju ojuti. Osa ayinyan ki ju akobelo. Awon lo'ndafa fun, Orisa-Nla
Oshereigbo, nijo ti awon eru re meteta saa.

The slow runner who runs like the chameleon, who does not go beyond the front of the house. The race of the toad which does not go beyond the water drain. The race of the cock-roach which does not go beyond the matchete case. That was the incantation with which Orunmila made divination for Orisa-Nla, when his three servants ran away. The three servants were the toad, the chameleon and the cockroach. After searching in vain for them, he invited one hundred and ninety-nine of the divinities excluding Orunmila, to assist him in finding them. They all searched for the three servants in vain without being able to find them. At that point, Elenini, the obstacle divinity advised Orisa-Nla to invite Orunmila for divination.

After divination, Orunmila advised Orisa-Nla to make three separate sacrifices. The sacrifices were accordingly prepared. Orunmila told Orisa-Nla to deliver them by himself. The first one was to be deposited at the foot of the tree in front of his house. As he was putting down the sacrifice with prayer for his escaped servants to return home to him, the chameleon retorted by begging him for forgiveness. The chameleon instantly returned to the house with him.

He was told to deliver the second sacrifice at the water drain leading outside from the kitchen of his house. As he again prayed for the return of his escaped servants, the toad also began to beg for forgiveness. The toad returned to the house with him.

Finally, he was told to bring his matchet case to be scraped into the third sacrifice. As he was scraping the matchete case, it shook the cockroach who was hiding inside the case and he fell to the ground asking for forgiveness for his misconduct.

Not being able to comprehend the instantaneous manifestation of the sacrifice, Orisa-Nla reacted by accusing Orunmila of being responsible for instigating the three servants to run away. Orunmila reacted by accusing Orisa-Nla of gross ingratitude. The argument attracted the other divinities, who, after hearing the two sides, out of envy, agreed with Orisa-Nla that it was indeed Orunmila who conspired with the three servants to escape.

Out of anger, Orunmila brought out his instrument of authority to proclaim that from that day, no sacrifice will again manifest on the very day it is made.

He Divined for Orisa to Make Sacrifice With His Dress

> *Osa-rete, Ogban inu eni ni ba ni asun baniji.*
> *Eda eni ni ba ni nishe ishegun bu a ba kofa titi lale.*
> *Bi a ba kofa le akoju she ni iyoni lenu.*
> *Adifa fun Orunmila nijo ti onlo ye okekponrin Orisa wo.*
> *Oni ki Orisa ru ebo.*
> *One's senses sleep and wake with one.*
> *One's guardian angel avenges for one.*
> *Too much knowledge of Ifa creates problems for one.*

These were the Awos who made divination for Orunmila when he was going to see the guardian angel of God. He told God to make sacrifice with his only white apparel and he did. After using the cloth to make sacrifice, Orunmila went away with it.

When the divinities trooped in to give morning greetings to God they found him without his traditional white apparel. When he explained that Orunmila took it away after using it to make sacrifice, all the divinities were infuriated over the apparent vindictiveness of Orunmila and they decided to ostracize him. As a punishment to him, Orunmila was subsequently enjoined by all the divinities to make a feast for them. He reacted by telling them that there were no gentlemen among them because they knew he lacked the wherewithal for feasting all of them. Nonetheless, he was determined to surprise them, if only as a means of establishing their gentry and lack of nobility.

When he sounded Ifa for directions, he was told to give a he-goat to Esu which he did. Thereafter Esu collected all the materials he required for the feast, much beyond the expectation of the divinities. The feast was prepared so elaborately that the divinities were all disappointed because they never expected Orunmila to be able to feast them so lavishly.

At divination, the person will be told that he or she is worrying over a seemingly difficult assignment. He can be reassured that if he gives a he-goat to Esu, he will perform the task to the amazement of his detractors.

The Divination He Made Before Leaving Heaven

Uyon mi oyon. Ekpo kii nyin eni lara.
Uyon mi oyon. Omi kii nyon eni lara.
Oil does not dry up the body. It cools it.
Water also cools the body.

Those were the Awos who made divination for Orunmila when he was coming to the world. He was advised to serve his guardian angel (Okekponrin in Yoruba or Ehi in Bini) and his head with a ram, melon seeds with its shells, unpeeled plantain, a goat and a hen, Esu with a he-goat; the unknown enemy with three cocks, three gourds of palm oil and three gourds of water; Ogun with a strong cock, big dog, tortoise and gourd of palm wine; and Osanyin with a dog, cock and tortoise. He was required to make the elaborate sacrifice because he would need the support of the divinities in weathering the storm of problems he was going to encounter on earth. Before leaving heaven, he also served Olokun with a pigeon and other materials.

He was born into a family where he became the only son, all the other children being females. He took to Ifa practice as soon as he grew up. He also took to trading on the side-line and he succeeded immensely in the two vocations. He eventually got married to the daughter of Olokun who enhanced his trading so successfully that his Ifa practice was totally marginalized. He became exceedingly wealthy through his trading and the active support of his wives. He had 201 wives in his harem and gave birth to an innumerable number of children. He was easily endowed with more fortune and fame then the king of his town.

Success was soon to breed envy and enmity. The enemies began their salvo by going to tell the king that Orunmila was usurping his authority and that he was freely engaging in human sacrifice. To substantiate their fabrication, they disclosed that there were two freshly beheaded corpses at the back of his house. Meanwhile, the enemies had exhumed two newly buried corpses from the public cemetery, cut off their heads and kept their beheaded bodies at the back of Orunmila's house. When the king sent the royal police to verify the allegations, the verifiers discovered the two beheaded corpses behind his house and he was instantly arrested and accused of engaging in human sacrifice. He was kept in prison to await trial and execution.

While he was in detention, his wives went to his Awos for divination. He told them to roast a rat and send it to him in prison to serve his head, promising to serve him with a goat if he survived the tribulations. Before doing the sacrifice, they were to give a he-goat to Esu. The sacrifice was accordingly made. After eating his he-goat, Esu went to the Oba in the guise of a visiting Ifa priest to warn him that, a cataclysm was imminent in his kingdom for putting Orunmila in detention because it was forbidden to incarcerate an Ifa priest. The visitor asked whether the Oba had thoroughly investigated the charges preferred against Orunmila.

In deference to the advice of Esu, the Oba invited representatives of his subjects from every street, hamlet, and village as well as Orunmila's wives and children to seek their opinion on his character and behavior. The first set of people to be questioned were members of his family. The Oba asked whether Orunmila had any divinity or charms for which he made human sacrifices. They all replied that not only had their father and husband never engaged in human sacrifice he had often said that Orunmila forbade human sacrifice. They insisted that before killing him for an offence he knew nothing about, the Oba should first kill of all them. The citizens who were assembled also confirmed that Orunmila was too inoffensive to touch a fly, let alone, a human being. They repeated the aphorism that Orunmila forbids killing human beings.

Meanwhile, after closely examining the beheaded corpses, some of the assembled citizens were able to identify them through the scars on their bodies that they were their recently buried relations. They proved their point by taking the palace police to the graves from which the corpses were exhumed by the mischief makers. With that information and corroboration, the accusers were instantly rounded up, charged, tried and sentenced to death by execution. Orunmila was not only released but given the title of the Shashere of the town.

Thereafter he made a large feast for the entire population. When this Ifa appears at Ugbodu, the person will be told to make sacrifice because he will have the problems that go with success. He will marry more than one woman and have many children.

He Made Divination for the Oloyan

Ti a ba ti kuro ninu ile, ibi ti a nlo, ti o ba ti nkini.
Ibi ti o ti kuro a jun a. Odifa fun Oloyan omo omi kikan
ti ntu aya ba ni asho.
When we travel away from home to a distant land,
We get to a point at which our destination is as far away as home.

These were the Awos who made divination for Oloyan. He was advised to make sacrifice with eight pigeons, a cock, and a he-goat, in order to avoid the unpleasant consequences of greed. He made the sacrifice but failed to add he-goat for Esu. The following day, he left with his son called Nkan to hunt in the forest. When he got to the forest, they saw plenty of animals on the other side of the river, but since the river was flooded they could not cross to the other side. While they were wondering what to do, Esu transfigured into a canoe paddler and offered to ferry them across the river, if they would reward him adequately. Oloyan promised to give an unspecified compensation to the boatman.

On getting to the other side of the river, he promised to reward the boatman on his way back. Meanwhile, Oloyan and his son killed plenty of animals which they ferried once more across with the help of the boatman. After taking the animals home, the boatman asked for his reward, but Oloyan continued to procrastinate. The boatman waited for his gratification for three months without getting anything. Thereafter, Esu caused the river to overflow its banks, thus generating a flood that engulfed the whole town. Oloyan lost his son and property to the flood for reneging.

When this Odu appears at divination, the person will be advised not to renege on his promise. If he had already broken a promise, he should make sacrifices to avoid courting the risk of fatal consequences.

He Made Divination for the People of Oyan and Their King the Oloyan

Igbin gbin yinkintin, awo Oloyan. Odifa fun Oloyan nijo ti.
Oloyan fi omi oju shubere aje. Aniki Oloyan ru ebo.

That was the Awo who made divination for Oloyan when he was poor. He was advised to make sacrifice with 16 rats, 16 fishes and 16 hens. He made the sacrifice after which he became wealthy, married many wives, had many wives, had many children and had plenty of money.

Egungun mogba mogba lo'ndifa fun won lo'de Oyan ni bi ti
ure gbogbo ti yan won loju kaaran kaanran. Ani ki won ru
ebo, ki won fi abo adiye ru ebo.

He made divination for the people of Oyan when they were anxious to have the good things of life. He advised them to make sacrifice with a hen. They made the sacrifice and the children of prosperity that had previously deserted the town began to return.

When it appears at divination, the person will be advised to make sacrifice so that prosperity may return to his life.

Chapter 12

OSA-EKA

He Made Divination for Obe-Esilo

Osaka Araka. Odifa fun obe esilo o mba awon eji le ni
Erunwo. esilo lo si oko aloro odun. Won ni ki esilo ru ebo.

That was the Awo who made divination for the kitchen knife used for peeling yams and other food crops at home, when he was travelling in the company of 40 domestic appliances to the farm. Obe esilo went for divination and he was told to make sacrifice with a he-goat. After making the sacrifice, he was advised not to accompany his colleagues to the farm but to remain at home.

When the efforts of his colleagues began to yield harvests, obe esilo became the first to taste them. He was the first to taste the products of the efforts of the cutlass, hoe, digger, carrier etc from the farm.

At divination, the person will be advised to make sacrifice for peace of mind, so that the benefit he is seeking from a distance will come to meet him at home.

He Made Divination for Salubata

Osaka Araka. Odifa fun Salubata nijo to'nlo si ilu awusa.

He made divination for the wide slippers when he was travelling to the land of the Hausas. He was told to make sacrifice in order to become popular. He made the sacrifice and became the favorite of everyone in the place.

He Made Divination for the Calabash

Osaka, Awo Ugba. Odifa fun Ugba.

He made divination for the calabash when he was going to the farm during the planting season. He was told to make sacrifice with a knife (Obeke) and a cock. He made the sacrifice. At the end of the farming year, he produced several children who became the instruments of ornamentation.

He Made Divination for the Refuse Dump

Saka saka, soko soko awo etitan. Odifa fun eititan nijo tio lo si
kole orun bo wa si kole aye. Ani ki oru ebo.

He made divination for the garbage dump when he was coming from heaven. He was told to make sacrifice with he-goat to Esu and cock to his guardian angel. He did the sacrifice after which he was advised never to undermine anyone and not to live with a servant or maid.

On getting to the world he discovered that he was only given the rejects of other people. Not satisified with receiving disused and rotten materials, he decided to return to heaven to consult another diviner. He went to an awo called Igbodo, who told him that his lot had been designed and destined by his guardian angel and that nothing could be done to change his fate. With that, he returned to the world, where he continued to be the repository of all junks, garbage, trash and rotten dregs.

Very soon, he became so wealthy that people began to envy him. When he was feeling the pinch of the envy, he went once more for divination at which he was told to prepare his own Ogun shrine with a dog. After the sacrifice, Ogun became his body-guard, and Ogun was hurting and scaring off his assailants. Anyone who went to his house with bad intentions were often injured by broken bottles disused iron, nails and other hooks and thorns. Thereafter, he was left alone to thrive in peace and prosperity.

When it appears at Ugbodu, the person will be advised to serve; his head with a goat, Esu with he-goat and Ogun with dog. He will be assured of prosperity which will generate envy, but should not allow it to disturb him. At divination, the person should be told to serve; his head with a pigeon, Ogun with dog and Esu with he-goat, and be advised not to compete with anyone for anything because he will prosper in his own right.

Chapter **13**

OSA-ETURUKPON

He Made Divination for the Trumpet to Become Famous

Osa tuuru, Ipantuuru, babalawo ukpe. Odifa fun Ukpe nijo ti o
si kole orun bo wa si kole aye.

He made divination for the trumpet when she was coming to the world. She was advised to make sacrifice with: he-goat to Esu; cock to her head; and cock to Ogun in order to prosper, have many children and become famous on earth. She made the sacrifice. She came to the world at the same time as calabash and melon.

On getting to the world, she got married to Ogbe who gave her to the young palm tree (Okpe kete or Okhere) to look after. The branchs of the palm tree produced an enviroment for her to flourish and have many children. When her children matured for harvesting, Esu decided to compensate her for the sacrifice she made.

People had been looking for someone to herald important occasions. Esu advised them to invite the new arrivals to the world to find out which of them had a melodious voice. All the others tried and failed. When Ukpe's turn came to sing, the voice of her children was so impressive that they were instantly appointed as royal heralds to sing in praise of the king. Wherever the king went, ukpe was always infront to be carried by a human slave to herald his approach. They were also used as chronicles of important occasions in society. Ukpe therefore prospered through her children.

When it appears at Ugbodu, the person will be told to serve; his head with a cock, Esu with he-goat and to forbid drinking palm wine. He should be careful in relating with his brothers and sisters because they will pose unhealthy rivalry to him.

At divination, the person should be advised to serve his or her head with a cock and Ogun also with a cock. He should refrain from drinking alcohol.

He Made Divination for a Plant Called Kpanrikpan

Osa tuuru Ikpan tuuru. Odifa fun Ikpanrikpan onlo si eti odo,
onlo kpowole omo bibi.

He made divination for Kpanrikpan when she was going to settle down near the river. She was advised to make sacrifice with hen, pigeon and cutlass in order to survive human enemies and to avoid mass death for herself and her children. She did not bother to make the sacrifice.

On getting to the river, she multiplied quickly by having so many children who flocked around her. At the height of her prosperity Esu intervened to advise human beings that the approach to the river from where they fetched drinking water and fishes had become too infested with weeds. He advised them to use the matchet to clear the weeds. Subsequently, men used the cutlass to destroy Kpanrikpan and all her children.

At divination, the person will be advised to make sacrifice against the danger of mass destructin for himself / herself and children.

He Made Divination for the Head and the Mind

Osa kole inu. Eturukpon aya re Ilo la idi, Odifa fun
Ori, Obufun eden. Ebe la mbe ori inu ko ma ba to'de je.

Osa did not open his stomach and Eturukpon his wife did not open her anus. They made divination for the head and the mind. It is the mind we have to beseech and pet not to create problems for the head. They were both advised to make sacrifice so that the mind might not mislead the head.

The Divination He Made Before Leaving Heaven

Osa ologun erun. Eturukpan oloju olofa - were the two Awos who made divination for Orunmiila when he was coming to the world. He was told to serve: Esu with he-goat, his guardian angel with a ram, fish and rat; Elenini, the obstacle divinity with a goat in a feast and to obtain the blessings of Orisa with white pigeon, white cloth and white chalk. It took him a long time before completing the sacrifice after which he came to the world.

He started by operating as an itinerant Ifa priest who was moving from one place to the other. When he was not settling down properly, he had a dream in which his guardian angel advised him to stop roaming about and to settle down in one place. He was advised to serve Esu with a he-goat at a lake in which he was to leave his wearing apparel, hat and shoes, after taking his bath in it so that good fortune might stop passing him by. He was also required to serve Esu at the foot of an Iroko tree with a second he-goat and to have his bath there. After serving Esu at those two places, he was to serve his Ifa with a goat.

Since he could not imagine how he was to raise the money for the sacrifices, he ignored them entirely. For failing to make the sacrifice, Esu decided to tantalise him with wealth and opulence. Esu went to the household of the king and procurred an epidemic of cholera. Orunmila, in his capacity as the royal physician, was invited to help. Normally, he was often able to solve such problems without any difficulty, but this time around, he tried in vain for one month to abate the illness, but he failed woefully because the disease took many lives in the town. He was subsequently expelled from the palace without any compensation.

On his way home from the palace, Esu confronted him and told him that he failed because he did not give him a he-goat. He begged Esu to bear with him, but he refused. He tried to raise a loan to buy the he-goat, but no one agreed to lend him the money. Eventually, he stole a he-goat with which he served Esu. As soon as he offered it to Esu, he was apprehended for stealing and severely beaten as a common thief.

After eating the he-goat, Esu went back to tell the Oba that the difficulties in the town were not abating because he did not treat Orunmila well. Esu told the Oba that Orunmila was the only physician who could stop the epidemic. The Oba subsequently sent for him and presented him with gifts comprising; 2 men, 2 women, 2 cows, 2 goats, 2 he-goats, 2 hens, and 2 bags of money; promising to give him more and to make him a chief, if he could abate the epidemic.

Orunmila then went into the bush to collect the appropriate leaves after giving the two he-goats to Esu at the lake and at the foot of the iroko tree. After eating the 2 he-goats, Esu went to where he knotted the problem that caused the epidemic and untied it. Orunmila prepared the medicines for all the afflicted persons to drink and bathe with the water he got from the lake. Before the following morning, relief had come to everyone and the disease stopped afflicting anyone else. In a matter of days, the problem was over and every chief in the town sprayed Orunmila with gifts. He became very famous and prosperous.

At Ugbodu, the person should be told to make the special sacrifice at the lake and at the foot of the Iroko tree.

Chapter 14
OSA-OSE
OSA-SESESE

He Divined for 76 Bush Rats in Heaven

Osa she, irin she. Irin she, Irin kese kese. Ni ese Olude.

These were the Awos who made divination for seventy-six bush rats. They were advised to only eku oyo that made the make sacrifice to survive the evil designs of enemies, with okro, twine, blade, sheer butter (Ori-oyo) It was sacrifice. The rest became victims to mankind, while no body touches eku-oyo to this day.

When it appears at divination, the person will be advised to make sacrifice in order to survive the evil designs of powerful enemies.

He Made Divination for the Bird Called Eluulu and the Snake

Osa sese, Odifa fun Eluulu, Obufun Ejo.

He made divination for Eluulu when she was coming to the world. She was told to make sacrifice in order to prosper on earth. On getting to the world, she began to have children. After having her first child, it had eye trouble which was making him blind, and which made Eluulu to go to Orunmila for divination. She met the snake in Orunmila's place who came with a different problem. He complained that he came to the world without knowing how to mate his wife to have children. Orunmila told the snake that the only way he could make love to his wife was by biting her to put her into comatose. After making love to her in her state of unconsciousness, Orunmila taught him the leaves to squeeze into her eyes to revive her. That is what the snake does to this day.

As soon as the snake left, Eluulu told Orunmila that her child was virtually blind and needed his help on how to restore sight to it. Orunmila told her to use the same leaf that he taught the snake to use to revive his wife after mating her. The leaves are found wherever Eluulu hatches her eggs. It is used for restoring sight to the blind. Occasionally, when Eluulu is looking for the leaves and finds them with the snake, she will kill the snake, no matter how big, to collect the leaves from him.

When this ifa appears at Ugbodu, the person will be told to wash his head with the appropriate leaves to be collected by the Ifa priest and a he-goat, on Esu shrine, adding parrot's feather and cowries. He should also be advised to beware of friends. At divination, the person should be told to refrain from betting with anyone. He should beware of friends and serve Esu with a he goat in order to realise his ambitions.

He Made Divination for Two Neighboring Farmers

He made divination for Uri and Olobahun when they were sharing the same boundary in their farms. They were told to make sacrifice with he-goat to Esu in order to prosper through their farming. Uri made the sacrifice after which he was advised to be hospitable to visitors. He was told to give food to anyone who visited him in his farm or in his house. On the other hand, Olobahun failed to make the sacrifice, prefering as always to rely on his wits.

After making the sacrifice, Esu decided to help Uri in his farming chores. The following morning, Esu visited Uri in the farm in the guise of a helpless cripple. Remembering the advice he was given at divination, he gave roasted yam and palm oil to the cripple. After eating, Uri did as he was told and instantaneously, a number of men appeared to help in clearing the farm. At the end of the day, they had cleared enough space for ten farmers. When Uri was about to go home, the criplple told him to hit his waist with the handle of his hoe and all the helping hands disappeared and the cripple crawled away.

That operation repeated itself throughout the chores and the farming year and people were wondering how Uri was able to have such a large farm and the prolific harvests. Later in the year, it was time for barning the yams. After barning his yams, with the help of his mysterious helpers, Uri was fatigued and decided to have a rest the next day, following a frightening dream he had in the night. He went to Orunmila for divination and he was told that trouble was imminent, because he was going to be the victim of a false accusation which could cost him his life. To fend off the eventuality, he was told to serve Esu very quickly with a he-goat and to refrain from going to his farm for seven days.

After serving Esu, he was to serve his head with a guinea-fowl, 201 pieces of coconuts, white and red kolanuts, and to serve his father with the leg of an antelope and pounded yam. After making all the sacrifices, he was to weep round his house in the night.

Following the departure of Uri, Olobahun also came to Orunmila for divination, in order to know the secret of the success of his farming neighbor. Orunmila told him to serve Esu with a he-goat and to serve his mind with pounded yam and a soup prepared with the leg of antelope to parry the risk of losing his life through the words of his mouth. He made a jest of Orunmila by saying that if he wanted meat, he could not get it from him.

Meanwhile, Uri served his head and decided not to go to his farm for the next seven days. During Uri's short break from his farm, the cripple visited his farm and he hailed on Uri, but got no reply. As he was crawling away from Uri's farm, he strayed into Olobahun's farm. Instead of entertaining the cripple as Uri used to do, Olobahun accused him of partiality. When the cripple asked him for food, he had none to give. Nonetheless, the cripple told him to touch his waist with the handle of his hoe. Instead of touching his waist mildly, Olobahun dealt a fatal blow on the cripple which instantly killed him.

Olobahun carried the corpse of the cripple and positioned it on the yam barn of Uri and went to Uri's house to tell him that an intruder was removing the yams he had barned. Without remembering the advice he had been given by Orunmila not to go to his farm for seven days, he left in fury for the farm with his gun, followed by Olobahun. When they got to Uri's farm, Olobahun pointed at the man he had positioned on his barn as if removing yams.

Without knowing that it was the corpse of his benefactor, the cripple, Uri shot at him and the corpse fell to the ground. When they both got to the barn, Uri discovered that it was his benevolent cripple he had shot, and he burst into tears and began to weep. Esu quickly influenced his next reaction by advising him to go and report his action to the Oba. He carried the corpse of the cripple to the palace and reported to the Oba how he came to shoot him, although he could not imagine how the cripple was able to climb the barn unaided. The Oba reminded Uri that he (the Oba) was the only authority that could deprive anyone of the right to continue to live and that any other person comiting murder had to pay with his own life.

Almost immediately, Esu influenced the Shashere who reminded the Oba of the sumptuous homage that Uri used to make to him after every harvest and hunting expedition, and of the Oba's erstwhile promise to confer a chieftaincy title on him. The Oba reacted by proclaiming that having pronounced the death sentence on Uri, he could not retract it, but that having also promised to confer a chieftaincy title on him, he would not renege on it. He immediately conferred a chieftaincy title on Uri, and told him to celebrate the conferment after which he was to surrender himself for execution.

Uri thanked the Oba and he led a dance procession throughout the town subsequently. Olobahun did not know what transpired at the palace because he stealthily withdrew from the scene of the drama he had orchestrated. His first intimation of what transpired at the palace was when he subsequently saw Uri at the head of a triumphal procession. Since he could not believe what he saw, he decided to find out who was the new chief at the head of the procession. When it dawned on him loud and clear that it was Uri, the supposed victim of his own treachery, he was overwhelmed with envy. Thinking that Uri had been compensated for killing the cripple, he decided to correct the mistaken notions of the Oba. He quickly raced to the palace and on getting there, he sought audience with the king. He went on his knees to announce that he had just discovered that the Oba compensated the wrong person for killing the cripple.

Everyone, including the Oba was taken aback when Olobahun professed that he was the one who killed the cripple and that he also positioned his corpse on the barn of Uri's farm. Thereafter, he continued he went to Uri's house to lie to him that someone was stealing yam from his farm, and that Uri reacted instinctively by picking up his gun and shooting the already dead corpse of the cripple when he got to the farm. Olobahun asked the Oba, how else would it have been possible for the limbless cripple to climb the barn, where he was shot by Uri long after he was dead by his own (Olobahun's) hand? He therefore insisted that he was the rightful candidate for the compensatory cheiftaincy conferment.

The Oba and his chiefs were puzzled by the anti-climax, but decided to wait for a decision after Uri's return from his procession. However, Olobahun was not in a mood to wait. He raced towards the direction of the procession and met Uri on his way to the palace, where he was escorted by Olobahun, who told him to dismount from the horse and surrender the paraphernalia of the chieftaincy to him because he was the rightful owner of the title, being the one who killed the cripple.

While agreeing with him, Uri begged Olobahun to exercise patience to enable him to pay the final obeisance to the Oba before surrenering the title to him. When Uri got to the palace, he paid the final respect to the Oba and his chiefs. Thereafter, the Oba invited Olobahun to repeat his story. Once more, he narrated how the cripple came to his farm after hailing in vain for Uri, who had not been coming to his farm for some days. He went on to add that on his way home, the cripple stopped over in his own farm for the first time ever, and asked for food. When he had no food to give him, the cripple told him to hit his waist with the handle of his hoe. He hit his waist with the handle of his hoe, so hard that he fell down and died, after which he deposited his corpse on Uri's barn. Eventually, he went to Uri's house to lure him to come and attack the "thief" who was stealing yam from his farm. Uri believed him and loaded his gun and returned with him to the farm. On getting to the farm he pointed at the corpse of the cripple he had positioned on the barn and Uri shot the corpse. He emphasized that he was the one who killed the cripple before Uri shot his corpse post-humously, and that he was therefore the rightful candidate for the chief-taincy title wrongfully conferred on Uri.

The Oba called on the chiefs for their opinion, and they all said in unison that the matter had decided itself. They explained that since Olobahun had openly admitted the murder of the cripple, he and not Uri was the culprit to be executed. Uri was discharged and acquitted at once.

At divination, the person will be told to make the sacrifice that Uri made and not to go to his place of work for seven days after completing the sacrifices. He should arrange to have his Ifa over the seven day period.

The Divination He Made Before Leaving Heaven

Orunmila mi sere lere, misere.

That was the Awo who made divination for Orunmila when he was coming to the world. He was advised to make sacrifice with: a ram, guinea-fowl and tortoise to his guardian angel (okekponrin); one he-goat to Esu; and to feast the 200 divinities with a dog, cock, gourd of palm wine, gourd of palm oil, white cloth and red cloth.

Since he did not have money for the sacrifice, he borrowed it from Elenini (Idoboo) the obstacle divinity. After making the sacrifice, he came to the world in the company of a represen-tative of the divinities. He had been advised at divination that he was not to be engaged in any other profession on earth apart from the practice of Ifism.

On getting to the world, he abandoned the representative of the divinities who came to assist him on earth. He also neglected the practice of Ifism. Consequently, a settled life eluded him on earth, because he could not afford to have a wife, bear children or build a house of his own. One day, he met an awo called Aganmurere who took a liking to Osa-Ose and engaged him as a personal assistant. Meanwhile, the Awo told him that his life had been listless because he had not only failed to tread the path of his destiny, but also neglected to link up with the divine representative that accompanied him to the world. Aganmurere told him to become his understudy in the art and practice of Ifism, but that before settling down to that vocation, he was advised to return to his home base (Idile in Yoruba and Igiogbe in Bini) to rendezvous with the divine representative who accompanied him to earth.

On his part, after waiting in vain to link up with Osa-Ose, the divine representative had decided to take a permanent abode in the forest from where he often came to the town to operate. He was advised to travel with a dog, cock, gourd of palm wine and white and red cloth which he was to present to the divine representative when they met. On getting to his home town, he was told about a strange deity who used to come from the forest to dance in the town from time to time. WIthout waiting for his next visit to the town, Osa-Ose decided to comb the forest for him. After a long exploration in the forest, he came to a deserted hut where he met the skeleton of the man's corpse because he had long died.

Osa-Ose cleared the bush around the hut and used the man's skull to prepare a shrine which he served with all the materials he brought, while spreading the red and white cloth around it. While he was making the sacrifice, the 200 divinities heard his prayers in heaven and agreed to send back their representative to him once more. Before allowing the representative to set out from heaven, Elenini, the obstacle divinity insisted on having his loan to Osa-Ose be repaid first.

Eventually, the divine representative met Osa-Ose at the shrine and reminded him of his indebtedness to Elenini while emphasizing that nothing would turn out well for him until he repaid it. He quickly returned home to collect the money for repaying the debt. Upon his return to the hut, he gave the money to the deity who advised Osa-Ose to take to the practice of Ifism, but to visit him at the hut from time to time.

After settling his scores with destiny, Osa-Ose began to flourish as an Ifa priest with the active moral support of the deity. He became so effective and famous as an Ifa priest that Aganmurere stopped coming from heaven, while leaving the practice to Osa-Ose. He was eventually able to raise a large family, build a big house and to take a chieftaincy title.

At Ugbodu, the person should find out the divinity that came with him to the earth, repay his debt to Elenini and serve Ifa conscientiously.

He Made Divination for Ogun to Prosper

Saka saka, libi libi soko tuuru tuuru. Odifa fun Ogun omo
ni jan-ole. O lo ba Alade mu ile ni'le aro. Ebo aje ni ki
oru o, ki a tun lo bo ogun. Akuko adiye lo fi bo ogun. A mu
eyele bo olokun.

These were the Awos who made divination for Ogun when he was going to apply to the king for a piece of land on which to build his factory. He was told to make sacrifice with cock to Ogun and pigeon to Olokun in order to become wealthy. He made the sacrifice and Ogun's life was transformed to one of eternal opulence.

When it appears at divination, the person will be advised to exercise patience because prosperity is on its way to him or her, provided he or she makes the necessary sacrifice.

Chapter 15

OSA-OFUN

He Made Divination for the Animal Called Ikeeghe and the Eagle

Boba fumi ni te mi. Emi a fun eni tire. What ever you do for me, I will do for you, was the Awo who made divination for the animal called ikeeghe in Yoruba or Akhakhua in Bini, who is wont to build several houses, while taking turns to live in them. He also divined for the Eagle, when both of them were anxious to have children. They were told to bring a hen each for preparing the sacrifice to enable them to have children. They both made the sacrifice.

After the sacrifice, they both had two children each. The eagle built her house on top of the oak tree while Ikeeghe built her house at the foot of the same tree. The hawk was friendly with the eagle, but was a dead enemy to ikeeghe. When the hawk heard that the Eagle had given birth to two children, she visited her friend who told her that her neighbor ikeeghe had also given birth to two children. On that note, the hawk asked the Eagle what time her neighbor was often at home. Without knowing that the hawk and ikeeghe were sworn enemies, the Eagle told her that her neighbor was always in all day except at noon when she went out to look for food.

The following morning, the Hawk took a position near the oak tree from where she saw ikeeghe leaving her house. As soon as she left, the hawk moved in to make away with one of Ikeeghe's two children. When she returned home to see that one of her children had been stolen, she ran to Orunmila who told her to serve Esu with a he-goat, and palm oil. After eating his he-goat, Esu went to the Hawk's house on top of the Iroko tree and lined it with palm oil from the ground to the home of the Hawk where she too had her two children.

As soon as the Hawk left home in search of food, soldier ants followed the palm oil trail right up to her house where they met and consumed her two children. Meanwhile, the Hawk went in search of the remaining child of Ikeeghe. Before then Ikeeghe had built several other houses and kept her remaining child in one of them. After searching in vain for the child of Ikeeghe, the Hawk flew back home only to discover that her home had been taken over by soldier ants. She flew back to tell the eagle that she could not find her two children "Mi O ri Omo oyen". That was how the Hawk paid for aggressing Ikeeghe who upon hearing about the tragedy which befell her adversary, began to sing in praise of the Awo made divination and sacrifice for her.

When this odu appears at divination, the person should be told to make two sacrifices; one for having children, and the second for protecting the children from the evil intentions of an enemy who is a witch.

He Divined for Ogun and Uja When They Were Coming From Heaven

When Ogun and Uja his wife were coming to the world, they were advised to serve each other's head with a cock. He refused to do any sacrifice. However, Uja called one of her children called Ejida - Totoda and with him, she served their head with a cock.

On getting to the world, Ogun was not recognised. He helped all and sundry, but no one showed any appreciation. When other divinities went out dancing, they pulled large crowds, but when it was Ogun's turn to dance, people were running away from him. Meanwhile Uja suggested that he should dress his son Ejida-Totoda to go out dancing. His son instantly became a crowd puller.

In disgust, Ogun took to the production of decoratory ornamentations, which people bought readily. His products made him to become very wealthy and popular.

At Ugbodu, the person should prepare his own Ogun with a dog, and serve his head and that of his wife with a cock. If he has no wife, he should serve his head with that of his Arugba, the woman or girl who accompanied him to Ugbodu. At divination, the person should be advised to serve Ogun with a dog and his head with a cock in order to achieve his objectives.

The Divination He Made Before Leaving Heaven

Osa lo efun, Osa lo osun, Osa lo mariwo ye ye ye.

The Awo who uses white chalk, the Awo who uses camwood, and the Awo who uses palm frond, were the people who made divnation for Orunmila when he was coming to the world. They advised him to serve: Esu with a he-goat, his guardian angel with a goat, hen and pigeon; Ogun with a cock, and Olokun with a pigeon. He made all the sacrifices.

On getting to the world, he married Olokun's daughter, gave birth to a daughter who was a Sango priestess while he acquired fame and fortune as an Ifa priest. He was so resoundingly successful that Orisa-Nla appointed him Osafun, as one of the leaders of the six cardinal points of the earth - what the Yorubas call Igharafa-mefa and the Binis call Edion ne'han.

At Ugbodu, the person should have his own Ogun, Sango and Olokun in addition to Ifa. He will prosper in life provided he serves Ifa well. At divination, the person should be told to have his own Ifa and to serve Ogun, Esu, Sango and Olokun in order to have his prosperity consolidated.

He Made Divination for the Hunter, The Farmer and the Awo

*Osafun roju. Odifa fun Ode, obufun ogbe, otun dafun Awo
okpe. A ki awon meteta ru ebo nitori amubo.*

He made divination for the hunter, the farmer and the Ifa priest all of whom were advised to make sacrifice to avert the risk of unconsumated fortune. They were required to make sacrifie with a he-goat toEsu. The hunter and farmer refused to make the sacrifice, but the Ifa priest did his own sacrifice.

Soon afterward, the hunter went to the forest where he shot a deer. At the same time, the son of Orisa was ill in heaven and the physicans taking care of him had asked for the blood of a deer to cure the illness. After unsuccessfully scanning the forests of heaven for a deer, the knights of Orisa's household took a position at the boundary of heaven and earth, from where they targeted the hunter with their telescope. Not long afterwards, they rendezvous with the hunter who agreed to drain the blood of the deer for them to take away in exchange for three casks of unsplit kolanut. The hunter put the kolanut in his hunting bag and left for home.

He subsequently stopped over at the farmer's farm, who gave him roasted yams to eat. After eating, he also drank palm wine. To show his appreciation, he gave the three casks of kolanut to the farmer and left for home. When the farmer was subsequently returning home, he heard the sound of drumming from the direction of the Ifa priest's house. He was performing his annual Ifa Festival and there was plenty to eat and drink. The farmer stopped over and was entertained hospitably. As the farmer was leaving, he gave the three casks of kolanuts he was given by the hunter to the Ifa priest on the grounds that he had plenty of kolanuts in his house and since he knew that the Ifa priest traditionally used plenty of kolanuts in his work. The Ifa priest thanked the farmer and he left.

Three days after the feast, the Ifa priest got a knife to split one of the three kolanut casks given to him by the farmer. As he was splitting the cask, money began to gush out of it. The second cask positioned a palatial building standing by the side of the house of the Ifa priest, while the third one produced all descriptions of clothes and apparels. Thus, the Ifa priest who made the sacrifice suddenly became the most prosperous man in the town and the Oba soon confered on him the title of the Shasere of the kingdom, which made him the second-in-command to the Oba.

Long afterward, the hunter returned to the forest where he met the heavenly knights who had given him the three casks of kolanut as recompense for giving them the blood of the deer he shot. They were surprised to find him still hunting. Out of curiousity they asked him what he did with the kolanuts they gave him. They were amazed to hear his reply that he presented them to the farmer. The leader of the heavenly knights instinctively proclaimed that no one would ever be able to prosper on earth through hunting, as a full-time profession. They did not explain their reaction to his behavior.

After his reNdezvous with the heavenly knight, who, unknown to him, came from heaven, he went to enquire from the farmer what he did with the three kolanut casks he gave him years before at his farm. When the farmer replied that he gave them to the Ifa priest, the hunter repeated the proclaimation made to him, that no one would ever be able to prosper from cottage farming as a full-time profession. He explained that that was the curse he got from the people who presented the kolanut casks to him.

Eventually, the farmer was too scared of the status of the Ifa priest to ask him what he did with the kolanuts, but when he eventually mustered the courage to face him, he replied that he used them to make the sacrifice prescribed for them at divination. That was when the farmer regreted his failure to make sacrifice because he readily surmised a causal relationship between the sacrifice made by the Ifa priest and the change in his fortune.

When this odu appears at divination, the person should be advised to have his own Ifa if he does not already have one, and to give a he-goat to Esu. If he is not inclined to having his own Ifa, he should serve Ifa with a goat, and Esu with a he-goat to avert the risk of diverting the fortune due to him, to someone else. He should be advised never to part with any gift given to him no matter how inconsequential it may seem.

He Made Divination for the Woman Who Divorced her Husband

Osafun, Safun, emi k o safun. Oko ki fi ibi woroko kole
Odifa fun shudi rodo. Awo shudi rodo ko okore si le.
O nshe abe kele kele kiri.

Run from him. I will not run from him. The hoe does not use its mouth to clear the grass on the ground without a handle. Those were the Awos who made divination for a divorcee who deserted her husband. She was advised that unless she made sacrifice, she would never again be able to settle down with any husband. She failed to make the sacrifice. Try as she did to link up for keeps with any other man, she often ran out of luck. She eventually settled down to full-time prostitution, in the course of which she contacted venereal disease that terminated her life prematurely.

If this odu appears for a woman at divination, she will be told not to market herself in the light of her beauty, lest she will contact venereal disease and become an object of ridicle later in life.

Made Divination with Ale the Son of Death and Ojiyan, the Son of Orunmila

Sa ale fun, Sa alosun. sa ani mariwo ye ye ye.
Ale omo iku, Ojiyan omo Orunmila. Iki ojiyan ko ma ojiyan
Ijo kon soso le logbon ni osu ule sorun. Adifa fun omo iku.
Abufun omo Orunmila. Awon mejeji won jon se ore.

Mark with chalk, mark with camwood, and decorate with palm frond. Ale, (with whom no one argues) the son of Death and Ojiyan (the argumentator) the son of Orunmila, were both friends. Ale visited Ojiyan, and they both went for divination to an Awo called "Don't argue". They were advised to make sacrifice with a he-goat and a gourd of palm oil to avert the consequences of a fatalistic argument.

Before they had the opportunity of making the sacrifice, Ale came out of the house the following night and asked Ojiyan what day the moon was going to appear. The host replied that the moon traditionally appeared every thirty-one days. Ale his visitor retorted that the moon appeared evey thirty days. The argument was so intense that Ale left for home the following morning to report to Death, his father, that his friend Ojiyan had been arguing with him on the day the moon was due to appear. At that time Orunmila was away on tour.

Since it was forbidden to argue with Ale, his father was annoyed and got his club and left for

Orunmila's house to kill Ojiyan. Death arrived at the same time that Orunmila returned home from his tour. When he saw Death in a combative mood, he asked him what the matter was and he replied that he came to eliminate Ojiyan for daring to argue with his son, which was an abomination. Orunmila intervened by asking Death whether he had verified the onus of truth in the matter, and he replied that it was not necessary to find out who told the truth and who told a lie before concluding that Ojiyan had argued with Ale. On that note, Death argued with Orunmila that Ojiyan could only rightly be adjudged as being an argumentator if he argued blindly on the side of falsehood, and that the victim would only deserve to die if he was proved to have lied. Between Death and Orunmila, with the caveat that if the moon appeared on the 30th day, Ojiyan would die, and he would earn his freedom if it appeared as he predicted on the 31st day.

Meanwhile, Orunmila called his son to explain what happened. After giving his father the details, Ojiyan recalled what the Awo had told them to do at divination. Orunmila proceeded without any delay to make the sacrifice. After eating his he-goat, Esu went to the Moon's house in heaven to use palm oil to soil his only cloth with which he appears monthly. The Moon subsequently washed the cloth for as many times as Esu soiled it with palm oil. The last time, the Moon washed the cloth was just before sun set on the 30th day when he was due to appear. Since the cloth had no sunshine to dry it, it was too wet for him to wear. To make assurance doubly, Esu invoked the cloud to appear on the firmament, followed by a heavy rain that fell throughout the night. Even if the moon had the cloth with which to appear, the cloud and the heavy downpour, would have made him invisible. Nobody bothered to find out whether or not the moon appeared.

On the 31st day however, the rain stopped in the morning and the sun shone brightly. The Moon's cloth dried and he was able to appear in all his majesty in the evening on the 31st day. As people were hailing the Moon's appearance, they were at the same time exclaiming that after all, Ojiyan was right, thus winning his freedom from the cold hands of Death.

When this Odu appears at divination, the person will be told that he is an argumentator. He should immediately serve Esu with a he-goat and a bottle of palm oil to forestall the adverse consequences of arguing with a higher authority.

The Divination Made for Him When He Was Traveling Overseas

Sa fun mi. Emi ko sa efifun. That was the Awo who made divination for Orunmila before he traveled overseas. He was advised to make sacrifice with three pigeons, 3 cocks, and his big black apparel. He made the sacrifice but refused to part with his black apparel. Thereafter, he embarked on the journey.

The trip was reasonably problem-free and he realised plenty of gains in money and materials, but could not return home on schedule. When Esu was told that Orunmila had refused to make sacrifice with his black cloth, Esu unplugged the rain tap of the sky and it rained continuously for one month, causing a severe flooding which made it impossible for Orunmila to embark on his home-ward journey.

After waiting in vain for Orunmila to return home, his friend called Agbe went for divination at which he was advised to make sacrifice on behalf of his friend with a cock and his black apparel. After making the sacrifice, the Ifa priest gave a charm to Agbe to take to Orunmila. Agbe took the charm to Orunmila overseas. As soon as he used it, Agbe told him to pack his belongings in a big bag. Agbe touched Orunmila's head and feet, as well as his own and the bags. Instantly, they all disappeared and found themselves at Oke-jetti, Orunmila's home in Ife. That was how the miracle of disappearance started (Ide eyi ni awon yoruba fi ashe egbe).

When it appears at divination, for someone preparing to go on tour, he/she will be told to make sacrifice in order to return home safely.

Divined for Monkey When He Lied against Orisa

Osa fun was the Awo who made divination for Alakedun (Monkey) when he fabricated lies against Orisa. He was advised to make sacrifice to hinder the danger of getting into trouble through his utterances. He was required to make the sacrifice with a cock, roasted yam, palm oil and palm wine. He made the sacrifice.

Soon afterwards, he was walking one day in the forest when he came across Orisa with a plate of pap in his hand. Thinking that the plate contained palm wine, the Monkey ran to the divinities and told them, that contrary to popular belief, he met Orisa drinking palm wine in the forest. To assert the authenticity of his assertion he told them to follow him to the forest. The divinities followed him to the forest, where they met Orisa still holding the plate in hand.

When he saw them, Orisa asked what the fun was all about, and they told him that the monkey alleged that he was drinking palm wine in the forest. Orisa showed them the plate of pap he was holding. Seeing that he had lied, the monkey went on his knees to beg for forgiveness. Orisa forgave him, but proclaimed that for bothering the divinities needlessly, he, the monkey would never again have peace of mind throughout to eternity. That is why the monkey is eternally restless.

At divination, the person will be advised to watch his utterances to avoid getting into trouble. He should however make sacrifice to avoid becoming the victim of a vicious falsehood.

Chapter 1

ETURA-OGBE
ETURA-ELEJI
ETURA-ORILANA
ETURA-ARODEMI
ETURA-JOBI
ETURA-RINA

He Made Divination for Three Friends

Etura Arodemi made divination for Death, Ogun and Orunmila before their children went to the forest to fetch fire wood. They were to make sacrifice with cock, and roasted corn to avoid undoing themselves. Death and Ogun refused to make their sacrifices but Orunmila made his own.

One morning their children decided to go to the forest together to fetch fire-wood. Death's son was called Mogboferefere, while the son of Ogun was called Agbenmagbantan and the son of Orunmila was called Egodudu. After making his sacrifice, Orunmila told his son that when anyone asked him for his name, he should always call himself "Ignorance and Innocence", and that he was not to argue with anyone. The three friends left for the forest.

When they got to the three-road junction, they began to reason among themselves where they were to fetch fire-wood. The son of Death proposed that they should go to his father's farm, knowing fully well that it was forbidden for anyone to enter his father's farm. Before then Death had been anxious to know who was stealing from his farm. On that very day, Death had gone to his farm to lie an ambush against any intruder to his farm. Neither the son of Ogun nor the son of Orunmila knew that it was forbidden to enter Death's farm.

On getting to the farm, they began to cut fire-wood with an axe. After hitting the wood with the axe three times, Death heard the sound and held his cudgel to deal with the intruder. Meanwhile, the other two sent Orunmila's son to go and fetch the ropes with which they were to tie the fire-wood, while the son of Death was still cutting the wood.

When Death met the two boys beside the wood, they were mowing, he used his cudgel to hit the one who was doing the cutting, while hitting the one standing nearby on the leg. Incidentally, he was returning to his hut in the farm when the rain began to fall. At the same time, Orunmila's son was returning with the ropes he had fetched when the rain drove him to take shelter in the hut, where he met Death. When Death asked him who he was, he replied that he was innocent and ignorant. Asked what he was doing in the farm, he replied that it was his friend, Mogboferefere who invited them to come and fetch fire wood in his father's farm.

Confused at hearing the name of his son, Death entered the rain to go and verify the identity of the victims he had attacked. He was bewildered to see that his son was dead while Ogun's son was incapacitated with a broken leg. Realising that he had killed his son with his own hand, he remembered the warning he had been given at divination, to make sacrifice to avert the danger of undoing himself.

When this Ifa appears at Ugbodu, the person will be advised to serve Esu with a he-goat to avoid undoing himself. He should be advised to refrain from boasting and to beware of undertaking any major assignment with two friends in a trio, before making the sacrifice. If it does not rain on the day he went to Ugbodu, it will rain within seven days after that day. When it rains, he should enter the rain and allow its showers to drench him.

At divination, the person should be advised to serve Esu with a he-goat because of an impending visitor.

He Made Divination for the Head

*Etura Orimi gbemi. Ori lanade mi Orilana to
Ori eku ni lana keku. Ori eja ni lana keja.
Ori osan ni lana kosan. Ori oro ni lana koro.
Ibi usin ba do si ni omo araye lana nkan.
Ori obi ni lana ire kobi.*

*It was the head that paved the way to the world.
It was the head that brought salvation to the rat, fish, sherry,
edible fruits, kolanuts, birds, animals and humanity.*

That is why this Odu is called Etura Orilana. When it appears at divination, the person will be advised to make sacrifice with three cocks. He will serve his head with one cock, serve his late father (or father's head if alive) with the second cock and make sacrifice with the third cock for the Ifa priest to take away without killing it.

The Divination He Made Before Leaving Heaven

Alanoko lere mi alanoko. Ori obi ni a lano kobi was the Awo who made divination for Etura-Eleji when he was coming to the world. He was advised to make sacrifice with he-goat to Esu, and guinea-fowl to his head to prepare himself for the great work he was going to do on earth.

The Ifa priest made the sacrifice for him by collecting the leaves of Osan agbalumo, kola tree, and the leaves of another tree called . . . . in yoruba and Ogri in Bini, and making him to serve his head on a cirlce marked with white chalk and killing the guinea-fowl on them inside the circle. The leaves were subsequently ground with the head and blood of the guinea-fowl and used to prepare a special wand which was embedded in his head.

On getting to the world he began to practice Ifism and to trade on the side line, but he could not make ends meet. Meanwhile, he went for divination to find out why he was not making much progress. The Awos who made divination for him on that occasion were; Ofiki lawo Ofiki, Eji ale ano Ibara ni morun, Eji owuro oni Ibara ni mo dide. Oruko rimi eke lu-bebe. Agbo me so more lu momo. Awon ni won lo'ndifa fun Orunmila nijo ti ofe lo gba aya meta; Bejide omo olokun, koriko sugbe ' nini omo orisa, kpelu gbirada omo aje.

He was at the time trading in fowls. He was told to make sacrifice with a he-goat to Esu and to serve Ifa with a hen. He did the sacrifice, after which he went to the market of Oja-ojigbomekon-Akira with 201 fowls for sale. On getting to the market he sold all but three fowls, which was a record sale made possible with the help of Esu. Among those who bought the fowls were three maidens who came from heaven. They had vowed that they would only marry the man be he blind or crippled, who succeeded in knowing their names.

As Orunmila was trying to return home from the market, the three fowls cut lose and strayed to the direction of heaven. As he was pursuing the fowls he began to sing the following poem:

> *Mi O ri Sishe o,*
> *Mo O ri iba ti she o,*
> *Ori ire a she ni o,*

Meaning

> *I have not seen my 3 fowls,*
> *I do not know what to do,*
> *But my head will find them for me.*

When the three girls who were on their way back to heaven heard the strange song from the distance, they stopped to listen attentively. As Orunmila moved closer to them, they were astonished to know that the man was singing with their names in order of seniority. They began to wonder who it was that knew their heavenly names. They helped him to apprehend the three fowls, but gave him a pleasant surprise when they told him that they were going to marry him being the first man in heaven and on earth who succeeded in knowing their heavenly names. They immediately decided to accompany him to his house to become his wives.

Unknown to him however, the girls had three abominations: The senior of the three girls would instantly return to heave if the rain threatened before she got to her destination; the second one would also return to heaven if there was a tornado before getting to her destination, while the third one would return to heaven if the rain touched her before getting to her destination. Meanwhile, the clouds began to gather because Esu wanted to frighten Orunmila. Since it is forbidden for rain to beat Orunmila while travelling, he immediately put his left knee on the ground and marked the sign of this odu on the sand and began to chant the following incantation: which in effect were the names of the Awos who made divination and sacrifice for him:

Ofiki lawo Ofiki O.
Ofiki lawo Ofiki.
Eji ale ano ibara ni morun
Eji ale on Ibara ni mo dede obuko
Erimi eke lubebe kpo'mi.
Obuko me'so mo 're lu bebe.
Agbo rimi eke lu momo okpo mi.
Agb e somore olu mo mo.
Adifa fun oun Orunmila nijo ti emi.
fe gba omo olokun, omo orisa ati
Omo aje shaya.
Afoji foron fo ' mi do, Afoji foron...

When Esu heard the incantation, he smiled and wondered whether Orunmila was afraid. Thereafter, Esu sat on the rain, the cloud cleared and he was able to get home with the three girls. He subsequently began to live with them as his wives.

The three women became pregnant the following month before they had the opportunity of returning to heaven to receive the blessing of their parents for their marriage. On his part, he did not even bother to find out where they came from, let alone think of obtaining formal clearance from their parents. The result was that apart from his success in the fowl trading business, the prosperity of his wives which was meant to supplement his own, was held down in heaven and stopped from coming to meet them on earth. The women had three sons at about the same time and he began to have difficulties in feeding his large family. His three sons were named Ilelereji, Akoshe Yoyoyo and Ijenishe Regede.

Meanwhile, a visiting Awo from heaven called Ekun-da-ayo lule awo, called on Orunmila to make divination for him. He advised Orunmila to serve Ifa with a goat, but he could not afford it. Since he was anxious to make the sacrifice, he pledged his first son Ilele Reji to raise the loan for making the sacrifice. Five days after making the sacrifice, he sounded Ifa on whether or not the sacrifice manifested. Ifa told him that he was not yet satisified because he needed a second goat. Once again he used his second son Akoshe yoyoyo to pledge a second loan to buy the goat. At the end of another five days, he asked Ifa once again whether he was satisfied. Once more, Ifa asked for yet a third goat and a he-goat for Esu which he did by pledging his third son Ijeni-Sheregede for another loan.

Thereafter, the three women became so frustrated that they decided to return to heaven to ask their parents why they were suffering on earth. Before leaving, they told Orunmila that they were going to the market to see what they could do to retrieve their children from bondage. They were all in tears when they left the house. Three days after they left the house, the women did not return and Orunmila became so restive that he sounded Ifa once more on what became of the elaborate sacrifices he had made. Ifa told him to exercise patience because his sacirifces would soon manifest. He heaved a sigh of cold relief in a mood of total dejection.

Meanwhile, Orunmila's guardian angel (Ifa or Okekponrin) went to Orisa, Olokun and Aje in heaven to ask them whether they were not aware of their daughters' sufferings in the home of Orunmila on earth. That coincided with the time the three women arrived in heaven in tears over the desperate plight they were suffering on earth. That was the point at which the three women were cleared to return to earth with their prosperity.

On the other hand, after eating his he-goat, Esu rose up to create upheaval in the kingdom of Ife and there was total confusion. That was the scenario in which Esu went to Olofin to ask him what he was doing to resolve the disruption afflicting his domain. Esu advised him to invite the three most popular Awos in the town to divine on what to do about the situation. In deference to the advice of the Counsellor, Olofin sent for Orunmila, Agbe and Aluko. At the same time, Esu to had been to heaven to ask Orisa why he was allowing his son-in-law to suffer on earth. Orisa reacted by giving Esu the middle of a tuber of yam to send to his son-in-law on earth. Instead of sending the half tuber of yam to Orunmila directly, he Esu prefered to make Orunmila work to earn it. This he did by going to hide it behind the door of the main bedroom of the Olofin.

That was the day on which the three Awos answered Olofin's invitation. Aluko and Agbe arrived at the palace very early in the morning. Orunmila left much later. On his way to the palace, he met Esu in the guise of the Awo called Ekun-do-ayo lule awo, and advised him that he was going to succeed in his mission to the palace, but that for his reward he was to ask for the half piece of yam at the back of the door to Olofin's bedroom, together with a cock. Even the Olofin was not aware of the presence of the half piece of yam in his room.

On getting to the palace, Agbe made divination and recommended sacrifice with a black goat in Olofin's zoological garden. The goat was given to him and he made sacirifce with it and left for home. Next, Aluko came in to recommend sacrifice with the red gown in Olofin's wardrobe. It was accordingly produced and after the sacrifice, he went away with the gown. When Orunmila made his divination later, he asked for sacrifice to Esu with a cock and the half piece of yam at the back of the door to Olofin's bedroom. Olofin produced the cock, but Orunmila insisted that Olofin should verify his assertion. Rather incredulously and reluctantly, Olofin went to his bedroom and was surprised to find the half piece of yam at the back of his bedroom door. As soon as Olofin removed the yam, Esu untied the knot with which he created problems in the kingdom, and life began immediately to return to normal.

Orunmila returned home to meet the daughter of Orisa back in the house. She had seen the goat that Agbe brought from Olofin's palace and the big red gown that Aluko brought from the palace. When her own husband was returning she was annoyed when she saw him returning home with a live cock on his shoulder and a half piece of yam in his bag. The woman was annoyed and yelled at him whether it was with such tenuous gifts that he was going to retrieve his three children from servitude. She subsequently decided to pack her belongings and leave his house for good unless he was able to return her son from bondage. However, Orunmila told her to put the yam he brought from the palace on the cooking pot before leaving, so that he could fire it by himself after she had left.

She proceeded to prepare the fire after which she brought out a knife to cut the yam before putting the pieces into the cooking pot. She became even more exasperated when the knife did not penetrate the yam while saying that even the yam he brought was not eatable. In anger, she hit the yam hard on the floor and it burst open, releasing its content of money, beads, clothes and all imaginable items of wealth. She instinctively hailed on her husband to come and see the miracle that was unfolding.

As if she called her mates when she hailed on Orunmila, the remaining two wives came with their large retinue of followers bringing their prosperity from heaven. In unison, Orunmila and his three wives started singing to their children who were in bondage.

Ilelereji ma ma i suun o o !
Akoshe yoyoyo ma ma i suun oo ! !
Ijeni sheregede mama i suun oo ! ! !
Ekun ma ti doyo ni'le Awo oo.

Meaning

My children, stop lamenting
Your sufferings are over because
happiness has wiped the tears from
the eyes of your parents.

The debts, owed by Orunmila were paid immediately and the children rejoined their parents. Thereafter, Orunmila and his family were translated into eternal and boundless wealth and opulence.

When this Ifa appears at Ugbodu, the person will be told that he will get married to three wives who will usher in prosperity to his life. He should serve Esu and his head always. The Ifa will be given three goats at intervals of five days.

At divination, the person should be told to have his own Ifa and to serve Esu with a he-goat. He will prosper through his marriage.

The Divination and Sacrifice He Made to Win a Crown

Ara kii kon lo'nshawo lo'de Igbago
Ekun lo'nde Ofe duwa si akon lode ominikun.
Oromu romu lo'nshawo lo'de sokpo
Awon lo'ndifa fun Orunmila nijo ti omu ade
lowo Alaafin, lo'de Oyo.

Those were the three Ifa priest who made divination and sacrifice for Eleji when he was going to win the crown from Alaafin of Oyo. At the height of his posperity, his guardian angel sent three Ifa priests to him from heaven. When the three Awos announced their arrival at his house, his attendants directed them to his palace. After giving them a warm reception, they decided to embark on divination. He did not know that they came from heaven.

At divination, they advised him to travel to the kingdom of Oyo after making sacrifice. He was told that he was going to see the apogee of his fortune and fame during the tour. Meanwhile, he was required to make sacrifice with, rat, fish and a ram to Ifa, dog to Ogun, and a he-goat to Esu. He made the sacrifices. After using the dog to serve Ogun, they prepared a special medicine and mounted it on the head of the dog. He was advised to travel the following morning to Oyo with the head of the dog inside his bag. Thereafter, he compensated the Awos and he left.

After the departure of the Awos, he felt disinclined to travel because he was already satisfied with the prosperity he had achieved. Nonetheless, as he was sleeping in the night, his guardian angel appeared to him in a dream directing him to heed the advice of the Awos and to travel to Oyo the following morning. Without disclosing his intentions to anyone, he left for Oyo as soon as the cock crowed the following morning.

As soon as he left home, Esu went to the palace of the Alaafin of Oyo and abducted the favorite dog of the Oba. When Alaafin woke up he could not find his pet-dog. The palace orderlies reported that someone had left the palace in the early hours of the morning with a bag believed to have contained the dog. The Alaafin instantly issued instructions for checkpoints to be mounted at all the main entrances to the town, and that all those leaving and entering the town should be thoroughly searched.

That was the state of affairs when Etura-Eleji arrived at the main entrance leading from Ife to Oyo late in the morning. When he was told to surrender his bag for checking, he complied without qualms. When the policemen examined his bag, they found the newly severed head of a dog with medicine mounted on it, with fresh blood oozing from it. He was instantly accused of stealing and killing the Alaafin's dog. When he tried to explain that he bought his dog from the market, the policemen slapped him, tied up his hand behind his back and matched him to the palace. He began to wonder whether he had not been the victim of some confidence thricksters who paraded themselves as Awos.

When he was eventually arraigned before the Alafin, without listening to any explanation from the accused person, let alone establish his identity, the king summarily sentenced him to death by execution. The royal executioners were instantly invited to carry out the execution. As Orunmila was being led to the execution chamber, Esu released the King's dog and it ran at once to the side of the Alaafin, who was so bewildered by his earlier miscarriage of justice that he sent words to the executioners not to carry out the sentence, because he wanted to interview the condemned prisoner. When Orunmila was re-arraigned before the Alaafin, the king told him that he apparently had a good head that had saved him from death at the nick of time. The king ordered that he be unchained and that the gag already tied to his mouth and the blind-fold on his eyes be removed.

It was at that point that the Alaafin asked for the identity of the accused person. When he identified himself as Etura-Eleji, the royal Ifa priest of Ife, Alaafin expressed his apologies and decided immediately to compensate him with a goat, a man, and a woman, to atone for the shabby treatment meted out to him. Orunmila replied in tears with the following song.

Ara kii kon lo'nshawo lo'de Igbago,
Ekun lo'de ofe duwa si akon lo'de ominikun
Oromu romu lo'nshawo lo'de Sokpo.
Awon meteta lo'ndifa fun un Orunmila nijo ti mo
nshawo lo so'de Oyo.
Alaafin da un lo le mu o oo. Orunmila

Almost immediately, Esu reacted by turning his eyes with fire on one side and blood flowing from the other side, followed by total darkness in the whole of Oyo. The Alaafin was startled from his throne by an earthquake which in a matter of minutes destroyed several houses and people in the town. The king began to beg Orunmila to soften up promising valuable items. As if to demonstrate that the compensation was inadequate, the harem of the King was instantly engulfed in a ball of fire. Alaafin agreed to divide the town into two and to give one part to Orunmila to administer. Once more, the earthquake affected the private chamber of the king and all the members of his household were buried in the debris.

That was the point at which Alaafin surrendered the crown and the throne to Orunmila. As soon as the crown was handed over to Orunmila, the Alaafin and his throne caved into bottomless precipice after which Esu agreed to a cease fire. It was from then on that a proclamation was made forbidding the binding in chains or detention of any Ifa priest. Thus began the maxim that the town which chains or forcibly detains an Ifa priest will not know any peace until he is released and compensated.

This Odu's Special Sacrifice for Prosperity

Orunmila ni ara, moni n kan eye.
Oni aje ti a ba wa ni ile eni, oni n kan e-ye ni.
Oni aya ti o ba wu ni ile eni, oni n kan e-ye ni.
Oni omo ti eni ba bi, oni n kan e-ye ni
Oni ile kiko, oni o hun e-ye ni.
Orunmila ti o ba ri be, kini a ma fi she?
Orunmila says it is an axiom. I replied it is a thing of joy.
Orunmila added that the presence of prosperity in a home.
Is a thing of joy. That if one has a wife, that gives birth to
a child, and is given a chieftaincy title of an elevation, it
is a thing of joy. When Orunmila was asked for the requisite
sacrifice, he declared that it would require two ducks.
Any female child born after the divination should be named
Ifayemi and a male child should be named Awoyemi or Ifadare.

At divination, the person should be advised to make sacrifice with 2 ducks, one for Ifa and the other to serve his head, so that whatever he or she tries his/her hand on will succeed because the duck never drowns in water.

Divined for a Brother and a Sister When They Were Looking for the Good Things of Life

Etura ra ra o dara - was the Awo who made divination for a brother and a sister respectively called Omonubi and Omolara, when they were anxious to make it in life. They were told to make sacrifice with rats, fishes, fowls and a he-goat. They made the sacrifice and prospered ever after.

When it appears at divination, the person will be advised that there is a catastrophe in the offing which can only be averted by fasting for Ifa.

This Odu's Special Sacrifice for Success in Life

Orunmila ni Orilana kpere. Moni orilana kpere.
Oni ori orogbo ni o ma nla ona fun Orogbo.
Oni ori obi ni o ma nla ona fun obi.
Oni ori osan ni o ma nla ona fun osan.
Oni ori iwowo ni o ma nla ona fun iwowo rin larin eranko.
Orunmila, iwo nshe n fo bi ade. Iwo nshe n fo bi eyo.
Orunmila proclaims that the future is bright. His priest
confirmed it. He explained that it is the head of the
bitter-kola that determines its course. The same is true
of the kolanut and the sherry. In the same way, it is true
of the grass-cutter that paves the way for other animals.
Orunmila finally declared that at the appearance of this
odu at Ugbodu and at divination, the person should serve his
head with many kolanuts in order to prosper in life.

He Made Divination for the Maggot

Akere mashogbara. O showo meji ni won nki ara won.
"Ku oja ti ta". Otoshi meji kpade. Won ko le da nkan.
egbe wa se. Won difa fun eruku, won bufun Egun iso-so.

The beautifully skinned frog and two friendly traders congratulated themselves for the successful sale of their wares. Those were the two awos who made divination for the maggot and the black ants, when they were coming to the world. They were both advised to make sacrifice to forestall the danger of having their children destroyed by the inhabitants of the world. They were required to make sacrifice with needles and dust. The black ants made the sacrifice but the Maggot did not.

On getting to the world, they began to have many children. As human beings and animals were wondering whether any of them had any alimentary value, Esu advised them that the children of the maggot were very nutritious, but warned them not to touch the black ants because of their toxic effect.

Those who neglected the advise of Esu and dared the black ants were stung by the probosis or needle with which their mother had made sacrifice in heaven. The victims of their bite had the bitten parts of their bodies swollen with severe pain. That is why the black ants are not edible to this day, whilst the palm tree maggots are delicious meals to men, animals and birds.

At divination, the person will be advised to make sacrifice in order to protect his or her children from the evil machination of enemies.

Chapter **2**

ETURA-OYEKU
ETURA-OGOKU
ETURA-ARIKU
ETURA-ARIKO
ETURA-AKPONKON

The Divination He Made Before Coming to the World

Mi ko li ku ekun lere. Mi ko li ku ekun, was the Awo who made divination for this Odu when he was coming from heaven. He was advised to make sacrifice with; a he-goat to Esu, and a dog, cock and tortoise to Ogun, in order to live a responsible life on earth. He made the sacrifice and left for the world.

He became an itinerant dancer, roaming about from one town to the other. For not being able to settle down to a profession, he became a laughing stock. During his dancing rounds, he tried his hands at divining but his predictions never came true. As he was dancing in a town on one occasion, he came across an Ifa priest who made divination for him. At divination, the Awo told him that he had forgotten the injunction he was given in heaven not to behave irresponsibly on earth. The Awo told him that he was advised in heaven neither to engage in dancing nor in drinking sprees. It was the transgression of these injunctions that prevented his previous sacrifice from manifesting. He was therefore required to make sacrifice to Esu with a he-goat and to use whatever he could afford to serve Ifa and to use the meat to feast the people around him.

On getting home he made the sacrifice to Ifa with a goat and a hen after serving Esu with a he-goat. He invited a large number of people who were feted with food and drinks. All his invitees remarked that for the first time he had done something responsible. That marked the beginning of his progress in life. He began to see clearly as an Ifa priest and his predictions were coming true while his sacrifices were manifesting. He was able to marry and to have children.

At Ugbodu, the person should be advised not to be gadding about but to settle down to a proper routine in order to prosper. At divination, the person should have his own Ifa in order to prosper in life.

He Made Sacrifice for Sankpana and Iya-Alaje

Etura Ogoku made divination for Sankpana and Iya-Alaje when they were both anxious to have spouses. He advised Sankpana to make sacrifice with a cock at home and a four-piece kolanut by the side of the road after which he would meet his live partner. He also advised Iya-Alaje to serve her guardian angel with a pigeon and her head with a hen in order to meet her live husband. They made the sacrifices.

Three days after making his own sacrifice, Sankpana set out on his practice as an Awo, playing oracle for people with cowries. When he got to the town of Ejigbo, people were streaming to him for divination, and he was giving them satisfaction. One of the people who came to him for divination was Iya-Alaje. After playing oracle for her, he told her that she had no husband, but reassured her that she was about to get married and to start having children, provided she served her head with a hen.

When she confirmed that she had just made the sacrifice, he told her that her days of anxiety over a spouse were over. In turn, she asked him for his wife and Sankpana replied that he had none.

With that, she formally proposed to marry him and he agreed by embracing her. After spending the night with him, she went home the following day to pack her belongings to join him as man and wife. Their marriage marked the beginning of their prosperity.

When this Ifa appears at Ugbodu, the person will be advised to prepare his own Sankpana shrine and keep it at a conspicuous place for people to see. Thereafter, he should serve his head with a cock. At divination, the person will be advised to serve Esu with a he-goat to avert the risk of losing a fine opportunity to others.

Divined for Mooye, the Wife of Orunmila

Arira O shaya gomugo gun okpe. Odifa fun Mooye
ti'nshe aya Agboniregun. A ni ki o ru ebo tori
oro ale ko a so fun obinrin na ko jo wo ale re.

The broad-chested Ifa priest looking like an ape was the Awo who made divination for Mooye, the wife of Orunmila when she was having a difficult labor as she was about to deliver a child. Orunmila had become so worried when Mooye could not deliver after three days of labor. That was when he invited the Awo to make divination for her. The Awo told her that she had been unfaithful to her husband and that unless she confessed the abomination, she could not deliver and would die.

While she was still strong enough to talk, she denied doing anything wrong. Thereafter, she began to discharge blood and water which de-hydrated her so much that she lapsed into coma-tose.

That was the point at which Orunmila began to sing the following song to persuade her to make a clean breast of whatever she did because she was too dear to him to be left to die;

Arira Mooye, bi o ba bi eji-ogbe lo fe bi,
Arira Mooye, bi o ba ku kee wi o, Arira Mooye.

He sang with the names of his sixteen opostles (Olodus) beseeching her to mention who-ever it was that had an affair with her, because he was prepared to forgive her. That demon-strated how forebearing and forgiving Orunmila can be.

At that stage, the woman gathered enough strength to mention the name of her lover and she was able to deliver safely.

When this odu appears for a woman at divination, she will be told that she had been unfaith-ful to her husband and should confess the act to avert the risk of death.

He Made Divination for Okponremi, the Daughter of Aremonijan

Etura yereku, Oye yereku, made divination for Okponremi, the daughter of Aremonijan, who was given in marriage to Orunmila. She ate a meal comprising of rat, fish and goat meat. As soon as she finished eating, she started raining insults on Orunmila. She eventually left Orunmila. When Orunmila sounded Okekponrin, he was told to make sacrifice with the duck, who neither sleeps by day nor by night.

Thereafter, the woman found it difficult to sleep and she began to emaciate as a result of her chronic insomnia. When her father observed the deterioration in his daughter's physique, he went for divination and was told that unless she returned to Orunmila, she would not get well and would die in the end. Thereafter, she went to apologise to Orunmila and to beg for forgiveness. She agreed and went to beg him for forgiveness to take her back after which she became well.

When it appears at divination, the person will be advised to advise his daughter not to leave her husband because she will be forced to return when between the devil and the deep blue sea.

Divined for Awogboro the Trumpeter

Etura kon go go go - made divination for Awogboro the trumpeter, when he was so pugna-cious that the burden of sudden death hung over his head, like the damoclean sword. He was advised to make sacrifice with a he-goat, a hen, a sword and his own wearing apparel. He was the trumpetter of his country's armed forces and all of them were advised to make similar sacri-fices. Awogboro was the only one who made the sacrifice.

When they subsequently got to the battle field, Awogboro blew the trumpet as soon as they encountered the ambush laid by enemy forces. The surprise attack led to the death of the soldiers, and only a handful of them including Awogboro survived unscathed.

When it appears at divination, the person will be warned that death is in the offing. He or she should make sacrifice to avert the danger of untimely death.

Chapter 3

ETURA-IWORI
ETURA-AWOYE
ETURA-OLE

He Made Divination for the Snail

Etura-Awoye made divination for the Snail, when she was losing her children after giving birth to them. Orunmila advised her to make sacrifice with a hen and a bag and she did it. Thereafter, he advised her to be hiding her eggs before hatching them into children. She was given the bag which she carried about on her body. When it was time to hatch the eggs, she followed the advice of Orunmila and hid the children in a hole.

Incidentally, she loved trading and money more than her children. When the children left their shells, they could not find their mother to feed them. Consequently, they went about stealing food from wherever they could find it.

One day, they went to the house of the Pawpaw to steal food. To teach their mother a lesson, the pawpaw incarcerated the snail's children under her mortar. When the snail returned from the market, she trailed her children to the home of the pawpaw where she found them under detention. When she asked the Pawpaw what offence her children committed, she explained that they came to steal in her house. She successfully begged for their release. When she went to the market again, the children went to steal from Osan-Agbalumo after which their mother abandoned them.

At Ugbodu, the person will serve the Ifa with 16 snails in order to avoid embarrassment from his children. He should give proper attention to the up-bringing of his children to avoid the danger of forcing them to become morally depraved.

At divination, the person should serve Ogun with a cock to avoid an unpleasant incident.

He Made Divination for the Ground and the Sky

Etura gamuga, Iwori gamuga, Okan gamuga laga ileke

Etura rose up, Iwori rose up and both of them climbed up to a beaded chair. That was the Awo who made divination for the ground, trees and ropes, and man and woman. The sets of pairs were all advised to make sacrifice in order to prevent the danger of fighting with each other. They were required to serve their heads. The ground was told to serve his head with a guinea-fowl, while the sky was told to serve his head with a pigeon. They both did the sacrifice together. The tree was told to serve his head with a cock while the rope was told to serve his head with a pigeon. They did not do the sacrifice. The two hills between a valley were told to join hands to buy a guinea-fowl to serve their heads together. They bought the guinea-fowl and served their head together. The man was told to serve his head with a cock while the woman was told to serve her head with a hen. They failed to perform the sacrifice.

That is why the pairs who made their sacrifices do not quarrel between themselves to this day, while those who failed to perform their sacrifices are always antagonistic to each other.

When it appears at divination for a man and his wife, they will be advised to serve their heads respectively with a cock and a hen on the top of a hill. If it appears as Ayeo, they should also serve Esu with a he-goat and extinguished fire-wood to avoid the risk of being on each other's throat. If it appears for a man or a woman, he or she should be asked whether he or she is part of a pair, either as twins, brother and sister, or brothers or sisters. For easy identification, one of them will have a deformed tooth or an open space between two teeth.

He Divined for the White Man When Coming from Heaven

Atanrere tanrere. Odifa fun afin-oyibo ni jo ti o wa mu use Igbameraye.

That was the Awo who made divination for the white man when he was coming to the world without the garb of poverty. He was advised to make sacrifice with beans, sugar cane, pine apples, and coconuts. He made the sacrifice.

He landed in the world on the land beyond the deserts and the seas, or Igbehin-okun, where he began to prosper after three years.

At divination, the person will be told that he or she is proposing to travel to a place by the side of a sea or river. He or she will benefit from the journey provided sacrifice is made to Esu and the water divinity before leaving. Nothing with blood or oil should be used for the sacrifice except white materials.

He Made Divination for Ogbese and Oshun When They were Competing for Seniority

Etura ole, Iwori ole. Ole meji. nja ni abe idiye. Idiye ko wo.
Be ni, ole meji ko da ara won, awon ni won loon difa fun Ogbere
ati Oshun.

Those were the two Awos who made divination for Ogbere and Oshun when they were contesting for seniority. They were advised to make sacrifice with plenty of Akara. Right from the venue of the divination, they were boasting and swearing at each other until they eventually agreed to meet for a duel to test each other's prowess in five days time.

Before the appointed day, Ogbere returned for divination and he was advised to make sacrifice and he served Esu with a he-goat and akara.

On the appointed day, Ogbere flooded the house of Oshun thus winning supremacy over the vanquished Oshun. That was how the saying began, "Ogbere fi kekere se egbon Oshun". That is, "Ogbere river swalloped Oshun to win supremacy over him".

When it appears at divination, the person will be advised to make sacrifice to avert the risk of losing supremacy to a junior person.

He Made Divination for Adeduntan

Etura gan ga, Iwori gan ga, awo Adeduntan, wondafa fun
Adeduntan, omo ewuru dagba ni oke.

They made divination for a woman called Adeduntan. She was advised to make sacrifice to avert the danger of miscarriage of her pregnancy. She was required to make sacrifice with a tuber of water yam which she had at home, adding a rabbit, snail and he-goat. Since she was disinclined to part with the water yam, she refused to make the sacrifice.

Subsequently, anytime she contemplated cooking the water yam, Esu would blot the idea from her memory. Meanwhile, the water yam (ishu ewura) began to germinate at the back of her house where it was kept. As the stem of the yam grew in height, the pregnancy of Adeduntan began to recede in size and to detoriate. She became worried and her anxiety sent her back to the Ifa priest who reminded her of the sacrifice she failed to make. It was at that point that she made the sacrifice, adding the water yam.

Thereafter, her pregnancy resumed development and in the fullness of time, she delivered a healthy child. At divination the person will be told to make sacrifice so that his wife's pregnancy might not abort. Ditto for a pregnant woman.

Chapter 4

ETURA-IDI

He Divined for the Pregnant Woman and for Olobahun

Etura-yedi was the Awo who made divination for Olobahun and a pregnant woman. Olobahun was told to make sacrifice to avert the danger of premature death. He was required to make sacrifice so that his inner head (mind) might not destroy the outer head. Since he normally prefers to rely on his wits, he refused to make sacrifice.

On her part, the pregnant woman was advised to make sacrifice to forestall the risk of becoming the victim of an offence she knew nothing about. She made the sacrifice.

Meanwhile, Olobahun felled a tree to block the only thoroughfare to the farms and the market. The tree had a big hole in it and everybody passing the road had to stretch out his or her legs over the tree thus exposing the genitals. Olobahun hid himself inside the hold of the fallen tree and brought out his penis through the hole. In that way, he was effectively making instant love to every woman who had to stretch her legs over the tree.

As a pregnant woman was passing over the fallen tree on her way to the market, Esu cajoled Olobahun to believe that the last woman had passed to the market, and he felt that all was clear for him to come out. As he was coming out of the hole, the pregnant woman saw him and raised an alarm that she had caught him *flagrante delecto*, the unscrupulous man who had been polluting the pride of the women of the town passing that way to the farms and the markets. Olobahun was instantly apprehended by the men who were coming behind the pregnant woman.

He was subsequently arraigned before the royal court where he was summarily tried and executed at the Ogun shrine.

When this Ifa appears at Ugbodu, the person will be advised to serve; his head with a cock, and Ogun with a tortoise within three days, to avoid becoming the victim of a vicious and undeniable falsehood. The sacrifices will be made at the Ifa shrine. At divination, the person should be advised to serve his head and Ogun with whatever he or she could afford. He or she will also serve Esu with the skull of a he-goat and promise to thank Esu with a live he-goat upon succeeding in a proposed venture.

He Made Divination for the He-goat When he was Arranging to get Married

Etura di, kankan di. Odifa fun Itu toni o unlofe aya.

He made divination for the he-goat when he was arranging to marry. When he proposed to the woman, she did not respond reassuringly. He decided to go to Orunmila for divination, who told him to make sacrifice with the equivalent of 30k. Instead of going to make the sacrifice by himself, he gave 45k to his mother to make it on his behalf. The mother made the sacrifice with 15k, keeping 30k to herself. Since she only made half sacrifice, it did not manifest.

After losing the woman to another man, he went to Orunmila to query why his sacrifice did not materialise. Orunmila explained that his mother was responsible for his problem because she only made half of the sacrifice with 15k. On getting home, he challenged his mother for cheating, thus making him to lose his intended spouse to another man. He challenged the mother with the words "WO BE EBO JE" and in the process attacked his mother and raped her. Thereafter, he told the mother that since she too was a woman, he would continue to make love to her from that day. That was how the he-goat established the incestuous tradition of making a wife of his mother.

When this odu appears at divination, the person will be told to make sacrifice if he is proposing to marry a woman in order to obviate the risk of losing her to a rival suitor. He or she should endeavour not to make sacrifice through a proxy in order to succeed.

Divined for Baata to Excel all other Musical Instruments

Etura di, kankan di, babalawo Baata, Odifa fun Baata, Abufun
gbogbo ilu to ku.

He made divination for the two-sided base drum and all other drums. The Oloye had invited all of them because he wanted to appoint a leader among them. Before honoring the invitation, all of them went to Orunmila for divination. He advised each of them to make sacrifice with calico cloth and a cock. They derided the advice by saying that there was no time one went to Orunmila without requiring one to make sacrifice. With the exception of Baata, all the others decided not to make the sacrifice.

Meanwhile, all of them left for the Oloye's palace on the appointed day. After allowing them to leave their homes but before getting to the venue of the contest, Esu caused the rain to start falling but before the rain started, he gave to Baata the calico with which he made sacrifice to cover up his head. Since they had no where to take shelter, they were all thoroughly drenched by the rain. By the time they got to Oloye's palace, they were all shivering from chill and loss of voice.

At the time of their arrival, the Oba was already annoyed for keeping him waiting for so long. He told each of them to start dancing and singing. They were able to dance, but practically all of them had lost their voices so much that the Oloye was disgusted by the cacophony of their sounds. He was about to leave them in anger when he was told that it remained one of them who had not performed. That was when Baata took the stage. He removed the calico with which he had covered his head during the rain and began to sing in praise of the Awo who made divination and sacrifice for him:

"etura di, kankan di, Etura di, kankan di"

and the sound was so melodious that their host had no difficulty in proclaiming Baata as the king of all musical instruments.

When it appears at divination, the person will be told that he or she is preparing for a conference or contest with other colleagues. He or she should make sacrifice before going and forewarned that it would rain before the contest, but should avoid being beaten by it.

He Made Divination for the Elephant and the Pit

Etura ye di. Awo erin, odifa fun erin, abufun ofin. O ni ki
awon mejeji rubo nitori akoba. Sugbon won o ru ebo na.
Obuko ni ebo re.

He made divination for the Elephant (Erin) and the Pit (Ofin) advising them to make sacrifice to prevent the danger of having a misfortune mightier than themselves. Since the Elephant could not imagine what other force was greater than himself in the forest, he was not inclined to do the sacrifice. On his part, the Pit boasted that neither death nor illness could overcome him, and since he was capable of swallowing up whoever dared to engage him in combat, he did not see the need for any sacrifice. Each of them was required to serve Esu with a he-goat, but they refused to do it.

On being told that Erin and Ofin refused to heed the advice to make sacrifice, Esu decided to teach them a hard lesson. One morning, while he was taking a walk, Esu lured the Elephant to stroll by the side of the Pit. As the Elephant moved near the Pit, Esu blinked his eyes to him which made him so dazed and dazzled that he strode into the Pit. The Pit was so happy with his big catch that he began to make a jest of Orunmila who had advised him to make an unecessary sacrifice.

From that morning until the evening, the Elephant battled with the Pit to make a get-away. In the wake of the combat, the Elephant broke the precipices supporting the cliff around the pit. The cliff hanger gave way stimulating an avalanche which instantly buried the elephant and closed the Pit for good. Thus, both the Elephant and the Pit battled each other to death for failing to make sacrifice. That is why it is often said that a crater that kills an elephant not only cannot kill another animal, but also dies with it.

When this odu appears at divination, the person should be told to serve Esu quickly with a he-goat to forestall the danger of sudden death to himself or a close relation. At Ugbodu the Awo will obtain the appropriate leaves to prepare for him to have a bath inside a pit, while mounting the relevant leaves of this odu on the fresh skull of the he-goat and positioned on the shrine of Esu with a U-bolt. One of the things to be used for mounting the skull of the he-goat will be something which the person will pick from the pit after having his bath in it.

Divination Made for Orunmila When He Travelled with Other Divinities

Etura di, kankan di. Odifa fun Orunmila ni'jo ti omba
awon omo erumole lo si ile obinrin gbondu gbondu.

He made divination for Orunmila before accompanying the other divinities to the land of women, where thre were no men. The other divinities had been to the town without being able to make any impression on the women. That was when they decided to return home to invite Orunmila, the wisdom diviner.

At divination, he was advised to make sacrifice with drum, gong, maracas and trumpet. With music and dancing he was able to cajole the women to return home with the divinities.

When it appears at divination, the person will be told that he or she will come across a prospective spouse who had rebuffed the advances of other suitors. He or she should make sacrifice because he or she will be attracted to marry him or her.

He Made Divination for the Musical Drums

Etura-idi, Goinidi, Adada-idi, were the Awos who made divination for the Musical Drums when they were travelling to the town of Ile-Ipe. They were advised to make sacrifice so that they might return home with plenty of gifts. They made the sacrifice.

When they got to Ile-Ipe, they began to entertain with an essemble which attracted many people. They sang and danced right up to the Oba's palace during which they attracted a large crowd of people who were spraying money and gifts on them. They sang to the beating of the drum thus:

Mo ti she'bo etura idi, Goin goin di
Alada idi, goin goin di.

That is the sound of the drums to this day. At divination, the person should make sacrifice in order to obtain the fortune destined for him when working far away from his/her home town.

He Made Divination for the Chameleon

The same Awos made divination for the Chameleon who was advised to make sacrifice to avoid experiencing any suffering whatsoever. He was required to make sacrifice with cloths of assorted colors and a cock. He made the sacrifice. That was how the chameleon was endowed with the rare privilege of receiving his food through the air.

When it appears at divination, the person will be advised to make sacrifice in order to receive the special blessing of God and to live a problem-free life.

He Made Divination for the Bass Drum

Etura-idi, Goin goin-idi. Adadaidi - were the Awos who made divination for the bass-drum when he was going to war in the town of Ile-Ikpe. He was told to make sacrifice in order to gain advantages from the journey to the war-front. He was advised to make sacrifice with a pigeon, a he-goat and twines. He made the sacrifice before leaving for the war-front.

On getting there, he met the two opposing forces engaged in a ferocious combat. As if oblivious to the reality of the bellicose situation, he began to dance and to sing, to the admiration of the combatants. Esu amplified the echo of his song and dance and instinctively, the combatants dropped their bows and arrows and began to dance to the alluring tune of his music.

Meanwhile, they stopped fighting and in unison, joined his procession to return home in peace to the tune of his music - Mo ti shebo Etura di, Etura di goin goin di. Aladi, goin goin di, which ended the war.

At divination, the person will be advised to make sacrifice and to take a job far away from the land of his birth in order to prosper.

Chapter 5

ETURA-OBARA
ETURA-ARABA
ETURA-BA-BA-BA

Divined for the Bird called Ako When Indebted to Olokun

Ewe ti a se ki 'run. Oro ti a mo tele ki i ni eni lara.
Adifa fun Ako ni jo ti onje gbese lowo Olokun ati Orisa.
Ebo niko ru o.

A leaf plucked does not grow again. The information already known does not come as a surprise. Those were the Awos who made divination for Ako (Erigoin in Bini) when he was indebted to Orisa and Olokun to the tune of six bags of money (Oke owo mefa). He borrowed the money for trading and the business collapsed. When he found himself unable to repay the debt, he began to hide from place to place. Subsequently, he was able to raise half of the loan and he decided to go to Orunmila for advice on whether to repay half of the loan to each of his creditors or to repay one of them in full until he could raise money for the balance.

After divination, Orunmila told him not to repay any of the loans, but to make sacrifice to Esu with the money he had, adding a dress made with plantain leaves which was to be burnt on Esu shrine. He accepted the advice and made the sacrifice. Thereafter, Orunmila told him to go and tell Olokun that he was indebted to both Orisa and himself, but that following a solemn appeal, Orisa had forgiven him the debt, and to ask how Olokun could help him since he had no money for repayment.

The following morning, he got dressed in velvet clothes into which Esu had turned the dress of plantain leaves with which he made sacrifice, and got drummers to accompany him to Olokun's place. On getting there, Ako began to dance in praise of God not only for the gorgeous dress he was wearing but also his debt forgiveness. The melody of the music attracted Olokun to come out to see who the singer and dancer was. As soon as Olokun came out, he added a refrain to his song in which he made a solemn appeal to him for loan forgiveness because God had extended the same compassion on him. Olokun replied that although God was his father and creator, if he could forgive his loan, he could do more being "richer than Orisa". Not only did Olokun forgive the loan, he also endowed Ako with more gifts and money.

After expressing his profound gratitude to Olokun, he led the dancing troupe to God's divine palace where Ako prostrated to thank the Almighty Father for being so patient with him over his indebtedness. In a solemn song and dance, Ako appealed to God to accept half of the loan which he had been able to raise and to help him in thanking Olokun who had just forgiven the debt he also owed him, in addition to the gifts he gave to him. In response, God said that since He owned Olokun and all his wealth, He was also prepared to forgive Ako's indebtedness. With these blessings, Ako became very wealthy and respectable.

When this Ifa appears at Ugbodu, the person will be advised to serve his head with whatever he can afford preferably a guinea-fowl, and to serve Esu with a he-goat and a dress made with the leaves of plantain in order to obtain the blessing of people in high authority. At divination, the person will be told that he is indebted to two creditors. If he does not want to repay them, he should serve; his head with guinea-fowl, and Esu with he-goat and the debts would lapse.

He Divined for Ebo and Sigidi When They Contested for the Marriage of a Girl.

Etura ba ba ba made divination for Ebo (sacrifice) the son of Orunmila and Sigidi (charms) the son of Osanyin when they both contested for the hands of a spinster in the divine household of God. The girl could not make a choice between the ajility of Sigidi and the serenity of Ebo, and therefore appealed to the Almighty Father to make a choice for her. Meanwhile, God invited the two contestants and appointed a date for them to come and demonstrate their credentials and eligibility for the girl's hands in marriage. They were told to return for the contest after three days.

On getting home, Ebo went to his father for advice and he was told to give a he-goat to Esu before going for the contest. He made the offering without any delay. On the third day, Sigidi got dressed in his diabolical outfit and he began the contest by demonstrating very amusing and entertaining magical feasts. He transfigured himself into a bird that flew round the podium to the delight of all the spectators. At another point, he suspended himself in the air and danced airborne for a long time without touching the ground with his feet. The climax of his performance came when Esu entered his mind and persuaded him to transfigure into a giant mouse which moved to salute all the spectators. At that point, Esu transfigured into a cat which gripped the mouse and made away with it. Since people thought that the apprehension of the rat by the cat was another scene in the drama, nobody moved to rescue the rat.

After waiting in vain for a long time for the cat and the mouse to return, God declared the contest closed by inviting Ebo to take the girl away to live with her as man and wife.

At divination, the person will be told that he or she is contesting for a favor with someone else. He or she should make sacrifice in order to win the contest.

He Made Divination for Onibedo, the Supporter of the Yam

Ewe ti a se ki 'run. Oro ti a ti mo tele ki 'nini lara.
Adifa fun Onibedo ti a ni ko ru ebo ki won ma ge ese re danu.

A leaf plucket from the plant does not grow again. An information already known does not make news. Those were the two Awos who made divination for Onibedo (Isaa or Eghee in Bini) the yound stick used for supporting a germinating yam plant. He was advised to make sacrifice to avert the risk of having his legs cut off. He was advised to make sacrifices with someone else's matchet that he had in his custody. He did not make the sacrifice because he was too much in love with the cutlass to part with it.

When the yam was planted in the farm, the farmer began to wonder how to support it when it germinated. Esu intervened to advise the farmer to cut the young sticks abounding in the bush round his farm to support the yam. Thus, the cutlass was used to cut the legs of the sticks to provide support to the germinating yams.

At divination, the person should be told to make sacrifice to prevent the danger of sudden death, or matchet attack.

The Divination Made for Him When Coming to the World

Etura ba Abara ba, were the Awos who made divination for this odu when he was coming from heaven. He was advised to serve his head and guardian angel with guinea-fowl and dried rolled fish; Esu with a he-goat; and Ogun with a cock. He did the sacrifices before leaving for the world.

On getting to the world he became so successful as an Ifa priest that he became the royal diviner to the Oba of his town. He made his debut in the palace by helping the barren favorite wife of the Oba to start having children. He prepared the medicine that helped the woman to have children, in the cemetery. To show his appreciation, the Oba built a house for him to live in. He was eventually made the Araba-Olotu-Awo, the head of all the Ifa priests.

When this Ifa appears at Ugbodu, the person will be told to make the above-mentioned sacrifices in order to excel in his work.

He Divined for the Penis and the Vulva to Gain Universal Honor and Respect

Etura ba ba ba was the awo who made divination for the vulva when she did not have a settled abode. She had been to the head, shoulder, chest, abdomen and waist to accommodate her, but they all refused because they had been warned by Orunmila not to grant lodging to visitors. That was when she decided to go to Orunmila for divination. She was told to serve Esu with a black he-goat and a black piece of cloth, after which she was to serve her head with a hen, coconut and white and red kolanuts.

She went to Orunmila to make the sacrifice to Esu and she was told that she had to serve her head by herself in a secluded place. Since she had previously been rebuffed by other parts of the body, Esu advised her to go to the secluded abode of the outer pelvis of the cavity between the human legs. On getting to the home of the pelvis, the vulva did not get an easy reception because like all other parts of the body, she too had been told not to accommodate any lodger in order to avert the risk of being completely over-shadowed and marginalised by the visitor. The vulva appealed passionately to the pelvis that she was only looking for a temporary abode in which to serve her head.

The pelvis eventually allowed the Vulva to serve her head on the outer fringes of her own house. As soon as she sat down to serve her head, Esu gave her the black cloth with which she made sacrifice to screen herself from public view. After the sacrifice, the pelvis told the vulva to leave her house, but she persuaded her host to let her stay overnight because of the convention requiring one to stay wherever one serves one's head and guardian angel, overnight. Before the following morning, Esu used the skin of the black he-goat with which the Vulva made sacrifice to glue her inseparably to the outer fringes of the abode of the pelvis (akata in Yoruba and Akhara in Bini) where she has remained ever since.

The vulva and the penis had all along been platonic friends. When the penis did not see the vulva for a long time, he was eventually told that she had taken permanent residence with the female pelvis. When he went to the Pelvis's house to look for the vulva, the pelvis closed the gate to her house.

That was when he too decided to go to Orunmila for advice and he was told to perform the same sacrifice that his friend the vulva made. He quickly did the sacrifice and thereafter, Esu persuaded the female pelvis to let in the penis of the male pelvis. After a brief meeting, the Penis left, leaving something for the vulva to keep which became a child after nine months.

Thereafter, Esu went to block the passage between heaven and earth thus making it impossible for people to go and come between heaven and earth to ask God for children.

Subsequently, Esu proclaimed that anyone looking for children should go to the male and female genitals. That was how they both got universal honor and respectability.

At divination, the person should be told to serve Esu with a he-goat in order to become prosperous and popular.

He Divined for Orunmila to Produce Children Who Were to Become Fathers

Araba ni baba, Araba ni baba. Eni ti a ba ba li aba ni baba eni.

Those were the Awos who made divination for Orunmila when he was going to produce children who were to become fathers. He was advised to make sacrifice with leather fans. (Abebe in Yoruba and Ezuzu in Bini), fly whisk (or horse tail) (Urukere or Oroke). He did the sacrifice. That is why all adherents of Orunmila who have their own Ifa are called Babalawo.

When it appears at divination, the person will be advised to learn to give honor and respect to his or her elders so that he or she too will reach the ripe old age to be refered to as an elder. He will become a prominent personality in his community.

He Made Divination for Alaraba

Abi irukere jonwonron, Babalawo Alaraba, Odifa fun Alaraba.

He made divination for Alaraba to make sacrifice to ward off the danger of sudden death through an inconsequential insect or animal. He was required to make sacrifice with his wearing clothes and a sheep. When he saw that the diviner was wearing wretched clothes, he concluded that the man wanted clothes with which to change his tattered ones. He therefore refused to make the sacrifice.

A few days later, as he moved out of his house in the night to ease himself, he stepped on a scorpion which stung him. Before the following morning, he died.

When it appears at divination, the person will be advised to make sacrifice in order to prevent the danger of sudden death.

.

Chapter 6

ETURA-OKONRON
ETURA-TIKU

He Made Divination for the Rat, Fish and Bird

Etura re re re, Okonron re re re. Odifa fun eku, obufun
eja, otun bufun eye nijo ti awon meteta ti kole orun
bo wa si kole aye.

He made divination for the rat, fish and bird when they were coming to the world. They were advised to serve their heads with palm fruits and to avert the risk of being attracted by other people's food. They did not make the sacrifice.

When they got to the world, Esu advised mankind that palm fruits were the favorite food of all three of them. Fishermen began to use palm fruits for setting nets to catch fishes, while trap setters used palm fruits for baiting rats and birds into traps. That is why it is other people's food that entice the three of them to their deaths, to this day.

At the appearance of this Ifa at divination or during initiation into Ifism, the person will immediately serve Esu with rat, fish, bird and he-goat to forestall the danger of eating poisoned food outside.

Divination for the Male and Female Genitals

Ake ke ti 'nke igi ni nu igbo, Ohun ni so igbo do oloni.
Ba laumo akpa ni so ashe da ototo eniyan. Adifa fun obo,
Omo ariyo oshu. Abufun oko, omo agana ere. Eyi ti o tori
omo dafa.

The axe which fells trees in the forest turns them to someone's property. Menstruation is the forerunner and midwife of mankind. These were the Awos who made divination for the Vulva to become alluring to the male sight. They also made divination for the Penis to become the father of humanity. They were both advised to make sacrifice with pig's meat, rat and fish. They made the sacrifice and became the parents of mankind.

At divination, the person will be told to make sacrifice because he/she is going to have many children.

The Divination He Made Before Leaving Heaven

Iwaju iroko rege. Eyin iroko rege rege. Adifa fun Orunmila
ni jo ti o ti kole orun bowa si kole aye.

They were the Awos who made divination for this odu when he was coming to the world. They told him that he was going to be the victim of a spiteful falsehood on earth and that to thwart the evil machinations of his enemies, he was required to make sacrifices to; Sango with a cock, camwood, bitter kola, kolanuts, ekuru, akara and eko; and Ogun with a cock, gourd of palm wine and blacksmiths scissors; and Esu with a he-goat. After making the sacrifices he went to seek and obtain God's blessings to survive the turbulence and tribulations of life on earth. Just before leaving for earth his guardian angel told him to make a special offering to the rubbish dump (Etitan or Otiku) with all remnants of food eaten in the house. He left for the world in the company of Sango and Ogun.

On getting to the world they all went their separate ways. Orunmila became an Ifa priest, but he was not doing very well. He was so poor that people soon accused him of being a witch and he was arraigned before the Oba who ordered him to re-appear for trial after eight days.

Meanwhile, he went for divination and he was told to serve Esu, Sango and Ogun. It was in the process of making the sacrifice that he met Sango and Ogun since they got to the world. On the day of the trial, Esu took over the mind of the judge at the trial. After hearing the case against him, the judge told him to defend himself and he said that he was a harmless Ifa priest who used his art to help people having problems. A number of witnesses were supoened by Esu to give testimony to the way he had used his Ifa practice to bring succour to their lives. Sango and Ogun also appeared to give testimony to his constructive application of Ifism.

Since no one was able to prove that he was a witch or that he used his powers destructively, the judge returned a no-case verdict in his favor. On the other hand, the Oba said that if he was able to help so many people with his Ifa practice, he should be able to help him as well. After the trial, he was made a royal diviner, and the Oba called him aside to tell him that he had long become impotent and wanted him to do whatever he could to restore his potency. When he made divination to find out the cause of the Oba's problem, he revealed that it was caused by one of his wives. He told the Oba to serve one of his Osanyin which was meant for checkmating danger called, Egbele kpota (Oghirare in Bini) with uncrowed cock, bitter kola, three-piece kola and crushed yam mixed with broken bones.

After making the sacrifice, Orunmila prepared the Iyerosun of his odu, and put it in a glass of water for the Oba to drink. Thereafter, any time the evil wife tried through witchcraft to manipulate the Oba's genitals, the Egbele kpota would threaten to arrest her and scare her away. Thus, the Oba was able to regain his potency. To show his appreciation, the Oba gave him five women who became his wives and five men who became his servants. He was also given 10 goats, 10 fowls and 10 bags of money in addition to a house which was built for him at the instance of the Oba Thereafter, all his accusers began to pay respects to him as he became famous and prosperous.

When this odu appears at an initiation ceremony, the person will be told to have his own Sango and Ogun shrines and to prepare his Esu without delay with a he-goat. He will be fore-warned of an arrest and trial which would be the prelude to his prosperity. At divination, the person will be told to serve Esu, Ogun Sango and Orisa so that what his enemies would plan to undermine him would become a blessing in disguise.

Divined for Him to Marry the Daughter of Olokun

He made sacrifice with 4 pigeons, guinea-fowl and white cloth which brought Olokun's daugh-ter into his life as his wife. Thereafter, his prosperity multiplied immensly. When this odu appears at divination, for a man, he will be told to make sacrifice because he will marry a woman whose star will bring prosperity to him. Ditto for a woman

Special Precaution Against Calamity

Orunmila ni eku, Moni Awishe.
Oni awishe eku ni eku yi o ko omo re sapamo si nitori iku.
Oni Awishe omo eja ni eja yi o ko omo re sakpamo si ni tori
awon dedo dedo.
Oni awashe omo eran ni eran yi o ko omo re sakpamo si ni tori iku.
Oni awashe omo eni ni omo eni yi o ko omo re kpamo si.
Orunmila, iwo n she n fo bi ede. Iwo n she n fo bi eye.
Oni ki a so fun eni ti o da oun, ki o ti ile kun re mo ori
ni ojo kan. Ki o ma si se jade. Ti o ba ti le she be ko
ni bo si owo iku. Be ni, ko si ni bo si owo ejo.

Orunmila pointed at the door, and he was told that the door was meant to be locked. He then added that it is by closing the doors that:- the rat protects its children from death; the fish protects its children from the fisherman; the animal protects its children from the trap set by the hunters; and human beings protect themselves from their enemies.

Orunmila subsequently explained that when this Ifa portends danger (or Ayeo) at divination, the person will be advised to stay indoors throughout the next day, to avoid getting into trouble.

Chapter 7

ETURA-IROSUN
ETURA-MOSUN
ETURA-OLOMU

Divined for the Ear When He Seduced the Mosquito's Wife

Eti ko le sun. Beni, Orun ko kun oju. Adifa fun Eti
ti o nlo gba iwuye aya efan

If the ear does not sleep, the eyes cannot sleep. That was the Awo who made divination for the Ear when he was going to seduce the wife of the Mosquito called Iwuye. The Ear was told to make sacrifice with a he-goat and a broom in order to minimise the nuisance value of the Mosquito. The Ear thought that the mosquito was too innocuous to pose any threat to him and so refused to make the sacrifice.

For failing to make sacrifice, Esu instigated the Mosquito to approach the Ear anytime the seducer of his wife tried to sleep. As soon as the Mosquito could muster the courage to dare the Ear, he went to him as he was trying to sleep crying "Wo gba Iwuye, Mo wa Iwuye - meaning You took Iwuye from me, I want my wife back. Although the Mosquito did not get back his wife, he nonetheless disturbed the Ear's sleep.

At divination, the person will be told to make sacrifice to minimize the inconvience from a helpless person whose spouse he or she has seduced.

The Divination He Made Before Leaving Heaven

Okee re ti do lale oyi shoko shoko shombe. Odifa fun Orunmila
nijo ti o kole orun bo wa si kole aye.

Those were the Awos who made divination for this Odu when he was coming to try to reform the world. When he heard of the extent to which evil had over-run the people of the earth, he was determined to come to make it a more liveable place. When he sought clearance from his guardian angel, he was told that he had no chance of succeeding where much more determined prophets and reformers had failed. His guardian angel however told him to go for divination on what to do in order to live long on earth. He was otherwise so useful in heaven that people did not want him to embark on a fruitless sojourn to earth. When he went to God for clearance, the Almighty Father told him that all the prophets who had gone to earth to reform it were not noted for any appreciable success, but that if he must go to earth for the same mission, he should go to Oyeku-meji for assistance.

When he went to Oyeku-meji he was advised to serve:- Esu with a he-goat, Ogun with palm wine, snails and a dog; and to feast the heavenly police. He made all the sacrifices and left for the world. All his efforts at reforming the earth were frustrated by Esu and his agents. Besides all the Awos on earth who considered him a threat, ploted to kill him. His enemies conspired with Ogun to eliminate him. When he made a morning divination, Ifa warned him that trouble was in the offing and that he should quickly give a he goat to Esu, and to stay in-doors at night. The chief of the heavenly police was at the same time visiting the earth.

The house of Orunmila had a tree of life (igi akoko in Yoruba and Ikhinmwin in Bini) in front of it. That was the description given to Ogun for attacking his house. On the other hand, the house of the Chief of Heaven's police force had a royal palm tree in front of it. Meanwhile, Ogun put on his fire dress which he wears when going to do battle. Before Ogun made his attack on the house with Igi akoko in front of it, Esu had transposed the tree with the royal palm tree in front of the house of the chief of Heaven's police. Ogun set the house on fire and as the chief of Heaven's police tried to escape to heaven, he was slaughtered by Ogun's soldiers, who surrounded the house.

After the operation, Esu changed the identification plants in front of the two houses to what they were before Ogun's onset. At day break, the conspirators were surprised to see that Ogun had apparently attacked the wrong house. When they queried Ogun for what he did, he confirmed that he attacked the house with the tree of life in front of it, and that if Orunmila survived the aggression, it was only because he could not have killed Orunmila anyway, because they came together from heaven and that he had in heaven enjoyed the sacrifice made by him and it was forbidden to kill anybody after enjoying his or her hospitality.

When this Odu appears at Ugbodu, the person will be advised to have his own Ogun shrine to support his Ifa because Ogun will assist Esu in frustrating the evil machinations of his enemies. He should be advised not to over-dramatise his reformist tendencies because it will cause a lot of problems for him.

He Made Divination for an Awo Called Idereluma

Oshe ni she iwaju ekun. A ba ma o ni igbehin oran.
O ton kpo kulu ko re 'bo a ba ma she. Adifa fun
Idereluma ti on lo she awo fun Onikpo.

Hissing precedes weeping. Regret is the culmination of mishap. The creatures of God could not know the sacrifice to be made against regret (Had I known). These were the Awos who made divination for an Awo alled Idereluma when he was going to work for the Oba of Ikpo. The Oba invited him to deprive him (Idereluma) of the crown and beads with which he was adorning himself In those days, successful Babalawos or Oba-Alawo as they were called, were known by the crowns and neck, wrist and ankle beads they wore, which made them look like Obas or Olojas. The Onikpo was determined to end the practice. He was told to make sacrifice before going, but he did not do it because he was sure of his survival techniques.

When Idereluma got to Onikpo's palace, the Oba appointed one of his most beautiful wives to be serving him with whatever he wanted, with special instructions to tempt him to seduce her. The woman was called Dede Oyin and she was enjoined to use herself to get the Awo into trouble in order to deprive him of his crown and beads. The woman was the only one who served him food, bathing water and all his requirements. She exploited the opportunity to make sensual overtures to him and he eventually succumbed by making love to her.

In the cause of the love-making, the woman took her time to cut off his wrist and ankle beads, which she sent to her husband. She did it over the span of his stay until she eventually succeeded in removing his crown. Thinking that the Awo might react violently if he realised that he had been deprived of his jewels, the Oba contrived a strategy for making him blind.

One night, as Dede Oyin was going for fresh sex rounds with him, she went with a needle which she concealed. As they were making love, the woman waited for him to reach orgasm before using the needle to blind him on both eyes, after which she pushed him aside leaving him helpless. From then on, he began to suffer. When people asked him what happened to his sight, crown and beads, he replied that he lost all of them to the Onikpo. It was from then on that Awos ceased to be addressed as Oba Alawos, and stopped wearing crowns.

When this Odu appears as Ayeo at divination, the person will be advised not to undertake a journey he is proposing to make. If it is Uree, he should make sacrifice before going, to avert the danger of being lured into a trap. He should be advised not to make love to any woman in the place throughout the tour.

He Made Divination for Iwa to Have Children

Etura ko roko. Irosun ko bere, Adifa fun Iya olomo mewa.

Etura does not go to the farm. Irosun does not bend down to work. These were the Awos who made divination for Iwa when she was coming to the world. She was told to serve her guardian angel with a goat and to serve Esu with a he-goat in order to have children on earth who would serve her at old age. She made the sacrifice to her guardian angel but not the one to Esu.

On getting to the world, she had ten children, who turned out to be insubordinate and uncaring to their mother. When she became too old to help herself, the children offered no assistance. Her last son called Adeshomoju went for divination on behalf of their mother and he was told to serve Esu with a he-goat. After making the sacrifice, Esu told him to fetch her mother a chewing stick, kolanut and drinking water. By the time he got to her mother's bedside with the three materials, she was already dead. These are not only the three materials people eat until they die but also the first thing the family asks for when a person dies.

At Ugbodu, the person will serve Ifa with a goat and Esu with a he-goat in order to live to have children who will look after him at old age. At divination, the person should serve Esu with a he-goat and his or her head with a pigeon. If it appears for someone anxious to have children, he or she will be advised to live near the sea or a big river after making sacrifice.

Divined for Oyadolu to Save Her Children From Dying

Okpeere ti do lale oyi. Shoko shoko shombe.
Adifa fun Oyadolu omo egbe te 're ni ojude onikpa
Agutan lo fi rubo ti tori omo.

They made divination for Oyadolu, one of the followers of Sankpana. She was advised to make sacrifice with a sheep (ewe) in order to prevent her children from dying before her and for herself to live to a ripe old age. She made the sacrifice. That is the same sacrifice that a person should be advised to make if death is foreboded at divination.

He Made Divination for the Star When Going to Marry the Moon

Etura ro ro, Irosun ro ro were the Awos who made divination for Agura (the Star) when he was going to marry Oshu (the Moon). He was advised to make sacrifice so that his wife may not outshine him. The Star refused to make the sacrifice.

On the other hand, the Moon also went for divination and she was advised to make sacrifice in order to command universal honor and dignity. She was required to make sacrifice with salt, honey, Camwood, shade, white cloth, red cloth and pigeons. She made the sacrifice.

When the star eventually married the moon, the people of heaven and earth only took notice of the wife and not the husband. The popularity of the Moon paled the Star into insignificance. That is why to this day, the Moon represents so many things to plants and animals, but the star is not used for any purpose with the solitary exception of latter-day astrology.

When it appears at divination for a man, he will be advised to make sacrifice to avert the risk of taking offence when his wife becomes much wealthier than himself, because it will promote the prosperity of the family. If it appears for a woman, she will be told that she will be wealthier than the husband, but should resist the temptation to over-reach herself with megalomania.

He Made Divination for Pagida

Etura gan ga, Irosun ganga. Okunrin kanga Kanga. kole digba
mo ekun ninu aga.

These were the Awos who made divination for Pagida when death was gunning for him. He was advised to make sacrifice to obviate the danger of sudden death. He was required to make sacrifice with a sheep and one of his big garments.

He refused to make the sacrifice because he did not want to part with his cherished robe. Not long afterwards, there was a tornado followed by thunder which struck him dead.

At divination, the person will be advised to make sacrifice to avert the danger of untimely death.

Chapter 8

ETURA-OWANRIN
ETURA-ALAKETU
ETURA-ALAKA

He Made Divination for Alligator, Crocodile and the Monitor

Etura rin rin rin, Owanrin sa sa sa - made divination for three brothers, the Alligator (Onne Wakaka in Yoruba and Agbaaka in Bini), Crocodile and the Monitor when they were coming to the world. Each of them was advised to serve Esu with a he-goat. The Alligator and the crocodile made the sacrifice, but the Monitor did not.

When they got to the world, they started having children. The Alligator and the Crocodile, both amphibians, lived mainly inside the water, while the monitor lived in the bush. Inside the river where the crocodile and the Alligator lived, also lived a python who used to make a terrifying noise whenever he had his bath in the morning by splashing his body on the water. The crocodile and the Alligator became so frightened that they went to Orunmila for divination on what to do to drive the terror from their habitat. They were advised to serve Esu with a he-goat. As soon as they left Orunmila's place, the Python also came for divination on what to do to expel two new intruders to his house, who were always watching him derisively each time he had his bath. He too was advised to make sacrifice with a he-goat to Esu. The other two did not make their sacrifices.

The following morning, they were once again startled by the thundering noise that was going on when the Python was having his bath. At that point, they decided that they had enough and left the area for a new abode, to save their lives. Their first inclination was to go and stay with their brother, the Monitor. Meanwhile the Monitor had blocked his two ears to prevent him from hearing the deafening noise that often came from the direction of the river, thus becoming totally deaf. When the Alligator and the Crocodile were running away from the river, they were pursued by the Python.

As they were running for their lives, they were hailing on the Monitor to run for his life because there was a war going on. But the Monitor did not hear their bellowing because he was already deaf. Thereafter, the Alligator ran into a cave while the crocodile took temporary refuge in a well. Subsequently, the Python caught up with the Monitor accusing him of being one of the intruders into his privacy. The Monitor told the Python that he was incapable of hearing whatever he said, and with these remarks, the Python took pity on him and left him alone. The exit of the Alligator and the Crocodile brought peace of mind and tranquility once more to the Python's habitat.

When this Ifa appears at Ugbodu, the person will be told to serve; the new Ifa with a crocodile and four snails, and Esu with a he-goat to fend off problems from his blood relations. At divination, the person will serve Esu with a he-goat to survive an impending disaster.

The Divination Ikin Made When Leaving Heaven

Erho ni a da ta arin - was the Awo who made divination for Ikin when he was coming to the world. He was told to make sacrifice to alleviate the problems he was going to have from enemies on earth. In that connection, he was required to serve Esu with a he-goat; his mind with a tortoise; enemies with a cock at a road junction, adding over-roasted yam, snail and three-piece kolanut; and his guardian angel with a goat, pigeon and snails. He was told that his most deadly enemies would be marble seeds (ishe ege in Yoruba and Akhue in Bini), ero mo don in Yoruba and Ise-Okhuen in Bini and pebbles. He made sacrifices before leaving for earth. Soon afterwards, he was followed by the three enemies who swore to frustrate Ikin's efforts on earth.

On getting to earth, they were all practicing divination in much the same way. Initially, the three rivals were even out shining Ikin and dispising him. In the wake of their derision of Orunmila, he ran into difficulties and lost all his clients. At a subsequent divination, he was required to serve Esu with a he-goat. After making the sacrifices, Esu created problems for the three of them. All the three of them went to Orunmila for divination and he advised each of them as follows:-

Marble seeds (Ishe - ege) -	to give up awo art and take to dancing which he does to this day.
Pebbles-	To give up awo practice and enter the river or the ground where he was to become a builder.
Ero mo odon (Ise Okhuen)-	to come and live with Orunmila to assist him at divination which is why he is used for divination by strong Ifa priests and Oraclists who divine by Ewawa.

That was how Ikin survived as the principal diviner in Ifism after dislodging his three enemies.

At Ugbodu, the person should make sacrifice to checkmate the evil intentions of three sworn enemies who followed him from heaven.

Divined for Olu-Jettu When His Subjects Abandoned Him

Etura-Alaketu made divination for the Olu of Jettu when his subjects rebelled against him. The obstacle divinity had formented confusion in the town and there was turmoil all around in the wake of which nobody was minding anybody while everybody was minding his/her own business. That was the setting in which the Oba of the town sent for Orunmila.

Before travelling, Orunmila made divination and he was required to give a small he-goat to Esu and to split it on Esu shrine, and to add the meat of antelope. On getting to Jettu, he made divination for the Oba, telling him to serve Esu with a he-goat so that he might discover the cause of their problems before the following morning. The sacrifice was made without any delay. As the sacrifice was being made on Esu shrine, one of the Oba's wives was spinning yarn at the court-yard of the harem.

After the sacrifice, Esu went to the woman to occupy her mind, which culminated in her decision to start singing.

"Oro kon bo lale Laketu"

After singing the song, apprising the Oba that a revelation was in the offing, people began to gather to hear what she was going to reveal. She started disclosing the meetings which the elders of the night often held nocturnally to cause problems in the town, adding that the two chiefs next in command to the Alaketu often attended those meetings. The woman soon began to make more revelations as if she was possessed. The Oba was subsequently invited to listen to her.

When the Oba shouted on her to confirm whether she realised the implications of what she was saying, she was startled back to her senses and she said that she did not say anything. In spite of her denial, the Oba immediately ordered the royal heralds to convene a meeting of all the chiefs and elders. As soon as the conference was assembled, the woman was invited to come forward to confirm what she had been saying. As she was moving to the rostrum, she transfigured into an antelope and escaped into the forest. That is why the people of Jettu are forbidden to eat antelope to this day.

In spite of the unexpected turn of events, the Oba called out the names of all the conspirators disclosed by the woman and made them to take an oath on the ground. They all took the oath and within a span of three months, many of them made open confessions and several others died one after the other. The number of casualties was so high that many of those who survived emigrated to settle elsewhere.

When this Odu appears at divination, the person will be told that he is the victim of enemies surrounding him and that his problems are being caused by the cult of witchcraft. He or she should make sacrifice and there would be a spate of open confessions and deaths among his enemies.

This Odu's Prescriptions for Alleviating Problems Caused by Enemies

Orunmila ni ele koro koro. Emi na ni ede gbede gbede ni 're.
Orunmila, kini a fi she. Bi Oba ri be, oni elede ni a ofi
ru ebo re. A o tun lo fi abo adiye bo ifa.

Orunmila declared that there was a strong and different problem. I retorted that it could be made easy and soft. He asked what was to be used to soften the difficulty. I replied that I had no clue, and he prescribed that the sacrifice required a pig to serve Ifa in addition to a hen.

If this odu appears at divination for an invalid, the man should be advised to arrange to have his own Ifa. If he already has Ifa, he should learn the fundamental principles of divination in Ifism. If it appears for a female invalid, she will be advised either to marry a man having his own Ifa if a spinster, or to persuade her husband to have his own Ifa if married for their mutual benefit.

Divination for a Pregnant Woman

Omo yi o bi i ko elele. Odifa fun Ailele tori omo ninu
aboyun. Ebo tori omo ni aboyun ti a bi omo titun.
Obuko ni ebo tabi elede. Awo a bere lowo ifa ewo la'ma lo.

A child shot out like the frond of the palm tree (ogoro) in several units, was the Awo who made diivination for Ailele when she was pregnant. She was advised to make sacrifice with either a he-goat or a pig (find out which to use from Ifa), in order to have a safe delivery or to avert the danger of still-birth. She made the sacrifice and delivered a healthy baby safely in the fullness of time.

At divination, for a pregnant woman or a nursing mother, she should be advised to make sacrifice to have a normal delivery or to avoid the death of her child. For a man, he should make the sacrifice for his wife.

Divined for the Generous Householder

Etura kpa eku, okpin fun ara ile re. O kpa eja.
okpin fun ara ile re. Be ni, Etura wa ge orin, ko ha fun ara ile re

Etura killed a rat and a fish and shared them with members of his household. When he brought chewing sticks from the bush, he failed to share them members of his household. They took umbrage to his niggardliness, which made him become ill. At a subsequent divination he was told that his illness was a function of his failure to share his chewing sticks. He made sacrifice and became well, after which he was advised to share whatever he brought from the bush, farm or outside, with members of his household.

At divination, the person should be told not to change his habitual disposition to benevolence and generosity and to take his wife into confidence as often as possible, because he lives in the midst of people much stronger than himself.

The Divination He Made to Become Prosperous Through Sedentary Work

Ewe lee, olele lee, Alele le ure. Adifa fun Orunmila nijo ti
baba ma nshawo imele ina.
Leaves I greet you, Pudding I greet you and I greet the drone.

These were the Awos who made divination for Orunmila when he was going to prosper through listless sedentary business. At divination, the person should be told that he or she is not destined to prosper through enervating or laborious work. He or she will make it through a seemingly calculated loafing business.

He Made Divination for Alaketu When He Was Going to be visited by Esu

Ki onile wo oju alejo. Ki alejo gbe ina wo oju onile.
Babalawo Alaketu, Odifa fun Alaketu.

The host should look at the face of his visitor while the visitor should look closely and examine a nocturnal visitor with light in order to identify the face of his guest.

That was the Awo who made divination for Alaketu, when he was going to receive Esu as a visitor. Alaketu was advised to be hospitable to his visitors and to make sacrifice with a strong he-goat to Esu in order to avert the danger of being embarrassed and the risk of losing his treasured belongings. He neither made the sacrifice nor heeded the advice.

One night there was a heavy rain which caused an overcast. That was the setting in which Esu transfigured into a chief to take shelter in the home of Alaketu. Esu was wearing a necklace made of red pepper round his neck. Without looking carefully at the face of his visitor, Alaketu let him in, but did nothing to entertain the visitor. His visitor went to bed with an empty stomach. When Esu woke up the following morning, he yelled out that the beads he wore to Alaketu's house had been stolen. Esu caused a pandemonium which attracted neighbors and passers-by. Esu caused more furore by disclosing that he entered the house with a boxload of beads which had mysteriously disappeared.

The enormity of the allegations attracted the chiefs who immediately remited the matter for adjudication to the Alaafin of Oyo. At the palace, Alaketu disclosed that what he saw his visitor wearing when he admitted him into his house looked like pepper seeds. On the other hand, Esu asked whether it was feasible or convenient for anyone to wear pepper fruits when it was raining heavily. Meanwhile, the king ordered the palace police to go and search Alaketu's house for any beads.

At the same time, Esu had positioned a boxload of beads and a necklace of beads at the private room of Alaketu. After a thorough search, the palace police discovered the beads in the private chamber of the Alaketu and they brought them to the palace. Since Alaketu could not explain how the beads found their way to his private chamber, the king concluded that he was guilty of robbing his visitor and ordered that all his belongings should be forfeited to Esu, the visitor. That was when Alaketu realised that he was paying a heavy price for refusing to make sacrifice and failing to heed divinational advice.

When this odu appears at divination, the person should be advised to serve Esu with a he-goat and a necklace made from red pepper fruits which he would wear on his neck to be removed by the Ifa priest during the sacrifice at Esu shrine. He should also be advised to be hospitable to his visitors, to avert the danger of being robbed of his treasured assets.

This Odu's Special Sacrifice for Prosperity

Orunmila ni shi shi. Moni go go

Orunmila recommends sacrifice with a sheep and the appropriate
ayajo leaves.
Oni nse ni agutan ma nshi fun oloko nigbati yio
kpa je. Orunmila je ki aje shi gogo wa ba mi.
Ewo dewe a la shi gogo ti aje t'omo
Shigo go wa ba mi ala shi gogo.
Gbogbo ire shigo go wa ba mi.
Ewe alashi go go ni ewe ewe ifa yi.

The divinee besought Orunmila to bring the good things of life to him or her, including but not limited to money, children, peace of mind and fame, but in all, humility and courtesy.

When this odu therefore appears at divination, the person will be advised to be humble and courteous while in the company or midst of elders to receive all the good things of life.

Chapter 9

ETURA-OGUNDA
ETURA-ARIRA
ETURA-TAKUTA SOLE
ETURA-TA-GITAN

He Made Divination for the Parasite Plant and the Star

*A le mi ni ile aje, mo bo si ile ileke. Odifa fun Afuma ti
yi o je Oba igi oko. Abufun irawo so so ti yi o je Oba lorun.*

I was driven out of the house of money and I ended up in the house of beads and jewels. That was the awo who made divination for the parasite plant (Afuma in Yoruba and Osee in Bini) to become king of plants in the forest. He also divined for the Star to become the King of the sky. They were told to make sacrifice.

Afuma was advised to serve Esu with a he-goat and to make sacrifice with an egg at a road junction. After making the sacrifice he was advised never to hold meetings with anyone. Meanwhile, all the plants of the forest decided to be holding meetings alternately in the homes of the Iroko and the Oak trees. When Afuma was invited to be attending the meetings, he declined the invitation on the ground that he could not condescend to be holding meetings with his father's slaves.

The other plants were so infuriated by the derisive remarks of Afuma that they trooped to the divine chamber of God to ask Him whether he did indeed create them to be slaves of any particular plant. When God asked them the rationale of the question, they all explained that the inconsequentail Afuma refused to join their meeting because he could not condescend to relate with the slaves of his father. God told them to go and call the plant who made such a spiteful remark.

Before they got to Afuma's house, Esu had given him a bad chill and he was visibly ill. When the plants sent to invite him arrived to deliver God's invitation, he regreted that he was too ill to honor the invitation. Upon being told that Afuma was too ill to honor the invitation, God ordered them to fetch him by all means.

When they got back to Afuma's house the kolanut tree decided to carry him on his head to the venue of the meeting. When they got to the Divine chamber of God, the kolanut plant decided to put Afuma down on the ground but he bluntly refused to alight. At that point, God asked all the others how they got to the venue and they all replied that they came on their feet. When he put a second question as to how Afuma came to the conference, they answered that Afuma's father was the king of all plants and that he should remain in that position to eternity. That is why he grows on the top of other trees to this day, especially on the kolanut tree who carried him on his head that day.

On the other hand, the same Awo advised the Star to make sacrifice with a he-goat and a naked lamp. He made the sacrifice and became the king of the sky.

At Ugbodu, the person will be told to make sacrifice and to avoid holding meetings with anybody because he was destined for leadership positions. At divination, the person should be advised to make sacrifice in order to win a contest for a position of prestigeous authority or chieftaincy title.

The Divination Made for Him Before Leaving Heaven

Mi O rira Iere, mi Orira.
E ro ni ko'ro Orira.

Those were the Awos who made divination for Orunmila when he was coming to the world. He was told that he was going to occupy an indispensable position on earth and should therefore fortify himself against all problems that goes with success. He was specifically told to make sacrifice for long life and prosperity on earth and to ensure that his sexual potency remained healthy throughout his life. He was required to make the following sacrifices: to serve his guardian angel with a ram; to serve Esu with a he-goat adding a make-shift stool; akara, eko and ekuru; to make special Ifa sacrifice with castrated he-goat for potency; and to obtain clearance from God with a white pigeon. He made all the sacrifices before leaving heaven for the world.

On getting to earth, he lost no time in establishing his fame as an effective and proficient Ifa priest. Meanwhile, there was so much turbulence on earth because of the actions of evil minded men that God invited the two hundred divinities to meet him at Orita-Ijaloko. When Orunmila consulted his Okeponrin on what to do, he was advised not to go on schedule, but that if he desperately wanted to go, he was to ride there on a ram after giving a he-goat to Esu.

Olokun's daughter Aje also went for divination and she was told not to go but that if she must go, she should give a he-goat to Esu and serve her guardian angel with a goat and a cock. She did not do the sacrifice. When the others arrived at the venue of the meeting, God insisted that the meeting could not commence without the presence of Orunmila. Meanwhile, before leaving for the conference, Orunmila told Akpetebi to prepare food for him to hold for the journey. She refused to cook because she had to go to the market. Since he had been warned not to quarrel before going, he subsequently left on the back of a ram. There were seven shrines of the tree of life to pass before getting to Orita-Ijaloko. By the time the ram got to the seventh shrine, it hit its head on the tree and immediately walked home backwards.

Meanwhile, after waiting in vain for Orunmila to turn up for the meeting, the other divinities decided to disperse, leaving the daughter of Olokun alone with God. Back on earth, Esu went to blink his eyes to Akpetebi and as she was returning from the market, she was exhausted, felt drowsy and fell to the ground losing consciousness. Soon afterwards, Esu met her virtually dead, but got a stool, sat her down on it and prepared a tray in front of her as if she was selling akara, ekuru and eko by the side of the road. To give her a talking posture, Esu put a live frog in her mouth.

A little later, as Aje was returning from the venue of the meeting that never held, she met Orunmila's wife sitting beside her wares and asked after her husband. The frog in her mouth began to laugh scornfully at Olokun's daughter, and even spat on her.

As Aje moved to touch her, she fell down as if she had just died. From his hide-out, Esu came out to accuse Aje of murdering Orunmila's wife. One after the other, Aje surrendered each of her seven female followers to atone for Akpetebi's death but Esu insisted that their eyes did not match those of Orunmila's wife. She subsequently decided to settle the matter directly with Orunmila.

As soon as Aje left, Esu instantly appeared at Orunmila's house to brief him and to tell him that he should put the blame for Akpetebi's death on Esu who could not protect his wife as he was instructed to do. Before then, Orunmila had been told to decorate an apartment in his palatial house with white adornments because of the woman he was about to marry. When Aje subsequently arrived, Orunmila was in a hurry to entertain her lavishly, although she was more concerned with the problem of how she unintentionally killed Akpetebi. When she eventually summoned the courage to narrate how she pushed his wife to her death, Orunmila burst into tears, lamenting that far from blaming her, he only held Esu responsible for not being able to protect Akpetebi. He then vowed that Esu would never again enter his house.

At that point, Esu cried out from where he was squatting outside the house, while begging Orunmila for forgiveness. The cry of Esu quaked the very ground on which Aje was standing and she too began to weep. After giving all that she had to Orunmila, Esu was still crying. She ended the melodramatic scenario by bethrothing herself to Orunmila in marriage, in addition to her seven maidens. With her bethrothal, Esu stopped crying and tranquility returned to the scene. Aje was subsequently led to the decorated apartment where she began to live as Orunmila's wife.

Thereafter, Esu went to where Apetebi's unconscious body lay and used the appropriate leaves to bring her back to life. That is how Orunmila ended up having nine wives which is the characteristic of the children of this odu. With so many wives to cater for, Orunmila began to experience spasmodic bouts of sexual power failure. He had nonetheless become exceedingly famous and wealthy, but had to do something about his sporadic impotence.

He subsequently invited his Awos who told him to make sacrifice with a castrated he-goat and to take something from the seventh shrine on which his ram knocked its head before returning home backwards on the day of the conference that never was. He was required also to fetch the head of a boa, a python or boa constrictor and a cock. He produced all the materials and after obtaining the relevant leaves of this odu, the Awos killed the castrated he-goat for Ifa while the cock was slaughtered for Ogun. The testicles of the castrated he-goat and the cock were extracted and added to the heads of the boa and boa constrictor, put on the mortar and pounded thoroghly. The medicine was marked round Orunmila's waist, and the rest was mounted on the skin of the castrated he-goat with a brass scimitter any mytre on it (Ada and Eben in Bini with igheghan) The Mortar was finally washed and the water was used to wash the Ifa seeds (Ikin) and thereafter for him to bathe with it. He subsequently regained his potency.

When this Ifa appears at Ugbodu, the person will be told that he is likely to marry or have sexual relations with nine women, the second of which will come from the palace of Olokun to enrich him. He should endeavour to avoid attending meetings or belonging to social gathering in order not to suffer from sporadic sexual power failure, which he should forestall by preparing the special sacrifice (Ono-Ifa or Odiha) with the castrated he-goat after serving the Ifa with a ram. He will be a force to reckon with in the society.

He Made Divination for Alagemo, The Chameleon

Ariro or Alagemo was the favorite servant of God. He enjoyed the favored position of being God's closest confidant. That position generated considerable envy and enmity for him, and his detractors plotted to bear false witness against him. Meanwhile, as he was beginning to sense trouble he went to Orunmila who told him to serve Esu with a he-goat and Olokun with all the materials for sending gifts to the water divinity including cowries, white cloth, white chalk, white crushed yam and an image.

Meanwhile, his enemies went to inform God that the chameleon was usurping His divine position and authority. On hearing the accusation, God sent two executioners to go and deal with him. The executioners got hold of the chameleon, bound his hands and feet and jettisoned his corpse into the sea, after beating him mercilessly to death. Incidentally, in appreciation of the gifts which Alagemo often sent to the water divinity, neither sea nor river kills him. As soon as Olokun saw him floating on the water, he sent his body guards to rescue him.

He was eventually brought before Olokun who gave instant instructions that Alagemo should be moulded with inexhaustible prosperity. After being moulded with eternal opulence, Olokun advised him to return to life since it was not yet time for him to die. He was subsequently tossed to the surface of the water from where he swam to safety. The people who saw him on his way to his house went to tell God that Alagemo was still very much alive and well.

As the next day was the meeting of the divine council of heaven, God sent for Alagemo to be present at the meeting. He also sent for the people who were instructed to execute him. His executioners confirmed that they did not only beat the life out of him but also threw his corpse into the river and the corpse had actually gone under before they left the river. Their account was confirmed by Alagemo who lamented that without; investigating the allegation made against him by his accusers, giving him an opportunity to defend himself, taking account of his past perfor-mance, and viewing the accusation against the back-drop of his track record, God, the omniscent, condemned him to death. It was the superlative excellence and impartiality of providence through the instrumentality of Olokun that restored him to life in mysterious circumstances under the water. As if to state his case albeit *post facto*, he denied ever saying or doing anything or even thinking in terms of having the appearance of usurping the powers of the creator and master, and that he was ever so satisifed with the rare privilege of staying by God's side in putting the affairs of universal government right.

In his reaction, God reassured Alagemo that his experience was meant to enable him to realize that it is not the guilty alone that suffers, the innocent more often than not suffer for what they know nothing about. The experience was designed to enable the innocent, no matter how they might be badgered about, would always remain on their feet and live to a ripe old age. The Almighty Father proclaimed that the lives of innocent victims of falsehood would always be longer and more prosperous than those of their accusers. With that proclamation, God invited Alagemo to resume his eternal position by His side.

When this odu appears at divination, the person will be advised to make sacrifice against the danger of being made to suffer humiliation for an accusation he/she knows nothing about. He/she should make sacrifices to Esu and Olokun.

He Made Divination for Agbe When Going to the Farm

Igbe gidi ni a ba su kitikpa. Odifa fun Agbe ti o nlo
si oko aloro odun. Obuko ati eru ishu, ati oun ti enu
je gbogbo ni ebo re.

He made divination for Agbe when he was going to start a farm at the beginning of the new year. He made sacrifices with a he-goat, a pack of yam tubers and all eatable foodstuffs. He succeeded in having a rich harvest. At divination, the person will be told to make sacrifice before traveling in order to derive benefit from the journey.

He Made Divination for the Ironsmith

Gbogboro kun. lo ndifa fun Alagbede igba owuro.

He made divination for the ironsmith very early in the morning advising him to make sacrifice with a he-goat to thwart the difficulties that enemies were going to generate for him, most especially to avert the danger of bottom illness such as hyena. He made the sacrifice.

When it appears at divination, the person will be advised to make sacrifice in order to obviate the danger of bottom illness. If the divinee is a woman she will be advised to refrain from flirting in order to avert the danger of contacting veneral diseases. The same advice holds for a male divinee.

Divination for a Barren Woman to Have a Child

Orunmila ni Iraba, emi na ni Iraba. Iraba ni ishu n kpa tofi nta.
Iraba ni ogede n kpa ti o fi nso. Iraba ni agbado nkpa
ti o nfi nkpan omo. Ki a so fun aganbi kpe yio bi omo
ti o ba ru ebo. Ki a toju obinrin na o tori omo wa ni ile ara re.

Orunmila said circles on circles. The yam, plantain and maize all move in circles to bear fruits That was the incantation with which this odu made divination for a barren woman to have a child after making sacrifice.

When this odu appears at divination, for a man, he will be advised to take proper care of his wife because a child is following her. If sacrifice is made the woman will have a child before the end of the year.

Special Sacrifice for Harmony and Understanding

Orunmila ni emi mi yun, Moni emi ni yun. Orunmila ni emi mi yun
Moni emi ni yun. Oni Omo eja ko gbo ohun eja. Orunmila ni emi
mi oyun. Moni emi ni oyun. Oni omo eye ko gbo ohun eye.
Oni be ni omo eranko ko gbo ohun eranko. Omo eni ko gbo
ohun omo eni. Oni ikin ko gbo ohun oduso. Oduso ko gbo ohun
omo ikin. Oni aludun dun ko gbo ohun alayan. Alayan ko gbo ohun alaro.
Orunmila expressed gratitude to God for his life.
The Ifa priest made the same expression.
Orunmila observed that fishes do not understand themselves enough
to live a happier life.
He made the same obervation in respect of birds, animals and
mankind. Just as Ifa seeds do not understand their King, and the
king does not understand his followers. In like manner, the
drummer does not understand the reactions of his listeners, as
spectators do not understand the expressions of the drummer.
The Ifa priest said he did not understand the parables of Orunmila.
Orunmila explained that for human beings to live in harmony and
mutual understanding, it required sacrifice with a hen laying eggs,
and a rat called eku-akosi, because this specie of rat responds
promptly when its young ones are crying. The incantation for the
sacrifice is as follows: Ojo ti akosi ba ti ko, ila lehin ni o ma
n de inu. Akosi ki gbo kigbe omo re ki o dake. Ifa wa gbo ohun mi.
Eleye ile oyoro de ikin osa okpo gbo ohun mi.
Eleye ile oyoro ikin osa.

When it appears at divination, the person will be told that Orunmila has not been listening to his entreaties, because Ifa has turned a deaf ear to them. The person has previously been rude to his or her parents. The abovementioned sacrifice should be made so that his or her wishes might manifest.

Another Variation to the Exploits of Afuma, the Parasite Plant How Afumo Became the King of Plants

Oro gba gede gba was the awo who made divination for eighty forest, advising each of them to make sacrifice with a he-goat and parrot feathers to Esu, adding white cloth. All the plants refused to make the sacrifice with the exception of Afumo who made the sacrifice as was directed.

Meanwhile, Esu instigated a quarrel among the plants and they began to fight about who among them was the most senior. When the dispute aggravated into pandomonium, they all trooped to the Almighty Creator for a settlement. God told all of them to return after seven days for a decision, on who was their leader.

On the fourth day, Esu caused Afumo to have leg pains that made it impossible for him to walk. On the appointed day, Afumo was in severe pains and could not get up let alone walk to the venue of the conference. Meanwhile all the other plants were assembled and Esu transfigured into a knight of the heavenly grail. When God asked the plants whether they were all present, they all answered that they were all assembled. Esu however intervened to disclose that Afumo was not present. The other plants explained that he could not come because of his leg injury and that in any event, he was too inconsequential to bother about. The Almighty Father however insisted that unless all of them were assembled, He could not pronounce His judgment. The kolanut tree and Iroko then left to fetch Afumo.

Since he could not walk on his feet the kolanut plant decided to carry Afumo on his head. As soon as Afumo sat on Kolanut's head, Esu covered him up with the white cloth with which he had made sacrifice, placing a parrot's feather on his head. When they arrived at the venue, God asked the other plants who it was that, was clad in white cloth and wearing a parrot's feather. All the plants answered that it was Afumo. When the kola-tree wanted to put Afumo on the ground, God proclaimed that from then on, Afumo should no longer touch the ground with his feet except on the heads of other trees because he was the king of all plants. That is why Afumo only grows on top of other trees.

At divination, the person will be advised to make sacrifice in order to attain the leadership position awaiting him or her in the offing. He or she is endowed with leadership qualities and will attain it if he or she makes the foregoing sacrifice.

Chapter 10

ETURA-OSA

He Made Divination for the Hawk and the Hen

Iroko ni babalawo Asha. Odifa fun asha, Obufun abo
adiye ni jo ti awon mejeji fi omi oju shubere omo tuuru tu.

He made divination for the Hawk and the Hen when they were both anxious to have children. They were both advised to make sacrifice with ten different materials. As the stronger of the two sisters, the Hawk was able to fetch her 10 materials without any difficulties. As the weaker of the two, endowed with limited flying range, the Hen could only raise two materials.

After collecting her 10 materials, the Hawk asked the Hen whether she was ready for the sacrifice and she said she was not quite ready. However, the Hawk appealed to the Hen to take her 10 materials to Orunmila to make the sacrifice on her behalf, because she was too busy to have time to go by herself. The Hen readily agreed to oblige.

On getting to Orunmila's place, the hen transposed the Hawk's 10 materials to make her own sacrifice, while using her two materials to make the Hawk's sacrifice on her behalf. After making the sacrifice, Orunmila gave her the Iyerosun of one who made complete sacrifice with 10 materials, while also giving the Iyerosun of two materials to her to give to the Hawk.

A few day later, they began to lay eggs. The Hen laid ten eggs while the Hawk laid two eggs. In the fullness of time, the Hen hatched her ten eggs and brought forth ten chickens. On her part the Hawk hatched her two eggs and brought forth two children. Puzzled at the strange turn of events, the Hawk went in fury to Orunmila to find out why she had only two children after making full sacrifice with ten different materials. It was at that point that she was blamed for making her sacrifice through a proxy, and that the Hen presented two materials for sacrifice on her behalf while presenting all the ten materials for herself.

Since it was too late to swap or reverse their fates, the Hawk vowed from that day to feed her two children with the ten children of the Hen. As soon as the Hen brought out her ten children to the open, the Hawk dived down and picked up one of the children and the Hen cried, "Bi mo mo ma ba she bo ikoko koro yio" - meaning "If I had known, I would have made sacrifice with the ten materials prescribed by Ikoko. That was how the eternal war between the two sisters, the Hawk and the Hen originated. It also explains why the Hawk does not lay more than two eggs at a time.

At divination, the person will be advised to endeavour to do things fundamental to his or her life by him or herself. He or she should always make sacrifice by him or herself and not through anyone, no matter how close. Throughout the whole of that year he or she should not perform any chore through proxies to alleviate the risk of being cheated. If it is Ayeo, the person should be told to be satisfied with whatever he/she has and not to have an eye on stealing from anyone, to avoid disastrous consequences for his or her children. The person should be told to beware of a relation having two children because he or she is a witch, who can destroy his or her own children. In all cases, the person should make sacrifice.

The Divination He Made Before Leaving Heaven

Ogbe regede maa jebi keruku. Ugun orin rin rin okpa ori.
Akalamaigbo orin rin rin, Ogbi jolo so'run. Awon meteta lo'n
difa fun Orunmila ni jo ti oti si Kole orun bowa si kole aye.

Ogberede was not guilty when he went to carry the burden of death. The vulture worked so hard that he became bald. Akalamaigbo worked so hard that he too became bald and bearded. These were the three Awos who made divination for Orunmila when he was coming to the world.

He was told to make sacrifice to Esu with a he-goat; his guardian angel with a castrated he-goat; Uja with a hen; and to pay homage to the divinity of Death with a bundle of yam tubers, and fire wood. He was required to make these elaborate sacrifices to avoid premature death through ingratitude, and in order to live long on earth. He made all the sacrifices before coming to the world.

He was born with the name of Awodi, as the eldest son of Oshereigbo. He grew up to become an itinerant Ifa priest who travelled away from home most of the time. Nonetheless, he often brought elaborate gifts to his father anytime he came home. He had two other brothers called Ugun and Akala.

For a long time, a settled life eluded him, and he neither got married nor had children. He was far away from home on one occasion when his guardian angel admonished him in a dream for leading a listless life on earth. He was ordered to return home because his father was about to return to heaven. His guardian angel told him to return home in a hurry to sweep, scrub and clean the house for his father and to fetch fire wood for heating his room.

The following morning, he collected his belongings and left for home. On getting home, his junior brothers did not recognise him because they had not seen him for a long time. He met his father in an unkempt room inundated with smoke and ashes. As directed by his guardian angel, he swept the whole apartment, scrubbed the fire place, and dusted and cleaned up the entire place. Thereafter, he went to the forest to fetch firewood to prepare heating fire in the room.

As the father who was already blind from old age, was enjoying the heat from the fire place, he asked "Ere ni", that is who is it? and he replied to identify himself as his son Awodi. The father retorted to say that he was happy to know that he was at home to see him before returning home to heaven.

As soon as he was sure that they were alone, Oshereigbo told his eldest son the secret of how to survive the ordeal of the secret conclave by not taking any material prepared with palm oil into the place. He also disclosed that before the commencement of the coronation ceremonies, the shrine should be renovated with black dye stuff. After the disclosure, the father gave up the ghost.

Following the death of his father, Awodi went to tell his junior brothers that he was returning to his base and they bade him goodbye. When they got to their father's apartment, they saw the cleansing done by Awodi, but discovered that their father had passed away. Almost immediately, the two children alerted the surviving divinities that Oshereigbo had gone to meet his father in heaven. Since they all assured themselves that Awodi, the eldest son was never home, they called on Ugun the next one to make arrangements for the commencement of the funeral rites.

For the funeral ceremonies, Ugun slaughtered cows, goats, rams and fowls and they were cooked in the normal way with palm oil. He was meanwhile, told to retire into seclusion at the secret conclave of the coronation shrine where he was to stay alone for fourteen days. The only companions he was to have were to be the heavenly hosts who were to teach him the secrets of heaven and earth, and how to perform his role as leader of the Divinities on earth. Without knowing the do's and the don'ts of the conclave, he was served from the food prepared with palm oil.

In the night, while he was asleep, the elders of the night trooped into the secret conclave in the form of soldier ants. When they found the remnants of the palm oil prepared food, they ate up everything on sight including Ugun himself. When the conclave was opened on the fourteenth day to receive him, the people only found his bones, which was a clear indication that he was not conversant with the secret of survival at the conclave. It was the turn of Akala to enter the shrine. He too ended up the same way because he was not aware of the secrets of how to survive the ordeal of the conclave.

The divinities began to ponder on how to bring home the remaining and eldest son of Oshereigbo who was never home. While the sacrifice was being made at home, a parrot flew to his front and dropped a white feather which he interpreted to mean an invitation for him to return home. Without wasting a moment further, he raced home to meet the divinities, who immediately motioned him to enter the secret conclave at once. When he asked for his junior brothers he was told that they could not survive the rituals of the conclave.

Far from moving to the secret conclave as he was directed to do, he insisted on burying his father first, and he did so by slaughtering a cow and thirteen different animals and birds.

Before cooking the food, he proclaimed that no palm oil and pepper were to be used for preparing the food for his father's burial ceremonies. The only seasoning was to be done with ginger seeds (Ighere in Yoruba and Oziza in Bini). Although people wondered how food could be prepared without palm oil and pepper, his ruling was nonetheless respected.

After the completion of the funeral ceremonies, he served his Ifa and head as he was told to do at his family home (Idile or Ajule in Yoruba and Igiogbe in Bini) with a castrated he-goat, white pigeon, white cock and white hen. After the sacrifice which was also prepared without oil and pepper, he entered the secret conclave. His father had a mirror in his bedroom. Knowing that people could use it to spy on him while in the conclave, he took it with him. Before actually going into the conclave however, he ordered that the entire palace had to be renovated with black dyestuff right up to the conclave. Again, although people pondered over the wisdom of painting a house with black dyestuff instead of white during a funeral, his wish was carried out.

Finally, he gave orders that througout the fourteen days, neither oil nor pepper was to be used for preparing any food. The crushed yam (Elo or Obobo) which was to be sprayed daily round the house was to be white. People were astonished at the strange innovations he was introducing not knowing that he was acting on the advice of his father. That night he was locked away in the secret conclave for the next fourteen days. At the end of fourteen days, people rejoiced to see that he had survived the ordeal.

He was brought out to head a procession of dancing, singing and drumming to the coronation site and he sang:

> Ugun o rin rin rin, o kpa ori.
> Akalamaigbo o rin rin rin, Ogbi jolo so orun.
> Emi Awodi Orisa ni kon lu akon ni erin.
> Emi lo jo'ye aba mi ni gbegbe re.
> Ki'nla Awodi mu joye.
> Tubi Ture ni Awodi mu joye.

With that song of victory he led the procession to the coronation hall where he was formally crowned as the successor to his father. Orisa-Nla-Oshereigbo, and the Head and Leader of all the divinities on earth.

The Divination Made for Him When He Was Going to Work for King Onikaro of Ado

> Ogberegede majebi Keruku. Ireko te ilasa. Adifa fun
> Awodi Okpe nijo ti o fe lo shawo fun Onikaro.

These were the two Awos who made divination for Awodi when he was going to help the wives of the Onikaro to have male children. He was advised to make sacrifice with a he-goat, gourd of water, an axe, a scissors and a parrot's feather, in order to survive the ordeal he was going to go through on account of a wicked falsehood and an ingratitude to his benevolence. He was also advised to serve his head with a white pigeon.

He did all the sacrifices and left for Ado to meet Onikaro, Oba Ado Ajuwaleke. Awodi had a protruded navel and as he began to have children after the death of his father he had become a specialist in preparing medicines for women to have children. That was the connection in which the Oba of Ado heard of him and sent for him. On getting to Ado, he prepared medicine for the favorite wife of the Oba and she became pregnant. Three months later, he left for home.

In the fullness of time the woman gave birth to a male child. But tongues began to wag because of the close resemblance between Awodi's and the child's navels. Three years after the child was born, the Oba sent for Awodi at Ife to come and receive his reward. His chiefs then came out openly to protest that Awodi did not deserve any compensation for polluting the Oba's wife and putting her in the family way.

When Awodi received the Oba's invitation, he invited his Awos for divination and he was fore-warned that this time, he was going to answer the call of death unless he made sacrifice. He was told to make sacrifice with; a he-goat to Esu, a pigeon to Ifa and a cock, dog, tortoise and 2 giant scissors to Ogun. After the sacrifice the Awos prepared the scissors for him to be using for picking anything instead of using his hands.

On getting to Ado, the people had prepared a giant burn-fire for him to enter for a trial by ordeal. He was told that it was strongly suspected that he had an illicit love affair with the Oba's wife before she became pregnant in the light of the strong resemblance between himself and the child with special reference to their navels. He was therefore required to fetch the brass bangle inside the burning fire. If he was innocent, he would survive the ordeal but if he was guilty, he could lose his life in the ordeal. That was in spite of the woman's denial of having any sexual relationship with Awodi who only helped her.

Without any hesitation whatsoever, he called on his father and his guardian angel to guide him through the ordeal. In consonance with the advice at divination he held his scissors in hand, and dared the fire but it was too hot him. After making two abortive efforts, he called on Esu to help him out because he sensed that strong forces were working against him. Esu responded and without being seen by other people, Esu put out the fire at the point where the brass metal lay under the fire, thus clearing the way for him to pick it up with his scissors. At the production of the brass metal, his innocence was hailed with a thunderous applause. He survived the ordeal without a scratch or a blister, except that he emerged from the fire with the pigmentation of his complexion turning from fair to black.

As his gifts were being assembled, he refused to touch any of it but proclaimed that from then on all Obas in Benin would always have navels, which explains why the the regalia of a Benin King always has a protrusion near the navel.

At divination, the person should be advised to make sacrifice to survive a false accusation which he or she may not be able to deny.

He Made Divination for Ogun When Going to War

Okpa teere kon, Amudi wondon, Adifa fun Ogun nijoti o n
gbo'gunronron muron odo. Ogun fe gbe Arire Omo le shaya.

That was the Awo who made divination for Ogun when he washed on the spring river, where he met to marry the daughter of Olokun. He was told to serve his guardian angel with a dog, cock and tortoise, and Esu with a he-goat. He made the sacrifices and left for the spring river where lives Aire Omo Ire, the daughter of Olokun.

All the men around had approached her for marriage but she rebuffed all their overtures. As soon as Ogun popped the question, she readily agreed to marry him. After conquering the river town, Ogun returned home with Aire Omo Ire. Ogun soon discovered that she was a spoiled brat who knew how to do nothing else apart from having her bath very early in the morning and rubbing her skin with camwood. Nonetheless, all the men of Ire were annoyed because the girl agreed to marry Ogun after rejecting all of them.

Meanwhile, it was time for Ogun to perform his annual festival, in connection with which he fetched 201 rats, 201 fishes, to be dried or smoked. As Ogun was going to the forest to hunt for the remaining birds and animals, he told the wife Aire Omo Ire to be putting fire to the drier to smoke the rats and fishes. As soon as Ogun left her at home, the aggrieved or derided men of Ire decided to take the opportunity to undo her, by burglarizing Ogun's house to steal all the rats and fishes under her care, leaving only two pieces crushed and smeared with camwood, her favorite pomade.

When she checked the drier the following morning to discover that all the rats and fishes had been robbed, she raised an alarm. But when the neighbors saw that the two remaining pairs of rats and fishes were daubed with camwood, they accused her of being responsible for the theft and warned her to replace them lest it would cost her life when Ogun returned home. She took the admonition seriously and decided to do something to replace them before her husband returned home.

First, she went to the bush to set several traps to catch rats. After catching 201 rats, she began to smoke them in the drier. Next, she went to the river to use net to catch fishes where she succeeded in netting in 200 fishes and took them home to the drier. As soon as she returned to the river to catch the last fish, her father's (Olokun) policemen apprehended her for running away from home without his authority. Nonetheless, she was waiting for her husband Ogun to come and retrieve her.

Seven days later, she sighted Ogun returning home with the animals from the forest and began to sing to him:

> Ogun oko mi, Eka bo okomi, Aire omo Ire.
> Omo ire jejeo, Aire omo ire.
> Oun tebiti oku gba eku, Ire omo ire.
> Omo ire jejeo, Aire omo ire.
> Oun gba wawo okugba eja. Aire omo ire.
> Omo ire je je o. Aire omo ire.

When Ogun looked back to identity the voice singing to him, he was surprised to see that it was his wife. When he returned her greetings, she could not answer because she was already under the spell of her father.

Meanwhile, he returned home to ask for his wife and the neighbors told him that she had escaped from the house after stealing the fishes and rats left under her care. Ogun retorted that she could not have stolen the fishes and the rats because they were all in the drier. He invited the neighbors to see for themselves and they were all surprised. He went to perform the ceremonies of his festival which lasted seven days.

After the end of the festival, he went to Orunmila to advise him on how to get back his wife. He was advised to serve Esu with a he-goat, a drum made with cocoyam leaves, three birds and a basket of palm kernels. He lost no time in making the sacrifices. After eating his he-goat, Esu went to enlist the support of the Eagle, and the cooperation of the Rabbit with the basket of palm kernels.

After accepting his offering, the Rabbit bored a hole from Ogun's house to Olokun's sitting room. He subsequently took a position from which to listen to developments. On his part, Esu took the chair and sat at a point near to Olokun's palace. At the same time, the Eagle stood on the top of a tree at the courtyard of Olokun's palace. As soon as he ensured that all the players in the drama had taken their assigned positions, Esu began to beat his drum to a song that evoked dancing:

> Sekure sekure, bere le o.
> Te ufu ri ere si nu ode o.
> Te u tu te re.

With that song accompanied by his drumming, he began to dance along and he was soon joined by a large crowd of singers and dancers. The dance procession was soon joined by several members of Olokun's household. The crowd-pulling music was subsequently joined by Aire Omo Ire and she too began to dance to the captivating melody of the music. As soon as the procession got past the quadrangle of Olokun's palace, the eagle swooped down from the tree and seized Aire Omo Ire and flew away with her to Ogun's house.

When Olokun saw the dramatic turn of events, he laughed contumeliously boasting that she was going to be useless to whoever seized her without seizing her from him with the fourteen materials which he brought from heaven. Unknown to Olokun however, the Rabbit was eaves-dropping on him and listened to every word he uttered.

On getting back to Ogun's house, she neither spoke nor ate let alone agree to make love to him. She became more or less a liability. Three days later, the Rabbit came to brief Ogun on what Olokun said, that he would have to buy Aire omo Ire with the fourteen materials he brought from heaven viz, white chalk, eagle feather, parrot's feather, brass ladder, bell, a bunch of keys, canoe and paddle, cowries, white cloth, white he-goat, white cock, maracas, metal scimitar and mitre, a special metal gong that makes musical sounds when divine dancers tie them to their feet, called sheke sheke in Yoruba and Eroro or Igheghan in Bini, and a metal chain.

Much as Ogun was prepared to send the materials to Olokun, he had no clue on the logistics of getting them to him. Once again, Ogun went to Orunmila for advice. Orunmila volunteered to take the materials and to lead Aire Omo Ire to and from Olokun's palace provided he could assemble singers, drummers and dancers to accompany him. This explains why no divine priest or priestess can complete his or her initiation ceremony without the active support and coopera-tion of Orunmila.

The following day, Orunmila fetched all the relevant leaves for the ceremony, put them in a small pot which he made Aire Omo Ire to carry on her head to the river, accompanied by a musical ensemble while Orunmila was carrying the tray containing the fourteen materials. On getting to the river, they met Olokun sitting on his throne where Orunmila appealed to him to accept the materials with which they came to buy Aire Omo Ire from him. He rejoiced that they knew what to do at last.

After Olokun agreed to receive them, Orunmila threw all of them into the river and asked Aire Omo the to fill the pot on her head with water from the river. As she was returning home to Ogun with the procession, Olokun called her name, Aire Omo Ire and she answered Ee yooh three times which were the first words she spoke since she was abducted by the Eagle.

When they got home, the now possessed Aire Omo Ire refused to surrender the pot, but after Orunmila used his Uranke to touch her, she simmered down and regained her normal senses. It was from then on that she began to live a normal life with Ogun as man and wife. That is why during initiation into Olokun cult it is necessary to take the daughter of Olokun to the river to complete her disengagement from the court of her father.

When this odu appears at divination for a man proposing to marry a woman, and if he is to marry her successfully, he must buy her from the water divinity. If it appears for a woman, she will be told that she does not have a settled life. If she is to settle down in life, she must have her Olokun shrine prepared for her.

He Made Divination for the Dog When Coming From Heaven

Etura maa saa, babalawo aja. Odifa fun Aja nijo ti on
ti kole orun bowa si kole aye.

He made divination for the dog when she was coming to the world. She was advised to make sacrifice with palm kernels, palm fruits and parrot's feather. She made the sacrifice without adding parrot's feather. She was required to make sacrifice with the parrot's feather to prevent her from having problems with bearing children.

On getting to the world, she befriended Esu who she visited daily for food, but whenever Esu visited the dog, she had no food to offer. Gradually, Esu began to keep her at arms length.

Meanwhile, she became pregnant. When it was time for her to deliver, she had a torturous labor, running from pillar to post until she went to Esu who asked her what Orunmila advised her to do when going to deliver a child. She replied that Orunmila advised her to put down a red parrot's feather and to deliver on it, but that she could not get a parrot's feather. Esu agreed to lend one to her which would enable her to make an easy delivery. Thereafter, Esu collected his parrot's feather from her. That explains why the dog does not put to birth in the presence of anybody.

When this Ifa appears at Ugbodu, the person will serve Ogun with a dog and be told to beware of friends much stronger than himself. He should serve Esu with a he-goat, palm kernels, palm fruits and parrot's feather.

At divination, the person will serve his/her head with a fowl and serve Ogun with a cock.

This Odu's Special Sacrifice to Overcome Enemies and Difficulties

Orunmila ni ti shan; Moni mo bo'la.
Oni laba-laba bo ni owo awon ti nkpa eye je.
Oni okun bo ni owo awon aje kokoro.
Orunmila ni ti shan; Mo ni mo bo la. Oni omo bi bo.
O bo ni owo awon tin run orin. Oni ekolo bo ni owo.
awon ti n je eran. Mo bo iku, mo bo ni owo aisan.
Omo bi bo boro no owo re omo bi bo.
Orunmila sneezed and the Ifa priest wished him God's blessing.
He disclosed that it was the sacrifices made by:
Butterfly that saved it from the jaws of meat consumers;
The millipede to thwart the evil designs of the soldier ants;
The cotton wool that delivered it from the hands of chewing
sticks;
The earthworm to escape the attention of meat eaters; and
Made his children and adherents to survive the cold hands of
death and sickness.

When this Ifa therefore appears at divination, the person will be told that he or she is operating in the midst of enemies. To survive their evil machinations, he should be advised to have his own Ifa. If a woman, she will get close to Orunmila to survive the difficulties besetting her.

The Divination Made for a Mother to Save Her Daughter From Death in Her Marital Home

Ashosho eye, Ashoro eye and Ogunrun eye o le she re she were the three Awos who made divination for the mother of a woman called Arola. She was advised to make sacrifice to save her daughter fom dying in the husband's house. She was advised to serve Esu with a he-goat and Ewusa (Walnuts (Okhue in Bini)). She ignored the advice and refused to make the sacrifice. Meanwhile, a basket of Ewusa was kept at the overhead counter in the living room of the house. While her senior mate was away to the market, Esu transfigured into an intruder who sneaked into the living room and stole all the walnuts in the basket, leaving the empty basket. That happened while Arola was sleeping.

When her senior mate returned from the market, she discovered that the contents of the basket had been removed. When she asked Arola what happened to the walnuts, she denied any knowledge because she had been sleeping when the Iyaale was away to the market. The senior mate in a mood that was suspicious of the innocence of her junior mate observed that nothing had ever been stolen from the house previously. Overwhelmed with the scornful remarks of her senior mate, Arola began to sing:

Arola, Arola Sogun run she she she.

As she was singing, she began to sink into a coma, because unknown to her senior mate, she had swallowed a toxic substance. As she lapsed into delirium, a message was sent to the mother, but Arola died before her mother's arrival. It was at that point that the woman wept for losing her daughter to her refusal for make the sacrifice prescribed at divination.

When this Odu therefore portends the danger of death (Or Ayeo) at divination, the person should be advised to make sacrifice to avoid the loss of a son or daughter. If it appears for a mother, she will be told to make sacrifice to save the life of her daughter in her marital home. If it appears for a husband, he will be told to make sacrifice to ward off the danger of sudden death to his wife.

Chapter 11

ETURA- IRETE
ETURA-AGO
ITONLO-ETURA-ITONLO
ETURA OLUGBA-ETE

Before mentioning the name of this Odu, spit out praying to Orunmila not to allow the words from one's mouth to kill one.

He Made Divination for the Cock

Etura Itonlo was the Awo who made divination for the Cock when he was coming to the world. He was advised make sacrifice with a piece of red cloth, palm fruits and a he-goat in order to avert the danger of being killed by the words of his mouth. He made a half-hearted sacrifice without adding a he-goat.

On getting to the world, he was not only very handsome but the red crown on his head made birds and animals to dread him. He became friendly with the Fox (Ufa in Yoruba and Umuokhokho in Bini). The fox was able to kill and feed on other birds but dared not to go near the cock.

One day, after discovering that the Fox was distancing himself from him, the Cock asked him what the matter was and the Fox explained that he was afraid of being harmed by the fire crown he was always wearing. The Cock laughed hilariously at the Fox. Asked what was so funny, the Cock explained that far from being hot and harmful, the crown on his head was as cool as the drinking water pot and as harmless as the sand of the earth. As if giving his secret away was not self-defeating enough, the Cock foolishly asked the Fox to touch his crown, which the latter discovered to be very cool indeed.

The following day, the Fox attacked the Cock through his crown, held it, tore it to pieces and killed him for his breakfast. As he was dying the Cock remembered what the Awo told him at divination and he cried "Itonlo ni re re rete O o Hoo". That is why one prays not to court death through the words of one's mouth. When this Odu appears at divination, the person should make sacrifice not to share the fatal experience of the Cock.

When it appears at Ugbodu, the person should quickly serve Ifa with a cock which is to be roasted and not cooked before being eaten, in order to obviate the danger of giving away his cherished and closely guarded secrets to his enemies. He should also serve Esu with a he-goat.

At divination, the person will serve; Esu with a he-goat and Ogun with a cock and advised to beware of enemies who are close to him in the guise of friendship.

He Made Divination for Three Sister-Birds

Obale sa gaara lo, ndifa fun Oge. Otirikpo lo'ndifa fun Olo
koshe. Ojuda ojura lo 'ndifa fun Oken ti o ma je oye babare
(Oloja Eye). Ebo oye ni ki a ru o.

Those were the Awos who made divination for the birds called; Oge in Yoruba and Ahianmwosa in Bini, Olokoshe in Yoruba and Alevbe in Bini; and Oken in Yoruba and Ogen in Bini, when they were about to take the throne of their father as the Head Chief of Birds.

They were told to make sacrifice with four pigeons at the bank of the river. The most senior of the three Olokoshe did not consider it necessary for him to make sacrifice since he was the heir apparent to his father's throne. The next most senior one, Oge refused to make sacrifice because the crown could not come to him when the heir apparent was alive and well. On the other hand, it was the most junior one, Oken who made the sacrifice.

After the Ifa priest Ojuda-Ojura made the sacrifice for him, he was required to take the four live pigeons to the bank of the river. As Oken was praying with the pigeons on the beach sand, he was apprehended by the guards of Olokun's palace who had been sent out to fetch four pigeons for sacrifice for the son of Olokun who was critically ill. When he bluntly refused to surrender them, he was instantly arrested and arraigned before the water divinity, accused of trespass.

On seeing him, Olokun reprimanded his guards for treating Oken shabbily. Thereafter, he appeased him and asked him the purpose for which he was making his sacrifice. He explained that Orunmila had advised him to make sacrifice in order to ascend to the throne of his father. Olokun retorted by assuring him that his sacrifice had materialized. It was at that point that he surrendered the pigeons to Olokun's body guards.

Meanwhile, Olokun ordered his followers to mould Oken with all items of prosperity. As soon as they began to mould him, long feathers protruded from his anus. When he eventually emerged at home, he was spontaneously acclaimed as the next king (or Oloja-Eye) of all birds. It is the long feathers of Oken that Kings and Head Chiefs in most parts of Yorubaland wear on their crowns.

When the odu appears at divination, the person will be told to make sacrifice in order to win an upcoming contest for a higher position. He should serve Esu with a he-goat and send four pigeons to the sea.

He Also Divined for Agbonrin, Agbe and Aluko

*Etura Irete lo 'ndifa fun Agbe, obufun Aluko, Otun bu
fun Agbonrin.*

He made divination for two other birds called Agbe and Aluko. He also divined for the Deer. They were all advised to make sacrifice to word-off the danger of death to be caused by human enemies. They did the sacrifice and escaped death.

At divination, the person will be advised to make sacrifice in order to survive an up-coming epidemic during that year.

He Also Made Divination for Ayinyan

*Etura re re re. Irete re re re. Babalawo Ayiyan, Odifa
fun Ayiyan.*

He made divination for the Cockroach advising him to make sacrifice to avert the danger of sudden death. He did not make the sacrifice.

Meanwhile, Esu advised the Fowl that the Cockroach was good for food. When the cockroach came out the following morning, the Fowl beaked him and he fell on his back and began to cry "Etura re re re". With that the fowl ate him up for an early breakfast.

When it appears at divination, the person will be advised to make sacrifice to avoid sudden death. If the divinee is proposing to travel, he or she should make sacrifice before leaving home in order to obviate the danger of accidental death during the journey.

The Divination He Made Before Leaving Heaven

*Edobi Ishu. Aboju regun regun. Odifa fun Orunmila nijo ti
ofe ti kole orun bowa si kole aye.*

The face of a half yam is smoother and more symetrical than the face of a whole yam. That was the name of the Awo who made divination for Orunmila when he was coming to the world. He was advised to make sacrifice in order to prosper on earth. He was required to make sacrifice with dog, cock, tortoise and a gourd of palm wine to Ogun; ram, cock, and snails to Sango; a pack of yams stacked in a basket at the road junction for Elenini, the Obstacle divinity; sixteen pigeons, sixteen cocks to Olokun; and two he-goats and a tortoise to Esu.

He tried to raise a loan to finance the sacrifice, but he could not make it. Since he was determined to go to the world, he decided to make as much sacrifice as he could afford. He served his guardian angel with a hen, rat and fish, gave the skull of a he-goat to Esu , sent white chalk, a pigeon, and a piece of white cloth to Olokun, while giving roasted yam and a gourd of palm wine to Ogun. For not making full sacrifices, Ogun decided to tie a chain to his waist to prevent him from going to the world. After roaming about in heaven, he went to God to report that Ogun had stopped him from going to earth by tying a chain to his waist. Since God does not stop anyone from carrying out his wish, he cleared and blessed Etura-Irete to go to the world to do the bit he could.

Eventually, without informing anyone, he ran away from heaven to the world, where he took to trading in addition to the practice of Ifism. After spending some time on earth without any visible sign of making it, he decided to return to heaven. Just as he was arranging to come to heaven, his guardian angel also turned up to meet him on earth to remind him of what he was supposed to do. Meanwhile, Elenini turned his attention to a different direction to ensure that his guardian angel and himself crossed ways without meeting.

As soon as he got to heaven, Ogun apprehended him once more, making him a servant in his household. When his guardian angel returned to heaven after failing to see him on earth, he set out to deliver him from servitude under Ogun. His guardian angel raised a loan on his behalf from Elenini for him to make the sacrifices prescribed for him. After making all the sacrifices, he received fresh clearance from God to return to earth.

On getting back to the world, he resumed his Awo practice and he began to prosper modestly, but he could never identify what tangible thing he did with the money he was making. He neither had a wife nor a child. Wondering why he was still not making it, he decided to go for divination at which he was reminded that he had not repaid the loan to his guardian angel in addition to a rat called Eku Olirin. He was told to repay the debt and to give two he-goats to Esu. After serving esu, he got the rat, used it to serve his Ifa privately and he proceeded to cook it by himself, since he neither had a wife not a servant to assist him. After cooking the rat in a soup, he added eko to it and shouted Ode Awo Eesu - signaling to the Awos that the food was ready.

When the Awos came in response to his call, they were surprised that it was a rat he invited them to come and eat with him. They were disappointed but could not refuse to eat the rat.

After eating the meat, they prayed for him to have a wife and a child before the next anniversary. After making the sacrifice, he went to the market where he met a young woman sitting at the foot of an iroko tree. After exchanging greetings with her, he told her that she was despondent because she had been trying in vain to have a child and that a child was close to her. The woman feeling reassured, confirmed that her main problem in life was how to bear a child. There and then, she promised to help him. She followed him home and they began to live as man and wife.

On getting home, he made divination and he was told to obtain Eku Olirin for the wife to serve Ifa, promising to thank Ifa with a goat and a hen if she became pregnant. He procurred the rat and after cooking with it, he again called Ode Awo Eeesu, and they came, ate the rat and had some drinks, praying for the woman to have a child before the end of the year.

Unknown to him, the wife came from the palace of Olokun in heaven and her name was Oja. On every market day, she always left empty-handed for the market, but invariably returned home with plenty of money. One month after they met, the woman became pregnant and in the fullness of time, she gave birth to a male child. He was now a rich man and his Ifa practice had made him equally wealthy and popular.

To mark the child's naming ceremony, he served Ifa with a goat, a pig, a hen, a fish, snail and a rat. When the Awos came this time in response to his call of Ode Awo eesu, they came to enjoy a proper feast.

During the next anniversary, he was already prosperous enough to serve Ifa with a cow, a pig, a ram and a goat. Every invitee had plenty to eat and drink. Meanwhile, he had many more children and built larger houses to accommodate his family. That was how this odu earned the sobriquet of Olomo yo yo the man endowed with many children. He subsequently became the wealthiest man in the town and he was made the Shashere of the town.

When this Ifa appears at Ugbodu, the person will be told to pay a debt he owes to his guardian angel and Elenini. He should immediately serve the Ifa with Eku Olirin and beseech Orunmila to make him prosperous enough to serve him with a cow. The next woman he meets after Ugbodu is his destined wife from the palace of Olokun. If he does not already have his own Ogun and Olokun shrines, he should arrange to have them soon after the Ifa initiation ceremony. The new wife he will come across will be a successful trader.

Divined for the Barrel, Clay pot and the Gourd When They Assailed the River

Ako elila ni a ti kekere ran imu.
Itiju wo eni ni orun ju eru.

Those were the Awos who made divination for the barrel, the clay pot and the gourd (Ikoko, Igba and keregbe) when they were going to wage war on the river. They were all advised to make sacrifice with pigeon to Esu for victory and safe return home. The barrel refused to make any sacrifice because he could not imagine how the river could ever dent his iron garment. The clay pot made sacrifice with the feathers of a pigeon, promising to give a live pigeon upon a safe return. It was only the gourd who made the prescribed sacrifice.

On getting to the war front, they aggressed the river. At the same time, Esu positioned the trunk of trees and stones to fight for the river. When the soldiers of the river engaged the gourd, he began to sing:

Mo gbon mo sa which reminded Esu that he had made sacrifice and he stayed afloat. On the other hand, the clay pot (Ikoko) cried:- Emi ti she bo, Igba kan gbudu gbudu and after staying afloat for some time he was engaged by the rock which broke him into pieces on the banks of the river. On his part, the barrel after being made to drink plenty of water, sank right down to the bed of the river never to surface again. Thus, it was only the gourd who survived the combat and he returned home safely.

At divination, the person will be advised not to undertake a proposed adventure without making sacrifice.

Special Sacrifice for Success in One's Endeavour

Orunmila ni ki Olugba ere. Moni olugba ere.

Orunmila told his priest to hail out, and the Ifa priest bellowed. Asked to explain the exclamation, Orunmila declared that rats, fishes, animals and infants all hail on their parents.

He prescribed sacrifice with a pigeon, because it is the only bird that flies fortune to the home with its wings, while chanting the following incantation:

Olugba ere wa sin mi
Olugba ere eku kuku gba
Ere wa je oka Olugba ere.

When this odu appears at divination, the person will be advised to make sacrifice with two pigeons in order to succeed in his work.

Chapter 12

ETURA-EKA

He Made Divination for the Oil bean Tree

Etura kpaa O sarejo. Eka kpaa o sare jo.

Those were the Awos who made divination for the Oil Bean Tree (Akpagha in Yoruba and Okpagha in Bini) when she was coming to the world. She was advised to make sacrifice to prevent her close relations from killing her children. She was required to make sacrifice with a he-goat to Esu and a cock to her head. She made the sacrifice and came to the world.

On getting to the world, she gave birth to several children. When it was time to hatch her children, she would shout Etura kpaa, or Eka kpaa - and the seeds would come down at a long distance from her house. That is why the seeds of the oil bean tree fall at least one hundred meters away from its foot.

Meanwhile, when her relations heard that she had produced several children, they went to visit her. These were the rabbit, the hare, the grass-cutter and the porcupine. When they asked to see her children, ostensibly for the purpose of feeding on them, she replied that they never lived with her. By the time, the enemies who wanted to eat them eventually saw them, they were already full blown plants. That was how the oil bean tree protected her children from the evil machinations of her relations. Even the rodents who dug their holes near her foot, could never see her children.

When this Ifa appears at Ugbodu, the person will be told to serve Ogun with a cock, Esu with a he-goat adding the hooks or spines of the porcupine (Ire in Yoruba and Okhaen in Bini), and a rabbit to the elders of the night. At divination, the person will be advised to serve; Esu with a he-goat and Ogun with a cock to fend off problems from close relations.

The Divination He Made Before Coming to the World

Oka 'le O A Ono was the Awo who made divination for this Odu before he came from heaven. He was advised to make sacrifice to his guardian angel with a goat, dried fish, fresh fish, hen, fresh rat; Esu with a he-goat, palm oil, hoe, sharp-pointed stick; Elenini (Idoboo) with disused machete, a basket; and a white chalk to obtain the blessing of Olodumare. He was required to make those sacrifices to alleviate the problems he was going to come across on earth and in order to live to a ripe old age.

He reacted negatively by saying that if the world was such a difficult place, all his colleagues who left previously without making such elaborate sacrifices would have returned long ago to heaven. When his guardian angel insisted that he was not going to allow him to leave for earth without making the sacrifices, he proceeded to raise a loan from Elenini (Idoboo) the Obstacle divinity to fund the sacrifices. He left for the world after making the sacrifices.

On getting to the world, he took to trading in addition to the practice of Ifism. He was making some money but he could not account for whatever he was doing with it, because Elenini was always seizing it from him. When he subsequently went for divination, he was told to repay the debt he owed to the Obstacle Divinity in heaven. He repaid it by making sacrifice with a basket containing a cock, and sixteen bags of money which was deposited at Orita-Ijaloko. He lived to a ripe old age but not in affluence.

He Made Divination for the People of Iroko and Eka

Okiti kpuke, Awo Eba ono. Odifa fun won lo'de Iroko.
Obufun won ni ode Eka to ri ogun omo araye.

He made divination for the people of Iroko and the people of Eka to forestall the wars they were going to have from the people of the world. They were required to make sacrifice with a he-goat, and a cock. The people of Iroko did not make the sacrifice, but the people of Eka made their own sacrifice.

At the outbreak of war, the people of Iroko decamped to emigrate to live with the people of Eka. When it appears at divination, the person will be advised to make sacrifice for progress.

This Odu's Special Sacrifice for Consolidating Fortune

Otura ka mi o serejo. Ami ni kini yi o fi serejo?
Orunmila ni ka fi ugbin bo ori ati ifa. Ni gba na ni eyi ti
o fo ka. Ni gba na ni yi o wa serejo. Ebo ki atun ru o.

Orunmila disclosed that what was to be used to gather one's fortunes together were snails to be used for serving both the head and Ifa after serving Esu as well.

When it appears at divination, the person should be told to serve Ifa, and his head so that his prosperity might be consolidated. If he does not already have Ifa, he should arrange to have one. For a woman, she will be told that she can only prosper if her husband has his own Ifa.

He Made Divination for the Hedgehog

Oruraka was the Awo who made divination for the hedgehog (Akika in Yoruba and Ekhui in Bini) when he was going to drink water in the river. He was told to make sacrifice to avoid taking the wrong route and running the risk of falling into a trap. He refused to make the sacrifice.

Without making the sacrifice, he went to the river and on the way, he was caught in a trap. For failing to heed the advice of the diviner, he became ashamed of himself and coiled up his body round the trap. That is why the hedghog rolls up his body as soon as it suspects the approach of danger.

At divination, the person will be advised to beware of falling into a trap of his or her enemies. To neutralize the evil contrivances of the enemies, he or she should serve Esu with a he-goat adding a twine.

Special Sacrifice Against Unconsumated Fortunes (Amubo)

Orunmila ni Otura ka, Moni o da nu wara.
Oni oun a fi eku ase she jo, Moni maa fi eku ase she jo.
Oni ki a wo aje ile olufe o daiye ti o nturake, ti o si
n danu wara.
Oni eku ase ni oun yi o fi she jo.
Orunmila advised the Ifa priest to stretch out his body.
The Ifa priest says it was a fruitless exercise.

Orunmila retorted that the incidence of abortive ventures could be corrected by making sacrifice with a squirrel. He added that the priest should look at the fame and fortune of Ife which has spread to the four winds, but which they have not put to advantage. He repeated that the direction of the tide could be changed by making sacrifice with a squirrel.

At divination, the person will be told that whatever he or she touches, misfires and fails, but that the situation could be corrected with appropriate sacrifice.

Chapter 13

ETURA-ETURUKPON
ETURA-TIKU
ETURA-OLOMU

He Made Divination for the Bird Called Dogi-Dokpe

Etura ba ti ye tiye. Odifa fun dogi dokpe tori oko riro.

He made divination for the bird called dogi-dokpe who dances with its tail/anus when standing on a tree. He was advised to make sacrifice to avert the risk of sporadic impotence. He was required to make sacrifice with a cock and a hen in order to remain potent throughout his life. He did not perform the sacrifice, and that is why it suffers from impotence for most of its life and when it stands on top of a tree, it pretends to be having sex with the tree by shaking its waist.

When it appears at divination, the person will be advised to make sacrifice in order to remain sexually potent throughout life.

The Divination He Made Before Leaving Heaven

Mi a tiku mo lere, Mi a tiku mo. Mi a tiku mo
Oun ko ki, oun lo 'ntiku mo.
What is considered to be disturbing.
What is it that one locks the door against, and heaps rubbish on it
to keep away, except death, rotten things or useless materials.

Those were the Awos who made divination for this odu when he was preparing to come to the world. He was advised to serve Esu with a he-goat and his guardian angel with a goat to avoid landing on earth in a difficult town where people do not make sacrifice, which would make him listless and unrecognised. He was also required to serve Ogun with a dog, cock, tortoise and a bag of money. Of all the sacrifices he was required to make, he only served Esu with a he-goat after begging his guardian angel to bear with him. He did not bother at all about Ogun.

He came out of the world in a town where people did not recognise the divinities, and where no sacrifices were traditionally made. Although he was required to serve Esu on getting to earth, the ecological profile of the environment in which he was born did not conduce to the making of divination and sacrifice. He was a lost sheep who grew up where Ifa practice was not known, let alone appreciated, which made him to live a wretched life throughout his short span on earth.

One night his guardian angel appeared and revealed to him that his problems arose from his failure to give him the wherewithal for buying him a more purposeful life on earth. Since he had no means of appreciating the significance of the dream, his guardian angel suborned Esu to deceive him to accompany him on an endless journey. Esu lured him on a journey to his guardian angel. When he appeared in heaven before his guardian angel, he was detained never to return to earth. He died in his sleep.

When this odu appears at Ugbodu, or at a naming ceremony divination, the person is un-doubtedly a fay. He will not live to an old age unless Ifa is prepared for him if a man, or she is made to marry a man with Ifa, if a woman.

He Made Divination for Ogun in Heaven

Etura-ba-turukpon was the Awo who made divination for the seven children of Ogun when they were coming to the world. The seven children were:- Ogun alade who eats cock; Ogun Alakama who eats ram; Ogun Ajero who eats he-goat; Ogun Gbeno Gbeno who drinks the water that flows down the stem of trees; Ogun Alara who eats dog; Ogun Gbejo Gbejo who eats snails and Ogun Lakola Otata Ginene, who feeds on human blood. Orunmila advised each of them to serve their heads with kolanuts after which they were to remain in-doors for three days. They served their heads alright but pondered on the advice to remain indoors for three days.

The seventh son of Ogun - (Ogun Lakola) wondered how he was going to feed and bathe in three days if he did not venture out since he traditionally bathes in and drinks human blood and feeds on human flesh.

The following day, he went out to look for food before coming to remain in the house. The other six remained in-doors in consonace with Orunmila's advice. It was during these three days that God gave them the secret of how to feed themselves without breaking his eternal injunction not to kill human beings while on earth.

After the end of the three days, they all went back to Orunmila who asked them the outcome of their recluse. The children of Ogun who preserved for the three days are those who use their powers constructively and have their shrines, priests and followers. Ogun Lakola, the man-eater, is dreaded, devoid of any shrine, priests or adherents. He is only known by the havoc he wreaks on his innocent victims. Orunmila however warned him never to tamper with his children and followers.

They came to the world to take advantage of the sacrifices they made and the advice they were given. When it appears at Ugbodu, the person should prepare his Ogun shrine to parry the risk of becoming very temperamental. At divination, the person should serve Ogun with a cock and his/her head also with a cock.

Incidentally, in a special revelation, Orunmila later disclosed to me that the white man was the product of the copulation of Lakola-otata-ginene, the 7th man-eating son of Ogun and the fair-skinned daughter of the Obstacle divinity (Elenini or Idoboo) called Afin-laarilo. He emphasised that most of the divinities created by God were dark, grey or brown skinned, except Elenini the obstacle. He went on to add that it was the curiosity-seeking Afinyibo who went to God to teach him how to create, without making sacrifice, which earned him the eternal curse of Esu, that whatever he learned from God would become his undoing on earth.

He Made Divination to Become a Head Chief

Oro ori ita, ko kpa w ewe. Atoshi aworo ko kpa ishe.
Awon ni won lo'ndifa fun Olomu. Aga omo ageshin won losi oko.
Ibayere yere teke leye - Odifa fun Ojiya jini jini ti o nbe
ni ode omu.

The plant which grows on a rock does not have strong branches. The poor can never perform better than the rich. Those were the two Awos who made divination for Olomu, who became a king in the Kwara State of Nigeria. They also made divination for the pauper who lived in the town of Omu.

Ojuya the pauper was advised to make sacrifice in order to achieve fortune, fame and recognition. He was required to make sacrifice with bush rat and palm kernel and he did it.

The Olomu of Omu was also advised to make a similar sacrifice to obviate the danger of being dethroned and replaced by an inconsequential character. He was required to make sacrifice with bush rat, his own cap, and a strong he-goat. He refused to make the sacrifice.

Meanwhile, Ojiya the pauper set a trap by the side of the road which subsequently caught a rat. When he went to watch the trap, he discovered that it had caught a rat. But as he moved to remove the rat, Esu intercepted him in the guise of a diviner and told him to leave the rat on the trap. Esu told him however to hide and watch the events that were going to transpire eventually.

At the same time, Esu cajoled the Olomu to visit his farm, which he immediately set out to do. On his way to the farm, the Olomu came across a trap which had caught a bush rat. Remembering at the instance of Esu that he had previously been advised to make sacrifice with a rat, the Olomu proceeded to remove the rat from the trap.

As he did so, Ojiya came out at the instance of Esu to accuse the Olomu of theft in the following words:

Olomu ole! Ibayere yere te keje. Esi ade ori re.
Ode mi kpa ewusa. Olomu ni o fun ibayere yere tekeleye.
Olomu Ole! Ibayere yere te keleye.

In the heat of the commotion, a knight from heaven emerged at the instance of Esu to find out the cause of the disturbance. Ojiya explained that the Olomu had stolen his rat, a charge which the king denied, because he had meanwhile hidden the rat under the cap on his head. Eventually, when Ojiya insisted that if the king opened his cap and there was no rat hidden under it, he should be summarily executed and the king should tread on his blood. On the other hand, if the rat was found under the cap, the king would surrender all his belongings including the throne in lieu of the death sentence since theft carried the death penalty.

When the Olomu subsequently removed his cap and the rat was found under it, he forfeited his crown and his horse to Ojiya who rode to the town to become the new Olomu of Omu. The embarrassment was so much for the Olomu that he committed suicide in the forest.

At divination, the person will be advised to make sacrifice to avoid losing his lofty position to a nonentity and an embarrassment that could make him/her to commit suicide.

Chapter 14

ETURA-OSE
ETURA-ALASHE
ETURA-ORI-WESE

He Divined for the Rabbit When He Was Coming to the World

Ashe una lo'mu jogbo. Ashe lo mu
gba le. Ashe ni iyo lo'dun ni nu obe.
The fire uses its authority to clear the bush, and to heat
the ground. The salt uses its authority to sweeten the soup.

Those were the Awos who made divination for the Rabbit when she was coming to the world. She was told to serve Esu with a he-goat and her mind with kolanut and salt to prevent the danger of running into difficulties through the words of her mouth. She made the sacrifices and came to the world.

While in the world, she shared the same accommodation with the grass-cutter (Oya in Yoruba and Evuato in Bini) who was a junior sister to the Tiger. When the grass-cutter delivered her babies, she sent the Rabbit to go and inform her brother, the Tiger, that she had put to birth and whether he could provide her children and herself accommodation in his house. The Grass-cutter told the Rabbit to take special note of the first and last words of her vicious brother, the Tiger.

When the Rabbit narrated the message to the Tiger, he replied, while licking his lips, that "the grass-cutter, his sister, with fats like oil, was welcome to his house." On hearing the reaction of her brother, she was left in no doubt that the Tiger looked forward to feasting on herself and her children.

After waiting in vain for the grass-cutter to show up in his house, the Tiger surmised that it was the Rabbit who scared her away by reporting his remarks verbatim. He subsequently went in search of the Rabbit. When he eventually caught up with the Rabbit, Esu directed her to run into a hole, but the Tiger succeeded in peeling her tail, but she escaped with her life. That is why the tail-end of the rabbit is white to this day.

When this odu appears at Ugbodu, the person should serve the Night with a rabbit and Esu with a he-goat and the skin or bone of a tiger in order to survive the witchcraft of his relations. At divination, the person should serve Esu with a pigeon and Ogun with a cock.

He Made Divination for the Monkey

Akan rin she she, Awo Alakedun. Odifa fun Alakedun to
tori tomo dafa. Ebo omo ni ki o ru o.

The crab moves from side to side, was the name of the Awo who made divination for the Monkey for the safety and survival of her children. She was told to make sacrifice with a rat called eku-emo, hen and snail. She made the sacrifice, which is why the children of the monkey do not fall from her hands when climbing a tree.

At divination, the person will be advised to make sacrifice to avoid loss of children.

The Divination Made for Him When He Was Coming From Heaven

Ase uno lo fi jogbo.   Ase Orunrun lo mu segun wo mu gbale.
Awon n won lo'ndifa fun Orunmila ni joti onti kole orun
bowa si kole aye.

It is the authority of Fire that it uses to burn the bush.
It is the authority of heat that it uses to dry up wet and
cold places.

Those were the two Awos who made divination for Orunmila when he was coming to the world. These Awos first made divination for Asori the father of Etura-Alashe, nicknamed the single tree that made a forest. He was told to make sacrifice because he was going to give birth to a son who was going to be greater than himself. He did not do the sacrifice.

His son Etura-Alashe also went to the same Awos when he was coming to the world. He was advised to serve his head and guardian angel together with tiger, coconut, crocodile and a goat, Esu with twohe-goats and Osanyin with cock and dog. He made the sacrifice but gave one he-goat to Esu, promising to give him the second one on getting to the earth.

He was born as the eldest son of Araba or Asori who was already very famous on earth. He was known by all the Obas of the known world, but he had the problem of not being given to making sacrifices. He had been advised to serve his guardian angel, his father and Esu, but he refused to do any of them.

That was when Esu set out to frustrate his efforts. Meanwhile, he was invited by the Olofin to come and cast lot for him(ibo or Iboo) in the palace. As soon as he got to the palace, he successfully revealed the puzzle he was invited to come and unravel. He was eventually asked to reveal what was going to happen momentarily. He predicted that as he was standing; some-one was going to come in with a live crocodile; another person was going to bring in a live tiger, and thereafter a heavy rain was going to fall. He offered to be executed if his three predictions failed to come true.

Meanwhile, Esu had taken up a position on the main high-way from where he conjured the rain to threaten. As the rain began to fall, the hunter bringing a crocodile to the palace decided to take shelter somewhere on the way. The hunter bringing the tiger also had a similar experience. Thereafter, there was a heavy downpour of rain. That is why when this odu appears at divination, the diviner can safely predict the approach of a heavy rain which would destroy many things.

Up to night fall, the first two predictions of Asori did not materialize. Asori was consequently pushed into the dungeon since it was forbidden to execute an Awo, but as soon as he entered the dungeon, he was swallowed up by the crocodile inside the place.

The following morning, the two hunters came in with the crocodile and the tiger. Although the events vindicated the predictions of Asori, nonetheless, they came in too late to save his life. At the same time, his son had become very famous as an Ifa priest. One day, the Olofin sent for Etura-Alashe for lot casting. Before answering the call he made divination and he was required to serve his head with a tiger, his Ifa with a crocodile, Esu with a he-goat, and his father with a dog and cock. He served Esu and his father, but could not immediately get hold of a tiger and a crocodile to serve his head and Ifa. He therefore improvised by serving them with kolanuts and wine, promising to serve them with the prescribed materials if he returned home triumphantly from the palace.

On getting to the palace, he met a large gathering of people. Before being told what he was invited for, he revealed the mystery he was required to disclose. People were not impressed because that was what his father did before his colossal failure. Once again, he was required to reveal what was going to happen for the rest of that day. He predicted that as he was standing, a hunter would bring two crocodiles to the palace, and that the biggest of the two would be for him and the other for the Oba. He added that a tiger and a tigress would be brought to the palace and the tiger would be for him while the Oba kept the tigress. He also predicted that there was going to be a heavy rain before the end of that day. He offered to be executed if his predictions failed to come true.

As soon as he took his seat, a visitor who was instantly heralded, brought two massive crocodiles. Etura-Alashe was accordingly given the biggest of the two. As the hunter was receiving his reward, the arrival of a second hunter was announced who came in with a tiger and a tigress. People were beginning to take a serious look at Etura-Alashe. As he was being given the male tiger, the sky opened up to usher in a heavy down-pour of rain. With the manifestations of all his predictions, the Oba made him the Prime Minister (Shashere) of the town and he returned home at the head of a large triumphant procession.

On getting home, he invited his Awos to assist him in serving his head and Ifa with the tiger and the crocodile in fulfilment of the promise he made before leaving for the palace. As the crocodile was being slaughtered for Ifa, a voice was heard from its bowels "emu suuru" - that is, handle softly. When the bowel was carefully opened, his father Asori jumped out and he embraced his son, that indeed he had exceled him because of the sacrifice he refused to make. He then joined his son in serving his head with the tiger. Asori lived for another four years before he finally died.

He Made Divination for a Woman Called Otuu

Akeke lo shudi dee re gbo kun. Odifa fun Otuu nijo ti o fi
ojojumo washe da nu. Oso fun kofi eku emo meta ru ebo. Ki
odi okpo Ifa mu, ki o lo ri omo bi.

The spinning Spindle (Akpe) tied a rope to its waist. That was the awo who made divination for Otuu when she was never missing her menstruation. She was advised to make sacrifice with three eku-emo rats in order to have a child. She was also advised to come close to Orunmila. She made the sacrifice and became pregnant the following month.

When it appears at divination for a woman, she will be advised to marry a man having his own Ifa, or to persuade her husband to have his own Ifa so that she can bear him a child.

Special Divination for Honor and Dignity

Ori re re a si she'yan la'forun bo wa'ye. A kii fi gberu si ni
o. Eyi ti Alara to yan waye, ko fi gbe ru sini o. Eyi ti Ajero
to yan waye, ko fi gbe ru si ni o. Eyi ti Orangun ni'le ile to
yan waye. Ko fi gberu si ni o. Eyi ti Orunmila to yan waye,
ko fi gberu si nio. Ebo ni o, ko tun fi eyele bo ori.

The good head chosen from the palace of God is not used for carrying any load in the service of anyone. The heads chosen by kings Alara, Ajero and Orangun Illa and by Orunmila are forbidden to carry load for anyone, just as the head of an ifa priest is not expected to carry any load in the service of anyone. The divinee should serve his or her head with a pigeon. At divination, the person should be told not to carry any load for anyone. He should perservere because he will prosper in the end.

Special Sacrifice for a Woman Anxious to Have a Child

Orunmila ni a wase, Moni Awase eku ni o fi ni oyun ti yi o fi
bi mo. Awase eja, eye, eran ni won fi ni oyun ti won yio fi
bi mo. Awase omo eni ni yio fi ni oyun ti yio fi bi mo.

Orunmila here discloses that it was after menstruation that rats, fishes, birds, animals and women, proceed to give birth to their young ones.

Orunmila prescribed sacrifice with one egg, ewe omo and ewe emu leaves. The incantation that goes with it is:

Bi emo ba mu ire re ki bo.
Bi adiye ba ti gun, ni she ni o ma fi a she oyun omo.

At divination, the person will be told that there is a woman currently menstruating. If she makes the foregoing sacrifice, she will certainly become pregnant.

Special Sacrifice for Prosperity

Orunmila ni etura shege, Moni oro ayo ni.
Oni kini a ri ti a n yo, ti a nkpa ariwo enu?
Moni aje tuntun ni o wo ile de.
Oni oro ayo ni ki a ma jo, ki a si ma yo.
Orunmila ni etura shege. Moni oro ayo ni.
Oni kini a ri ti a n yo, ti a nkpa ariwo enu?
Moni omo tuntun ni a bi. Oni oro ayo ni.
Orunmila ni etura shege, Moni oro ayo ni
Oni kini a ri ti a n yo, ti a si nkpa riwo enu?
Moni gbogbo ire tuntun ni o wole de. Oni oro ijo ati ayo ni.
Oni ti o ba to be, ki a ma kpariwo enu. Moni Orunmila ti o ba ribe
Kini awa yio fi she? Morontotu, Mokun otan leri.
Orunmila proclaimed that there is joy all around, and he asked
what was so pleasant as to generate so much ballyhooo?
The Ifa priest replied that prosperity had come to the house.
In answer to similar questions the priest also replied that a
bride had come into the house, which was followed subsequently
by the birth of a new child, followed by the entry of wealth
to the home. Orunmila agreed that those occurrences were
sufficient to justify eternal happiness. The priest then
asked him for the requisite sacrifice and Orunmila prescribed
sacrifice with a pigeon, and a white ram, which were produced.

As the sacrifice was being made, Orunmila chanted the following incantation:

Ereku reku ni eye le ma'nke
Mo ba ori rere yi wo ilu
Ori rere ni agba fi a nje ode ilu
Ma se ori rere ni ile yi
Ogede oyinbo de! Eni ato run gba iwa bo

Meaning:

The pigeon heralds the approach of prosperity to the house
The person will come to the world with a good head.
Just as the ram moves around in the town with a good head.
The person will prosper in the world because the Banana came
to the world with a good omen.

When this odu appears at divination, the person will be advised to make sacrifice with a white pigeon, a white ram and Banana so that the prosperity which is lurking around him might materialize and come within his grip.

Chapter 15
ETURA-OFUN

He Made Divination for the Albino (Afin or Eyaen) in Heaven

Etura Ofene. Ofene da gha arine afin e ji yo.

That was the Awo who made divination for the Albino when he was coming to the world. He was advised to serve Esu with a he-goat and to refrain from eating salt, okro and yesterday's soup. He made the sacrifice before coming to the world, where he avoided his taboos.

He got married, had children and prospered. When he was going to perform the new yam festival, his senior wife prepared an okro soup for him, but having dreamt about it in advance, he did not eat it. At the same time, he left the wife with the erroneous impression of having eaten it by covering up the soup some where.

After observing that nothing happened to him, she became curious. Eventually, he went to Orunmila to find out how to react to the situation. He was advised to serve his head with a cock. After making the sacrifice, the senior wife left him and he began to prosper more than ever before.

When this Ifa appears at Ugbodu, the person should serve Esu with he-goat and okro. Thereafter, he should refrain from eating okro soup and yesterday's soup. He will be fore-warned that his senior wife will not marry him to the end of his life. Whenever she decided to leave him, he should not do anything to discourage her. When it appears at divination, the person will serve Esu with a he-goat and his/her head with a cock.

He Divined for Meeriye to Obtain the Blessing of God

Dogi, awo eba ono. Odifa fun Meeriye nijo ti o ba won oluku re lo
si oko obaro.

Dogi, the road-side Ifa priest was the one who made divination for Meeriye when she followed her friends to the forest to fetch the fruits of a plant called Obaro in Yoruba and Oriema in Bini. She had previously been warned not to accompany anyone to the forest. When her friends continued to persuade her to go with them, she went to Orunmila, who advised her to make sacrifice before going with them. She made the sacrifice.

When they got to the bush, her friends were able to fetch baskets full of the fruits while she only succeeded in fetching a single fruit. On their way home they decided to stop by the side of the river to have their bath. As she was going into the river to swim, she placed her single fruit on her pad. While swimming she observed that some children came to the bank of the river apparently looking for something. Her curiousity was aggravated when the children left all the other fruits and picked her only one. She hurriedly came out to stop them from taking it, but they insisted on taking it, after which they ran away.

Not knowing who they were, she pursued them relentlessly until they got to the palace of God, from where they came. Meanwhile, she was brought before God as she continued to insist on retrieving her only fruit, and the Almighty Father told her not to return but to remain in His divine palace for seven days. During the seven days, she cleaned, swept and scrubbed the inner chambers of the palace, washed clothes and cooked food.

On the seventh day, as she was cooking in the kitchen, the rat came to ask her for melon pudding (Iru in Yoruba and Evbaire in Bini). She gave it to the rat who in appreciation, forewarned her that God would ask her to choose between two small calabashes in His treasury. The rat advised her to choose the dirtiest of the two calabashes and on getting back home, she was to close the door to her room for absolute privacy before hitting it on the floor.

When God subsequently asked her to choose one of the two calabashes inside the divine treasury, one of them was covered with jewels, while the second one was covered with smoke. In consonance with the rat's advice, she chose the dirty one. On getting home, she took it into her room and locked the door.

When she knocked it on the floor, all descriptions of wealth began to ooze out of it, comprising of plenty of money, jewels, clothes, animals, ivory, etc. When she hit it on the floor a second time, a row of house were positioned in front of her. She had suddenly become wonderfully wealthy. That was how God compensated her for her fruit and Meeriye became a force to reckon with.

At divination, the person will be advised that he/she will lose a valuable item, but should not worry unduly about it because it has been taken by the servants of God. God will eventually compensate him/her in multiples.

The Divination He Made Before Coming to the World

Enu Oge lo'nkpa Oge, was the Awo who made divination for Orunmila when he was leaving heaven. He was advised to make sacrifices in order to avert the risk of getting into trouble as a result of his utterances in his Ifa practice. He was required to feast the two hundred divinities with a goat, hen, in addition ten pieces of white and black cloth, and to serve Esu with a he-goat. He was also advised to serve Daylight with white by giving white chalk, white cloth and cowries. He was also advised to be giving white chalk to the day every morning before beginning his daily chores.

He finally left for the earth after making all the sacrifices. On getting to earth, he quickly established himself as an effective and famous Ifa priest, while out-shining all the Awos he met on earth. His predictions were always coming true, but his fame and fortune soon began to generate enmity for him. At the same time there was a popular uprising in the town when the citizens rebelled against their king. The Oba invited Orunmila for divination on how to contain the explosive situation. At divination, his own Odu appeared, and he advised the Oba to make sacrifice to quell the rebellion. The Oba was required to make sacrifice with a goat, a drum, a he-goat, white cloth, red cloth, plenty of cowries and black cloth. The sacrifice was instantly made. After the sacrifice, he advised the Oba to make a special regalia with red cloth - a tradition which is exclusive to the royalty.

As soon as Esu ate his he-goat, he went out the following night singing to the music of his drum that a destructive epidemic would afflict the town unless everyone went to the palace the following morning to apologize to the Oba. In the small hours of the morning, there was an earth tremor which shook every house in the town to their foundations, but there were no casualties except for the Olisa, the leader of the insurrection who was buried in the rubble. That was enough to give the citizens a preview or foretaste of what was in stock for them. The following morning, the Oba wore his newly made red outfit and the courtyard of his palace was filled with the men, women and children of the kingdom. As soon as the Oba appeared to receive them, all the people shouted 'K A B I Y E S I ! O B A B A ! The efficacy of the sacrifice enhanced the popularity of Orunmila but also earned him more enemies.

Meanwhile, he invited his Awos for augury, who disclosed that he had forgotten his injunction to give chalk to every new day in the morning. He was advised to make sacrifice with hen, cock, pigeon, piece of white, black and red cloth, plenty of chalk and a he-goat to Esu. He made the sacrifice. Eventually, his enemies came to him for a settlement. The Oba eventually made him the Oluwo of all diviners.

When this Ifa appears at Ugbodu, the person will be advised to make the special sacrifice in order to neutralize the enmity which his fortune and fame will generate for him.

He Made Divination for the Pauper to Prosper

Bi o ba funmi ni temi, Emi a fun e ni tere.

That was the poem with which Orunmila made divination for the pauper to prosper. The pauper was the only child of his parents, and he was friendly with the favorite servant of the Oba. Meanwhile, there was unusually intense heat of the sun which was making life intolerable in the town. The Oba invited all his diviners and seers to do something to appease the sun. While the Awos were divining on what to do about the situation, the pauper went about boasting that he was the only one capable of solving the problem. The Oba had promised to give a high chieftaincy title in addition to one hundred men, one hundred women, one hundred cows, one hundred goats, one hundred fowls and one hundred bags of money to whoever was able to force the sun to move upwards in the sky to cool the earth's ozone layer.

Meanwhile, the Oba set a date for the task to be performed. It was then he heard of the bluster of the Pauper, and he was invited to appear before the Oba. When he was subsequently arraigned before the Oba, he was about to disown the allegation when his friend eyed him to own up. The Oba retorted by telling him that if he was able to do it, he would immediately divide the kingdom and give him one half to administer, but that he would be executed if he failed. From the palace, he cried home to meet his mother, who was not amused at the prospect of losing her only child.

She immediately went to Orunmila, who after divination told her to make sacrifice with a bow and three brown he-goats, maracas and three cowries to Esu and a hen for Ifa.

The mother went home to produce the materials. After making the sacrifices, Orunmila prepared the bow (which was made from a stick cut from Irosun plant) and the arrows to spend three nights on the shrine of Esu, together with the maracas. He told her to come with her son to collect the materials on the eve of the appointed day. On the eve of the appointed day, Orunmila gave the Maracas to the mother and the bow and arrow to her son.

On the D - day, people were gathered. The elderly Awos who had volunteered to do the work, all tried but failed. The Pauper was finally invited to have a go at the sun. As he brought out his bow and arrow, his mother began to play with the maracas between her palms and to sing:

Eela o. Ela mosin ki awari baba lawo.
Bo ba ti fun mi ni temi, ma a fu eni tire.
Odafun omo mi atosi ti o ma to'jo.
Mo gbo, moru, mogbo tu lu esu.
Ebo fin, ebo mo fin okpo. Elumorere ebo lu arin
Ajagun tiinrin

That was the incantation Orunmila taught her to repeat before her son shot his arrow. As the son pulled the bow home to release the arrow, she said "Ofefe gbe mi dele". The first arrow got close to the sun before it returned. The second arrow hit the sun and returned. The third arrow hit the sun's bulls-eye and there was total darkness. When the sun re-emerged after its eclipse, it had been pushed to the distance it occupies from the earth to this day.

After performing the feat, the Olofin went back on his words and decided only to give the pauper a man, a woman and other gifts. Esu immediately intervened by yelling and it was echoed by Sango through thunder and lightening and where the thunder impacted on the palace grounds, caused a crater that consumed two hundred spectators. The incident scared the Olofin to submission and he quickly carried out his promise. In addition to making the Pauper the Shashere of Ife, he divided his kingdom, palace and harem into two and surrendered one half to him. The new Shashere then led a huge procession to his house.

When this Odu appears at divination, the person will be warned against the risk of locquaciousness to avoid getting into trouble that could cost him his life. In any event, if he is to benefit from his talkative disposition, he should have his own Ifa and give a he-goat, bow and arrow and maracas to Esu. He will prosper thereafter.

Special Sacrifice for Having Children

Etura fun yen yen. Oko firi fi asho gba. Odifa fun Ajiri eyi
she iya oloye. Ora gan, O ra 'kpata. Ori omo lehin adiye,

o bu si ekun. O ni be, Edumare lo she yi fun awon adiye. Won
she ni ki o ru ebo. Won ni ti o ba ti le ru ebo, Awon omo marun
ni yi o ma bi. Awon omomarun ni yi o joba ni oju re.

He made divination for Ajiri, the mother of Oloye who was already very old and wealthy enough to build and own a whole street. She was however still very anxious to have children, because she was barren and getting close to menopause. While taking a walk on the street one evening, she saw a hen cuddling to her chicken and she stopped and began to weep. She asked in her melancholia, why had God done so much to make the hen to have a full and happy life, and given her not even a single child to make her happy? It was in that state of depression that Etura-Ofun saw her and invited her to his house for divination.

After making divination, he reassured her that if she could make sacrifice, she would have five male children who would all become kings in her life time. She was required to make sacrifice with a he-goat, mortar, white yam (Ishu-Iolo) hand-loom (Agbo gboro) for weaving cloth, and five small gourds (irere). She made the sacrifice, after which she became pregnant. In the fullness of time, she gave birth to a male child who was named Oloye. She had four additional male children in quick succession who were respectively named; Oloja odo, Osolo, Irere, Oloja-igbehin.

Over time but while she was still alive, all her five children became kings of different places. When she eventually went to thank Orunmila, she sang in praise of Ifa as follows:
Etura fun yinrin yinrin. Oko fiirifi a shogba. Odifa fun mi
Ajiri tin she iya oloye. Mo gbo riru ebo
Mo run, mo gbo eruatu kesu, mo tu.
Ko i kpe. Ko i jina. Wa ba mi lokpo lokpo ire omo.

When this Ifa appears at divination, the person will be told that he or she has a nagging problem, but that with sacrifice, he or she will see happier days.

He Divined for Ojola Gidigba, the King of Snakes

Kpelebe a bidi soro, was the Awo who made divination for Ojola gidigba (bigbon) the king of snakes. He was told to make sacrifice to avert the risk of severe illness for his children. He was required to make sacrifice with his wearing apparel, a fowl, plenty of loaded materials (konu kofo in Yoruba).

He made the sacrifice. The appropriate medicines (ayajo) was prepared for the children to use in rubbing their bodies. That is why snakes do not fall sick. Rather, they exude their scales to renew their lives.

At divination, the person will be told to make sacrifice to avert the danger of illness or death.

IFISM

THE COMPLETE WORKS
OF ORUNMILA

VOLUME THIRTEEN

THE ODUS OF IRETE

Chapter 1

IRETE-OGBE
IRETE-TE-NU-OLU

Divined for Orisa When He Was Having Stomach Ache

Eji ni mo oju eji. Ole ni mo ese ole. Agbagidigidi
ni mo ese arawon lori akpata. Awoni won lo'ndifa fun
Orisa ti inu re maa run ni ugba kugba ti o ma mu emu
okpe. Won difa fun Nana kpakpakurudu ti'nshe wole wode Orisa.

The trickster recognised the style of the fraudster. The robber discerns the foot ptint of the elders on the surface of a stone. These were the Awos who advised Orisa when he was often developing stomach upset after privately drinking palm wine. Orisa does not drink in the presence of anyone except in strict privacy. Nana Kpakpa Kuurudu was the personal servant of Orisa who used to tap the palm wine from the bush and keep it in the inner chamber. However, it soon became apparent that Orisa often developed stomach trouble after drinking the palm wine. He subsequently invited his Counsellors who advised him to instruct Nana kpakpa kuurudu to encircle the gourd of palm wine with a layer of salt. Unknown to anyone, it was a snail, which Orisa forbids, who was often moving in to sample the palm wine, which was responsible for Orisa's incessant stomach upset.

The following morning, the personal assistant of Orisa was given a bag of salt to use in encircling the gourd container after tapping the palm wine. At the same time, the ant-hill (Okiti-ogan or ite) went to his diviner called Ero kongon gon gon for divination and he was told to make sacrifice to Esu with a he-goat, a hoe and a sharp pointed stick, to forestall the danger of strife to be brought by a lodger with the curse of God on his head. He did not bother to make the sacrifice. A plant called Iyanrin gia gia gia in Yoruba was advised to make sacrifice to Esu with a he-goat, cutlass and crushed yam to prevent a hard luck case from endangering his life with his own problems. He also refused to make the sacrifice. The deformed tree (igiabuwo in Yoruba and Erhan no gbu kpo in Bini) was also advised by Ero kon Fuuu to make sacrifice to Esu with he-goat, dried palm leaves and crushed yam to hinder any danger that his tenants would create for him for their failure to make sacrifice. At the same time, the big and small bats (adiden and oloja wonron in Yoruba and Eguen and owo in Bini) were also told at divination to serve Esu with he-goat and 201 needles. The big bats did not make the sacrifice, but the small bats did theirs.

Meanwhile, the snail left his house in the small hours of the morning to go to the home of the palm tree. As he tried to move to sample the wine inside the gourd, the salt encircling the gourd and venomous to him poisoned his lips. As the toxic effect ran through his alimentary metabolism, he began to discharge slimmy liquid which trailed his movement after the event to wherever he moved to in search of detoxication. In his last death throes, he sought solace in the home of Okiki-ogan, the anthill, who refused to accommodate him in the deference to the warning he was given at divination. However, the saliva secretion trailing his movement had already made an indelible track into and out of his house. He next crawled to the home of Iyanriyan plant, who also refused to ollige, but not before the salivation of the snail had indicated his trail in and out of his house.

The salt on his lips was becoming clear before the snail arrived for refuge in the home of the deformed tree. He went into the hold in his house to rest there. When Nana-kpakpakuurudu got to the palm tree the following day to collect the wine, he observed the mouth-trail of the snail which confirmed that he was the culprit who had been stealing the wine all the time. The palm wine tapper went to report his findings to Orisa, who immediately asked for volunteers who could search and apprehend the snail wherever he was hiding. Ogun was the first to volunteer to undertake the task.

He assembled his soldiers to accompany him in trailing the movement of the snail through his saliva marks on the ground. When he trailed the movement to the home of Okiti-Ogan, they used hoes and shovels to break down his house before they discovered that the snail had subsequently moved out through the back door of the Ant-hill's house. That however was after completely levelling his house. Next, they trailed snail's movement to Iyanrinyan's house and used the cutlass to mow down his house before they discovered that the culprit moved beyond his house. They trailed the movement of the snail eventually to the home of the deformed tree, and they used dried palm leaves to set it on fire.

As soon as all the 201 small bats (adiden or Eguen) were warned by Esu of the approaching danger, all of them abandoned their landlord and flew to safety. On the other hand, all the 201 big bats (Oloja wonron or Owo) having been hypnotised by Esu into a heavy dew of slumber were all roasted alive. Subsequently, after being burnt to its foundation, the deformed tree died and fell to the ground. Ogun's soldiers were able to collect the casualties of the conflagration, comprising the 201 big bats and the snail. The were all carefully stacked in a bag to be carried to Orisa.

On their return journey, they were already very hungry and tired and Ogun decided to call at his mother, Idaagba so they could find something to eat. She gave them the little food she had at home, while she asked them what they had in their bag. When they told her that they had roasted bats in it, she asked for one of them, but her son refused to give her, because Orisa was already aware of the number of bats in the bag.

While Ogun and his soldiers were eating, his mother stole one of the bats and folded it in the loin cloth she tied round her waist. When Ogun and his troops finished eating, they took up the bag and made straight for the palace of Orisa. On getting there, they reported mission accomplished. Orisa thanked Ogun for solving the problem, not only for bringing the culprit's corpse, but also those of 201 bats. However, when the bats were counted, one of them was missing. Ogun confirmed Orisa's affirmation that they counted 201 bats and wondered what happened to one of them.

The embarrassment was too much for Ogun to take lying down when Orisa asked him whether they stopped anywhere? Ogun confirmed that they stopped to have a bite in his mother's house. In a delirious mood, Ogun brought out his fighting arrow (Oso-Uhi in Yoruba and Ekpede in Bini) and vowed to trace the whereabout of the missing bat. He then stretched out the weapon and commanded it to go and attack whereever the bat was. The weapon flew up and down the sky in search of the missing bat. At the same time, just as her son's weapon was flying over the roof of her house, Ogun's mother came out to the back of her house to split fire wood. The Oso-Uhi targetted the missing bat in her loin and hit her on the head and she died instantly. As soon as she died, the bat was transfixed on her chest.

When Orisa was subsequently told about what happened to Ogun's mother, he ordered that she should be revived by Ogun. However, Ogun begged to decline because she had disgraced him. Ogun subsequently proclaimed that if anyone was invoking him for quick action, he should be told to kill the culprit like he killed his own mother.

At the appearance of this Ifa at Ugbodu, an Ogun shrine should be prepared for the new Ifa immediately and Esu should be served with he-goat adding a big bat. At divination, the person should serve Esu with a bat and Ogun with a cock to avert the risk of any embarrassment. The person will be told to beware of the thief in his house. The Ifa priest can say that a clay pot has been used to cover up snails at the back of the divinee's house. If it is Ayeo, the person should be told that a hen has roosted its eggs in the house. He or she should not allow the hen to hatch its eggs lest it would stimulate an outbreak of epidemic disease of disastrous proportions.

He made divination for Olokun When His Fortunes Waned

Isekpe igi ma lu gho ghagha. Uti igi mu lu ge idi.
Ikoko didu Awo orita. Awon meteta lo'nshe Ifa fun Olokun
nijo ti won so fun wi kpe ko le ila mo.

The branches of used fire wood are brought from the farm in scattered units. The stem of the fire wood and the black clay pots left at a road junction were the Awos, who made divination for Olokun when his fortunes were flagging and he was short of water. After divination, they told him that "his prosperity was gone for good. As he was trying to cooperate with the inevitable, he came across another Awo called Ota kpelebe inu omi ko mo kpe Orunrun kpaa to'ode - meaning The stone emerged in the river does not know that the heat of the sun is heating the stone exposed on the surface. The Awo reassured him after divination that he was going to be very prosperous and full again, provided he was able to make sacrifice. He was required to make sacrifice with he-goat to Esu and with sixteen white pigeons, a piece of white cloth and eight white kolanuts.

He produced the materials and made the sacrifice. After making the sacrifice, the Awo gave two of the pigeons to Olokun to serve his head with them on getting home. As he was praying with the two pigeons in his house, they both flew away from his hands, which made him to become even more despondent. Three month later the two pigeons flew back and stood in front of Olokun's house. As he was about to catch them they flew off once more. At that point, he threw up his hands in dispair as he lamented the amount he spent for the sacrifice.

Meanwhile, Esu invited all the rivers and accused them of abandoning their eldest brother Olokun in his moment of despondence because he was poor. All the rivers reacted by convening a conference at which they all decided to visit Olokun. As soon as they all turned towards the direction of Olokun, Esu blew at them proclaiming that from that moment all the rivers would always turn towards the direction of Olokun's house never again to return to their own homes. That was when all the rivers of this world began to turn towards the direction of the sea.

As they were moving to Olokun's house, they met the three Awos who made the first negative and daunting divination for Olokun and carried them off their feet. They began to cry to Olokun for help, but their voices were dwarfed and rendered inaudible by the sound of the rivers' movement and they drowned into the depths of the Ocean. Subsequently, the rivers also met the last Awo who made the encouraging divination and sacrifice for Olokun, but as they tried to carry him, Olokun told them to leave him alone because that was his benefactor. At the height of his property, Olokun proclaimed that no matter how big a tree or wood may be, they would always be sunk in the depths of the river or sea, but that no matter how small a stone may be, no sea or river would ever be able to carry it. As soon as his life became properous again, Olokun invited his last Awo (Ota kpelebe inu omi ko mo kpe orunrun kpaa to'de) to live with him as his diviner. That is how pebbles and stones came to dwell in water.

When this odu appears at divination, person will be told to buy an elderly goat to serve his Ifa in order to live to a ripe old age. He should also make sacrifice with four pigeons, out of which the Awo would give him two to serve his head after which he will rear them and not kill them. If the person does not have his own Ifa, he should arrange to have one.

Another Variation of How Ategbe Divined for Olokun to Regain Opulence When All But One of His Wives Deserted him

Ategbe awo Olokun, Odifa fun Olokun ni jo ti ayare
merin fi si 'le. Ebo ni o ru o.

Ategbe was the Awo who made divination for Olokun when property made him to become pompous and vain-glorious. The Awo advised him to offer a he-goat to Esu and to make sacrifice with 16 pigeons, a 10 metre piece of white cloth, 16 bags money and a gourd of palm wine. He was advised to stop taking alcholic drinks after making the sacrifice. Olokun not only refused to make the sacrifice, but continued with his intoxicating drinks.

Meanwhile, Esu decided to teach him the lesson often learnt the hard way by all those who look down on him. He went to dam the flow of wealth to him. As no new wealth moved in to replenish his resources, he soon depleted his savings and sank into the depths of abject penury. In other words, Esu dyked the flow of water from the rivers while at the same time plugging the rain-pipe of the sky. As a result of which there was continuous draught for three years.

That was the state of affairs in which four of his wives left him. The wives who left him were, Oburo (Oriema in Bini). Teteregun (Ukhuroho in Bini), Aabo (Ebo in Bini) and (Iranmwinran in

Bini). The only wife who stuck it out with him was Aromi (Etebetebe in Bini). She refused to leave because she remembered how prosporous he was when she married him. Olokun's problems arose from his egotistic narissism and self-worship which made him to look down on all other divinities because of his wealth.

When she found herself alone with her husband, Aromi decided to go to Ategbe for divination. She was told to make the same sacrifice that her husband refused to make. She went out to borrow money to buy the materials for the sacrifice. This was at a point when Olokun was almost dried up from dehydration and draught. Ategbe gave the he-goat to Esu and prepared the sacrifice by putting the appropriate leaves into two clay pots which he concealed behind a fence prepared with four sticks stuck to the ground and covered with the white cloth. When the people who had written off Olokun as a finished man saw the rectangular tent of white cloth, they ran back, thinking he was already dead and that his corpse was hidden behind the white mask.

After eating his he-goat, Esu removed the materials with which he dyked the flow of homage from the rivers while at the same time, unplugging the rain-tap of the sky. As water was moving into Olokun's house from rivers, it was also raining non-stop for fourteen days. At the end of fourteen days, Olokun became so full again that he began to overflow his banks. His prosperity had returned. When the four wives who deserted him saw and heard the vibrations of his resurgence, they tried for a comeback, but he told each of them never again to come near his house. One of the wives called Iranwinran in Bini refused to leave his house, but Olokun proclaimed that she could only stay on the outer fringes (surface) of the house, but would never have any roots in his house anymore. That is why it is the plant that grows on top of rivers and seas without having any roots on the bed of the water. By the same proclamation, Olokun declared Aromi (Tebetebe) his favorite wife to eternity, giving her the freedom to enter any part of his domain.

At the end of the year, Olokun made a thanksgiving feast in honor of Ategbe, at the end of which he gave him beads, plenty of money, goats, clothes and several jewels.

He Made Divination for the Walnut Plant

Moshe tere tere Mo gbu ji. Awo Etura ti ankpe Asala,
nijo ti on fi omi oju shubere omo tuurutu. Ebo lo'n ru o.

He made divination for the Walnut when she was anxious to have children. She was advised to make sacrifice with a he-goat, a three year old cock, crushed yam and her own machet. The he-goat was given to Esu and the cock was used to prepare a special medicine for her. She subsequently became pregnant and gave birth at the same time to hundreds of children. unfortunately the people and animals of the world did not know the utility value of the Walnut's children.

Meanwhile, Esu invited people to roast or cook the fruits of the walnut to eat. When they saw how tasty the fruits were, the people cleared the bush, encircling the walnut to preserve her to bear fruits annually. That was how the walnut became famous through her children.

When this Ifa appears at Ugbodu, the person will be told to make sacrifice in order to achieve fame and fortune in life. He should forbid eating walnuts.

The Divination He Made When Coming to the World

Ajilolo nire, mi elajilo je. Lo ti tan ni ijilo udi. Lojo loro
nire mi alajilo. Lo'ko ni jolo Obo. Igbawe ojilo. Awonlo'n
difa fun Orunmila ni Ojo ti onti kole orun bowa si kole aye. Ebo
lo'nru o.

The prosperity of the world is extant, but he only visits those destined to prosper. That is why the crooked plank or wood stay longer on the roof of a building. The seat enjoys the prosperity of the buttocks just as the penis enjoys the pleasure of the vulva. Those were the Awos who made divination for Orunmila when he was leaving heaven. He was advised to make sacrifice in order to be able to wear the crown he was carrying to earth. He was required to make sacrifice with he-goat, a pack of yams, a tuber of cocoyam, a cock, a snail, camwood, and salt. He did the sacrifice.

Thereafter, he came to the world where he met several Awo stronger than himself. He began to have problems created for him by the stronger Awos as soon as they recognised his leadership qualities and esoteric prowess. When he divined through Ikin divination, Ifa told him to offer a rabbit to the elders of the night and to grind the bark of sasswood (Obo in Yoruba and Iyin in Bini) to prepare the Iyerson or divination powder on the sacrifical pot. Thereafter, he was to deposit it at a road junction in the night. After multiplying the sacrifice ten-fold, Esu lured all of Orunmila's night enemies to feast on it.

After eating the sacrifice, they all had bouts of diarrhea which purged them of all their bad intentions towards Orunmila. Thereafter, his fame began to blossom and he became so prosperous and popular that he was eventually given the crown of Oke-Mesi.

When it appears at divination, the person will be told to make sacrifice in order to wear the crown he or she brought from heaven. If the man does not already have Ifa, he should arrange to have it in order to prosper. He should also serve a divinity close to him but which he has for long ignored. It is served with white materials and people wear white dress serving it amidst dancing and drumming after the operation. The rain will beat those coming from the shrine.

He Made Divination for the Kings of Owo and Benin

Agbaro O lo'lo. Agbaro o lo'da, on fi enu gbe'le bi osa-sara, were the Awos who made divination for the Olowo of Owo Akpakudu fi enu jo oko, sugban ko ni iru bi to ti oko - were the two Awos who made divination for the Oba of Benin. They were both advised to make sacrifice with white moin-moin, a pigeon and a strong he-goat. The Olowo of Owo made the sacrifice but the Oba of Benin did not.

After preparing the sacrifice, the Awos told the Olowo to carry it by himself and deposit it in his father's farm. As he was putting down the sacrifice in the farm, he saw a bird on the ground and caught it with a view to send it to his children to play with. As he was carrying the bird home, it spoke to him in the following words:- semi je je o. Iwo ma mu mi lo si le. Meaning, Handle me gently and take me to your house. As he was getting home, the bird spoke once more - wa ikoko nla kan, fi mi kpamo si ninu, si fun mi ni ekuru fun fun. Gbe mi kpamo si inu iyara kan. Ti o ba di aro, iwo wa wo mi. The bird told the Oba to keep him in a big clay pot and feed him with white moyin moyin in his private room.

He told him to keep the pot containing him in a separate room where the Oba alone was to look him up every morning. The Oba who was now very curious followed the advice of the bird scrupulously. When the Olowo went to see the bird the following morning, he was astonished to see that the bird was standing on a pot full of money. The Oba was now taking and keeping the money collected from the pot every morning. He soon became extremely wealthy, which changed his life style completely so much that the Oba of Benin noticed the salutory change in the fortunes of his friend.

Meanwhile, the Oba of Benin sent spies to Owo to confirm the positive signals he was getting about the dramatic opulence of the Olowo of Owo. The spies came back to report that there were signs of prosperity in Owo which made the Oba of Benin to decide to visit his friend at Owo. The Olowo had been advised at divination not to reveal the secret of the bird to anyone. When the Oba of Benin saw the prosperity of the Olowo he besought him to take him in on the secret of his new-found-wealth. The Olowo bluntly refused in consonance with his divinational advice. The Oba of Benin reminded the Olowo that their relationship transcended that of "anyone". With that, the Olowo decided to take his friend on board. The following morning, the Olowo invited the Oba of Benin to accompany him to the room where the money spinning bird was lodged. It was in his presence that the Olowo harvested the money from the pot that morning. There and then, the Oba of Benin successfully persuaded his host to lend him the bird for only five months after which he would return it.

The Oba of Benin went home with the bird and the pot but after keeping it for five months, he refused to return it to the Olowo. When the owner of the bird insisted on having the bird, there was a quarrel which culminated in the decision of the Oba of Benin to wage a war on Owo. As the threat of military invasion loomed over his kingdom, the Olowo returned to his Awos, who reminded him of the maxim that over generosity begets ingratitude. He was advised to make sacrifice with 40 sheep, the horn of a deer, white cloth and plenty of money. He made the sacrifice very quickly, and he was advised to carry it to his boundary with Benin. Ase was prepared on the deer's horn and he was told to use it every morning to make the following proclamation: Ti o baje wi pe emi ni mo she Oba ado yi, ki Oba Ado yi shegun mi. Ti a ba si je wi pe Oba Ado yi mi o she mi. Emi ni ki o shegun re ni oni. Meaning - If I was the one who wronged the Oba of Benin, let him defeat me in the up-coming military encounter. If not let providence decide in my favor.

In the ensuring military confrontation, the forces of Owo were able to penetrate into the city of Benin and in the scuffle, the bird was killed. When the odu appears at divination, the person will be told that he will become rich in money, but should not reveal his secret to anyone. He should also refrain from lending money to anybody, because it would generate unnecessary enmity. He should however make sacrifice with a sheep, white pigeon, deer's horn and white cloth.

The Sacrifice Ategbe Made for Olokun to Regain Prosperity

Ishekpe wonron awo olokun.   Itikirimi, awo olokun. Otakpete
Bebeyi bebeyi, ekikwu ti n se owogbo gbogbo, awo olokun.

These were the Awos who made divination for the water divinity when his life was dull and poor. He was advised to make sacrifice with all edible foodstuffs, a hoe, a cutlass and a strong he-goat. He made the sacrifice and thereafter, Esu unpluged the rain tap of heaven and it rained consecutively for 40 days and 40 nights. Thus, Olokun's life became full once more.

At divination, the person should be told not to be upset by temporary setbacks. He should make sacrifice and all would be well again.

Chapter **2**

IRETE-OYEKU

He Made Divination for Morning and Evening

Ale bidi brikpe, Owuro yereku yereku, were the Awos who made divination for Morning and Evening. Each of them was advised to make sacrifice to Esu with a he-goat, cotton wool and walking stick inorder to live to a ripe old age. Only Evening made the sacrifice. Morning considered himself too handsome and popular to bother about any sacrifice.

Morning was the first to be born, and was so handsome and popular that everybody hailed him. He was however soon abandoned because people had to go to their daily chores to settle down with him. Thus, Evening came to have many more admirers and followers then Morning since people pray for their Evening to be more rewarding and prosperous than the Morning of their lives.

When this odu appears at divination, the person will be advised to make sacrifice for a prosperous and lasting evening. A child born at this time should be called Alejuaro in Yoruba or Otasowie in Bini.

He Made Divination for the Bird's Kindred When They Were Leaving Heaven

"Irete she biri biri. Oyeku she yereku, made divination for one hundred and sixty birds of the bird family when they were coming to the world. They were told to make sacrifice with he-goat to Esu and to serve their head with kolanuts. They made the sacrifice. The bat was the last bird to come to the earth where he told all the birds that God had decreed that all birds having no ears should stop having children. He also went to the animals to announce that any animal with ears and teeth should start procreating only by laying eggs. He was the only creature endowed with the features of mammals and birds. For the next three years birds could not have children while animals with teeth continued to bear children.

Meanwhile, the birds trooped to heaven to protest to God for promulgating such a discriminatory decree against them. In reply, God told them that He neither made such decree nor sent the bat any message to that effect. God revealed that the bat stole the teeth He had earmarked for the goat. Meanwhile, God proclaimed that from then on, all birds with no ears should continue to procreate by laying and hatching eggs. Animals with teeth should continue to procreate through conception and delivery through the womb, while condeming the bat to vomit through the mouth whatever he ate with the teeth he stole from heaven.

When this Ifa appears at Ugbodu, the person should serve Esu with a small he-goat which would be split on the shrine, to avert the danger of a malicious falsehood. At divination, the person will serve Esu with a he-goat to prevent the danger of being poisoned through food.

The Divination He Made Before Leaving Heaven

Iya omo ko fi 'nu han omo. Inu jin ju afi lo.

A mother does not open her mind to the child. The mind is deeper than the well. Those were the two Awos who made divination for Orunmila when he was coming to the world. He was told to make sacrifice to Ifa with a goat, Esu with a he-goat and his guardian angel with a guinea-fowl and eggs to protect him from the problems of witchcraft inside and outside. He was also required to make a special sacrifice with the leg of antelope, a thunder-stone, plenty of wine, and to prepare an amulet for him to take to earth. When the amulet was being made, the Awo marked all the two hundred and fifty six odus of Orunmila on the Ifa tray and they never saw daylight until they finished preparing it. He was not allowed to go outside the house when it was being pre-pared. Thereafter, he came to the world.

On getting to the world he was doing very well as an Ifa priest. He married and had children, but his mother, being a witch was always procuring illness for his children. He made divination at which he was required to serve the night with a rabbit and all edibles. After making the sacrifice, he had to deposit it on the way to his mother's farm. Thereafter the problem from witchraft abated.

When this Odu appears at Ugbodu the person will have to serve Ifa with a goat and add the heart, parts of the liver and intestine, the eyes and ears of the goat to a rabbit for the night to prevent problems from the cult of witchcraft. When it appears as Ayeo at divination, the person will be told that his/her mother is worrying him or her through witchcraft. If the divinee is a woman, she will be told that her mother is the one preventing her from having children. She should make the night sacrifice and keep it near the mother's house or farm.

He Made Divination for a Woman Called Osun-Onibuola

*Ote yereku, Obi mi birikpe. Ukoko Ekuru, abuodi yereku
yereku. Adifa fun Osun Onibuola, nijo ti olo gbe ugba oje
re ni odo Orunmila.
He moved with a bent waist, and he was pushed to straighten up.*

The pot of pudding had an awkward bottom. Those were the Awos who made divination for a woman called Osun-Oni-buola, the wife of Orunmila who was a very wealthy trader when she was treating her husband with contempt. Since he realized that it was her wealth that made her to treat him with derision, Orunmila made her trading to slow down. She went to all lengths to correct the imbalance in her business fortunes, but all to no avail. She was subsequently advised to apologise to Orunmila who told her to make sacrifice with a goat and a pot of pudding (Ekuru or Emieki), after warning her never again to allow her business success to make her pompous. Her business began to progress thereafter.

If it appears at divination for a woman, she will be told that she is disrespectful to her husband. She should make sacrifice to Ifa and apologise to her husband. If it appears for a man, he will be told he is ignoring Orunmila. He should serve Ifa with a goat to open his blocked fortunes. If he does not already have Ifa, he should arrange to have one in order to prosper in life.

He Made Divination for Olofin to Prosper

Mote o she yereku. Erin yi olo gbiri gbiri jako.
Odifa fun Olofin nijo ti ofi omi oju shubare aje.
I treaded on the ground and it caved in.
The elephant moved its mortar-legs through the farm.

Those were the Awos who made divination for Olofin when he was seeking prosperity. He was advised to serve Esu with a he-goat. He made the sacrifice and he became prosperous.

He Made Divination for The Ship

Otemi yereku, Oyimi biri kpe, were the two Awos who made divination for the ship as a mass carrier to prevent the danger of capsizing. He was told to make sacrifice with a cock, wooden spoon and a long stick. He made the sacrifice.

Subsequently, when he set sail he began to sing in praise of the two Awos who made divination and sacrifice for him thus:-

Otemi yereku, Oyimi biri kpe.
At divination, the person will be advised to make sacrifice before travelling by any means of transportation to abviate the danger of an accident.

The Same Awo Made Divination for the Boa And The Python

Otemi yereku, Oyimi birikpe, also made divination for the Boa (Oka, omo Oluwo) and the Python (Ere, Omo ojugbona). The same Awos also made divination for the snail (Igbin amure nana) when the first two divinees were jealous of his iron dress and sought how to take it from him because neither rain nor the sun affected him. They were all advised to make sacrifice with cock to Sango adding bitter kola and camwood. But the first two, thinking that the snail was an easy prey, refused to make sacrifice. The snail however made the sacrifice.

When the Boa and the Python eventually launched an attack on the Snail, he cried out:

Otemi yereku o, Oyimi birikpe o.
Awon lo ndifa fun Oka, omo Oluwo, won bufun
Ere omo ojugbono, won tu bufun oun Amure.
Sango gba mi o, gbami mokin ari, abami

ni owo ara eni ti n she ibi.

He was making a distress call to Sango to come to his rescue. When Sango heard the cry, he became delirious. After lightening had identified the two assailants of the Snail, Sango released two missiles (thunder) which struck the Boa and the Python to death. That explains why to this day Sango does not strike at the snail.

When it appears at divination, the person will be advised to refrain from cheating and tale-bearing. He should heed the advice he will be given at divination.

Chapter 3

IRETE-IWORI
IRETE-AJERO
IRETE-NTE-AWOYE

He Made Divination For The Pigeon When She Was Coming to the World

Odi, Ofun Laba. Odi, Aba lase Otete di edi. Those were the Awos who made divination for the Pigeon when she was coming to the world. She was advised to serve her head with white kolanut in order to succeed on earth. She made the sacrifice before leaving for the world. Her brother remained in heaven while she came to the world.

On getting to earth, she could not find a suitable husband to marry. Out of frustration, she returned to heaven to ask God why she could not find a husband on earth. God told her that he created them in pairs but that she left her opposite number behind when she left for earth. The pigeon subsequently returned with her brother to earth after which she began to have children. That is why the pigeon never mates with any other male except with the ones sharing the same parents with her. It was the pigeon who introduced twin-birth to the world.

When this Ifa appears at Ugbodu, the person should be advised to rear pigeons after serving his or her head with them. He should always listen to advice and not to rely solely on his intelligence. If he is not one of a twin birth, he will certainly have twin children. At divination, the person should be advised to serve his/her head with white kolanuts, before embarking on a proposed journey.

The Divination He Made Before Leaving Heaven

Baba Orunmila Olotunraye she Otu orunshe Obu Ifa fun eyon meta - was the Awo who made divination for him when he was coming to the world. He was advised to make sacrifice against the incidence of gratitude from his beneficiaries. He was required to make sacrifice with a goat, hen, rat and fish to his guardian angel and to serve Esu with a he-goat. He made the sacrifice.

On getting to earth, he had three pupils learning Ifism from him called Ukpen, Ayire and

Okpeluju (Amenmen, Uwowe and Udin in Bini). He had only one son. He was often shuttling between heaven and earth for his Ifa practice.

On one occasion he travelled to heaven. After completing the task for which he was invited to heaven, the divinities refused to allow him to return to earth because they considered him more useful to heaven than to earth. Meanwhile, his son began to worry about the unusually long stay of his father in heaven. Anxious to learn Ifism, his son was advised by the mother to approach one of his father's surrogates, Ukpen (or Ameme) for tuition.

When he approached Ukpen, he told Orunmila's son that the course would cost him 201 men, 201 women, 201 cows, 201 goats and 201 each of fowls, pigeons, rats, fishes, cowries, parrot's feathers and yam tubers. When he reported to his mother, she told him that Ukpen was being greedy because his father did not demand such requirements from him before teaching the art and practice of Ifism. She subsequently advised the son to approach Ayire, who enumerated the same requirements as Ukpen. He eventually went to Okpeluju who demanded 2 each of cows, goats, fowls, tortoises, pigeons, rat, fish, mats, cutlasses and bags of money. When he reported to his mother, she confirmed that Okpeluju was right.

The following morning, his mother collected the materials and invited Okpeluju to come in for the ceremony. He performed the ceremony by using one each of the materials for the sacrifice while taking away the second lots. On the fifth day of the initiation ceremony, Orunmila returned from heaven, his wife and son were relieved to see him back. When they told him of their experience with his surrogates, he was surprised to observe that it was Okpeluju, his most junior surrogate who had honesty and integrity to do the right thing in his absence. He immediately instructed his son to invite the three of them to see him without delay.

When Okpeluju was coming to honor the invitation he came with all the single units of the materials that remained, wondering whether he had made a mistake. As soon as they were all assembled, they paid the customary respects to Orunmila, while Okpeluju surrendered the materials he brought with him to Ornmila. Orunmila subsequently asked Ukpen and Ayire whether he initiated them unto Ifism with units of 201 materials. In fury, he cursed Ukpen with his brass wand of authority that the Ifa he prepared for him would melt in his hands and that on his part, Ayiree would never be used for anything useful and constructive to all eternity. Simultaneously, Ornmila declared that the Ifa he prepared for Okpeluju would forever make him prosperous from his head to his feet and from generation to posterity. He then faced his son that for seeking to maintain his tradition he would always relish in opulence. With that he decided to retire for good to heaven, leaving his son to continue his good work on earth, after authorising Okpeluju to retain the materials he brought to him.

That was the origin of the tradition of using pairs of materials for initiation into Ifism, with one to be half taken away by the Ifa patron. Ukpen and Ayiree are never used for any tangible purpose.

When this odu appears at divination, the person should be told to have his own Ifa immediately and to refrain from greediness in order to prosper in life.

He Made Divination for the Son of Sango

*Odiye o fi mu fele jeun. Odifa fun Sarolu, omo arira lufe ni ti
oju rire gbogbo nkpan.*

The fowl blows its nose on the ground in search of food.

That was the Awo who made divination for Sarolu, the son of Sango at Ife when he had struggled in vain to prosper. He was down and out. After divination, he was advised to make sacrifice with hen, cock, pigeon, kolanut and palm oil. He made the sacrifice and he became affluent and well-off.

He Made Divination for Shomolu to Have Children

*Odi ofun laba. Odi, aba lase. O tete di edi. Iroko de lebo.
Oba ara orun sa ila. Odifa fun Shomolu ti 'nti omi oju
shubere omo. Ebo ni omo ni ki oru.
He was tied up, and he got one part.
He was tied up, and it gave him authority. He got to the foot
of the Iroko tree before those who were going to make sacrifice.
He had a demarcation line with heaven.*

Those were the Awos who made divination for Shomolu when she was desperate to have children. She was advised to make sacrifice for child birth with a hen, 4 snails, 4 rats and 4 fishes. She made the sacrifice and began to have children.

He Made Divination for Anibire

*Ki Irete wo rin rin. Emi ni ki Irete wo rin rin.
Ariwo rin rin ni ikin fi kpa omo eja.
Bi omo eniyan ba ji, bi o ba wo rin rin ti o ma rin.
Iku yio kpa. Oluwo re re ko ru ebo tori iku.
Adifa fun Anibire, omo iron ni a tiba owuro.
Irete was advised to watch his movements.
I also told him to watch his movements.*

It was the rat and the fish who did not watch their movements in the morning that got killed before the end of the day. When a person looks carefully before leaping, premature death will be kept at bay. Those were the Awos who made divination for Anibire, the son of all those who set out for their daily chores in the morning. He was told to make sacrifice to obviate the danger of sudden death.

When it appears at divination as Ayeo, portending danger, the person will be told to make sacrifice to check-mate death.

Special Divination for Child-Birth

Orunmila ni ole keregun. Moni Oshukpa Irete ntewori ni o nron.
Oni o nron fun won ni ilu omo eku, Gbogbo aiye omo eku dara.
Oni o nron fun won ni ilu eja, Aiye omo eja dara.
Oni o nron fun won ni ilu eye, Aiye omo eye dara.
Oni o nron fun won ni ilu omo eranko, Aiye omo eranko dara.
Oni o nron fun won ni ilu omo eni, Aiye omo eni dara.
Oni o nron si ile akakpo, ti oun, Oni oun ni akakpo yi o
fi tu la, ti ofi tu yebe yebe.
Orunmila ni akakpo, Moni Oluwesin, Oni okpe segi,
Moni ikin owo mi a dayo.

Orunmila says that the birth of the children of rats, fishes, birds, animals and human beings brought multiplication and prosperity to them. He adds that as his own parents gave birth to him, so will the divinee expect a child to be born to him or her.

When it appears for a pregnant woman, she will be advised to make sacrifice with rabbit, a hen laying eggs, honey, palm oil and white cloth so that she may have a safe and painless delivery.

He Made Divination for Shugunrinmi, The Wife of Orunmila

Omo kpe ni o nit kekere di ogun mo ara, Mariwo okpe ti
nu ita re she bi omo titun was si'le aiye. Those were the Awos who made divination for Shogunrinmi, the wife of Orunmila. Orunmila had been told to make sacrifice to prevent his wife from leaving him, but he refused to make the sacrifice.

Subsequently, Orunmila travelled out for Ifa practice telling his wife that he was going to be away for four days. As soon as he left, Esu instigated the wife to pack everything including his Ifa and she escaped from his house. As soon as he got a premonition on what was happening at home, he sounded Ifa who reminded him of the sacrifice he failed to make before leaving home. It was at that point that he made the sacrifice to Esu with a he-goat, a cock, and twines.

As the wife was travelling with her very heavy load on her head, Esu used the twine with which Orunmila made sacrifice to fasten her feet and she fell to the ground and became unconscious. People who saw her on the way, took her into their house and went in search of Orunmila to come to the aid of his wife.

She was still unconscious when Orunmila arrived at the scene. On getting to the place, he touched her with his fly whisk (horse tail) and called her name three times, after which she answered. When she came to, Orunmila got her to return bag and baggage with him to the house.

When this Odu appears for a man at divination, he will be told to make sacrifice to stop his wife from deserting him. If the divinee is a woman, she will be told not to leave her husband because circumstances will compel her to return to his house.

Chapter 4

IRETE-IDI

He Made Divination for Six Sisters, the Flames, Honey-womb, worm, heat and the Garbage Dump

Tendi, Tendi, awo abo adiye, Odifa fun adiye, obufun
Otitan, atun bufun ekpara ati owo.

He made divination for the hen and the refuse-dump, as well as for the fire flames of dried palm branches, honey comb and bee, worm and heat, all sisters. He also made divination for the palm tree and the palm climbers, both sisters. Each of them was advised to serve Esu with a he-goat and Ifa with a guinea-fowl. They all refused to make the sacrifice with the exception of the garbage dump, who made her own sacrifice.

Meanwhile, Etitan and Adiye made a bargain for the hen to be going to spoil food in the house so that the damaged food might be sent to the refuse dump for them to share subsequently. In consonance with the agreement, the hen began to putrefy food items in the house after which they were sent to the garbage dump. Contrary to the term of the agreement, the refuse dump was singularly consuming all the food sent to her in the wake of the damage being done by the hen.

When the hen subsequently asked the refuse dump to produce the food she had been sending to her, the latter could not explain. The Hen eventually resolved to be scattering the house of the refuse dump in search of her children (worms) to feed on. That is the endless war which the hen wages on the garbage dump to this day.

In the same manner, the palm tree climber was so jealous of the success of her sister, the palm tree, that she aided and abetted human beings to destroy her sister's children (palm fruits); the hot water destroyed the children of the worm, her sister, and the fire flame waged war on her sister by burning up her children, and the fire flame waged war on her sister by burning up her children (honey). All the casualties of the fraticidal wars ended up in the home of the rubbish dump who used them to feed her children, but the action of the hen only scratched the surface of the Refuse dump's prosperity, being the only one who made sacrifice.

When this Ifa appears at Ugbodu, the person will be warned to beware of his brothers and sisters. He should serve Esu with a he-goat, palm tree climber, honey comb, fire flame prepared from dried palm branches and rotten meat with worms. He should also serve the new Ifa with a castrated he-goat to forestall the irresolvable dispute that is bound to erupt between his brothers and or sisters and himself. The special sacrifice of this Odu is made by preparing the appropriate leaves for the son of the Odu to have a bath on the refuse dump with a hen, white cloth, cowries and his mud image in order to survive the evil machinations of his enemies. At divination, the person should serve Esu with a he-goat and the ancilliary materials to avert trouble from relations.

He Made Divination for the Head When Going on Tour

Oni mi ge ori, Ola mi ha ori, Otunla mi fo ori gbo
erun shuku shuku, Adifa fun Ori, o nshawo lo si ilu Onigaga-nigogo.

I will cut a chewing stick today, scrape the bark off tomorrow and chew it to clean my teeth the day after tomorrow. Those were the Awos who made divination for the Head when he was travelling for Awo practice to the head of Onigaga-nigogo. He was advised to make sacrifice with a he-goat to Esu and he did. That made him the only divinity that is capable of providing enduring salvation throughout his children's sojourn on earth.

He Made Divination for Olakpade

Ki iwo tedi, ki emi tedi, Oka ko kporun lo run.
Adifa fun Olakpade, omo Akpanroro lo 'de ti o nfi omi oju
ahu bere oje.

You treaded on it. Let me tread on it. The Boa does not bend his body over his neck. Those were the Awos who made divination for Olokpade, whose complexion was as fair as palm oil, when he was desperately looking for money. He was told to make sacrifice and he did. Thereafter, he became wealthy.

The Divination He Made Before Leaving Heaven

Nyain Nyain awo iyanrin. Ajija gororo awodi oro.
Aba elegigi , Oruko ale. Awon metata lo'ndifa fun
Orunmila nijko ti onti kole orun bo wa si ko le aye.

The Awos nicknamed Wind, water and ground, were the three Awos who made divination for Orunmila when he was coming to the world. They advised him to make sacrifice with snail's shell, snake's scales and a he-goat to Esu. He made the sacrifice before coming to the world.

On getting to the world, he took to trading in addition to the practice of Ifism. He was successful in both vocations. On one occasion when he travelled for his business, the Awos in the place decided to disrupt his journey with the rain on account of the size of the gifts he was taking home from his Ifa practice. As the rain threatened to fall, he began to repeat the following incantation:- Aigugbin je ekagha re. He was asking the rain whether he is capable of eating the snail and its shell. The rain reacted by receding to heaven. Next, they provoked the wind to fight him with a tornado. Once again, he humoured the wind by challenging whether he eats the snake and its scales "Aije ejo je uke luku re." Finally, they incited the ground to open up to conume him. Once more, he humoured the ground to close its mouth by asking him whether he eats the tortoise and its shell - "Aije ahun ju gba re". The ground responded by praying for him to outlive his enemies, and that from that day, he should touch him with whatever he did so that it might materialize. That is why an Awo is required to touch any sacrifice on the ground before going to deliver it. Thereafter, he was able to get home safely.

He Made Divnation for the Rat Not to Marry a Woman Stronger Than Himself

This odu made divination for the Rat, advising him to make sacrifice to avert the danger of marrying a wife stronger than himself. He was required to serve Esu with a he-goat adding elubo and yam called akpamisesan. He refused to make the sacrifice. When the Rat subsequently went to the market, he met Ologbo (cat) a very pretty woman and offered to marry her. The cat responded favourably and they got married.

One day, the Rat spoke angrily to his wife, but when the cat brought out her ferocious eye-balls, the rat blushed. On a subsequent occasion, when the Rat tried to establish his masculine superiority, the cat again brought out her vicious eyes and as the Rat tried to escape, she gripped him with her hitherto hidden left hand claws and killed her husband.

When this Ifa appears at Ugbodu, the man should be told to make sacrifice either to forestall the risk of marrying a woman who is capable of killing him, or to survive her ferocity if he has already married such a woman for a wife, because he is destined to marry a woman of that ilk, and the marriage will be childless.

He Made Divination for the Mother of Osho

Tedi simi, ki emi na tedi si o. Eni ti eshin te omo
re kpa, Oun ni won fi je ashikpa. Adifa fun Iya osho.

Deal with me and let me deal with you. The person whose child was trampled.

Those were the Awos who made divination for the mother of Osho to have a child whose name was going to endure eternally. She was required to make sacrifice with three cocks and three bows and arrows. She made the sacrifice and subsequently gave birth to Osho. When he grew up, he became a hunter.

As he was away on a hunting expedition on one occasion, he came to a town called Ilu-Ika which had an endemic problem. A mysterious bird used to come to the town periodically to make calamitous cries which often led to the death of one hundred persons. As soon as the people saw Osho with a gun, they asked him whether he could assist them in killing a bird that used to cry havoc in the town. When he promised to try his best, they took him to the Oba's palace. It was at the palace that he was told that all known hunters had tried in vain to kill it. When he confirmed to the Oba that he had up to that time never missed his target, he was promised a reward of half of the town if he succeeded. Meanwhile, he was given an accommodation in the palace, while awaiting the next visit of the bird.

Three days later, the bird showed up on top of the oak tree at the entrance to the town. Osho brought out his bow and arrows and after a short incantation released the arrow without looking at the bird. The multitude of people who gathered to watch the spectacle gave Osho a rousing plaudit when they saw the bird diving down with the arrow piercing its heart as it fell to the ground dead.

News of the death of the bird caused a commotion in the town as people surged forward not only to see the dead bird but also the hunter who succeeded in killing it. Meanwhile, Osho was made the Prime Minister of the town and his achievement has kept his name alive ever since. The name of Osho remains a legend in the town of Ilu-Eka to this day.

He Made Divination for the Greedy Hunter Who Failed to Make Sacrifice

Ate nla ma ya gbangba, was the Awo who made divination for the hunter who never shared the meat of his game with his neighbors. He was advised to make sacrifice and he refused. When he subsequently went to the forest, he killed an antelope and on getting home, he threw it at his wife before entering the house.

When Esu was told that Arayagba refused to make sacrifice, he went to wait for him at the back of his house. As soon as he threw the antelope to his wife, Esu turned it into a stone which crushed the woman to death. He did not know what happened. Later, he called on his wife to bring food to him and there was no response. He was stunned when he found the wife dead beside a big stone.

His alarm attracted neighbors who accused him of killng his wife and marched him to the Oba's palace. Asked why he killed his wife with a stone, he explained that in consonance with his tradition, it was the antelope he brought from the forest that he threw to his wife and not a stone. When the Oba asked him whether he owed any debt of sacrifice, he confirmed that he failed to abide by the advice of Orunmila and that was the price he had to pay. He sang - Ate nli maya gbangba ni odifa fun oun Arayagba. Mogbo riru ebo, emi o ru. Mogbo eru a tu kesu, emi kotu, ko i kpe, ko i jino. Ifa wa she bi ala. He said that he failed to make the sacrifice prescribed at divination. Since the law had to take its course, he was executed.

At divination, the person will be advised not to answer calls made from outside when he is inside his house. He should peep out through the window to see who is calling him. He should however make sacrifice with a sheep to avert the danger of head injury which could cause his death. The blood of the sheep will be spilled on a big stone and given to him to throw into the river, to alleviate the eventuality.

Chapter **5**

IRETE-OBARA
IRETE-ALAO
IRETE-OLOBA

He Made Divination for the Bird Called Ogbigbo or Thiokam

Te 'bara ki ekuro ni be. Odifa fun Ogbigbo niwanran ti
'nlo si oko aloro odun. A ni ko ru ebo.

Stay briefly and move on, was the name of the Awo who made divnation for a bird called Ogbigbo (Owonwon in Bini) or the Tiokam when he was going to start a new farm at the beginning of the year. He was advised to make sacrifice in order to return home peacefully. He made the sacrifice and returned home in one piece after his farming chores.

When it appears at divination for a person who is proposing to travel, he or she will be advised to make sacrifice before leaving home. If it appears for a woman who is contemplating to leave her husband, she should be advised not to do so without making sacrifice.

He Divined for Light and His Brother, the Termite

Irete ba ba ba, Obara ro ro ro, made divination for light and termite who were brothers. The termite was advised to make sacrifice in order to return home alive from a trip he was proposing to under-take. He was required to serve his head with a pigeon, but he travelled without making the sacrifice. The Light was also told to make sacrifice in order to see himself instead of providing illumination for others to see themselves. He too did not make the sacrifice.

When the Termite was travelling, he only went out with the dress he was wearing. During the journey, the rain fell heavily and his single dress was drenched. When he removed the dress to dry up, it was thrown away by Esu and he could not find his way home on foot. That is why termites are unable to find their way home after flying out.

Light, his brother, was told to go and look for Termite. He was able to find him and show him his way to a new home, but in the process Light forgot himself and no one went to look for him.

At Ugbodu, the person should serve his head with a cock and a termite, and should not travel without making the sacrifice. Make an overnight oil lamp for Esu after serving him with a he-goat. At divination, serve Esu with a he-goat before embarking on a proposed journey.

The Divination He Made Before Leaving Heaven

Te 'bara ki ekuro nibe was the Awo who made divination for Irete Obara when he was coming to the world. He was advised to serve Esu with a he-goat, Ogun with a cock and his guardian angel with a goat. He made the sacrifice and came to the world, after seeking and receiving the blessing of God.

He Made Divination for Oloba-Ahun

Agba ninu sise. Oran ko ton ni 'le yi boro boro.

As the royal diviner, he made divination for Ahun who was the Chief Page of the Oba, advising him to serve Esu with a he-goat to parry the danger of sudden death. Oloba was characteristically very intelligent which endeared him to all and sundry, but on the other hand he was not given to making sacrifice. He did not make the sacrifice before he left on an errand to the town of Oba on behalf of oba. That was when Esu decided to frame him up. On his way to the town of Oba, he decided to impersonate the Oba by adorning himself with a seemingly beaded outfit with red fruits looking like beads. He was accordingly given the honor and reception befitting a king. Instead of staying for a few days and leaving, the lavish hospitality he was given, lured him into staying much longer.

After five days, the fruits with which he adorned his regalia began to shrink and to dry up. As soon as he noticed the deterioration in the texture of the fruits, he decided to set the guest house on fire, which burnt up his outfit. The following day, he told the Oloja of Oba that they had to replace the beaded dress he brought. But when the Oloja sent messengers to retrieve the beads from the inferno, there were no traces of beads. Meanwhile, the Oloja sent errand men to Ife to find out from the Olofin whether he knew the Oba who was visiting them on his behalf. "Of course", he said. He only sent his Chief Page whose return was long overdue. The Olofin sent his royal constables to verify the situation at Oba.

When the policemen got to Oba, they discovered that it was Ahun the Chief Page of the Olofin who was impersonating the oba. He was tantalizingly nicknamed the Oloba of Oba during his trial. While the trial was in progress, his wife ran to Orunmila to make the sacrifice her husband had earlier refused to make. After eating his he-goat, Esu went to Olofin in the guise of a visiting diviner and queried him for trying to execute Ahun who had previously served him so dutifully and loyally. The diviner prophesied to Olofin that if the man was executed, there would be a calamity of unimaginable proportions throughout the kingdom of Ife.

Although, Oloba was previously sentenced to death by execution, the Olofin granted him an immediate reprieve, warning him not to repeat that mistake ever again.

When it appears at divination, the person should be advised to make sacrifice to avert the risk of sudden death.

He Made Divination for the Barren Woman to Have a Child

In a poetic dialogue with his followers, Orunmila said that the original crowned kings of Ijero, Ilara and Ila-Orangun were all children of Orunmila, born of the same mother. It was the same medication prepared for the same woman that Irete-Oloba used for a barren woman who came to him for divination. That was after she had been told to go and serve the Esu shrine of an unknown person with a rabbit and a rat because no one ever heard of a barren rabbit or rat.

The following month, the woman became pregnant and in the fullness of time, she gave birth to a male child who was named Ifatoba.

At divination for a woman anxious to have a child, the Ifa priest should perform the same sacrifice for her and her first child will be a male who will be named Ifatoba.

He Made Divination for Alao

Ogon yi O lo lo di na. Agba ninu ohun sise.
Oran ko ton ni 'le yi boro boro. Adifa fun Alao
to fi okun sorun to fi ara re bo ifa to ke be bi ewure.

Those were the surrogates of Irete-Oloba who made divination for Alao who offered himself for sacrifice to Ifa in the likeness of a goat. He had been told at divination to serve Ifa with a goat, and to offer another goat to Ifa after five days. He served Ifa with the first goat and removed the skin.

On the fifth day, he told his wife to sweep and scrub the house. Thereafter, he wrapped his body with the dried skin of the first goat and with a kolanut in hand, called on Ifa to accept the second goat. He actually cried Mee like a goat, when he was praying.

After splitting the kolanut for Ifa, he told his wife to prepare pounded yam with the skin of the goat. They ate the food and went to sleep. The following morning Alao did not wake up, having died over night in his sleep. As people were wondering about what might have caused Alao's death, his wife narrated how he served Ifa the previous evening. People blamed him for bringing death upon himself because he preferred to cheat instead of making the prescribed sacrifice.

At divination, the person should be advised to serve Ifa with a goat and to refrain from trying to be clever-clever. If the divinee is an invalid, and it portends death (Ayeo), the person should make his last will because his fate is beyond redemption.

Chapter 6

IRETE-OKONRON
IRETE-EGE

He Made Divination for the Rope and The Wooden Fastener

Irete lo lo lo, Okonron ke ke ke - was the Awo who made divination for the Rope and the Fastener in Yoruba and Ukeke in Bini. They were advised to serve Esu with a he-goat. The Fastener made his sacrifice but the Rope did not. Consequently, after the Rope was used to tie any object, the Fastener would be made to sit on top of him as a knot. Not satisfied with his subordinate role, the Rope decided to abandon the Fastener to return to his home town, the Bush in- order to live with the plants, his brothers. Thereafter anyone who wanted to use the Rope had to go to the Bush to fetch him.

Meanwhile, the plants discovered that the presence of the Rope in their midst was creating problems for them. Any time the Rope was being removed from the Bush he pulled several plants with him. He was told by the plants to leave the bush and he went to the farm where he was also compelled for similar reasons, to leave.

Alone and abandoned by all his relations, the Rope returned to Orunmila, who reminded him of the sacrifice he failed to make. He subsequently made the sacrifice after which he had a settled existence. He was often invited to all important occasions marked by human beings in towns and villages.

At Ugbodu, the person should be advised neither to serve anyone nor to give out his children in servitude. He should serve Ogun with cock and Esu with he-goat. At divination, the person should serve Esu with a he-goat and his head with a cock to avert the danger of being ostracized by his or her associates and relations.

He Made Divination for the Penis and the Vulva

Oyeye moko. Erubo dee, were the Awos who made divination for the male and female genitals to be rid of their physical handicap. The Penis had no head and the Vulva had no eyes or orifice. The Penis was told to make sacrifice to ogun with cock and roasted yam while the

Vulva was told to serve Ifa with a hen and a snail, honey, sugar cane and palm oil. They both made the sacrifices.

As the Penis was leaving Ogun's house after making his sacrifice, Ogun used his knife to remove the veil covering the head of the penis. The Penis had a lot of pain from the attack, but as soon as the pain abated, he became more active. When he subsequently met the blind Vulva he collided with her, causing her to instantly open her eyes. The cutting of the veil covering the head of the Penis became the process of circumcision, while the collision between the two genitals has since become the disvirginity of the vulva.

The Divination He Made Before Leaving Heaven

Oyeye mo ko. Erubo dee, were the Awos who made divination for this Odu when he was coming to the world. He was advised to make sacrifice in order to prevent the danger of being killed by a woman and to remain actively potent throughout his life. He was required to serve: Esu with a he-goat; his guardian angel with castrated he-goat, electric fish, and a cock. He left for the world without making the sacrifice.

He became a practicing Ifa priest on earth and he had initial success. At the height of his success, Esu pushed a woman to marry him. The woman was much stronger than himself. After living with the woman for some time, he became sexually impotent. He approached several physicans for help to no avail. He finally went for divination and he was told to serve; Esu with a he-goat, and Ifa with castrated he-goat, electric fish, cock and pigeon. He made the sacrifice after which the Awos prepared a special belt for him to be tying round his waist. It was prepared with the genitals of the birds and animals with which he made sacrifice, in addition to the appropriate leaves. Part of the medicine was given to him to eat in a soup and to add to soap for bathing, while the rest was mounted on the skull of the castrated he-goat to be kept at his Ifa shrine.

Soon after the sacrifice was made, his wife left him unceremoniously. That paradoxically was after he regained his potency. He subsequently married other women and had several children.

When this Ifa appears at divination or Ugbodu for a man, he will be told to make sacrifice to avert the danger of committing suicide when he becomes impotent.

He Made Divination for the Mother of Adeyosola

Ki Irete ko lu arankan si 'risi. Odifa fun Yeye Adeyosola
Ebo tori iku omo re yi oru o.

Let Irete play a musical instrument called Arankan in Yoruba and Akpata in Bini to the end, was the name of the Awo who made divination for the mother of Adeyosola. She was told to make sacrifice to save the life of her daughter and her other children. She made the sacrifice with a he-goat, rat, fish, rabbit, kolanut and palm oil, after which she lost no child.

When it appears at divination, the person will be advised to make sacrifice to avoid losing any of his or her children. He or she should be told to advise the children to be humble.

If it appears as Ayeo, the person will be told to ask his or her son to have Ifa, and for his or her unmarried daughter to marry a man having his own Ifa.

Divined for Elekolo Not to Give her Daughter in Marriage Outside His Town

Aferege eyige, Odifa fun Elekolo

That was the Awo who made divination for Elekolo, advising him to make sacrifice with a sheep and a piece of white cloth to avert the danger of losing his daughter. He was also advised not to give his daughter in marriage to any husband outside his town. He had the intention of making the sacrifice but procrastinated on it for so long that he eventually forgot about it.

Meanwhile, a young man called Ege from the town of Taji offered to marry Elekolo's daughter. At the same time, Esu blotted out the memory of the advice given to him not to give his daughter in marriage to any man outside his town. He agreed to give his daughter in marriage to Ege.

As soon as she got to the town of Taji, she became ill within the first week of her arrival. When her condition began to deteriorate, she was taken back to her father. No sooner did they arrive at her father's house, she gave up the ghost. It was at that point that Elekolo remembered the sacrifice he did not make and the advice he did not heed.

She was buried in front of the father's house with a warning inscribed on her tomb that anyone who sits on it will be fined a ram and that anyone who put any calabash on the tomb will be fined a hen. That is why Elekolo is greeted with the words "Omo elege", who forbids the use of Calabash.

When this Odu appears at divination, for a woman, she will be advised not to travel outside her home town throughout the rest of that year. If she is a spinster, she should be warned never to marry outside her home town. If it appears for a father, he will be advised to make the above sacrifice and not to give his daughter in marriage outside his home town.

Chapter 7

IRETE-IROSUN
ATENUROSUN
IRETE-ERIJIYAN

He Made Divination for Oloba-Aghun, the Womaniser

Ada ko-bo. Odifa fun Oloba-aghun nijo to 'nshawo losi ilu
Obinrin gbadu gbandu. Won i ko ru ebo ko to lo. Ko ru ebo na.
Won tun so fun kpe okpe kan ombe ni ojude ilu obinrin yen.

The eunuch was the Awo who made divination for Oloba-aghun when he was travelling to the land of women, where there were no men. He was advised to make sacrifice before going. He was required to serve Esu with a he-goat and palm fruits. He was also told that he would see a palm tree in the town with ripe fruits. If he wanted to eat palm fruits, he was to pick from the fallen ones and not to climb the palm tree. He however failed to make sacrifice before leaving for the town.

On getting to the town he found the palm tree with several fruits that had fallen to the ground around it. He was given a rousing welcome by all the women of the town. While in the town, he began to sleep and copulate with the women one after the other until Esu decided to punish him for failing to make sacrifice. One morning, Esu waited for Oloba-aghun at the foot of the palm tree. When he got to the foot of the palm tree to pick up some of the fallen fruits, Esu challenged him for picking the "dirty" fallen fruits when there were cleaner and more delicious ones on top of the palm tree. Esu elated him by remarking that it was denigrating for the husband of all the women in the town to eat dirty fruits picked from the ground instead of plucking those on top of the tree.

Acting on the advice of Esu, Oloba-Aghun climbed the palm tree and plucked several fruits into his bag after eating as much as he could. As he was climbing down the tree, he discovered that his penis was no longer in a position to make love to any woman.

Later that night, the woman whose turn it was to sleep with him came to meet him. When the woman discovered that he was not able to make love to her, she turned him into a tortoise and threw him into the bush.

When this Odu appears at divination for a woman, she will be advised to make sacrifice and told not to allow a light skinned man to make love to her. If it appears for a man, he will be told to serve Esu before embarking on a proposed tour. While in the town, he should not make love to a light complexioned woman, and should refrain from; eating palm fruits, pottage and banana, and from wearing red clothes during the tour.

The Divination Made for Him Before Leaving Heaven

Baba bolo bolo bolo was the Awo who made divnation for Orunmila before coming to the world. He was advised to make sacrifice in order to survive the problems he was going to have from women, who would be much stronger than himself. He was required to serve: his guardian angel with a goat, hen, rat and fish; Esu with a he-goat, giant needle, comb, pad, rafia bag and a wooden tray (   ) in Yoruba and Atete in Bini). He made the sacrifice after which he came to the world.

On getting to the world, he did not do so well as an Ifa priest. He therefore went for divination and he was told to serve: Esu with a he-goat, black thread, comb and needle; Ogun with a cock; and Ifa with a hen. He could not affort to finance the sacrifice. He only gave black thread and needle to Esu, promising to bring a he-goat as soon as he could afford one.

The following morning, he left for the market. At the same time, the wives of death, Witchcraft and Disease respectively came to the market to sell he-goat, cock and hen for one bag of money each. The three fearsome divinities all corked their wives' mouths with leaves, warning them never to speak to anyone before returning from the market to heaven.

On his way to the market, Atenurosun met each of the three women on their way to the market. He told them to take what they were selling (he-goat, cock and hen) to his house and that he would come and pay them upon his return from the king's palace.

After waiting in his house for him to return home, the women became hungry. They searched through the house and found some yam tubers, which they cooked, ate and kept a part for him. After eating, they went to the back of the house where they found needle, thread and comb on Esu shrine, which they collected to weave their hairs mutually.

At dusk, he returned to the house apologising to the women for keeping them waiting, which resulted from being delayed at the palace. He proceeded at once to serve; Esu with a he-goat, Ogun with the cock, and Ifa with the hen. Thereafter, he ate the food prepared for him by the women. After eating they asked him to pay for the materials and he persuaded them to wait until the morning, since it was in any case too late for them to return home. When it was time to sleep, he spread out a mat in the sitting room on which they all slept. In the night, he made love to each of the three women, in the wake of which they could no longer return to their husbands.

The following morning, death, wizard and diseases asked after their wives and they were told that they were seen to have gone to one man's house the previous day. They all decided to find out what man was bold enough to keep their wives over-night. Meanwhile, the women told Atenurosun who their husbands were and he became so scared that he went immediately to his Awo for divination. He was told to obtain three pads, three bags each containing one bag of money, three wooden trays and a chicken and place them at the road junction near the market, after giving another he-goat to Esu.

He immediately went to the street to capture the first he-goat he came across and used it to serve Esu. Thereafter, he took the other materials to the road junction. After eating his he-goat, Esu hid near the road junction at which Atenurosun deposited his sacrifice. At the same time, Death got his club and set out to do battle with whoever was keeping his wife. Esu had meanwhile used the skull of the he-goat to prepare a stud near the road junction. As Death was getting to the road junction, he knocked his feet on the stud, which jerked him to see the bag and tray looking like those of his wife. When he picked up the bag, he discovered that it contained one bag of money, which he surmised, his wife received for the sale of the he-goat she took to the market. He then wondered whether his wife must have been murdered. He subsequently collected the materials and returned home to heaven.

After successfully deceiving Death, Esu arranged similar ploys to put off the Wizard and Diseases. All of them gave up on their wives for dead and returned home with the money and materials they found at the road junction. Subsequently, Esu went to Orunmila's house to announce that the husbands of the three women had surrendered them to misadventure.

The women were called:

Death's wife	-	Adesina (Akpako)
Wizard's wife	-	Aderunla (Uroke)
Disease's wife	-	Tamukokoro (Oroke)

That was how Orunmila married three wives at the same time, which marked the beginning of his prosperity. When this Ifa appears at Ugbodu, the person should prepare this special sacrifice, because he would marry three women in his life in very difficult circumstances.

He Made Divination for Olofin to Save His Children's Lives

Ateninurosun a buru buru buru buru ti o ka ba ki she
Ojoni. Buru buru ti ere ba ki Ishe ojo ni o. Odifa fun Olofin
La'gba yi gba Ufe Kiri biti, to ri iku omore ka ru ebo Esu.
The boa who roosts quietly on a calm spot is not doing so out of fear.
The python who roosts quietly on a calm spot is not doing it out of fear.

Those were the Awos who made divination for Olofin in Ife. He was told to make sacrifice with a pig to save the lives of his children. The sacrifice was made by digging a hole at the entrance to his palace and his ikin (Okekporin) was put inside the hold. The pig was slaughtered on top of it inside the hole. After the sacrifice, the Okeponrin was left in the hole until the following moring. The Okekponrin was removed and the hole was covered up, containing the head of the pig.

At divination, for a man, he will be told that his life and his house are not settled. If he has Ifa, he should make the foregoing sacrifice to prolong his life and those of his children. If he does not have Ifa, he should have one and make the above sacrifice on the last day of the intitiation ceremony.

He Made Divination For The Greedy Fisherman

Ko kpo to, lo 'nkpa Olowo.
Ko si ra ra, lo 'nkpa talika.
Awon ni won lo 'ndifa fun A kpeja ti ogbo
Ohun Ayare ti o si di Atosi.
Avarice destroys the rich, while deprivation kills the pauper.

Those were the two Awos who made divination for the Fisherman when he was poor but who took his wife into confidence on everything he did. He was advised to send gifts to Olokun with fourteen different materials, including a white cock, and to serve Esu with a he-goat. He was particularly advised to beware of the danger of cupidity.

On getting home, he told his wife what he was told to do. His wife sanctioned the advice and the sacrifice was made. After completing the sacrifice, he began to fare better in his fishing business and he began to breathe the cool air of opulence.

Subsequently, his wife told him to go for consultation once more with Orunmila, on what to do to become the Oba of the town. After divination, Orunmila advised him to serve the river in which he was fishing with a ram, so that people might be serving him. He did the sacrifice after clearing it with his wife.

Three days later, his net caught a talking fish. As he was about to kill the fish, the fish told him to set him free, but to make any wish he desired. He told the fish that he wanted to become an Oba. The fish agreed to help him after which he released it to return to the water. Before returning home from the river, his house was filled with people who came to rejoice with him because the lot had fallen on him to be made the next Oba, the former one having recently joined his ancestors. He was subsequently crowned as the Oba and he stopped fishing.

Three months after his coronation, his wife directed him to meet Orunmila once more to tell him what to do in order to become the next man to God. At divination, Orunmila told him that there was no sacrifice to be done except to return home to sack his wife if he was to endure in his regal position and prosperity.

On getting home, he told his wife what Orunmila directed him to do, and the wife retorted that Orunmila had apparently lost his senses. The wife warned him never to go back to Orunmila, but to return to the talking fish for advice.

The following morning, he returned to the river and hailed on the fish with its code name of Amiegho! When it appeared, he told the fish that he wanted to become the second-in-command (sic) to God. The fish told him to return home to the position of God's second-in -command. On getting home, he found his life back to the penury he was in before he went to Orunmila in the first instance. He met his wife in the kitchen of their ramshackled house. That was the stage at which he wanted to estrange his wife. As he began to beat her, she told him not to blame her for subjugating his masculine authority to her feminine fickle-mindedness. When he subsequently went back to Orunmila, he was reminded of his last advice that there were no more sacrifices for him to make apart from divorcing his wife. That was how he returned to penury.

At Ugbodu, the person should serve; the new Ifa with a ram and Esu with a he-goat, to avert the danger of being misled by his wife. At divination, the person should serve Esu with a he-goat and Olokun with 14 materials including white cock and be told that his prosperity lies in living near the sea or river.

Orunmila's Special Sacrifice For His Odu

Orunmila ni aru. Mo ni a ru ra ra.
Oni ki a mu iru iyo, ata rodo, ekpo, ati iru wa,
ki a fi she 'bo, ni tori gbo ure kpelu ishegun ota.

Orunmila says that when this Odu appears at Ugbodu, the person should be advised to make special sacrifice with melon sauce (iru in Yoruba and evba-rhie Bini), salt, pepper, palm oil, and mat in order to:

i)   thwart the evil machinations of his enemies;
ii)   checkmate any danger that would have disturbed his life; and
iii) to ward off any harm that he would have come across.

When making the sacrifice, the Ifa priest should chant the following incantation: Ewe di ewe. Shegun shete temi. Igbati mo ba ti de, Emi ni yi o she won ni ote - meaning "Add leaves together, grind them, add the Iyerosun of this odu and in the end, you will overcome your enemies.

He Divined for Sango When He Was Suffering

Ate ni nu irosun. Ba bu bu, Oba ni abe efolo. Efifi ni
uyi ino. Ije ni uyi orun. Ki a ri Ogun, ki a ma saa.
Oun ni uyi okuntin.

Those were the Awos who made divination for Orunmila when he was going to use forty cowries to prepare Ifa for Sango when he was suffering. Orunmila sewed the 40 cowries to a piece of red cloth and gave it to Sango to wear in order to prosper.

In the process of dancing about, Sango became possessed and began to divine for people wherever he went and realised a lot of money which made him to become opulent. Before leaving for his dancing spree, he left his two sons called Kawo and Kabiyesi under the care of Orunmila.

When Sango was returning home, he went to challenge Orunmila that he had become richer than himself. Orunmila reminded him that it was forbidden for anyone to bite the finger that fed him. When Sango saw how well his two sons looked as a mark of the good care that Orunmila took of them, he went on his knees to apologise to his benefactor for his show of ingratitude.

At divination, the person should be advised never to be ungrateful to his/her benefactor.

Chapter 8

IRETE-OWANRIN
IRETE-ARIN
IRETE-OGEGE
IRETE-OLOTA

He Made Divination for the Monitor

Irete ge ge ge, Owanrin go go go - were the two Awos who made divination for the Monitor (Aghanrighan in Yoruba and Aleekpa or Omiamwenze in Bini) when he wAs coming to the world. He was advised to serve his head on the bank of the river with two pigeons, 2 guinea fowls and kolanuts. He did the sacrifice. He was however strongly advised never to live with any of his relations while on earth.

On getting to the world, he raised a family and was doing pretty well. Meanwhile, the crocodile, his relation approached the Monitor to grant him temporary accommodation because his house had been destroyed by a hurricane. Forgetting that he had been warned against that kind of hospitality, he agreed to accommodate his brother. Soon afterwards, the crocodile told the Monitor that he had discovered an eternal source of food supply. Thereafter, the two of them began to feed from that source.

One day, the crocodile went to Orunmila for divination on what to do to drive the Monitor out of his house, so that he could occupy it alone. He was told to serve Esu with a he-goat and to forbid eating rotten food. While he was procrastinating on when to make the sacrifice, the Monitor had a dream in which he was being pursued by an assailant. As soon as he woke up, he raced to Orunmila's house for divination, where he was told that war was imminent, and that he ran the risk of being driven out of his house unless he made sacrifice. He was required to serve Esu with a he-goat, and rotten rat in order that his enemy might be checkmated and exposed. He did the sacrifice almost immediately.

As soon as the Monitor made his sacrifice, he went home while the Crocodile was also on his way to Orunmil's place to make his own sacrifice. Meanwhile, in view of the maxim that first in sacrifice is first in manifestation, Esu used a metal hook to set a trap on the way with a rotten rat. After making the sacrifice, the Crocodile was returning home when he saw a rotten rat on the way. Forgetting the advice to refrain from eating rotten food, he could not resist the temptation to eat the rotten rat. The metal hook got stuck in his throat and he struggled to death.

After waiting in vain for the Crocodile to return home, the Monitor went out to look for him. He was astonished to find the corpse of his brother by the side of the road. When he saw the rat with which he made sacrifice in the Crocodile's mouth, he realised that his brother to whom he extended hospitality against advice, was his unknown enemy. Thus, sacrifice had manifested for the first to perform it.

When this Ifa appears at Ugbodu, the person should serve the Ifa with a crocodile, Esu with he-goat, metal hook, and rotten rat; and Ogun with a cock. At divination, the person should serve Esu with a he-goat and rotten meat.

The Divination He Made Before Leaving Heaven

Ti Akiko ba ki, ojo a ma.

When the cock crows, a new day will dawn. That was the name of the Awo who made divination for Orunmila when he was coming to the world. He was advised to make sacrifice to preclude the danger of untimely death through his own child. He was required to serve: Esu with a he-goat, 7 thorny sticks, white cloth, snail, rat and fish; his guardian angel with ram, hen, tortoise and snails. He did the sacrifice and left for the world where he became a practicing Ifa priest.

On getting to the world, he became a popular Ifa priest. One day, Olota invited him to find out the cause of the socio-political turbulence in his kingdom. Before going to the palace, he sounded Ifa who told him to serve Esu with a single rat. He made the sacrifice and went to the palace. At the palace divination, he disclosed that there was a visitor from heaven who was an agent of the Obstacle divinity sent to cause confusion on earth. He advised the Olota to serve Esu with a he-goat and Elenini with a cock, a tortoise and all available edible foodstuffs at the main junction in the town. Orunmila was advised to return to the palace in three day's time for the sacrifice. Thereafter, he returned to his house.

As soon as Orunmila got home, a man (who, unknown to him was Elenini's agent) came to have Orunmila prepare Ifa for him. He made the arrangements for the initiation ceremony without any delay. Three days later, Orunmila went to the palace to perform the sacrifice for Olota. The sacrifice to Elenini was deposited at the main junction of the town. The effect of the sacrifice was that as soon as Elenini's agent saw it, he would die and return to heaven. On his part, having discovered through his esotoric vision that Orunmila was responsible for exposing him, he also firmed up plans to return to heaven with him.

On the seventh day, the initiation ceremony was over and he had to follow the initiate home with his Ifa. At that morning's divination however, Orunmila was required to serve Esu with a he-goat before leaving home. He made the sacrifice after which he left with the initiate or his Ifa child

(The person who takes Ifa is regarded as the Ifa son of the man who prepared it for him). It was on that occasion that it occured to Orunmila to ask the man where he lived. The man replied that he lived at the boundry between heaven and earth.

At that stage, they had already left Orunmila's house and Orunmila realized too late that he was not prepared for such a long journey. Not knowing what next to do, Orunmila resigned himself to the fate that awaited him. It was time for Esu to come to his rescue. Orunmila decided to buy a few things from the market. Before getting to the market, they had to pass through the main road junction on which Elenini's sacrifice was deposited. When they got to the junction, the man's attention was directed by Esu to the sacrifice. As soon as he saw it, he fell to the ground and died on the spot. It was then that Orunmila realised who his Ifa son was - the agent of Elenini and how close he came to death because the man was taking him to heaven but for the timely intervention of Esu. Thereafter, peace and tranquility returned to the town of Ota.

When this Odu appears at Ugbodu, the Ifa father should suspend the ceremony and make his own sacrifice to Esu and Elenini before completing the initiation to avoid the risk of untimely death. In that situation, the Ifa patron will serve Esu with a cock and not a he-goat. The person will have two baths in the market and at a road junction.

He Made Divination for the King of Ife (Olofin)

Ogege, Ogogo, Oye a gbe nu odu soro. Adifa fun Olofin nijo
to'nlo si oko aloro odun.

The bird who spoke from the clay pot was the Awo who made divination for the king of Ife when he was going to start a new farm at the beginning of the year. He was going with his children to the farm.

Suddenly, the children who were walking in front of him ran back because they saw an unusually big bird. When the Olofin saw his children running back, he went forward to find out what was frightening about the bird. As he tried to move back, the bird spoke to him, telling him to carry him to his house. Accordingly, the Olofin took the bird home where he kept it in a large pot called Odu where the bird began to lay eggs daily. It was a pleasant surprise when the Olofin discovered that the eggs laid by the bird were beads, which he began to use to prepare regalia, crowns and shoes for sale to the other Obas of the known world.

One day, the Alaafin of Oyo visited Olofin in Ife to find out the secret of the latter's new found prosperity. Instead of concealing his secret, the King of Ife took his visitor to see the bead-laying bird. Thereafter, the King of Oyo succeeded in persuading his Ife counterpart to lend the bird to him for some time. The king of Ife agreed to oblige.

On getting home to see the immense value of the bird, the king of Oyo decided not to return it to the king of Ife. When the King of Ife persistently demanded the return of the bird, the King of Oyo decided to wage war on Ife. When the Olofin heard of the bellicose stance of his Oyo counterpart, he invited Orunmila for divination. He was advised to make sacrifice, which he made. In the ensuing military encounter, the armed forces of Ife defeated the Oyo agressors, but the king of Ife did not get back the bird.

When this Odu appears at divination, the person should be told not to reveal the secret of his success to anyone, to obviate the risk of being deprived of either his hen that lays the golden eggs, or of his life.

The Divination He Made Before Going to Ota

A nte ni'le, Owanrisi ni. Adifa fun Orunmila nijoti
on shawo lo si ilu Ota.

It was being designed on the ground and he bent his head to reflect on it. Those were the two Awos who made divination for Orunmila when he was going to practice Ifism in the town of Ota. He was advised to serve Esu with a he-goat before leaving and he made the sacrifice.

On his way to Ota he came across an intersection of four roads, and not having been to the town before that day, he did not know which way to take and he did not find anyone to ask for directions. Meanwhile, he sat by the road side until he found people returning from Oa who showed him the way to the town. Before getting to the town, it was nightfall and he came across an oak tree and sat down to rest.

As soon as he sat down, he heard voices from the top of the tree. There was a meeting of the elders of the night in progress at the top of the tree. No sooner did he sit down to rest, than he heard someone remarking at the top of the tree that a spy was eavesdropping on their discussions at the base of the tree. Almost immediately, someone spoke to him with an incantation and the following conversation ensued:

They said - Omu so - meaning - I have thrown a missile,
He replied - Omu HAN - meaning - I have caught it.
When the former asked him what he used to catch the missile, he
replied that he used a needle.

Once more, they said - Omu Soo - meaning - I have shot it.
and he replied - Omu HEE - Meaning - I picked it up.

When they asked him what he picked up, he replied that it was an egg.

They further asked him what he used to pick up the egg and he replied that it was a cotton wool.

At that point, they came down from the top of the tree to exchange pleasantries with him. From there they led him to the town and gave him a befitting lodging and hospitality. He made plenty of money in the town because he was reputed to be the first Awo to come and operate successfully in the town of Ota which was famous for being the haven of witchcraft.

Before he returned home, he advised them to build a special house for their nocturnal meeting and to stop meeting on top of trees. The Hall was accordingly built and it was called ULEDI.

When this odu appears at divination for an impending journey, the person should make sacrifice before going in order to survive the tests he is bound to have there.

He Divined for ABI When She Had No Child

Afari ko ru igi egun. O beru beru ko ro oko ni idi agbon.
Abere to so fin, O tan yanron, o tan yanran. Awon ni won lo'ndi
fa fun Abi, nijo ti o nke wi kpe ko ri omo bi.
A bald-headed person does not carry a thorny wood on his head.
A coward cannot make his farm under a coconut tree.
The needle seeks no permission before piercing through a piece
of cloth.

Those were the Awos who made divination for Abi when she was desperate to have a child. She was advised to make sacrifice with 3 bitter kolanuts, 3 alligator peppers, one goat and a skull of two other goats, three bags of money and one cowrie. She made the sacrifice after which she was assured that she would have three children whose fame would be recognised all over the world.

Thereafter, her first son was called Ogbo, the second was called Oni and the third, a girl was called Erelu. They became the founders of the first sign of three, with which they and their offspring would recognise each other as belonging to the same family tree. They were required to greet each other with the call sign of "Eta ijosi da?" Meaning "where are the trio". That is why it is said that it take two cult (Ogboni) members to recognise the third one.

When this Odu appears at Ugbodu or divination, the person will be advised to become a member of the Ogboni fraternity in order to prosper in life.

Divined for Orunmila When He Went to Work at Ota

Iwo leye, ki emi leye. Eje ki o so fun eye meji ki
won se inule kpakpo tori ki won ma ba dale ara won.

Those were the Awos who made divination for Orunmila when he went for divination to Ota. He was advised to practice Ifism at Ota without risking his life. He was however told that if he insisted on going, he should make sacrifice with two rabbits and 2 pigeons. One of the rabbits was cooked for him to eat while the second was prepared for him to travel with to Ota.

On getting to Ota, he was given an accommodation in the king's palace, where the elders susbsequently sent people to welcome him formally. As he was entertaining his visitors, they heard a strange sound from the direction of his bag (Akpominijekun) crying "Siun". The sound reassured his visitors that he belonged to the cult of witchcraft.

Subsequently, they asked for food and he gave them the rabbit inside his bag, in the process of which another sound echoed from his stomach. In a spontaneous demonstration of oneness, the visitors greeted him with the exclamation of "Baba O". He was eventually given the chieftaincy title of the "Ajana of Ota". That is why Ifa priests applaud Ifa with the words, "Ifa kpele o Ajana Ota."

At divination, the person will be advised to make sacrifice with a rabbit and plenty of palm oil in order to avert any disturbance from the elders of the night.

Chapter 9

IRETE-OGUNDA
IRETE-OGUNRERE
IRETE-OYAO
IRETE-EGUNRE

He Made Divination for the Porcupine and His Wife

Ohun rire lo'n yo obi la akpo
Ofo buruku lo'n yo ifa ore ja'de la'kpa. Adifa fun Ighogho
(Osorhue in Bini) kpelu iya re.
It is a good word that brings out kolanut from the pocket.
It is a bad word that brings out a fighting weapon from the bag.

Those were the Awos who made divination for the Porcupine and his wife. The wife was pregnant at a time when there was famine in heaven and on earth. The Porcupine decided to go to Orunmila for divination on what to do to feed his family. He was told to serve Ogun with a tortoise and Esu with a he-goat, three arrows and pieces of yam, plantain and corn. He had no money for the sacrifice, but he served Esu with yam, plantain, corn and three arrows, promising to give Esu the he-goat as soon as he could afford it. He also served Ogun with wine and kolanut.

Not long afterwards, his wife put to birth. The following morning he sharpened his matchet and his hunting instrument and made for the forest in search of food. Before leaving, he told his wife that if he succeeded he would return home, if not, he bade her farewell. For the whole day he was cutting a path through the forest. When it was night-fall, he stopped to rest and sleep. The following morning, he continued with his path-cutting until midday, when he came across a farm having yams, plantain and corn in abudance. He knelt down to pray for the owner of the farm after which he ate some corn because he was already very hungry. After eating, he plucked some corn and plantain into his bag, adding tubers of yam. He got to his house in the evening and his wife was relieved and happy to see him back. They continued to feed on the stock of food he brought.

As the stock was about to be exhausted, he took his bag and went back to the farm. On getting there, he knelt down once more to pray for the owner of the farm before removing as much foodstuff as he could carry. After repeating the journey several times to the farm, the farmer was beginning to notice that someone was stealing foodcrops from his farm. When the farmer discovered the route that the intruder took to his farm, he thought of setting a trap on it but Esu changed his mind and he decided to hide and see who the thief was.

The following day, the Porcupine returned to the farm with his bag. As the farmer aimed to shoot him, he was taken aback when he saw the intruder going on his knees to pray for the owner of the farm, prior to taking just 2 tubers of yam, some corn, and plantain. The farmer was so disarmed by the good wishes made for him by the porcupine that he could not shoot. The farmer watched several repetitions of the exercise until he took the situation for granted.

One day, the Porcupine's wife challenged him for coming home with only a few food crops at a time. He retorted by saying that he was taking the foodstuffs from someone else's farm because he did not own a farm himself and that in the circumstances he had to act with his discretion to avoid provoking the owner of the farm. Not satisfied with his explanation, the wife placed a parcel of ashes in his bag to trail the route he took to wherever he was getting the foodstuffs. As soon as he left for the bush, the wife decided later to go after him by following the trail of ashes.

When he got to the farm, as he was about to kneel down to pray, he heard footsteps and was surprised to see his wife. When he asked her what she came out for, she replied that she came to help him. Thereafter, he knelt down in his usual tradition to pray for the owner of the farm. His action annoyed his wife and without knowing that the owner of the farm was watching them, she proceeded to destroy the crops indiscriminately, while insulting and cursing the farmer in the process. The farmer was exasperated by the destruction and provocative action of the Porcupine's wife remarking that if he spared her life, she would finish his farm in no time. Upon hearing this, the farmer pulled the trigger and shot her. The male porcupine ran away leaving his dead wife behind.

When this Ifa appears at Ugbodu, the special sacrifice will be made in the farm, so that the person may live long.

The Divination He Made Before Leaving Heaven

Okiti baba ni kpe kun okpokpo. Odifa fun Orunmila nijo ti onti kole orun bowa si kole aye. The huge anthill is the bench mark for sighting the distance.

That was the Awo who made divination for Orunmila when he was coming to the world. He was advised to make sacrifice to hinder the danger of being killed by Ogun on earth and to prevent death through a woman. He was required to make sacrifice to Esu with a he-goat and a parcel of ashes; Ogun with cock and tortoise; and the unknown enemy was not to be eaten but to be left where he was to bathe in the forest. He made all the sacrifices after which he was warned against the risk of showing ingratitude to his benefactors. He subsequently left for the world.

On getting to the world, he took to hunting. He prepared an over-head counter round iroko tree in the heart of the forest which he used as the staging post for his hunting. He however began to notice the foot-prints of animals at the foot of the iroko tree. Unknown to him, that was the spot at which the animals of the forest held their meetings every five days. Incidentally, try as he did to meet or see them, he never did. Due to some mysterious reason he was always falling asleep on top of the counter just before the animals started their meetings. He would awaken as soon as they dispersed. The puzzlement urged him to go to Orunmila for divination and he was told to make sacrifices to Ogun with a cock and Esu with a black hen. He did the sacrifice.

Five days later, he returned to his hunting base to watch for game. As the animals were about to begin their meeting, he was falling asleep, but Esu startled him with his bow. He was astonished to see a huge assemblage of all the animals in the forest. As soon as they realised that he was seeing them, they sent a wasp to bite him, but he did not react. A swarm of bees was sent to attack him and he bore it. Eventually, they sent cough to irritate his throat. This time, he could not resist the urge to cough, which eventually gave him away.

With that he was invited to join them after which they asked why he was spying on them. He explained that far from spying on them, he was a hunter and where they found him was his hunting stand. He informed them that he had seen animal footprints around the tree without knowing what was going on there. Thereafter they initiated him as a member of their club and he was given clearance to attend their meetings every five days. He was present when they tried all the animals who had transgressed their rules and two antelopes were sentenced to death. The condemned antelopes were subsequently slaughtered at their shrine while they gave their corpses to the hunter without their heads. On getting home he explained to his wife that the gunshot severed the heads of the antelopes.

Five days later, he was also given the corpses of one deer and one bush goat which were executed. Once more he had to take them away without their heads. When he got home with two more headless game, the wife's curiousity was ignited and she was determined to find out what was happening to the heads of the animals her husband was bringing home. When he left for the forest after the next five days, she trailed him until she arrived at his staging post on the steps of the Iroko tree. When he asked her what she was doing in the forest, she explained that she came to assist him in searching for the heads of the animals he had brought home. Instead of asking her to return home immediately, he allowed her to have her way when she insisted on staying to watch developments.

Not long afterwards, the animals were assembled for their meeting, and the hunter was once more invited to join them. He went to the meeting without his wife, but no sooner did the meeting commence one of the animals shouted that another human being was around. They sent the wasp to search for the presence of an intruder, but as soon as it bit her, she shouted and they invited her for questioning. When she explained that she was the hunter's wife, they immediately turned on him to explain why he brought his wife to spy on them. It was the turn of the wife to explain that far from inviting her to come with him, her husband did not know that she was trailing him to the forest. She went on to explain that what made her curious was the headless animals her husband was bringing home. Since she was not satisfied with his explanations that it was his bullets that were severing their heads from their bodies, she came to see for herself.

Meanwhile, she was told that she had to pay a commensurate price for her snooping curiousity. They made her to drink the blood in their pot, but as she was about to faint, her husband begged the animals to spare her life. In deference to his appeal, they proclaimed that she would never be able to remember or recall what she saw at the conference, but that from then to eternity she would always return to them part of the blood she drank - which approximates to the feminine menstruation every month.

When this Ifa appears at Ugbodu, the person will be told that he will have cause to belong to a secret society or cult but that he should never tell the secret to his wife. He should make sacrifice to prosper through his membership of the cult. He should be given a bath in the forest by the Ifa priest.

At divination, the person should serve Esu with a he-goat and Ogun with a cock in order to avoid the danger of sudden death.

The Divination He Made When Eziza Came to Challenge Him

Irete-Ogunrere made divination for himself when he was going to be challenged by Eziza. The night before Eziza came to him, he had a dream in which he saw two kolanuts, one white and one brown wrapped in separate parcels. When he sounded Ifa the following morning, he was advised to serve his head with wine, alligator pepper and kolanut in order to triumph in a n imminent challenge. He had scarcely made the sacrifice when someone knocked at his door.

He met the man at the door and after exchanging greetings the visitor introduced himself as Eziza, the priest of the Wind divinity. He lied to Orunmila that he had just prepared a medicine which he kept in the different parcels and that he wanted to make divination to find out whether they would be efficacious. Orunmila began by enquiring from Ifa whether the two parcels were what he had dreamt of the previous night. At that point he gave Eziza a piece of the kolanut and some seeds of alligator pepper with which he had just served his head.

After allowing the visitor to eat the kolanut, he faced him squarely, and told him that what he had just eaten were meant to disclose to him the true content of his parcels, and that he thought he could fault him lying that they contained medicine. He therefore categorically confirmed that what he had in the two parcels were white kolanuts and alligator pepper. Orunmila told him that he wondered why anyone would like to try him when he had neither boasted nor competed with anybody.

Eziza reacted by turning himself into a dog, and Orunmila used his divination tray to mark the odu with which God created the dog and commanded Ogun to eat the dog if he failed to turn to his human self. Almost immediately, the dog turned back to Eziza. Not satisfied with the trauncing he had got, Eziza transfigured into a hurricane that blew off the roof of

Orunmila's house. With his divination tray (Akpako) still in hand, Orunmila began his incantation. "Ole, gbudugbudu. Elu Ojiji firi naa jo fidan. Aa duro ho he gbe ruko ma yi. Ona kpe ese merindilogun lo mu wa si aye to fi ku eyo kon so so. Agogo shere agbara". Meaning - "You thief, the drum that has no hole under it, the shadow that kills in the full view of everybody, the man who stands by the iroko tree without falling. Have you forgotten that you came to the world with sixteen legs, out of which you only have one left? The gong who exhibits his strength".

With that, Eziza returned the roof to Orunmila's house and assumed his human figure. He was thoroughly humoured and deflated because the effect of the incantation unwound the key of his powers. He went on his knees to apologise to Orunmila, promising to serve him at his beck and call from then on.

When this Ifa appears at Ugbodu, the person should prepare Eziza shrine for his Ifa and be advised never to offend his Ifa father (the man who prepared the Ifa for him). He should serve; Ogun with a dog, Esu with a he-goat, and his head with two guinea fowls. He should either completely refrain from eating kolanuts or forbid eating any kolanut given to him by any other person apart from the ones he buys for himself.

He Divined for Three Trap Setters

ete regun abeso juwenu. Adifa fun Olomo Ashi'ni,
abufun Egbire owo, atun bufun omo titun Arimewe/Arimooran.

That was the Awo who made divination for three trap setters who were never catching any animals with their traps. They subsequently went to Orunmila for divination. He prepared the required devices for them and they promised to send him the leg of the first animal they caught with their traps.

Five days later, their trap caught a deer and they thought it was too much for them to send the leg to Orunmila. They subsequently contrived a strategy for concealing their catch from Orunmila since they had to pass through his house. They decided to dress the deer like a human corpse since they were aware that Orunmila forbade to see a human corpse.

Meanwhile, Esu and the head of the cult of witchcraft were visiting Orunmila in the morning. As he was escorting the visitors away from his house, he saw his three beneficiaries coming with what looked like a human corpse, and shouting " Oku mbo o, Ogbe kuro lone ", meaning " We are carrying a human corpse, laymen, get out of the way." When Orunmila and his two visitors heard the warning they entered the bush and hid their faces. Nonetheless, the king of witchcraft opened the two ears at the back of his head to see what they were carrying. With his esoteric hind sight, he was able to see that far from carrying a human corpse, they are in fact carrying a dead deer, a fact which he subsequently disclosed to Esu and Orunmila as soon as the carriers passed by.

Since Orunmila recognized the three young men as trap setters who promised to send him the leg of the first animal they caught with their trap, he surmised that they feigned carrying a human corpse, as a ploy for absolving themselves from the promise. To deliberate on the action of the three young men, Orunmila and his two visitors returned to his house. When the witch heard the report of Orunmila he was annoyed and proposed that they should be taught the hard lesson of those who in bad faith, renege on promises made in good faith. He proposed that he would take the senior one of the three; Esu should take the second one; while Orunmila was to take the most junior one. At the same time, they admonished their chicken-hearted and ever-forgiving host not to let them down. Akpetebi, Orunmila's wife was present when their strategy for punishing the three scoundrels was being firmed up.

As soon as he left Orunmila's house, the witch went to the house of the three young men. He was looking at them when they were butchering the deer. He also saw them extracting the small parts with which to cook a soup to eat pounded yam. As soon as the eldest of the three took a piece of the meat into his mouth, the witch cryptical punched him on the throat and he began to choak. In a matter of minutes he lost his breath and choked to death. His death created a pandomonium in the locality.

The following day, Esu went to their house and watched the sympathisers coming into and leaving the house. Meanwhile, the people set out to eat. He focused his gaze on his victim and as he took a helping of food into his mouth. Esu unscrutably hit him on the stomach and he began to complain of stomach upset. In a matter of minutes, he began to vomit blood and before anyone could do anything to help him, he died. Following the death of his two elder brothers, Omotitun the junior one began to run from pillar to post, knowing that it was reasonable to imagine that it was his turn to die, having drawn a positive correlation between the deer incident and their deaths.

The following morning, he was wondering whether or not to go and make a clean breast on the matter to Orunmila when he met Orunmila's wife on her way to the river. He was now weeping helplessly and akpetebi stopped to ask him what the matter was? He explained that he was about to die because his two elder brothers had died in quick succession. Akpetebi only gave him a cold comfort by confirming his fears which she attributed to their bad faith and greediness. She reminded him of their promise to send the leg of the first animal they caught to her husband. Omotitun instinctively went on his knees to beg Akpetebi to advise him on what to do to atone for their treachery. She sympathised with him and proposed that he should immediately remit the remnants of the meat of the deer and a bundle of yam tubers to Orunmila, and to beg for forgiveness.

He quickly raced home to parcel what remained of the deer in addition to a bundle of yams to Orunmila. When he got to Orunmila's house, he prostrated on his stomach begging for forgiveness. Orunmila however insisted on knowing how he found out the cause of their plight and Omotitun explained that it was Akpetebi who told him about it and advised him on how to atone for their bad faith. With that disclosure, Orunmila told him that he was forgiven and could go home because Akpetebi had, through her betrayal of trust, absolved him of his bond and would have to carry the death burden. As soon as Omotitun left, Orunmila sat down in fury to wait for his wife to return from the river.

As his wife was returning from the river with the pot of water on her head, Orunmila commanded her to wait outside. He reproached her for betraying his confidence by revealing to Omotitun the discussion he had with his friends, when she knew that they had already accused him of chicken-heartedness. He subsequently used his wand of authority (ASE) to conjure her to remain transfixed and to dry up on the spot with the pot on her head to eternity. Thus, she transfigured into what the Yorubas now call Teteregun, that is, the type of palm tree which carries a load on its head.

When this odu appear at divination, the person will be advised to use a pebble to touch his or her mouth and to throw it away, praying not to be destroyed by the words coming out of his or her mouth. If it appears as Ayeo for a woman she will be told that she has betrayed her husband and if he has Orunmila, she should appease him with a soup and pounded yam prepared with the foot of a deer. At the same time, she will give a he-goat to Esu and a rabbit to the night. If it is Uree, she will be warned never to disclose what she knows about her husband.

This Odu's Special Sacrifice for Saving One's Life

Orunmila ni iyawo fere. Moni iyawo fere. Oni,
Iyawo asin ni o fi nkpa eku. Iyawo osa ni o fi nkpa eye.
Iyawo ekun ni o fi nkpa eran. Iyawo aje ni o fi nkpa eni.
Orunmila eulogised alacrity, and I also praised agility.
Orunmila then explained that it is with agility and alacrity
that the pointed-nosed cannibal rat kills other rats;
the hawk succeeds in killing other birds;
the tiger is able to kill other animals; and
the witch succeeds in killing human beings.
Orunmila therefore recommends that to be able to save one's self from evil forces, one should
make sacrifice with palm kernels, salt, and a he-goat to Esu with the incantation.
When food is being cooked, the cook is the first to sample the taste.
Although the eyes are the first to see the river,
It is the feet that touches it first.

He Divined for the Monkey Family Not to be Greedy

Ohun rere ni o ma nyo ni akpo.
Ohun buburu ni o ma nyo ifon jade ninu akpo. Awon lo'ndifa
fun Ologbon jinire.
It is good words that bring kolanuts from the bag.
It is bad words that bring arrows from its' case.

Those were the two awos who made divination for the red male and female monkeys. They were advised to make sacrifice with garden eggs (agbede in Yoruba) cock, ashes and a porous bag. The male monkey made the sacrifice but the female one refused to make it.

Meanwhile, the male monkey went out into the bush in search of food with which to feed his family. On getting to a maize farm, he went on his knees to pray for the owner of the farm. He begged God to protect the farmer from the cold hands of death and stife, so that he would live through the year to make another farm the following year. Thereafter, he plucked a few of the ripe maize and took them home for his family to eat. The male monkey susbsequently made it a regular habit to pluck maize from the farm after praying for its owner.

Meanwhile, the farmer observed that an unauthorized intruder was regularly plucking maize from his farm He then enlisted the services of a hunter to search and kill the intruder. However, when the hunter got to the farm, he took a vantage position from which to watch the approch of any intruder. He was disarmed by the sight of a monkey who knelt down to pray for the owner of the farm before plucking a few maize that he carried home. The hunter was too compassionate to shoot.

When the farmer noticed the incompetence of the hunter to deal with the intruder, he admonished and threatened to terminate his services if he failed to abate the nuisance. Thereafter, the hunter decided to deal with the situation more positively. At the same time, the wife of the monkey was accusing him of not coming home with enough maize to feed the family. She therefore decided to trail him to the farm by putting ashes inside her husband's pourous bag. The ashes trailed behind him when he next went to the farm and the wife followed the ash-trail to the farm.

When the male monkey got to the farm, he went through his habitual ritual of praying first for the farmer. As the hunter took his gun to shoot, the female monkey emerged blaming her husband for his meekness and cowardice. She proceeded to pluck the maize indiscriminately. The hunter had no hesitation in pulling the trigger on the female monkey. After shooting her, she dropped dead and the male monkey ran home.

When the hunter moved to take the dead monkey home in his bag, he heard a voice from her stomach which warned him not to take her home. He therefore butchered her and found a talking calabash in her stomach. The calabash warned the hunter not to take it home until he had fetched a piece of white cloth, a drum and a gong.

The hunter went home to fetch the materials and he was accompanied by other people to the farm. As soon as the calabash was put in the white cloth, it began to sing the music of the town. As soon as they got to the town, the calabash told them to build a shrine for it which was to be called Orisa Oko, which is served to this day.

At divination, the person will be told to serve Orisa Oko and to watch his utterances to avoid being killed by the words of his/her mouth. If the divinee is a man, he will be advised to make the above sacrifice to avert the danger of death through the action of his wife.

Chapter 10

IRETE-OSA
AROTESA

The Divination He Made Before Leaving Heaven

gba yeke yeke, Awo Iranyin, odifa fun Orunmila
nijo ti onti kole Orun bowa si kole aye.

That was the Awo who made divination for the Odu when he was coming to the world. He was told to make the following sacrifices:- to Esu with he-goat, tortoise and white cloth, pigeon and cowries; to his guardian angel with a ram, pigeon, cock - which were left unkilled at the junction of heaven and earth, and Olokun with white cock, white chalk, white cloth and cowries. He made   all the sacrifices before coming to the world. At the same time the daughter of Olokun left for the world.

He got to the world and became an Ifa priest. It was not long before he met the daughter of Olokun who was a trader and they got married. They were quite prosperous but had no child. When he eventually went for divination, he was told that he forgot to serve Osanyin/Osun in heaven. He was advised to serve Osun with a dog, tortoise, and a cock. He made the sacrifice. The following month his wife became pregnant and in the fullness of time she gave birth to a female child who was named Ayo. They had many other children and they prospered.

The Contest for Leadership Between Esu and the Divinities

This odu reveals the story of what happened when the divinities decided to use the process of feasting to determine seniority. At a meeting of the divinities, Orisa-Nla proclaimed that each of them should take turns feasting the others in their home at every meeting. Orisa-Nla announced that he was going to host the first meeting and feast.

While they were deliberating on the matter, Esu appeared to warn them that if they did not want to provoke his wrath, they should allow him to host the first feast and meeting. While they were all hushing him down, he proclaimed that not even God, their creator and father had any claim to seniority over him. He reminded them that they all met him on the swamps while they were descending from the top of the palm tree when they all came from heaven. Since no one was prepared to take his threat seriously, Esu withdrew from the meeting. Thereafter, Orisa-Nla told the other divinities to be prepared for his feast at the next meeting.

On the appointed day, Orisa-Nla had prepared an elaborate feast of inexhaustable food and drinks and the table was set. As soon as they were all assembled, Orisa-Nla brought out kolanuts to pray. As he was breaking the kolanuts, there was screaming, yelling and hysteria from Orisa-Nla's harem. Two of his young children had been attacked by convulsion and before help could reach them, they died. The feast was subsequently abandoned, giving way to gloom and misery.

At the next meeting, it was the turn of Ogun and the same incident was repeated as the host lost two children to convulsion, which subsequently disrupted the feast from materialising. The incident was repeated in the homes of Olokun, Sango and Osanyin until it came the turn of Orunmila. Before embarking on his feast, Orunmila made divination, and was told to make sacrifice with a he-goat and the bronze images of a man, the lead casting of a woman, and the mud images of male and female rabbits. He was advised to deposit the images on the shrine of Esu and to shed the blood of the he-goat on them. After making the sacrifice, he proceeded to prepare for his feast.

Once again as soon as the divinities were assembled, Orisa-Nla was splitting the kolanuts when an uproar was heard from the backyard of Orunmila's house. Two of his children, a boy and a girl had developed convulsion, but as soon as the divinities came out to see them, the children sneezed and became well. Esu had meanwhile relieved them of the convulsion in deference to the sacrifice he made. At the same time, they saw the bronze image of the man dancing with the lead image of the woman while the mud images of male and female rabbits were also dancing at the rubbish dump (Etitan or Otiku) at the back of Orunmila's house. While they were watching the mysterious images, Esu invited fowls and goats to destroy the food prepared for the feast which thus became a non-event.

At that point, Esu reappeared to renew his boast that unless they all conceded seniority to him by inviting him to start the feasting, none of them would succeed in hosting one effectively. There being no other option left, Esu was invited to host the next feast.

On his feast day, Esu prepared inexhaustible food and drinks and all the divinities ate and drank to their satisfaction. After the feast, Esu brought out the bronze and lead with which Orunmila made sacrifice and told the divinities to melt them down for use as money. Thus, it was Esu who produced the bronze, copper and lead from which money was manufactured as a medium of exchange, replacing the cowries created by God. That is why Orunmila has revealed that Esu was the one who created money, and why it is that money serves, makes, destroys and kills humanity, depending on the role one allows it to play in one's life.

When this odu appears at Ugbodu and at divination, the person should be advised to refrain from any contest for superiority with anyone because it is heads you lose and tails you lose. He should serve Esu with a he-goat and the images of a male and a female to prevent loss of children.

He Divined for the Divinity of the Night When He Was Leaving Heaven

Bi ore le tu ka ki o tuka. Bi ore ba le ba je, ki o baje
Adifa fun Awon iyami Oshoronga
bowa si kole aye.
If a friend prefers to revere in wickedness, let him remain abominable.
If he prefers to be nasty, let him remain repulsive.

Those were the two awos who made divination for the divinity of Witchcraft, when he was coming to the world. He was advised to make sacrifice with a goat, yam and a gourd of palm oil. He made the sacrifice.

On getting to the world, he discovered that wickedness had quicker reward than benevolence. He therefore decided to practice iniquity and atrocity, just as he was notorious for, in heaven. They began by killing Ogun's son called Oriseku, followed by Orile-imere the son of Osanyin. When they wanted to take Afuwakpe, the son of Orunmila, he begged them to give him time to tell his father that he was returning to heaven at their instance and his wish was granted.

When he mentioned his plight to his father, he prepared a pot containing; a tuber called Abirishoko in Yoruba and Olikhoro in Bini, three eggs, three pebbles and three cowries. After preparing it with the iyerosun of this odu, he gave the pot to his son to ask the Elders of the Night to eat the contents before eating him. As they (eight of them) were eating the contents of the pot, an argument on seniority ensued among them. While they were fighting one another, Afuwakpe ran away.

At Ugbodu, the person will be advised not to belong to any meeting, and not to criticise the club of witchcraft. He should serve the night with a rabbit and the tuber of Abirishoko/Olikhoro.

The Divination Made for Him Before He Prospered

Arijanjanijan awo ile Orunmila. Odifa fun Orunmila nijo
ti onfi ogbon ara re ni kon she ofo arare. Ti ko
she ishe fun. Onfi ko'dun o faa ko to arawon. O ba
nkpe Arijanjankijan kpe kini o ti ri yi.

Arijanjankijan was a surrogate of Orunmila who divined from him when he preferred to rely on his intelligence for solving his problems. He pushed and pulled in several directions, but he could not make it. At his wit's end, he invited his surrogate for advice. Arijanjankijan told him to give a he-goat to Esu and a hen to the night. He did the sacrifice and things began to work out for him. Subsequently, he met his first wife who brought prosperity into his life.

At divination the person should be told to have his own Ifa in order to prosper.

He Divined for the Multi-purpose Diviner

A ro te sa Kobo. Bi olu odide. Bi akoba
de yeu. Adifa fun Shawa sheshigun ounti kole
orun bo wa si kole aye.
The one who sympathises profusely with the victim of his wickedness.
The king of Parrots. No one knows what is in an inner room without entering it.

Those were the Awos who made divination for the multi-facetted divine priest who was not only a witch doctor, but also a seer, diviner and an Ifa Priest. He was advised to make sacrifice and to beware of his junior brothers. He was advised not to live with any of his junior borthers, because their head was stronger than his own. If they lived together, his brother's head would kill him prematurely. He was told to have his own Ifa in order to live to a ripe old age. He made the sacrifices and heeded the advice and lived to a ripe old age.

When this Odu appears at divination, the person will be told to have his own Ifa in order to live long and to refrain from allowing his junior brother or sister to live with him on a permanent basis, to avoid being killed by the head of his junior. If the divinee is a woman, she will be given the same advice and told to be close to Orunmila.

He Made Divination for Olayoriju Omo Akpogbonshorun

Arotesa, Arotejo, Arotekpa kube, Ono se taara goke.

Those were the Awos who made divination for Olayoriju, the son of Akpogbonsherun who was advised to make sacrifice with six coconuts. He made the sacrifice. He also served Esu with a he-goat. He was told to serve his head with three of the coconuts. After the sacrifices, he began to prosper and sang in praise of Orunmila and the Ifa priests.

At divination, the person should be advised to make sacrifice so that his or her prosperity might blossom.

He Made Divination for Akerenikeyo to Take His Father's Crown

Arotesa, Arotejo, Arotekpakube Kube. Oro kan ni
be'le ti oju ogun lo.

Those were the Awos who made divination for Akerenikeyo when he was going to ascend the throne of his father. He was advised to make sacrifice with his wearing apparel, called kolokolo and a big he-goat. He did not only refuse to make the sacrifice but also began to boast that no one could deprive him of his father's throne, being the heir apparent.

When Esu was told that Akerenikeyo refused to make sacrifice, Esu cajoled him to start dancing to the tune of his drumming, two days before the coronation ceremonies were to begin. As he was dancing to the tune of Esu's drumming, Akere began to sing.

Leni Leni ni emi yio jo. Onishinko. Leni leni. Lola
Lola ni emi yio jo. Onishinko, lo'la lola

As he was dancing he also began to summersault. As he was dancing and summersaulting, Esu blinked his eyes to Akerenikeyo who instantly fell to the ground, fracturing his thigh bone. Following his physical handicap, the king makers subsequently announced that a partially crippled man could not be made king. His junior brother and a second son of his father was then crowned king.

At divination, the person should be advised to make sacrifice and not to allow over-confidence to deprive him of the benefit of an upcoming promotion or upliftment

Chapter 11

IRETE-ETURA
IRETE - ETURA
ESEKON-LA

He Made Divination for the Mouth and the Abdomen

Esekon tee lomi. Esekan Kpasa le Okiti. Odifa fun Enu,
Abufun inu nijo ti won ti kole orun bowa si kole aye,
Ebo aamubo ni Kiwon ru o.

One leg was inside the river, and the other was on the land. That was the Awo who made divination for the Mouth and the Abdomen when they were coming to the world. The stomach was advised to make sacrifice with spoiled things, rotten and disused materials and to give a he-goat to Esu. Before he reached Orunmila's place for the sacrifice the latter had already prepared a bag for him. The bag was given to Esu without the he-goat. Thereafter, he left for the world.

On getting to the world, nobody took notice of him. On the other hand, the Mouth also made divination with Orunmila. He was told to serve Ifa with a ram, and his head with white cock and white hen because he was going to be the spokesman of the entire bdy. He made the sacrifice and left for the world. He was told to steer clear of his relations on earth. He subsequently met the stomach who complained that he had been finding life difficult since coming to the world. Out of sympathy, the Mouth invited the stomach to live with him and the sacrifice made by the former subsequently benefitted the two of them. They cooperated so effectively that they became very friendly, although the Mouth never knew the content of the bag which Orunmila gave to the Stomach.

That is why no one fully knows the nature of his or her fellow man and woman to this day, because nobody knows the content of the stomach's bag. In contrast, the Mouth is ever so plain and friendly with everybody.

When it appears at Ugbodu, the person should be advised to beware of relations but should serve Esu and the Night. At divination, the person should serve the head with a cock and Esu with a he-goat.

The Divination He Made for the Mother of Okpere

*Kpeje fuuru kpeje. Adifa fun okpere to'nshe wole wode Orisa
to ni oun ko mo ewu. Bi oju ba mo okpere yi o jade si ajude
iya're. A a ni ko se'wu. Kewu, do se'wu ke wu.*

That was the Awo who made divination for the mother of the bird called Okpere (Ukpomobie in Bini). As soon as the bird woke up in the morning he would start shouting - There is no trouble, no trouble, no trouble. His mother tried in vain to stop him from making that kind of announcement.

Meanwhile, the bigger and carnivorous birds began to search for the abode of the bird who was always making those "no trouble" announcements to find out the source of his strength. The Hawk decided to do a reconnaissance tour to locate the bird's where about.

At the same time the mother of the bird realising that her son's boasting was bound to get him into trouble sooner than later decided to go to Orunmila for divination. At divination, she was told that trouble was already in the offing and that she could only make sacrifice to minimize the effect and not to avoid. She was told to make sacrifice with an egg and cotton wool. She made the sacrifice immediately.

The following morning, Okpere came out again and began his day as usual by shouting "Ko se'wu kewu". Unknown to him the Hawk was watching him. Before he shouted a third time, the Hawk grabbed him by his two feet while his head was facing downwards and flew away with him. Esu immediately intervened by advising the Hawk that by seizing him, Okpere would realize that there could be trouble, and that he would have learnt his lesson. He should therefore drop him to crash on the ground.

The Hawk heeded the advice of Esu and dropped Okpere. As he was falling to the ground, Esu used the cotton wool with which his mother made sacrifice to cushion his impact on the ground and Okpere fell on the cotton wool without sustaining any injury. As soon as he fell to the ground, he ran into the safety of his mother's house. From then on, he changed his tune to "Shaorao, ewu mbe, ewu mbe ewumbe", meaning, watch out, there is trouble, there is trouble, trouble, trouble, trouble" which has remained the call sign of Okpere to this day.

At divination, the person will be told to keep a close watch on his/her young stubborn and swanky child who will talk his way into trouble. If it is Uree, the person should make sacrifice with an egg and cotton wool. If it is Ayeo, it means that witches have already slated him for elimination and the sacrifice should be made on that day so that he or she might survive an inevitable illness.

The Divination He Made Before Leaving Heaven

Ose kan te lomi, Esekan kpasa le okiti.

One leg inside the river and one leg on the land was the name of the Awo who made divination for Irete-Etura when he was coming to the world. He was advised to make sacrifice with: one hen, four snails, a goat, tortoise, rat and fish to his guardian angel (Okekponrin); cock , tortoise and black cloth to Osanyin/Osun. He was required to do the sacrifice to alleviate the problems he was going to have in bearing children, and in order to prosper on earth. He made the sacrifices and left for earth. Before leaving, he was advised that in addition to his Ifa practices, he should also have his own Ogun and Osun shrines on earth.

On getting to earth, he took to the practice of Ifism, but he was not doing very well. He could not even afford to marry. The two divine priests, who came to the world at the same time with him, Ogun and Osanyin were also loafing about with no settled life.

One night, his guardian angel appeared to him to remind him that he had forgotten the two divinities who accompanied him to the world and that without their cooperation, he would not make it on earth. When he woke up in the morning, he decided to sound his okekponrin and his own Ifa appeared on the tray. He was told to serve his Ifa with a goat, and to use the meat to prepare a feast for the people around him. He made the sacrifice and invited plenty of people to the feast. Some of his invitees were making jest of him by querying why he had to make such an elaborate feast when he had no family of his own.

Among the invitees were two stange figures who lived in the town, but who had never met him. It turned out later that they were Ogun and Osanyin priests and that their guardian angels had also appeared to them in dreams, directing them to attend the feast that Orunmila was going to throw. After eating and drinking at Orunmila's house, the two divine priests were drunk and in their delirum, they began to say sooths as if possessed. They divined for Orunmila telling him to serve Ogun and Osun respectively with a dog, cock, tortoise and palm wine. They also divined for themselves to serve their guardian angels.

After the feast, Orunmila arranged to know their houses and they subsequently assisted him in preparing his Ogun and Osun shrines. Incidentally, although Orunmila later told them the divination they made for themselves during trances. They however failed to make the sacrifices to their guardian angels.

On the other hand, three months after making his sacrifice and feast, the Olofin bethrothed his daughter to Orunmila to compensate him for the efficacious divination and sacrifice he made for him. As their friendship solidified, Orunmila was able to persuade his two friends to make their sacrifices, after which, they too became married. Incidentally, for a whole year after their marriage, none of them had been able to put his wife in the family way.

How Orunmila had his First Child

Back in heaven, his guardian angel was anxious to send a child to him on earth. One morning, three children were parading the quarter occupied by the guardian angels when Orunmila's guardian angel invited them and persuade them to go to his son and his friends on earth. They agreed but told the guardian angel that they were fays and were going for a short sojourn on earth. Nonetheless, he convinced them to go and that if his son knew what to do, he should be able to detain the child to outlive him on earth.

After the three children left Orunmila's guardian angel, they subsequently met the guardian angels of Ogun and Osun who made similar appeals to them.

Before they left heaven, they went to their own guardian angels for clearance. The eldest of the three was called Ajifono who promised to go to Ogun on earth and that he would return to heaven on the day his father would perform his naming ceremony. The second one was called Okpadeere who promised to go to Osanyin and that he too would return to heaven on the day his father performed his naming ceremony. The third one was called Ajidibo who promised to go to Orunmila, and vowed to return to heaven on the day his father performed his naming ceremony divination. The three children were fays and were leaving for earth from the land of fays. (Ile-imere in Yoruba or Evbo- Igbakhuan in Bini).

Back on earth, Ogun's wife was the first to become pregnant, followed by Osun's wife and finally followed by Orunmila's wife. The problem with Ogun and Osun is that they behave like the mirror who can see the problems of others but not their own. On his part, as soon as his wife became pregnant, Orunmila made divination to find out the kind of child that was coming to him. His own Odu again appeared which meant that the child was a fay. *At this point, it should be emphasized that if this Odu appears at Ugbodu, the man is a fay and the requisite sacrifices should be made to give him a long span of life on earth. He will also marry a fay and his children or many of them would also be fays.*

At divination, his Okekponrin (Ikin divination which can only be revealed to those who have been to the secret initiation conclave of Ugbodu), told him to serve Esu at once with a stool, four U-bolts, three cudgels and a he-goat, so that Esu might arrest the child to remain on earth because he was a fay. His ifa also told him never to perform any naming ceremony feast or divination and to mark the birth of the child, and more importantly, he should prepare Ifa for the child before he was born. He was also informed that for as long as he lived, he should not ask the child to do ibo divination (Dibo in Yoruba and Yan-Uta in Bini).

In the fullness of time, Ogun's wife delivered a male child and he was very happy. A week later, Osun's wife also delivered a male child, and he too was very happy. They decided that they would not perform the naming ceremony feasts until Orunmila's wife also delivered. Three months after the birth of Osun's child, Orunmila's wife finally gave birth also to a male child.

A week after the birth of Orunmila's child, Ogun decided to perform the feast marking the naming ceremony of his much desired child. He went to the forest to hunt for all kinds of animals from grass-cutter to an antelope, bush pig, deer and buffalo. He also tapped palm wine in abundance for the occasion. On the day of the feast, the food had been cooked and the table was set while the wines were ready. He invited the Shashere of Ife to be the chairman of the occasion. As the Shashere was praying with the kolanuts, the mother of the child was holding him on her lap. As the first kolanut was being broken, the child began to shiver on her mother's lap and when she noticed that his eyes had gone white, she cried out. The child had developed convulsion and he died almost immediately.

The ceremony became a non-event. The experience of Ogun did not teach Osun any lesson because he went ahead to fix the naming ceremony of his own son for the next fortnight. He also went to great lengths to prepare a feast to mark the occasion. As if history was repeating itself, Osun had the same experience as Ogun. Meanwhile, Ajifono the son of Ogun after dying, went to the boundary of heaven and earth to wait for his two other friends. As the naming ceremony of Okpadeere, the son of Osun was about to commence, Ajifono began to sing as follows:

> *"Emi Ajifono omo Ogun ti duro al Orita-Ijaloko. Emina*
> *kpe e o, iwo Okpadeere ke so omo Osanyin.*
> *Omo ru e 'gege wa bo ba mi o o". As he was singing the song*
> *repeatedly, the son of Osun got the message.*

As the food was being dealt out to the invitees the child turned his eyes and before the mother realised what was happening, he died, bringing the ceremony to an abrupt end. All eyes were now on the son of Orunmila. Contrary to all expectations, Orunmila refused tp do any naming ceremony. In spite of the absence of any ceremony, his son's two colleagues stood at the boundary of heaven and earth (Orita-Ijaloko) to be hailing on him to join them.

As soon as Ajidibo, the son of Orunmila heard the song, he developed a chill. It was at that point that Esu got his club and went to drive away the sons of Ogun and Osun towards heaven. As soon as his two friends left, the son of Orunmila became well, because Esu had nailed him down on the stool to sit and live with his parents.

The sacrifice made by Orunmila before the child was born is this Odu's specical sacrifice for detaining a fay to live with his parents on earth. He had several other children subsequently.

When this Odu appears at Ugbodu or at a naming ceremony divination, the person should be known as a fay. Arrangements should be made without delay to make the sacrifice to make the person stay on earth.

The Divination He Made for Sango

Esekonla made divination for Sango when he was having problems on earth. He too had forgotten his heavenly vows. The fact that Orunmila was the only one who kept his own child after the deaths of the children of Ogun and Osun made him more popular than ever before. Sango had no wife and no child. He decided to go to Orunmila for divination. He was told not to marry a light-complexioned woman, but that he should serve his guardian angel with a red cock, uncut calabash with long neck (ishere) wooden tray, a wooden stool with no hole in it, camwood, alligator pepper, bitter kola and kolanuts to enable his life to sit properly. He went home to make the sacrifice.

Not long after he made the sacrifice, he met a pretty light complexioned woman, who, un-known to him, was the daughter of the divinity of death. He was swept off his senses by the ensnaring beauty of the woman and when he proposed to her, she agreed right away and he took her home to live with her. That night, he made love to her and the following morning, she was already pregnant and having signs of labor.

Once again, Sango raced back to Orunmila for divination and he advised him to serve Esu with seven he-goats at once. Orunmila predicted that the woman was going to give birth to a male child, but that he should make the sacrifice before she delivered. Sango had no intention of making the sacrifice because he made a jest of Orunmila that by asking him to make sacrifice with seven he-goats, he was looking for meat with which to feed his family and he was not going to get it from him.

As the sun was setting on that day, the woman went into labor and gave birth to a male child. Sango rejoiced that in spite of not serving Esu with seven he-goats, his wife had delivered safely. When the child cried out, it provoked tremors and shockwaves. In the evening of that day, there was a cry from Sango's house because both the mother and child had died as suddenly as they came into Sango's life.

At divination for marriage, the person will be told that the woman he has in mind is a fay and if she is fair in complexion, he should not marry her. If it appears for a pregnant woman, the husband will be told to serve Esu with a live he-goat and six skulls of he-goats, so that the mother and the child (who will be male) might live.

He Made Divination for the Olofin

Esekonla, awo olofin, Odifa fun Ule gingirin,
Iyale olofin. Abufun Oro'jo, tiin she Iyawo Olofin.
Aniki Olofin ru ebo.

This odu made divination for two of Olofin's wives, the senior wife, who was hot-tempered, and for the junior cool-headed wife who was pregnant. As the pregnant wife was about to deliver, her senior mate came to support her. She made the junior one to believe that she had to be blindfolded as part of the delivery process. As soon as she delivered the child, the senior mate covered the child's mouth to stop it from crying. Thereafter, she choked the innocent baby to death and it was subsequently cast away. Ule-giriri repeated the same process on two subsequent deliveries by Oroojo.

After the loss of the third child, the mother of Oroojo went to Orunmila for divination, at which she was told to give a he-goat to Esu and she did. When Oroojo was delivering her third pregnancy, her senior mate had got a calabash ready. This time Esu changed her mind and she did not kill the child right away. Instead, she inserted a stone covered in blood between Oroojo's lap to give the appearance that she gave birth to a stone, while covering the real child up in a calabash.

When the lamentations were all over, she carried the calabash containing the child to an anthill and dropped it inside. Unknown to her however, a palm wine tapper saw her dropping the calabash into the open ant-hill. As soon as she left, the palm wine tapper climbed down to see what the calabash contained. He was astonished to see that it contained a newly born baby who was still alive. He took the baby home and asked one of his wives to bring him up with her breast-milk because she too had just delivered. It was a baby boy.

The palm wine tapper and his wife took good care of the child who grew up to bear a keen resemblance to his father, the Olofin. As soon as the child grew up to be an adult, the palm wine tapper told the young man, who was hitherto never told about his paternity to attend a ceremony at Olofin's palace. He looked so much like the Olofin that everybody exclaimed "When did Kabiyesi have this child?". As if to confirm their indications, the palm wine tapper asked both King and Chiefs whose resemblance the child bore and they all confirmed unanimously that he was the carbon copy of Olofin.

The palm wine tapper proceeded to narrate how eighteen years before, he saw Ule girigiri the lyale of Olofin deposit a calabash inside an ant-hill. When he came down to verify the content of the calabash, he saw a newly born baby boy. Since then he had been taking care of the child. When lyale was invited to explain, she confirmed the palm wine tapper's story, adding that she was also responsible for killing the first two children of Oroojo because she did not want her to have a child in the royal household. She was summarily tried and executed and Oroojo was made to take her place.

The palm wine tapper was aptly rewarded with gifts and a chieftaincy title. At the death of the Olofin the child was crowned to succeed his father.

When this odu appears at divination for a woman, she should be told that she had child bearing problems and should ask her mother to go and make divination for her, in additon to giving a he-goat to Esu. The skull of the he-goat will be mounted with Ifa medicine with the appropriate leaves including ewe-lakparada, and kept in an ant-hill on the way to her husband's home town or village because that is where her senior mate prepared the medicine that prevented her from having a living child.

This Odu's Special Sacrifice for Prosperity

Orunmila ni ese kan tan ni mo'na. Oni ese kan tan ti Aworogun
na ni yi o fi ri ire ni idi Ogun re. Oni ese kan tan ti akakpo
ti oun na. Oni rere ni yi o ma fi ri.

Orunmila proclaimed that when he stretches out his legs it portends the advent of good fortune because the legs stretched out by Aworogun signifies the crowning of his efforts with prosperity, just as the stretching out of his legs by his Ifa priest marks the beginning of his success. He however added that the sacrifice should be made with plenty of pigeons, because pigeons use their wings to fly prosperity into the house of their owner.

At divination, the person will be advised to make sacrifice in order to succeed in his ventures.

Divined for Orunmila Before Travelling to Ekiti

Ese kan gbu lomi. Ese kan gbu le'kiti.

Those were the awos who made divination for Orunmila before he travelled to Ekiti to abate an infanticidal epidemic. He was told to make sacrifice with six chains, a chicken and any thorny plant. He made the sacrifice.

On getting to Ekiti, he made sacrifice with he-goat to Esu and the epidemic abated. The children immediately stopped dying.

At divination, the person should be advised to make sacrifice to prevent the danger of multiple children's death.

Chapter 12

IRETE-EKA
ATEKA

He Made Divination for the Tongue When in the Midst of Enemies

*Irete adoko babalawo Uwan. Odifa fn Uwan nijo to mbe
laarinrin ota. Wo ni ebo nikiwonru. Ugbu ni ebo re eku,
eja eko akara ati ebo adiye.*

He made divination for the Tongue who lived in the midst of enemies who were posised to destroy him. He was told to make sacrifice with four snails, rat, fish, hen, eko and akara. The Tongue made the sacrifice after which all his enemies who were waiting to eliminate him were pinned down by Esu to remain immobile in their positions. Thus, the Tongue began to move freely without any harm from his enemies. His enemies were the teeth surrounding him.

At divination the person will be told that he or she is surrounded by closely related enemies. If he/she is able to make sacrifice, he or she will survive or even outlive the enemies. That is why teeth pulled off from the jaw leaving the Tongue to live with the head to the end of life.

He Made Divination For The Okro When She Was Going to the Farm

*Ateka teka, babalawo Illa, Odifa fun illa nijo ti o nlo si
oko alore odun. Won ni ki illa ru ebo. Illa ko ru ebo na.*

He made divination for the Okro when she was going to the farm to avert the danger of sudden death after having children. She did not do the sacrifice. In the farm, she grew to be very beautiful and so tall, that the farmer had to bend her down to cut her fruits after which she was discarded to wither away.

At divination, the person will be told to make sacrifice and advised not to be insubordinate to his or her superior, bosses, landlord, spouse and seniors, lest force will be used to supress him/her to submission.

The Divination He Made Before Leaving Heaven

*Kakara mukokoro, awo oyi oba Orunmila. Je ki mi ri to ma
gbamila. Awon ni won lo'ndifa fun Orunmila nijo to'nti kole
orun bowa si kola aye.*

Here comes Irete Eka, Oh ye awo of the wind divinity, let me find the Awo who will save my life. Those were the Awos who made divination for Irete-Eka when he was coming to the world. He had been to several diviners who could not satisfy him. He subsequently came across the wind diviner, who was suspended in the air. The diviner advised him to make sacrifice to obviate the danger of returning from the earth in a hurry. He was advised to serve: his guardian angel with a ram and four snails; Ogun with a cock, dog and tortoise; Esu with a he-goat ; the Death divinity with a millipede and to bring him (the wind awo) two pigeons because he was going to one of those to help him on earth.

He made all the sacrifices except that he could not find a millipede. After eating his he-goat however, Esu set fire to the place where millipedes were, and seven of them ran out helter-skelter. Ateka took one of them to the divinity of death who was very happy to have it because he had for long been searching for one. Death prayed for him to remain fresh and young while on earth, while promising never to come to his direction, unless when he was fed up with life on earth. The wind diviner also advised him to speak to him always by blowing chalk and salt to him through the air.

His style of awo practice soon brought him at odds with the more elderly awos he met on earth and they began to gun for him. He was a considerate Awo who demanded modest fees for his services, in contrast to the extortionate fees traditionally demanded by other Awos. He was always falling ill. He then invoked his heavenly awo through the wind with chalk and salt on his palm. The awo subsequently visited his house in the company of another Awo called Aganmurere. They both prepared leaves for him to bathe, after which they assured him that no enemy would ever be able to harm him any more.

Thereafter, the awo returned to heaven leaving his partner, Aganmurere to stay with him to the end of his life. It is this leaf going by the name of Aganmurere that this odu uses to perform miracles. This event marked the beginning of good health and prosperity for him. After trying in vain to bother him thereafter, the other awos began to befriend him. They actually began to learn from him because he outlived all of them to a ripe old age. He only died when he was tired of living in old age.

When this ifa comes out at Ugbodu, the person should make the above sacrifces in order to live to a ripe old age. He will be battered and bruised by the enemies in the midst of whom he will live, but with sacrifices, edurance and a refusal to return tit for tat, he will outlive all of them.

He Made Divination for the Farmer

*Ateka, awo Ogbe, odifa fun Ogbe. Ani ki o fi akuko bo ori re
ati ogun. Oru ebo no.*

He made divination for the farmer, advising him to serve, his head with a cock, and Ogun with another cock. He made the sacrifices. Thereafter, his farming became very prosperous because in addition to crop farming, he was also engaged in livestock farming in fowls and goats. He had three sons, one who took to farming like his father, the second took to trading, while the third one became a musician. The three children were subsequently advised to serve their heads together with a goat. Although the eldest one bought the goat single-handed, the other two refused to turn up for the sacrifice. He had to serve his head alone although he added the prayers for his junior brothers. He eventually became the repository of the proceeds of the efforts of the others and he became the tree on which all the birds came to feed.

At Ugbodu, the person should serve his head with a goat while calling his brothers to join him for the sacrifice. He should also serve the Night with a hen. At divination, the person should serve Esu with a he-goat in order to prosper in his work.

He Made Divination for Olawunmi of the Town of Ikpakpo

> Kpete ebole, Ebole ikpete, Olukiri, bifi kashu olele
> Ka fi idi sha eku. Kashu olele. Ka fi idi sha eja.
> Kasha olele Ka fi idi sha eja. Adifa fun Olawinmi lode
> ikpakpo. Omo egunyan Kpakpo, fun osho ilemu. Emi
> ko o gunyan oba loshe. Emi ko bo Orisa odi funooni.
> Ega she she. Kini woni moshe ni ile yi mo re.
> The ground with hillocks. The thing that rolls. Prepare
> pudding to feed the enemies who behave repectively like;
> snake, rat and fish.

These were the awos who made divination for Olawunmi who lived in the town of Ikpakpo. The person who prepares pounded yam to feed the enemy at home. I did not prepare seedless pounded yam for the Oba. I did not serve his divinity for the Ooni of Ife in the wrong way. What wrong do you people accuse me of doing in life? He was however told to make sacrifice with white , yellow and black bean pudding (Ekuru or Olele in Yoruba and Emieki-ere in Bini). The sacrifice was made by putting each color pudding in different containers, adding a rat, fish and snake respectively to each container.

At divination, the person will be told that he has three enemies; one smallish like rat, the next one with body as smooth as a fish, and the third one as thin and tall as a snake. He should make the above sacrifice. If it appears for a woman, the awo should make additional sacrifice with a guinea-fowl so that she can settle down in marriage.

Sacrifice to Be Made Before Travelling

> Orunmila ni kale kiribiti. Moni ikale keregun
> Olota ka le, o ni a ma wa si odo.
> Oni rin rin kale. O ni ki a ma wa si ilu owo.
> Oni oshe kale. Oni ki a ma si ode ila.
> Oluwuku kale. Oni ki a ma wa si ode ona oke. Ijere.

Alamoye kale. Oi ki a ma wa si ilu Ara.
Bebe kale. Oni ki a ma wa si ilu oyo.
Oni Sango kale. Oni ki a ma wa si ilu koso.
Orunmila ikale kiribiti. Moni ikale keregun.
Oni oun ti ka Orunmila, oni oun kale.
Oni so wi kpe ki won ma si oke jeti.
Orunmila proclaimed that it was not safe to travel.
The priest repeated the same warning.
Several Kings were advised that it was not safe to
embark on any journey. The advice was given to:-
the Olota not to travel, to Ado, Owo, Illa,
Ijero, Ara, Oyo, and Koso town.

Orunmila however advised that whenever it became inevitable to travel to the places mentioned, sacrifice should be made with rat, fish and meat to Ifa for a safe journey.

At divination, the person should be advised to make sacrifice before setting out for a proposed journey.

He Made Divination for Crown Prince Ikukpolarun Aremu

Atekun 'le nkanle. Orekan l'an kan ikan.
Ate l'an ka igi agaba a bi ehin Kokoko.

Those were the Awos who made divination for Ikukpolarun Aremu Eleka, the crown prince. He was advised to make sacrifice with a white ram, hedge-hog (Akika in Yoruba) and plenty of assorted white clothes in order to inherit the wealth of his father. He made the sacrifice, after which he became a wealthy king following the demise of his father.

At his coronation, he sang a in praise of Ifa priests as follows:

Atekale l'anka ila
Ate kala ni a nka ikon
Ate kala ni a nka igi ogba
Abehin ki koko ni won she ifa fun mi.
Mo ngbo riru ebo mo ru.
Mo nbgo eru ata ke'su mo ntu.
Koi kpe, koi jina. Ifa wa she bi ala.

At divination, the person will be advised to make sacrifice to regain the lost glory of his family.

Chapter 13

IRETE-ETURUKPON

He Made Divination for the Pigeon When She Offended Death

*Irete tutu begidi. Odifa fun erukuku ta bi eyele nijo
to'nlo bu uku la bagbe. Iwo iku a beri sirigidi.*

That was the Awo who made divination for the Pigeon when she was going to insult the divinity of Death. She despised Death by calling him a big-headed monster. In view of the fact that she had previously made sacrifice, Death was not able to do anything to chastise her. She had earlier made pre-emptive sacrifice with a guinea fowl.

When this odu therefore appears at divination, the person should be told to make sacrifice with a hen or a guinea-fowl to forestall any problems that would have culminated in the wake of an insult to a higher and stronger authority. The sacrifice is made to Ifa.

He Divined for the Porcupine (Ire or Okhaen)

*Akparafa, ekparefa teere le 'ti omi. Odifa fun Ire
(Okkaen) to'n te gbigbona, to'nte gbigbe, to'n tunbo tawa ti etiti
Oni ki alado te titu dain, Ire nte titu dain dain*

The thiny plank used to bailey-bridge a river, was the name of the Awo who made divination for the Porcupine (Ire in Yoruba and Okhaein in Bini) when he was behaving in-transigently and heartlessly. He was advised to make sacrifice in order to cool off and to live long. He subsequently lived a tranquil and inoffensive life, which gave him a trouble -free life eventually, because long life only goes with cool-headedness and inoffensiveness.

At divination, the person should be told to make sacrifice and stop fishing in troubled waters so that prosperity and peace would come to him/her in the evening of his or her life.

The Divination He Made Before Leaving Heaven

Aro konron okpa ugba, odifa fun Orunmila nijo to'nti kole
orun bowa si kole aye.

One missile which killed two hundred victims was the name of the Awo who made divination for this odu when he was coming to the world. He was advised to serve: his guardian angel with four pigeons, four snails, rat, fish and a bag of cowries; Esu with a he-goat; Sango with cock; Olokun with the fourteen traditional materials including pigeon; and Elenini with all edible food-stuffs. He ended up by obtaining blessing and clearance from God, who advised him not to do anything disgraceful on earth because he wasa man of honour. He made the sacrifice before leaving for the world.

He was an intial success story from the outset. Incidentally, he failed to add a cock and rotten material to the sacrifice to Elenini (Idoboo) in heaven, for which the obstacle divinity held his fortune to ransome in heaven. He soon ran into difficulties when Elenini plugged the tap from which his opulence was flowing. When he subsequently made divination, he was required to serve Elenini with a chicken, a rat, spoiled and rotten materials to be put in a calabash and deposited by himself at a road junction where he met a man who asked him for the remaining cock. He returned home to fetch the cock and the man received all the sacrificial materials from him and asked him to return home without looking back.

When he returned home, the Awos used drinking water sprayed on his body from their mouths to revoke the heavenly curse on him. He was astonished at the rate at which all the good things of life streamed to him after that day. He had plenty of wives and children and built many houses and was riding about on horses.

At Ugbodu, the man should make sacrifice so that his fortune held up by the obstacle divinity in heaven might be released to come to him. At divinition, the person will be told to serve; Esu with a he-goat, and Elinini with a cock, rat, fish and rotten materials at a road junction so that prosperity might find its way to him or her.

He Made Divination for the Prince of Iwo to Have a Child

Adagba gege kworun. That was the Awo who made divination for Omo Oliwo, (the prince of Iwo) to succeed in taking the throne of his father. After he became Oba, he had no children for a very long time. He subsequently sent errand men to comb the known world for Orunmila. At the subsequent divination, Orunmila told him that he had to go alone into recluse in the forest in order to be able to have a child. He pondered for a long time whether it was auspicious for an Oba to go into the forest in search of children. That night, his father appeared to him in a dream advising him to do whatever Orunmila told him to do.

At the instance of Orunmila, he served Esu with a he-goat. Thereafter Orunmila told him to enter the forest alone and continue exploring the forest until he came across a forest fountain (Omi-ugbogi in Yoruba and Ohiame in Bini), where he was to have his bath before returning home. Meanwhile, as the Oliwo of Iwo left for the forest, Orunmila returned home. On his way home, he met the Princess of Offa, who appealed to him for divination on what to do to have a child. After divination, Orunmila also advised her to enter the forest from which she was not to return until she saw a fountain on which to have a bath. She was however also required to serve Esu with he-goat before making for the forest.

As soon as the Oba of Iwo and the Princess of Offa entered the forest from different directions, Esu commanded all the fountain in the forest to conceal themselves beneath the ground. The two of them combed the forest for fountains for three years without coming across one. Their people had given them up for dead and and a regent was appointed to administer the affairs of Iwo. They did not appoint a new Oba because at divination, they were often assured that their Oba was alive and well and would turn up one day after a long sojourn to the forest. Meanwhile, the Oba's clothes had turned into shreads and his body had become as hairy as that of a gorilla. The same thing was happening to the princess of Offa who was now going naked as a female gorilla.

One day, Esu asked one fountain to open up in front of the princess of Iwo. She was released to come across it. As she was having her bath in it, she sighted a gorilla looking like a man coming towards the same fountain. They were both naked. As they were attracted to each other, their genitals stood erect. Without any ceremonies and without asking any questions, they made love. Thereafter, they began to move together, not in search of home, but in search of where they could live together because they had given up all thoughts of returning to their respective homes.

It was much later that they formally introduced themselves. That was when they got to Orita-Ijaloko where they met Orunmila who divined separately for the two of them. They recognized him but he could not recognize them because he assumed that they gorillas. When they greeted him, he stopped to recieve the greetings and asked them to identity themselves. He could not believe his ears when they told him who they were. The woman was now at an advanced stage of pregancy. He hurriedly made divination for them and told them to make sacrifice with two he-goats.

Since they did not have the where-with-all for purchasing two he-goats, he told them to wait until dusk to steal the he-goats. The sacrifice was made in the night with small he-goats that Esu had to eat alone. By the small hours of the morning, Esu had cleared all the hairs on their bodies and provided them decent clothes to wear. Before dawn, the Oba of Iwo found himself sitting at the popular Osanyin shrine of the town of Iwo, while the princess of Iwo found herself at her forefather's shrine in Offa.

Eventually, amidst pomp and pageantry, the princess of Otta was led by a huge procession to Iwo. The Oba of Iwo was meanwhile discovered and hailed by his people. As he was being led to his palace, the pregnant princess of Offa was entering the town of Iwo. They eventually met to become king and queen. In the fullness of time, she gave birth to male child and they invited Orunmila to perform the naming ceremony divination and preside over the consequential town-wide feast. The child was however very hairy and Orunmila prepared leaves and camwood to be rubbing his body after which the hairs withered away.

After rewarding Orunmila appropriately, the king of Iwo proclaimed that the fountain on which the queen and himself met, should become the shrine of Osanyin for the people of Iwo. They had seven children on the whole and they lived and ruled until all the hairs of their bodies turned grey.

When this odu appears at Ugbodu, the person must be made to have a bath in a forest fountain and should have his own Osanyin/Osun and Sango shrines. He will have difficulty initally in having chidren but he will enjoy a blissful evening. At divintion, the person will be advised to have his own Ifa which will be washed with water taken from a forest fountain. After washing the Ikin with the water, he will bathe with it for seven days.

He Made Divination for Masquerades

Irete rin rin rin, Etutu le le le - were the Awos who made divination for the Masquerade who used to dance about during his annual festival. He was advised to serve Esu with a he-goat to avert the danger of falling down when dancing. Traditionally, a masquerade who falls down during performance will not live to the end of that year. He was also advised to serve his head with a cock. He served Esu, but not his head.

At the subsequent festival, he fell down during performance and he could not rise up any-more. That became the first masquerade shrine on earth. People who were desirous of children and money went to serve him with the song:-

> Gbayigha gbanyigha. Gbangho gbamo.
> meaning - Give us money and children.

When it appears at Ugbodu, the person should serve his head with a cock while backing the Ifa and quickly prepare his Esu with a he-goat. At divination, the person should serve; his/her head with a cock/hen and Esu with with a he-goat to avert the danger of sudden death.

Specical Sacrifice Against Infectious Disease

> Orunmila Oni atetu, Mo ni atetu. Oni atetu omo eku
> Kiikpa omo eku. Atetu omo eja ko ni kpa omo eja
> Atetu omo eran ko ni kpa eran.
> Atetu omo eni ko ni kpa omo eni.
> Ato igbin kii kpa igbin.

Orunmila proclaimed that there was an incidence of gonorrhea around and his Ifa priest confirmed it. He however advised sacrifice because gonorrhea does not kill rats, fishes, animals, snails and human beings. He prescribed sacrifice with plenty of palm wine, shea butter (Ori-eyo) and snails.

At divination, the person should be asked whether he or she is suffering form any veneral disease. If not, he or she should make preventive sacrifice.

Chapter 14

IRETE-OSE
IRETE-ALAJE
IRETE-SEKPERE
URU-EKUN

He Made Divination for the Tiger

Ojo Kata Kata Kata. Ofaa ole de ekun, were the Awos who made divination for the Tiger advising him to have his own Ifa. The tiger was prepared to have his ifa, but insisted that the initiation ceremony had to take place in his own house. Since Orunmila doe not believe in impossibilities, he made divination for himself on what to do to avert any harm in the Tiger's house. Ifa advised him to give a he-goat to Esu and to add his own blood to the sacrifice. He was also required to have his bath with sixteen snails and a basket by the side of the road, in order to return home safely. He made the sacrifice before leaving home.

On getting to the Tiger's house, he enumerated the materials for preparing Ifa for him to comprise: two goats, two hens, two tortoises, two snails, two pieces of white cloth, two cutlasses, two hoes, two mats, two legs of bush-goat, two raffia mats (aghen) two legs of deer, two legs of monkey, six red parrot feathers, fourteen tubers of yam, plenty of cowries, plenty of kolanuts, a plate or calabash with a lid, two rats, two fishes and two pigeons. They are the traditional materials used for initiation into Ifism. The Tiger was able to produce all the materials.

During divination at Ugbodu, Irete-Ose came out for the Tiger, which was a warning to Orunmila that the Tiger (his Ifa son) would try to kil him at the end of the ceremony. Thereafter, Orunmila asked the Tiger to produce his multi-colored dress with which he used to do havoc. He brought it out and Orunmila kept it - as a ploy for taming the Tiger's ferocity. At the end of the seven day ceremony, Orunmila had to return home with one each of the initiation materials and the Tiger (his Ifa son) had to follow him home to serve his own Ifa with the goat. Before leaving his house, the Tiger had already left Orunmila in no doubt that he was not going to take kindly to the idea of being deprived of all his belongings in the name of initiation into Ifism.

On their way to Orunmila's house, as soon as they entered the forest, the Tiger sought an excuse to ease himself and to enter the bush, from which he soon returned in fury to attack Orunmila. With the use of the appropriate incantation, Esu produced an even fiercer tiger, who engaged the one that assailed Orunmila. The Esu-produced tiger was able to subdue and kill the Tiger who tried to attack Orunmila. Orunmila was thereafter able to reach home with the materials and used another he-goat to thank Esu for saving his life. As he was putting the butchered goat inside the Ifa plate, he sang, "Ekun kpe'kun je, eron le ekun. Ereron le'kun je. Ekun kpe'kun je, ereron lekun je. That is the song for putting meat into Ifa plate to this day.

That is why, as soon as this Ifa appears at Ugbodu, the Ifa father should immediately serve his own Ifa with 16 snails and add the leaves of his Ifa to the liquid from the snails to have a bath. After he should give a he-goat and his own blood to Esu. He can return to complete the ceremony after making his own sacrifice. The fact remains however that sooner than later, the person for which this Ifa appears at Ugbodu will try to beat or kill his Ifa father.

The Divination He Made Before Leaving Heaven

Ojo Kata Kata Kate, Ofaa ale de ekun, were the Awos who made divination for Orunmila when he was coming to the world. He was advised to make sacrifice to: his guardian angel with a goat, hen, tortoise and a pigeon; Esu with two he-goats; to buy his life from Ogun with a dog, cock and tortoise; and to feast the divinities with a gourd of palm oil. He was required to make such elaborate sacrifice because his Ifa practice was going to create lots of problems for him on earth and in order to live to a ripe old age on earth. He borrowed money to make all the sacrifices before coming to the world because he was going to have wives and children much stronger than himself.

On getting to the world, he took to his Ifa practice and got married to the daughter of Olokun who took to petty trading. He had many children who turned out to be very insubordinate when they grew up. His wife and children subsequently took a confrontational stance against him. He was himself very harsh, which made many people to distance themselves away from him. Eventually, he met an Awo who told him that far from being the peace-maker he vowed to be on earth, he was becoming very pugacious. He was told to make sacrifice with a goat, knife, snails, 201 kolanuts, and white cloth.

After the sacrifice was prepared, the Awo got relevant leaves, ground them with the blood of the goat and mounted it on the head of the goat and covered it with the white cloth for him to keep on his Ifa shrine. Thereafter, he simmered down and all his enemies began to run into difficulties. He began to command the respect of the people around him and his family became more submissive. He was not exceptionally rich and did not have many children.

At Ugbodu, the person should be told to make sacrifice to avert the danger of becoming too aggressive for the comfort of those around him.

He Made Divination for a Girl who Came From Heaven

Irete sekpere made divination for young girl who came from heaven to cause havoc on earth. She was a ruthless witch who sought to destroy everyone and everything around her. At divination, Orunmila told her that she was going to settle down with a third husband and that she had to curb her destructive tendencies. She was required to serve, her head with a hen and Esu with a he-goat. She served her head but not Esu.

Subsequently, she met Osanyin or Osun who married her without knowing her because she was very pretty. Following the marriage the fortunes of Osanyin began to deterioate. She killed all his children and drove away his other wives with her witchcraft powers. After reducing Osanyin to abject penury, she left him to go and marry Sango.

She did the same havoc to Sango, who drove her away before she could do more damage. She subsequently met Ogun and married him. Ogun was always going to war and leaving her at home. When Ogun returned from war on one occasion he foresaw that the woman had concluded arrangements to kill his eldest son. Ogun however lost no time in warning her that before she touched any of his children, she would have to die first. Thereafter, Ogun called her late in the night and had her chained up in such a way that she could no longer attend the meetings of the club of withcraft.

Thereafter, she was effectively humoured and she became Uja, the wife of Ogun and began to help him in all constructive engagements.

At Ugbodu, the person will be very stubborn and heady. He should serve his head with a guinea-fowl and the new Ifa with a white goat and prepare Ogun shrine for his Ifa with a dog and cock.

At divination, the person should serve; Ogun with a dog to prevent witches from holding meetings in his house and his head with a cock.

He Made Divination for Ajibola When He Was Moving With Witches

Ohun kon soso laja fo. Adifa fun Ajibola ti'nshe ore awon
eleye. Ebo aje niki o ru o.

The gong only speaks one word. That was the name of the Awo who made divnation for Ajibola when he was moving with members of the club of witchcraft. He was told to serve; Esu with a black hen and the elders of the night with a rabbit to avoid being killed through witchcraft. He made the sacrifices and stopped moving with them.

When it appears at divination, the person will be told that he is moving with a friend who is a witch and that to avoid being killed through witchcraft, he should make sacrifice. If the divination comes out for a sick person, he will be told that his illness was caused by witches and should make sacrifice to get well.

He Made Divination for Omo-Lahere The Workaholic

Ikan-yere lofo ri she aje lo'na oke ekpelisa
Odifa fun Omo Lahere eyi ti ushe uya nigba eru ti a ni ki
Oru ebo to ba di igba ojo - Ara a'ro. Ebo Niki oru o.

The seeds used for making gourd maracas, uses its head to produce money in its country, but later found money after being sewn up. That was the name of the Awo who made divination for omo-Lahere who was working so hard that he was not resting. He was told to make sacrifice and to rest as often as possible and in order to have peace of mind and prosperity during the rainy season. He made the sacrifice and prospered in peace and tranquility.

When it appears at divination, the person will be advised to exercise patience because he will eventually prosper.

He Made Divination for Onigbolo Si Gbolo

> Alilere ori. Odifa fun Onigbolo si gbolo. Eyi ti a ni
> ko she ebo tori idalo to'nlo tori ki oba bo wale re.

Alilere was the Awo who made divination for Onigbolo si gbolo who was advised to make sacrifice in order to return safely from a trip he was undertaking. He did the sacrifice and travelled out. He was so successful in the trip that he came home with plenty of gifts and money.

The Divination He Made Before Prospering

> Ogidiri gbo. Odifa fun Orunmila baba fi omi oju shubere
> aje, ati omo, ati gbogbo ure.

Ogidiri gbo made divination for this Odu when he was anxious for money, children and prosperity. He was advised to make sacrifice and he did, after which his desires came true.

At divination, the person should be told that he is anxious to have something. He should make sacrifice in order to achieve the objective.

Special Sacrifice Against Imminent Danger

> Orunmila ni hu. Moni eru ba mi. Oni Ifa wo ni mo da ti
> eru ba mi. Mo ni Irete oke ni. Oni she ni ki emi
> mi riru ebo. Oni she ni ki emi mo eru atu ke'su.

Orunmila exclaimed "HU". The Ifa priest retorted that he was frightened. Orunmila asked for the Ifa that appeared that made him to be afraid, and the priest replied that it was Irete-Oke. Orunmila told him that instead of being frightened, he should make sacrifice with pig, the appropriate leaves, snails, shea butter (Ori-Oyo) thorny leaves and water leaves.

The sacrifice was prepared with the following incantation:
Ero ni ti te te. Ero ni ti odon fon. Igin Ki je aye igbona Aja bale ro roife. Ibi ti awo ba ti de ki gbogbo ibe di ero Iroko ma so ele. Ero ni ki iroko so Ero.

When it appears at divination, the person if a man will be advised to have his own Ifa who will solve all his problems. If it comes out for a woman, she will be advised if a spinster to marry an Ifa man, and if married to persuade her husband to have his own ifa.

Special Sacrifice of this Odu for Prosperity

Orunmila ni Agokela. Moni Agokela. Oni ki a mu nkan
ebo re wa. A mu eku, oni ki nshe eku. A mu eja. Oni
mo je wo obun, ki iwo da aso ro mi. Oni a fi eni
ti o ba ni okpolokpo eyele ati ekuru funfun. Moni
Orunmila a ri a ko de. O ni eri ti o gun okela, ki a
ma kpe ni, Irete-oke. Idi eyi ni a fi nkpe ni Irete-oke.
Orunmila proclaimed success, and his priest confirmed it.

Orunmila aksed the priest to name the sacrifice required for success. The priest enumerated; rat, fish, and meat, all of which Orunmila rejected. He subsequently prescribed sacrifice with plenty of pigeons and white bean pudding (ekuru funfun). They were produced and after the sacrifice, Orunmila proclaimed that "Anyone who succeeds in climbing the ladder of prosperity should be called Irete-Oke".

When it appears at divination, the person will be advised to build his house on top of a hill in order to prosper

Chapter 15

IRETE-OFUN
IRETE-AFUN

He Made Divination For Palm Tree

Atemu mi ateyo, ojojumo ni omo araye kpere te ati te'ni mu
Ori eni ni ko'ni yo.
Deep it into the depth and into the sacrifice.
No day passes without mankind thinking of sinking one into
the precipice.
It is one's head that saves one from all the evil designs of
mankind.

Those were the Awos who made divination for the palm tree when she was coming from heaven. She was advised to make sacrifice in order to minimise the problems of living on earth. She was advised to make sacrifice with white cloth, hen, rat, fish, salt, eko and akara and to serve her head with a pigeon. She refused to make the sacrifice because she was sure that her indispensability and beauty would see through all obstacles. She was born at the same time with two hundred divinities, because she provided them passage through water to the world.

On getting to the world, she had a beautiful face and breast. All the men wooed her, but she rebuffed all of them. The Thicket (Eti) decided to attack and besiege her. That was when she invited her brothers and sisters to sit down to serve her head with her. After the sacrifice, they began to dance. When it was the turn of Fire to dance, he warned all those attacking his sister (palm tree) to withdraw or face his wrath. As he started dancing, Fire engaged the Thicket (Eti) and burnt him up. As Fire was dancing, he sang:-

"Wele wele ni ino njo - to ba to ke bu yaya".
Thereafter, the palm tree had a better lease on life.

At Ugbodu, the person should serve his head with a pigeon and Esu with a he-goat. At divination, the person will serve Ogun with a cock and his/her head with another cock.

He Made Divination for Orunmila

Okiti kpuke ao eba ono. Odifa fun Orunmila nijo to'nlo bo
Oshun ati Orisa.

He made divination for Orunmila when he was going to offer sacrifice to Osun and Orisa. People began to make jest of him for serving Ifa, Orisa and Osun all at the same time. He told the jesters to mind their own business while he was minding his own. He eventually prospered to the astonishment of those who laughed at him. At divination, the person should be advised not to listen to those dispising him because his success will keep them quiet, provided he makes sacrifice.

Special Poem Against Fear

Atefun shun. Mi atefun shun. Oni omo eku kii ke fiin fiin
Ki a tori ti be tori re bo erun.
Atefun shun. Mi atefun shun. Omo eja kii ke fiin fiin ka to
ri re bo run.
Beni omo eye. Kii ke fiin fiin ka to ri re bo 'run
Boni Omo eniyan kii ke fiin fiin ko to ri re bo'run

The swamp gives way when treaded on. The children of the rat, fish, bird and mankind cannot be eaten up without being captured and roasted, merely because they cry seemingly helplessly.

When this odu appears at divination, the person will be told that he is emotionally disturbed about something and that he is not feeling freely at ease. He/she should be advised to make sacrifice after which he or she should behave and speak boldly beacause nothing will happen to him or her.

The Divination He made When Leaving Heaven

Aro fifun da didun. Aro didun da fifun.
Those were the two Awos who made divination for this odu when he was coming to the world. He was advised to make adequate preparations because he was going to have a difficult time on earth especially as he was destined to make other people's problem his problem. He was advised to make the following sacrifices: to serve Esu with a he-goat; his guardian angel with a ram, hen and snail; to serve the voice of people at the road junction with 16 pigeons and a piece of white cloth; and to obtain the blessing of God. He made all the sacrifices before coming to the world.

On getting to the world, he became an Ifa priest and all his predictions often came true. In spite of his effectiveness, his life was listless and colorless. He could neither afford a family nor to build a house. His mother was a woman called Iwa, (Uyinmwen in Bini) who was very poor, and Atefun was her only child. Atefun was very friendly with the son of Olofin and they were always together. Olofin had a black loin cloth which he often wore when in a state of melancholy. He also had several livestocks comprising; two hundred and one cows, two hundred and one goats, two hundred and one sheep and two hundred and one fowls which were grazed by four shepherds.

One day, as Atefun was joking with his friend the son of Olofin, he expressed a desire that if Olofin could give him four each of his various livestocks, he would have been able to clean his black misfortune cloth to become white. The prince asked him pointedly whether he was capable of performing the feat and Atefun confirmed categorically that he could do it. The prince quickly ran home to alert his father, the Oba who immediately sent for Atefun. When his mother heard that her son was being invited for questioning, she became scared.

When Atefun got to the palace, a large crowd was already gathered to hear his wonder-story. When asked by the Oba to confirm that he was capable of washing his black misfortune cloth to turn white, he explained that although he said it jocularly, nonetheless, if it was considered an important issue he would do it provided he would be commensurately compensated. He was told to prepare for the operation in seven days time. The Olofin told him that if he succeeded in performing the feat, he would give Atefun half of the kingdom to administer, but that if he failed , he would be executed. He became so downcast that he ran home to tell his mother how he had talked himself into trouble. The mother burst into tears at the prospect of losing her only child. She quickly ran to Orunmila for divination.

At divination, the Odu of Atefun came out, which indicated that the young man had for long ignored his Okekponrin - and that he was not practicing Ifa in the proper way. Orunmila reassured the woman that her son could perform the feat provided she was prepared to make sacrifice with; a ram to Ifa adding a ten metre piece of white cloth, and a he-goat to Esu. She was told that on the day of the operation, she was to put the ten metre piece of white cloth into a pot adding four rats and deposit on the swamp of the river. Although people were already ridiculing Atefun for allowing his locquaciousness to run riot, the mother proceeded all the same to make the sacrifices.

On the seventh day, Atefun went to the palace and the Olofin, where he was given the black cloth and plenty of soap for the operation, while sending for verifiers to go with him to the river to watch the operation. The verifiers were laughing him to scorn all the way to the river. When they got to the river, he started to wash the black cloth, while the four verifiers stood in close watch. It was time for Esu to work for the sacrifice he had enjoyed. He began by releasing the four rats with which Atefun made sacrifice, in the midst of the four verifiers, which they immediately identified as the four species of rats that Olofin had been finding for sacrifice. They left their beat and pursued the rats because the Oba had promised to adequately compensate whoever was able to fetch the rats.

While the four verifiers were busy pursuing the rats, the mother of Atefun came in from her hide-out in the swamps, gave the ten metre piece of white cloth to his son and took the ten metre piece of black cloth from him. Thereafter, she immediately left for home while his son continued to wash the white cloth. Meanwhile, the verifiers returned after congratulating themselves for being able to apprehend the four rats. They were astonished to see that Atefun was now washing a white cloth, and that the black cloth had already turned to white. They told him not to continue washing because he had succeeded in turning the cloth from black to white.

When he returned to the palace, there was general amazement to see him returning with a white cloth, which Esu had meanwhile fixed in the shape and size of the black cloth. The Chiefs brought out a tape and measured the white cloth and it coinded with the dimension of the black cloth. Olofin however said that he would allow some grace period to elapse to see whether no other misfortune would befall him, before paying the compensation to Atefun. Almost immediately, Esu turned his two eyes, which provoked tremors and shockwaves throughout the grounds of the palace. With that Olofin was jolted back into his senses and he immediately promulgated a decree making Atefun the Ojugbona of the kingdom of Ife. Atefun was charged with the responsibility of administering half of the kingdom and was translated into eternal prosperity.

When this Ifa appears at Ugbodu, the person should be told to make sacrifice so that his locquacious disposition might become a blessing. He should serve Ifa conscientiously because it will bring him prosperity. At divination, the man will be advised to have his own Ifa and for the woman, to get close to Ifa to avert the risk of getting into trouble through his/her utterances.

He Divined for Orunmila When He Went to the Land of Albinos

> *Bi oju ba ti kpon eni ni akponju. Awo iro ni o mu*
> *ni nshe. O difa fun Orunmila ni ojo to'nlo she awo*
> *fun awon ni ilu afin. Won ni ki Orunmila ru ebo na.*

Anyone who is in a hurry in life ends up with misfortune. That was the Awo who made divination for Orunmila when he travelled for Ifa practice in the land of the Albinos. He was required to make sacrifice with pigeon and plenty of fowls. He made the sacrifice before leaving for the journey.

After divination, he told them to make sacrifice with plenty of fruits, black hen, goat, sheep and a cow. They produced the materials and Orunmila prepared the sacrifice with the appropriate leaves for them to bathe with. They all bathed with the water and on the following morning, all their skins turned dark like that of Orunmila. He however told them not to bathe again until after seven days. Thereafter, he returned to Oke-jetti. Those who had their bath after five days, got their color scheme changing from black to their original albino pigmentation. They trooped back to Orunmila and he repeated the sacrifice for those affected.

At divination, the person should be advised to be satisified with what God has given to him or her, and should not attempt to change the designs of the Almighty Creator.